LITERARY
FORTIFICATIONS

"Portrait imaginaire de D.A.F. de Sade" (1938) by Man Ray. Private Collection, reprinted by permission of the owner.

JOAN DEJEAN

LITERARY FORTIFICATIONS
Rousseau, Laclos, Sade

PRINCETON UNIVERSITY PRESS

Copyright © 1984 by Princeton University Press
Published by Princeton University Press,
41 William Street, Princeton, New Jersey 08540
In the United Kingdom:
Princeton University Press, Guildford, Surrey

ALL RIGHTS RESERVED
Library of Congress Cataloging in Publication Data
will be found on the last printed page of this book
ISBN 691-06611-6

Publication of this book has been
aided by the Ira O. Wade Fund

This book has been composed in Linotron Sabon
Clothbound editions of Princeton University Press books
are printed on acid-free paper, and binding materials
are chosen for strength and durability

Printed in the United States of America
by Princeton University Press
Princeton, New Jersey

IN MEMORY OF

KATE KEATING

Contents

CONTENTS

(3 traces of Vauban's fortifications follow page 54.)

A Note on References

Unless otherwise stated, references to the works of the central figures in this study are to the following editions:

Laclos. *Oeuvres complètes.* Edited by Laurent Versini. Paris: Gallimard, Bibliothèque de la Pléiade, 1979. In references to the *Liaisons*, I give letter number and page number.

Rousseau. *Oeuvres complètes.* 4 vols. Paris: Gallimard, Bibliothèque de la Pléiade, 1964-1969. I give volume and page number in parentheses in the text for all works except *Julie* (vol. 2 of the Pléiade edition) where I give part, letter, and page number. All references are given in Arabic numerals.

Sade. *Oeuvres complètes.* 15 vols. Paris: Au cercle du livre précieux, 1963-1964.

Vauban. *Oeuvres militaires.* Edited by Foissac. 3 vols. Paris: Magimel, 1795.
Vauban, sa famille et ses écrits. Edited by Rochas d'Aiglun. 2 vols. Paris: Berger-Levrault, 1910.

In citing Vauban's works, I refer whenever possible to the readily accessible Rochas d'Aiglun edition, otherwise to the Foissac edition.

When citing texts in French, I have reproduced the original spelling, accents, and punctuation. I have abbreviated certain titles (the *Liaisons*, the *120*). Unless otherwise stated, all books were published in Paris.

Acknowledgments

This study has benefited greatly from a number of careful and challenging readings. Jean Alter made helpful suggestions for revising early drafts of some of the chapters. English Showalter read the entire manuscript twice and gave indispensable advice at every stage of the book's preparation. I am indebted to him for his generous and painstaking attention. And to my favorite interlocutor and intellectual confidant, Charles Bernheimer— my first, my last, and my most demanding reader—I owe gratitude for his almost endless patience. My reading of *Salammbô* is influenced by his work on Flaubert, and the entire manuscript profited enormously from his questions and his suggestions.

A Morse Fellowship from Yale University made it possible for me to complete a first draft of the following study. A summer travel grant from the Council on the Humanities at Yale University allowed me to visit many of Vauban's fortifications. The Princeton University Committee on Research provided funds for the typing of the manuscript. To all those who made this support possible, I owe a debt of gratitude. I want to thank Elizabeth MacArthur for her scrupulous help in proofreading the manuscript. Finally, I am grateful to Elizabeth Powers for her valuable suggestions and careful assistance in the manuscript's preparation and to Jerry Sherwood for believing in the project from the start.

A longer version of my reading of *Psyché* in chapter 1 appeared in an issue of *L'Esprit créateur* edited by David Rubin. An earlier version of chapter 2 is included in *The Classical Sign*, a special number of *Semiotica* edited by Susan Tiefenbrun. A first version of part of chapter 4 was published in an issue of *Yale French Studies* edited by Barbara Johnson.

ACKNOWLEDGMENTS

Part of chapter 6 was originally published in *The Romanic Review*.

I would like to thank the Library of the University of Michigan for photographs from an edition of Vauban's works in their collections.

LITERARY
FORTIFICATIONS

Tout ce que vous lisez . . . dans le récit d'un narrateur militaire, les plus petits faits, les plus petits événements, ne sont que les signes d'une idée qu'il faut dégager et qui souvent en recouvre d'autres, comme dans un palimpseste. De sorte que vous avez un ensemble aussi intellectuel que n'importe quelle science ou n'importe quel art, et qui est satisfaisant pour l'esprit.

Proust, *Le Côté de Guermantes*

Introduction

During the past twenty years, the major figures of the French eighteenth century have been the object of a telling renewal of interest. Literary critics and historians have returned to them time and again in their efforts to uncover the origins of our modernity. Perhaps the most provocative contribution to this revitalization of Enlightenment studies has been what might be called—to borrow a term generally associated with only one of the schools I have in mind—the deconstruction(s) of eighteenth-century thought. The major recent figures of French intellectual life, including Derrida and Lacan, have been involved in endeavors that have in common a denunciation of idealized visions of eighteenth-century humanism. Perhaps the most visible proponent of a darker vision of the *Age des Lumières* is Michel Foucault who has laid the groundwork for a radical revision of our relationship to the Enlightenment. According to the terms of Foucault's critique, the French eighteenth century may have been an age of enlightened liberation, but simultaneously it invented new technologies of power and new modes of repression and made possible the creation of disciplinary societies.

In this study, I propose a view of three central eighteenth-century literary figures—Rousseau, Laclos, and Sade—that owes a great deal to the pessimistic evaluation of Enlightenment goals proposed by Foucault. In order to focus on the implications of the discourse of liberation in these three authors, I limit my consideration to their "novels" most directly concerned with what is perhaps the ultimate liberating discourse for the eighteenth century, pedagogy: Rousseau's *Julie* and *Emile,* Laclos's *Les Liaisons dangereuses,* and Sade's *Les 120 Journées de Sodome.* A study of their novelistic didacticism and their fictional re-creations of the pedagogical act

3

demonstrates that these key figures of the age whose mythical culmination is the destruction of a fortress, the Bastille, devoted themselves in their fiction—to translate Foucault's message into the vocabulary that dominates this study—to the creation of literary fortresses, texts dedicated to the constraint, control, and repression of all forces of (natural) disorder. Critics have long since ceased taking Rousseau at face value, that is, viewing him in his own terms, as a sort of literary innocent. Nevertheless, he is not considered a direct precursor of Laclos and Sade. On the contrary, Rousseau and Sade are commonly seen as polar opposites, and Laclos's Les Liaisons dangereuses is often read as a parody of Rousseau. Yet the relationship among the three novelists could be described as one of jealous proximity. Laclos saw how close Rousseau was to his own enterprise and was threatened by this incursion into his literary territory, whereas for Sade, Laclos played the role of the invader. What their works have in common, what I call their defensiveness, is an inevitable result of their authors' views concerning the role of nature and the natural within the framework of the novel. These views are best described not as pre-romantic, an adjective commonly chosen to characterize Rousseau and Sade, but rather as post-Classical. Each of these three novelists measures his accomplishments according to the standards created by the so-called Golden Age of French literature; each sets for himself the task of writing the next great French novel, of appropriating for himself the place in literary history reserved for Lafayette's heir.

Rousseau, Laclos, and Sade are semantically equivocal. They speak simultaneously with two voices, a voice of liberation and a voice of control. Traditionally, the voice of freedom has been privileged, and both Rousseau and Sade have been viewed as inaugurating liberating literary traditions. In this study, I stress the voice of repression in an attempt to demonstrate how both of them, like Laclos, remain essentially faithful to a typically Classical concern for order and control. Thus my reading of Les 120 Journées de Sodome runs against the current of recent Sade criticism, which has tended to follow Foucault's (paradoxical) lead. Foucault, who paints repressive images of many Classical thinkers, places Sade in the oxymoronic position of darkness enlightened and enlightening: "[L]'abîme d'en dessous le mal et qui était le mal lui-même vient de surgir dans la lumière du langage."[1] Furthermore, my reading of Rousseau intentionally repeats what Lawrence Stone, in a recent critique of what he terms Foucaultism, calls the major blindness of Foucault's model: "[I]t totally neglects the near-certainty of serious differences in beliefs and aims among the so-called controllers."[2] In other words, I take no account of intentions, in particular the distance that separates Rousseau's goals from Sade's. While I realize, for example, that Rousseau considered Julie's behavior with regard to other members of the Clarens community as an embodiment of the type of secularization of mythical power described in the *Contrat social,* I stress only the Sadean and sadistic implications of submerging the self in order to aggrandize it. My goal, in short, is to describe Rousseau, Laclos, and Sade as novelistic *strategists*—engineers in the first sense of the term, "plotter, layer of snares"—whose textual enterprise is driven by the desire to make their territory secure.

In chapter 3, "The Oblique Way: Defensive Swerves," I discuss Freud's use, in *Beyond the Pleasure Principle,* of an amoeba-like figure as a metaphor for the psyche and its double defensive shields. Freud's description of the double structure of these defenses provides a basis for characterizing the defensive text, for it, like Freud's psyche-amoeba, is both internally and externally defended. As a result of its internal system of defenses, the characters it presents are preoccupied with protecting themselves against the power of the other. They form relationships based on aggression: the principal goal of

---

[1] Foucault, *Naissance de la clinique* (Presses Universitaires de France, hereafter PUF, 1963), p. 197. See also his description of Sade's work as totally enlightened—"il n'y a pas d'ombre chez Sade"—at the culmination of *Histoire de la folie à l'âge classique* (Gallimard, 1972), p. 553.

[2] *New York Review of Books,* 31 Mar. 1983, p. 44.

INTRODUCTION

those relationships is the engulfment or absorption of the other
and therefore the elimination of the threat posed by that other.
In defensive texts, as in French Classical theater, nothing happens before the readers' eyes. We are confronted instead with
various accounts of events that have already taken place (or,
on occasion, of events that are unfolding, as when Saint-Preux
writes in Julie's closet or Valmont on Emilie's back). All these
novels adopt the distanced narrative stance associated with
collections of tales like the *Arabian Nights,* but they do so in
order to reverse the pattern established by Scheherazade. In
them, storytelling does not function to put off death, but
rather to revenge the storyteller by bringing on death and
destruction. The defensive text is also externally fortified, in
the sense that its author has protected it against the threat of
invasion by the reader. These texts have in common with the
classics of French literature an appearance of rigorous clarity
and limpid transparency, yet they are in reality so ambiguous,
so equivocal, that they invite contradictory, yet mutually ir-
refutable readings. This is the impact of textual fortifications:
they render the text invulnerable behind a wall of irreconcil-
able readings. Thus I say that Rousseau's texts are repressive,
but know all the while that the contrary reading is prepared
for in the texts themselves, and that the question of whether
Laclos's novel is diabolic or angelic will remain incontro-
vertibly undecidable.

The major preoccupation in the defensive text—at times
the sole preoccupation—is strategic deployment. This is especially evident in the novels of Laclos and Sade, but it is no
less true of Rousseau's fictions. These texts are governed by
an all-consuming passion for defensive strategy. Their authors
and the characters they create share an obsession with strategic
perfection. They work to become all-seeing and all-powerful,
to perfect the ability to trap any victim in their snares. Both
the internal and the external fortifiers are constantly involved
in the task of making their defenses airtight.

The central metaphor for this study of literary defensiveness
is the fortress, and the strategist who is viewed as a model

for these builders of literary fortresses is the master fortifier of the French Classical age, Sébastien le Prestre de Vauban. I do not intend to suggest that history, or in this case military history, can provide an explanation for literary phenomena. For example, Laclos's biographical link with the art of fortification cannot explain the creation of his only novel. By the same token, the historical coexistence of the Vaubanian fortress and literary neoclassicism cannot be used to deduce the presence of some kind of inner logic that accounts for both phenomena. But in military practice during the Classical age (seventeenth and eighteenth centuries), the complex of fortifications Vauban developed constituted just the sort of strong model that literary Classicism did at the same period for the writers under consideration here. Vauban's work on defense offers concepts pertinent for the study of the literature that was worked out in the shadow of the Classical menace, and provides a rich source of metaphors and analogies for textual strategies.

In particular, I posit here a recurrent association between self-protectionism and (Classical) pedagogy. Rousseau, Laclos, and Sade are the literary heirs of Classicism, whose watchword was *plaire et instruire* (a maxim that eighteenth-century authors continued to repeat). The Enlightenment allegedly created a new pedagogy best represented by Rousseau's pedagogy of liberation. Yet the new pedagogy of the eighteenth century inevitably veers into protectionism. The intrinsic concern of Rousseau's master teacher (*gouverneur*) is identical to that of Vauban's *gouverneur* (the commanding officer of a fortified place), the defense of his territory (the space of teaching) against the threat of invasion.

What Foucault designates as the French Classical age is coextensive with the age of the fortress. During Louis XIV's reign, the advances in the technique of fortifications Vauban effected made siegecraft the dominant military art, and the engineer—defined at the period exclusively as "celuy qui invente, qui trace, et qui conduit des travaux et des ouvrages pour l'attaque, ou pour la défense des places" (Académie fran-

INTRODUCTION

çaise dictionary, 1694)—was the dominant figure in the military hierarchy, making Vauban, the master of the Sun King's siegecraft, the king's soldierly counterpart. This state of affairs continued throughout the eighteenth century, situated militarily in Vauban's shadow (and politically in Louis XIV's). It began to change near the end of the literary period dealt with in this study. Already the Trévoux dictionary (1771) gives two alternate meanings for "ingénieur," first as a term of artillery, designating the "ingénieur de feu," responsible for bombs and grenades; secondly, as a term of civil architecture, designating the ancestor of the civil engineer. Just as the period covered by this study came to a close, the infantry (Sade's specialty) won out under Napoleon over both the original *corps de génie* (the engineer of fortifications, Rousseau's familial profession) and the updated *ingénieur de feu* (artillery-*cum*-fortifications, Laclos's branch)—and Laclos lived both to test this new method of warfare and to see the end of the Golden Age of French military architecture. In the early nineteenth century, "engineer" would come to designate primarily the specialist in civil engineering.[3] The age of Vaubanian fortifications unfolds within strict chronological limits, but the concepts that can be associated with it, above all the control of natural forces by system, foreshadow many modern developments.

In an age when concern for protecting our frontiers has led us to assemble a "defensive" nuclear force sufficient to destroy the entire population of the globe many times over, Vauban's theories, and especially what I call the myth of Vauban, seem remarkably pertinent. Today as during the Classical age, the direct, one could say romantic, confrontation of field battles is not the central military preoccupation. We live in a new age of the fortress, for modern military architecture is a form of "bunker architecture,"[4] which hides our might in silos and

---

[3] In Vauban's/Louis's day, civil engineering was a mere sub-specialty of the *corps de génie*, a deviation of the talents of its engineers—witness Louis's use of military engineers for the colossal (and doomed) Maintenon aqueduct.

[4] I coin a term derived from Paul Virilio's *Bunker archéologie* (Centre Pompidou, 1975). See also his *Essai sur l'insécurité du territoire* (Stock, 1976).

8

underground fortresses, a development Vauban's fortified places, which are dug into and are almost one with the earth, foreshadow. Furthermore, we are not strangers to the phenomenon of a complex and allegedly flawless system of military defenses gone awry, to the vision of calculated perfection veering wildly out of control. Today, as in the France of the Golden Age of the Sun King's reign, we understand the concept that the strongest power should never decently be the aggressor; all we want to do is to protect ourselves. Yet in order to be secure, to safeguard our already superior strength and our status as strongest power, we must create a *numerically* superior system of defenses, somehow find the perfect system of defenses. So we build the MX missile[5] and silos to enclose it, as well as megaton bombs. We strive to outstrip the defensive strength of our nearest adversaries many times over, even as we speak of the balance of offensive and defensive forces. And all the while, just as happens to Vauban's system and to those of each of the literary fortifiers whose calculating systems follow his model, this defense proliferates endlessly, becoming a self-generating machine, a defensive machine that is alarmingly aggressive and bears an unsettling resemblance to offense. Of late, the origins of our modernity have often been traced to the French Classical age. It may be that we can also find there the origin of our current obsession with defense and our unspoken, implicit belief in the existence of a perfect system of defense, the protective system that would give us at long last (territorial) security.

Perhaps for literature, the central lesson of this camouflaged and shielded form of military confrontation is a lesson of secrecy and impenetrability. In siegecraft, the defender's position is the essence of voyeurism; those inside the fortress are rendered invisible by their fortifications, but everything outside is still visible to them through the fortress's deadly (and intentional) loopholes (*meurtrières*). In *The Freedom of French Classicism*, E.B.O. Borgerhoff proclaims his objective of dis-

[5] The MX is the latest descendant of the *boulet creux* Laclos invented to increase the Vaubanian fortress's defensive capabilities.

pelling the view of the French seventeenth century as characterized by its "remote pompousness and embalmed imperturbability"; he seeks to develop in its place a sense of the period's "vital complexity," of its authors' "sense of independence and freedom."[6] Yet the view of the literature of France's Golden Age that his work ultimately supports would seem to make him a precursor of Foucault: "[N]ot only the 'je ne sais quoi' but other ways of expressing and embracing the indefinable and the inexplicable were so inseparable from any discussion of literature as to make some critics and writers of the century seem guilty of a kind of partnership in secrecy, a kind of conspiracy to protect the ineffable" (p. ix). I have no quarrel with Borgerhoff's intriguing readings of Classical texts, but I do disagree with his calling a discourse of liberation what he himself feels to be a defensive conspiracy of silence. The Classical writers he analyzes do not tear down protective barriers; they erect them in order to defend the secret of their success.

Classical writers had an illustrious model for their endeavors, no less a figure than the monarch for whom Vauban built his extraordinary system of fortifications. One of the most significant recent trends in seventeenth-century French studies proposes a revised, one might say Foucaultian, image of the Sun King. Works such as Nicole Ferrier-Caverivière's *L'Image de Louis XIV dans la littérature française de 1660 à 1715* and Louis Marin's *Le Portrait du roi* chart the monarch's systematic mechanization of power. Ferrier-Caverivière—like others, including Voltaire, before her—sees 1678 as the turning point in Louis's reign. After that date the Sun King's rule—rather than the era of peace, plenitude, prosperity, and freedom it had promised to be—became instead an ever spreading system of control and repression, a colossal machine designed to reproduce, seemingly ad infinitum, frozen images of grandeur. After 1678, for example, a new Versailles rose up "où

---

[6] *The Freedom of French Classicism* (Princeton, N.J.: Princeton Univ. Press, 1950), pp. viii, 131.

la féerie et la fantaisie laissent la place au colossal, au majestueux, et à l'imposant."[7] Simultaneously, the king himself "a rompu avec un rythme d'existence vagabonde pour se figer dans le faste" (p. 163). The new palace, where nature was brought into line and made to conform to a system at the expense of superhuman labors (often effectuated by Vauban's men), provided a fitting setting for a monarch who was transforming himself into a secularly sacred and omnipotent idol. Louis walled himself in behind a series of dazzling façades, a self-protective machine that, like Vauban's outworks, proliferated endlessly. The Sun King's fortifications also had in common with Vauban's a reliance on secrecy. Louis's omnipotence—like that of Classical literature, as Borgerhoff's analyses demonstrate—depended on a cult, a conspiracy of silence, for its continued functioning. This absolute, impenetrable wall of silence allowed the monarch of Versailles to share in the invulnerability of the masters of a fortified place and bestowed on him the power of seeing while remaining himself invisible. A contemporary proponent of princely secrecy, Bouhours, aptly compared the monarch who relied on inscrutability to a deity resembling Pascal's *Deus absconditus*: both "gouverne[nt] le monde par des voyes inconnuës aux hommes."[8] According to Bouhours, secrecy is the essence both of sovereignty—"c'est une espece de souveraineté"—and of genius: "[I]l n'appartient qu'à un génie sublime et fait pour commander, de penetrer les desseins des autres, et de sçavoir cacher les siens" (pp. 163-64). In Louis XIV's France, the art of secrecy was brought to perfection, and as a result the king, "le coeur de l'empire," reached a defensive nirvana—"mais un coeur fidelle, impenétrable, et muni de tous costez du silence" (p. 168). Marin contends—and his argument parallels Borgerhoff's conclusion regarding Classical literature and criticism—that

[7] Ferrier-Caverivière, *L'Image de Louis XIV dans la littérature française de 1660 à 1715* (PUF, 1981), p. 164.
[8] Bouhours, *Entretiens d'Ariste et d'Eugène* (Mabre-Cramoisy, 1671), p. 165.

the ultimate secret this silent armature was designed to protect was the ineffable arcanum of the monarch's inner void:

> Si son secret, la pensée secrète de son secret, tellement secrète qu'il ne la pense pas, est qu'il n'est pas ce qu'il est, présence de son absence à soi, alors . . . le monarche absolu est un monument vide, un cénotaphe, un tombeau qui n'abrite aucun corps mais qui est dans sa vacuité même corps royal.[9]

In military terms, the secret of this hollow presence bears another translation: 1678 is a crucial date in the history of Louis XIV's reign because it marks the year of the peace of Nimwegen (Nimègue), but that so-called great peace is the single event that reveals most clearly the paradox at the heart of the Sun King, and of French Classicism as well. That allegedly peaceful, liberating juncture shows, in fact, Louis at his most warlike. The peace of Nimwegen is the origin of many of Vauban's theories and constructs, for he realized then, better than anyone else, that Louis had not ceased hostilities when he could have and had on the contrary put into function a war machine in which defense and offense were inextricably bound. The secret of Louis's inner void was that, from this point on, he had transformed himself into a Vaubanian fortress,[10] a defensive construct that, like our modern deterrent forces, was resolutely aggressive.

The splendor of Louis's dress and the glories of his palace were intended to deflect attention from his offensive activities, to render his critics not so much secretive as speechless. In one of her *Conversations nouvelles* entitled appropriately "De

---

[9] Marin, *Le Portrait du roi* (Editions de Minuit, 1981), p. 290. By the time of Louis XIV's death, his politics of majesty had brought France to such a state of financial ruin that the structure on which his power reposed, an empty center camouflaged by an intricate façade, ended in a striking reversal: the Sun King was buried incognito in order to protect his body from the anger of his no longer dazzled subjects.

[10] Whether Vauban provided a model for his king or whether the opposite was true is a subject I address in the first chapter.

la magnificence"—in which she, significantly, criticizes the
king for his growing preference for offense over defense—
Madeleine de Scudéry has a character explain to a newly
arrived noble curious about the latest diversion at Versailles,
"l'Appartement," that

> le Roy a surpassé tous ses Predecesseurs, et tous ceux
> des autres Rois; mais il ne pourra jamais se surpasser
> luy-même, et comme tout ce que nous en pourrions dire
> ne pourait l'égaler, preparons-nous à partir demain pour
> mener Philemon à l'Appartement, afin qu'il connoisse
> par ses propres yeux qu'il est au dessus de toute expres-
> sion, et qu'on ne peut jamais le bien representer.[11]

Scudéry unveils the functioning of the ineffable: Louis is so
perfect that he cannot even outdo himself, so no one else can
hope to describe his perfection. Faced with the phenomenon
of magnificence, all that the would-be commentator can do
is to let his eyes "know" and be enlightened by what is beyond
representation, and Scudéry makes it clear that this enlightenment is a form of blindness—"l'esprit s'eblouït comme les
yeux" (p. 7).

Sixteen seventy-eight also plays a significant role in French
literary history, for in March of that year the work generally
referred to as the first "modern" novel, *La Princesse de Clèves,*
was published (anonymously, as befits an age when secrecy
was considered the mark of both authority and genius). Its
author had a heritage of defensive military strategy: Lafayette's father, Marc Pioche de La Vergne, was an important
ingénieur des fortifications of the pre-Vauban generation and

---

[11] Scudéry, *Conversations nouvelles sur divers sujets* (Amsterdam: Wetstein et Desbordes, 1685), p. 52. *Représentation:* "Manière de vivre appar-
tenant à une personne distinguée par son rang . . . , sa fortune, manière de
vivre où l'on se tient comme dans une représentation théâtrale, soumis aux
regards du public" (Littré dictionary). According to the court aesthetics, the
code of behavior dominant at the time of the novel's genesis in France, the
meaning of representation was precisely the dazzling magnificence that cannot
be described or represented.

a sometime private tutor (*gouverneur*) in the art of siegecraft. In many ways, Louis's Vaubanian strategies provide a model for the French Classical novel (and I include in this category the eighteenth-century defensive texts that were written in the wake of Lafayette's masterpiece). The authors of these novels surrounded them with a façade so dazzling, so convincing, that readers can view a discourse of control and repression as a discourse of liberation, and their textual inner void, the enigma of their equivocacy, is thereby protected. As Sade himself realized—witness the incipit to *Les 120 Journées de Sodome*—the essence of Sadean strategy was foreshadowed by Louis's/Vauban's tactics. And perhaps the one point about their literary genealogy on which Rousseau, Laclos, and Sade agreed was that they were all Lafayette's heirs, hoping to inscribe their fictions in the wake of her masterpiece.

The modern novel was born in 1678 just as Louis XIV's reign veered into the domain of superhuman, all-controlling system. Too often, the history of the French novel is cut off from that myth of invulnerability and impenetrability, that is, the eighteenth-century novel is severed from its roots in Classicism and a detour made around it to link *La Princesse de Clèves* to the nineteenth-century novel (because both are in the third person, both are historical). Yet the origin of the major eighteenth-century texts to be examined here can be traced directly to 1678 because they were written in the aftermath of this Classical, Vaubanian myth of perfect control.

In the *Parallèle des Anciens et des Modernes*, Perrault lays bare the aggressive menace of the Golden Age of Classicism that would hang over subsequent writers of the Classical age. The image of the seventeenth-century modernist aesthetic he conveys is echoed by Sade in the opening of the *120*: "après [nous] le déluge." According to the reasoning of Perrault's moderns, the entire trajectory of world history has built up to its summit, the century of Louis le Grand, an age that owes its greatness to the greatness of its monarch. Moreover, within that splendid century, the absolute culmination of history can be precisely located, "l'âge viril" of Versailles's ruler (defined by Perrault as the period around 1678). Those who have lived through this period and who, with the king, are entering "dans la vieillesse" can know with absolute certainty that theirs is the ultimate, the last century, and that history will move downhill from this point: "[J]e prétens que l'avantage qu'a nostre siecle d'estre *venu le dernier*, . . . l'a rendu le plus sça-vant, le plus poli et le plus delicat de tous." This modernist optimism is grounded in a sense of relief for not having been born any later: "[J]'ai encore la joye de penser que vrai-semblablement nous n'avons pas beaucoup de choses à envier à ceux qui viendront après nous."[12] Small wonder that Vol-taire, that specialist of the century of Louis XIV, had the sense of living in an age of decline—witness the "épître dédica-toire" to *Les Lois de Minos*. Yet Voltaire responded only to the menace of seventeenth-century modernism; unlike Rous-seau, Laclos, and Sade, he failed to take up its challenge on the terrain the literary modernists of Classicism chose as their own. For Perrault, "l'âge viril" marked the apogee of history, and in literary terms it was noteworthy because the moderns invented a form unknown to the ancients, the novel. In order to return to the glory that was Versailles, eighteenth-century defensive authors had to understand the power of secrecy and outdo Louis/Vauban in the creation of protective strategies, all this in the literary domain that was the counterpart of the king's "âge viril," the modern-Classical novel.

The masterpieces of French Classicism have traditionally been referred to as "natural," this term being used in the sense of "limpid" or "transparent." Yet in the year of Perrault's *Parallèle des Anciens et des Modernes* (1692), Lafayette's nov-elistic teacher, Scudéry—herself the sister of the commanding officer of a fortified place—laid bare the link between the importance of nature in France's Golden Age and the dazzling rite of power crafted by its monarch. In a conversation in her last work, *Entretiens de morale*, Scudéry demonstrates that

---

[12] Perrault, *Parallèle des Anciens et des Modernes*, ed. Jauss (Munich: Eidos Verlag, 1964), pp. 114, 249, 125.

15

the goal of Louis's fortifications of secrecy is nothing less than the absolute domination of nature. The Sun King's latest *coup* has been staged at a banquet for the king and queen of England that one of Scudéry's interlocutors describes in these terms:

[J]e ne puis comprendre où l'on a pu trouver cette prodigieuse quantité de fleurs . . . , car quand la campagne n'en a plus, les jardins n'en ont guere, et il faut que LOUIS LE GRAND ait un pouvoir surnaturel qui force la Terre et le Soleil à contribuer à ses plaisirs, et à sa magnificence, comme il a celuy de forcer la Victoire à le suivre toûjours.[13]

As a result of Louis's machinations, what is admired as natural beauty is in fact nature reshaped according to the Sun King's desire, nature made to serve his magnificence, "les beautez de la nature que l'art a perfectionnées de nos jours" (p. 272). Furthermore, this natural beauty, far from being limpid and therefore knowable, must be situated in the domain of opaque secrecy: "C'est un secret qu'il s'est voulu reserver, . . . il faut toûjours soumettre sa raison à sa parole en raisonnant sur tant de merveilles incomprehensibles" (p. 274). Classical nature is anything but the product of spontaneous, instinctive, and therefore uncontrollable forces. "Le naturel" is nature transformed by man's art, allegedly irrepressible forces tamed by a powerful machine of grandeur that makes their arcane secrets known only to Versailles's master, who harnesses them to keep his public under his spell.

The critic who calls a French Classical text "natural" generally speaks from the point of view of Scudéry's interlocutors. For the critic, such an appraisal has in fact signified an admission of the reader's impotence: the critic means by this judgment that the text's plenitude is such that it has rendered him as speechless as the Sun King's commentators. The writer has written the critic out of the picture, and in so doing has

---

[13] Scudéry, "Des Fleurs et des Fruits," *Entretiens de morale* (Jean Anisson, 1692), pp. 269-70.

usurped his place, just as Louis le Grand preempted the narrative powers of those who sought to give his text written expression. The authors called most natural are those who have most successfully defeated interpretation because they are best protected against it. This protected, secret "naturalism" was an awesome model for the eighteenth-century writers who claimed to be (re)discovering nature. Since its origin, the novel has been judged the most natural of literary genres, for novelistic genius allegedly speaks with the voice of nature: "[L]e génie ne dira jamais mieux que la nature, mais il dira comme elle, dans des situations inventées," Staël proclaimed, echoing what had long since become a critical cliché.[14]

Also from the origin of the novel, this so-called limpid, natural style has allegedly existed primarily for one pedagogical purpose, the study of the human heart. Thus the great French tradition of the novel is considered that of the psychological novel, the "roman d'analyse," the tradition that leads (straight) from Lafayette to Rousseau, and it is assumed that later novelists aspire to greatness in the art in which these novelists excelled, that of exploring the human heart and creating a sentimental pedagogy. In his edition of Laclos's *Oeuvres complètes*, Laurent Versini voices his surprise that Laclos doesn't speak at greater length of Lafayette: "On est étonné de la discrétion avec laquelle Laclos fait allusion à Madame de La-fayette . . . la maitrîse de l'analyse étant dans *Les Liaisons dangereuses* l'aboutissement d'une tradition où son chef d'oeuvre occupe . . . une place capitale."[15] His astonishment seems ill-considered on two grounds. In the first place, Laclos's comprehension of the Classical strategy of secrecy leads him to suppress the names of many who provided models for his (novelistic) system. More significant, however, is Versini's misalignment of Lafayette's importance for Laclos. In the *Liaisons*, Laclos uses a four-part structure and an enigmatic ending reminiscent of *La Princesse de Clèves*, for what is essential

---

[14] Staël, preface to *Delphine* (Strasbourg: Treuttel et Wurtz, 1820), p. ix.
[15] Laclos, *Oeuvres complètes* (hereafter *O.c.*), p. 1145.

for him, and for Rousseau and Sade as well, is Lafayette's domination of the form of the novel, rather than her exploration of what Diderot would term, speaking of Richardson, previously hidden recesses of the human heart. For the eighteenth century, literary Classicism was synonymous with a perfectly functioning, all-controlling machine that disciplined form and fiction. For the novelist, Classicism meant an insistence on technique—on the how and why of what takes place, rather than on what is actually taking place—coupled with an insistence on the ordered placement of events. The French novelists who wrote in the shadow of the fortress of Classical literature sometimes revolted against the threatening model the so-called Golden Age represented—and Rousseau was perhaps the most vociferous of these critics—but they nevertheless translated the Classical pattern of self-protection into their fictions. The great French novelists of the Enlightenment are less concerned with teaching us more about the realm of human sensibility than with putting into operation an infallible system created to predict and control the shape of human behavior. They understand that in order to aspire to greatness in the French novelistic tradition, it is necessary to develop a science, a geometry, of the human heart, for the great French novel is dedicated to perfecting strategies of ordered, controlled placement. When the conflict between *esprit de géométrie* and *esprit de finesse* is played out within the territory of the French Classical novel, the *esprit de géométrie* (the voice of Vauban) always dominates.[16] Even Rousseau's fictions bear the stamp of a Vaubanian instinct, an instinct that eventually takes control over the voice of sentiment.

For the great (defensive) French novelist of the *Age des Lumières*, originality is not a question of emotional inven-

[16] Significantly, Fontenelle signs his eulogy of *La Princesse de Clèves* "un géomètre de Guyenne." In it, he praises the novel for its "charmes assez forts pour se faire sentir à des mathématiciens mêmes." Cited in Maurice Laugaa, *Lectures de Madame de Lafayette* (Colin, 1971), p. 22.

tiveness: Laclos, the novelistic ventriloquist, establishes himself as master of this tradition by reducing his characters'
passions to the already-said. He understood that "le naturel"
was not a sign of spontaneous genius, as early theorists of the
novel argued, but a product of systematization, a rigidly controlled and ordered construct. This view of the French novel
makes clear the centrality of Laclos's position and allows for
the recuperation of Sade's contribution as a novelist. In addition, it reveals the filiation leading, via Classicism and Rousseau, from both of them to the master of the *déjà-dit* and the
founding father of modernism, Flaubert.

I

Vauban's Fortresses and the Defense of French Classicism

Far rather do I believe that the high command has existed
from all eternity, and the decision to build the wall likewise. Unwitting peoples of the north, who imagined they
were the cause of it! Honest, unwitting Emperor, who
imagined he decreed it! We builders of the wall know
that it was not so and hold our tongues.

Franz Kafka, "The Great Wall of China"

The Genius of Louis's Machine

I read, some days past, that the man who ordered the
creation of the almost infinite wall of China was that
first Emperor, Shih Huang Ti, who also decreed that all
the books prior to him be burned. That these two vast
operations—the five to six hundred leagues of stone
opposing the barbarians, the rigorous abolition of history, that is, of the past—should originate in one person
and be in some way his attributes inexplicably satisfied
and, at the same time, disturbed me.

Jorge Luis Borges, "The Wall and the Books"

The Louvre's Grande Galerie may well be the most prestigious
exhibition space in France. Some years ago, a decision was
made to shift the paintings displayed there, so that a prime
section of this most illustrious museum walkway would be
given over to the masterpieces of the French Classical age.
During the reign of the master of ostentation, Louis XIV, the
gallery had already been used to display artistic chefs-d'oeuvre
that demonstrated national prestige. The area today devoted

to Poussin and Chardin was in the seventeenth century occupied by the scale models of fortified places, *plans-reliefs,*
that Vauban had constructed for his monarch in order to
provide him with a permanent, portable, and easily studied
record of each defensive complex. The miniature fortresses
Louis showed off as representative of his reign were no mere
utilitarian constructs. No expense had been spared to make
them not only accurate, but beautiful as well. Witness this
description by the curator of the museum in which they are
now housed:

> Le modelage général du relief est en bois. Les maisons
> et les monuments sont également en bois sculpté peint
> ou habillé de papier. Les arbres dont chaque essence est
> caractérisée sont en fil de fer et soie. La poudre de soie
> recouvre les prairies . . . et un mélange approprié de sable
> et de carton-pierre permet de caractériser les diverses
> roches.[1]

Upon receiving them the Sun King treated these miniatures
as works of art and displayed them to the assembled court to
be admired. Once installed in the Grande Galerie, however,
the scale models were intended to awe ("éblouir") their few
privileged spectators in a different manner. Access to the display was limited to those with the highest level of what we
today call security clearance: the king's signature was required
on each pass. As records of France's defensive might, the
plans-reliefs were shrouded in secrecy. The authority they gained
from the Sun King's classic strategy was only augmented on
the rare occasions when the veil was lifted. Thus in 1717 the
regent had Peter the Great taken to the gallery to prove to
him in the most succinct way possible that, even after his

[1] Michel Parent, *Vauban: Un encyclopédiste avant la lettre* (Berger-Levrault, 1982), p. 128. The text of this volume reproduces for the most part
that of *Vauban* (Fréal, 1971), a collaboration of Parent with Jacques Verroust.
All subsequent references will be labeled either Parent or Parent-Verroust
and will be given in the text as page numbers in parentheses, a practice I
follow with all works from which I quote several times.

21

death, Vauban continued to protect France (Parent, p. 128).
Inside the gallery and defended by military secrecy, the delicate
silk-clad miniatures were transformed into the representation
of an awesome military machine, the image of a deterrent
force then considered as dreadful as today's long-range missile
systems. In the process, as will become clear, they became true
artistic masterpieces, fulfilling the ultimate condition necessary for elevation to this status during the Sun King's reign.
The history of Vauban's scale models is faithful to the semantic origin of "machine." The Latin "machina" refers both
to a military machine and to a device or stratagem. Military
machines were devised by a *machinarius* or a *machinator*, an
engineer, that is, someone known for his *ingenium*, his natural
ability or genius. (In French, *ingenium* gave rise both to "génie"
and to "engin," military machine or ruse.) In seventeenth-
century France, all ingenious machinations, from ruses to industrial machines, functioned in some sense as artistic constructs. Machines of all kinds were appreciated as works of
genius, as achievements whose very ability to perform tasks
on a previously inconceivable scale and with superhuman efficiency lifted them out of the domain of the utilitarian and
into the realm of artistic creation. The theatrical machines
used in opera from which derives a concept of great importance for Classical literature, the *deus ex machina*, provide
the most obvious examples of artistic devices appreciated aesthetically because of their ingenious construction. The hydraulic machines built by Vauban's engineers in order to operate
Louis's lavish aquatic displays at Versailles are less obviously
artistic creations, but they, nevertheless, were admired by king
and court as though their aesthetic merits were as evident as
those of the fountains and ornamental lakes they made possible. The courtiers marveled at the waterworks because of
their sheer scale. The machine de Marly—whose functioning
attracted spectators as attentive as theatergoers—included an
aqueduct 643 meters long and 23 meters high, and 14 hydraulic wheels 12 meters in diameter. The never finished "grand
aqueduc de Maintenon" was to have had a total length of

4,600 meters; only the lower arcade, 975 meters long, was completed, with the efforts of 20,000 men and at a cost of nearly 9,000,000 francs.[2] These machines did more than fuel Versailles's spectacles and serve as spectacles in themselves. They functioned above all as signs of Louis's power, and of that of the *corps de génie* responsible for their invention. At Louis's court, power was beauty, and a machine that functioned on an enormous scale and at great expense was considered a glorious spectacle, even if, as in the case of the machine de Marly, its functioning was hardly a marvel of efficiency. Huet—a noted theoretician of the seventeenth-century novel—provides an apt characterization of this phenomenon of power become beautiful:

> Quoique les beautez naturelles soient préférables aux beautez de l'art, ce n'est pas pourtant le goût de ce siécle. Rien ne plaît s'il ne coûte. Une fontaine sortant à gros bouillons du pied d'un rocher, roulant sur un sablé doré, les plus claires et les plus fraîches eaux du monde, ne plaira pas tant aux gens de la Cour, qu'un jet d'eau puante et bourbeuse, tirée à grand frais de quelque grenouillière.[3]

As a result, even a quite humble machine, a machine that had at best an indirect connection to the spectacle of glory orchestrated at Versailles, the *machine à faire des bas de soie,* became a worthy subject for narrative and for aesthetic contemplation. In the *Parallèle des Anciens et des Modernes,*

---

[2] See Reginald Blomfield's *Sébastien Le Prestre de Vauban* (London: Methuen, 1938), p. 102. Racine wrote to Boileau: "J'ai fait le voyage de Maintenon et suis fort content des ouvrages que j'y ai vus: ils sont prodigieux et dignes, en vérité, de la magnificence du Roi" (*Oeuvres complètes* [Seuil, 1962], p. 377). My information for this chapter was obtained from a variety of sources. In addition to Blomfield and Parent-Verroust, the most helpful works on Vauban and his position in military history are Colonel Lazard's *Vauban* (Alcan, 1934) and Alfred Rebelliau's *Vauban* (Fayard, 1962). Christopher Duffy's *Fire and Stone: The Science of Fortress Warfare 1660-1860* (London: David and Charles, 1975) is an especially useful general survey.

[3] *Huetiana* (J. Estienne, 1722), p. 119.

Perrault cites many examples of technical progress as a demonstration of modern intellectual superiority. His description of the silk-stocking machine reveals the structure of power that made such mechanical functioning admirable. The machine is a spectacle because of its superhuman production level: "[elle] fait en un moment tous les divers mouvemens que font les mains [d'un Ouvrier] en un quart d'heure."[4] Furthermore—and for Perrault this is the mark of the "génie" and the "sagesse" of the engineer who, truly the god of this machine, "gave life" to it (p. 120)—this "astonishing" power is perfectly dominated by a system of indirect, impersonal control. The child who serves as the *infans in machina* by turning the wheel that operates the machine "understands nothing" about its functioning, so that, Perrault reasons, "du vent ou de l'eau tourneroient aussi bien [la roue] et avec moins de peine." Unlike the devices that brought divine spectacle to opera, there is no god in this machine, and that is precisely the origin of its powerful beauty.[5] Like the Sun King, the machine is a hollow construct, capable therefore of an inhuman, a superhuman, level of control and effectiveness.

Hydraulic machines, operatic machines, industrial machines, the royal machine—during France's Golden Age, the machine was an art form, a borderline art form because all these machines had both an aesthetic and a utilitarian function. In the case of the princely machine as much as in that of the operatic machine, the utilitarian function was the source of aesthetic pleasure. For Louis XIV and his moderns, art was an awesome, hollow construct that functioned as a sign of

---

[4] Perrault, *Parallèle,* ed. Jauss (Munich: Eidos Verlag, 1964), p. 120. The object the silk-stocking machine was designed to produce was a staple of the dazzling vestimentary façade adopted by king and courtier. "Les dentelles, le rabat, le fil, le passement, la coiffure désignent et indiquent cette multiplication et cette augmentation comme corps de pouvoir" (Marin, *Le Portrait du roi,* [Editions de Minuit, 1981] p. 36).

[5] In a fascinating study, *Le Roi machine* (Editions de Minuit, 1981), pp. 123-26, J.-M. Apostolidès analyzes the spectacle of machines during the Versailles period.

power. In this society that marveled at mechanical glory, it was fitting that the heart of the king's traditional home, the Louvre, should house the representation of the war machine without which all these diverse spectacles of power would have been meaningless. Vauban was the founding genius of the *corps de génie,* the century's most ingenious maker of *engins,* the machinator who devised the ruses that were the foundation of his king's war machine. Like his scale models, his military exploits were first an open source of astonishment and admiration. Then, also like his scale models, the strategies on which those exploits were based were shrouded in secrecy, making of Vauban not only a maker of machines that came to constitute a deterrent force, but a deterrent force in and of himself.

Vauban's *plans-reliefs* were the silk-clad miniaturization of a war machine that functioned on such a superhuman scale that it gave birth to a myth, the myth of a system of defenses so perfect that it could make France, like its king, an impregnable fortress.

—— ✳ ——

The Builder of the Wall

> Les génies lisent peu, pratiquent beaucoup, et se font
> d'eux-mêmes. Voyez César, Turenne, Vauban. . . . C'est
> la nature qui forme ces hommes rares-là.
> Denis Diderot, *Le Neveu de Rameau*

Evocations of the glory that was Versailles assign only a dark place in the Sun King's shadow to one of the individuals most responsible for the continued existence of that glory, Sébastien Le Prestre de Vauban, Louis XIV's *Commissaire général des fortifications.* Vauban's contemporaries were more generous in their estimation of the figure who would ultimately become a legend only for military history. Thus the arbiter of Classicism, Boileau, wrote to Racine: "C'est un des Hommes de

CHAPTER I

notre siècle à mon avis qui a le plus prodigieux mérite."⁶ Whereas most legends of the Versailles saga have been painstakingly dissected, one of the great myths of the Classical period in France has never been seriously explored: the creation of the perfect system of defenses. Yet the Sun King's master fortifier may well be the emblematic figure of what Michel Foucault considers the Classical era (the late seventeenth to the end of the eighteenth century). Militarily, Vauban's genius was indispensable to the success of his monarch's enterprise. Furthermore, at the end of Louis's reign and in the course of the eighteenth century Vauban's work came to be widely regarded as having almost magical powers that guaranteed France's protection. Finally, the complex of fortifications he developed to defend France against foreign invasion ultimately gave the country its modern shape, just as literary Classicism may have determined the future course of French literature.

The myth with which Vauban's name was synonymous, that of a perfect system of defenses, can be used to explore the intersection of military history and aesthetic history. Proust suggests that "tout ce que vous lisez . . . dans le récit d'un narrateur militaire, les plus petits faits, les plus petits événements, ne sont que les signes d'une idée qu'il faut dégager et qui souvent en recouvre d'autres, comme dans un palimpseste."⁷ A Proustian reading of the military history of the century of Louis XIV demonstrates that Classicism and defensive military strategies are homologous systems. As much as the triply unified play in five acts and alexandrines, the emblematic art form of the Versailles era is the Vaubanian fortress.

⁶ Letter, 26 May 1687, in Boileau, *Oeuvres,* ed. Adam and Escal (Gallimard, 1966), p. 735. Vauban's *Projet d'une dîme royale* has continued to receive attention from a wide audience, but it is only tangentially related to the military activity that is the foundation of his authority during the age of Classicism.
⁷ Proust, *Le Côté de Guermantes,* in *A la Recherche du temps perdu,* 3 vols. (Bibliothèque de la Pléiade, 1954), vol. 2, p. 109.

26

What has come to be known as the Golden Age of French art and literature was also the Golden Age of codification. Even if the dominant figures of the age of Louis XIV were not all makers of codes like Boileau, they both worked within the boundaries established by preexistent codes and worked to generalize the acceptance of these standards. Even within an artistic tradition as strictly governed by rules and hierarchies as the French, no period can equal the Golden Age for the seemingly unerring sense of limits and preference that then prevailed. Tragedy was superior to comedy, theater to the novel, formal "French" gardens were preferred to all other kinds—it seems as if all instinctively knew just what was best in every domain, and, furthermore, that those perceived as great heeded all prescriptions, rather than striving to bend or break them. In this context, Vauban can be considered Boileau's military counterpart. He codified the disparate fragments that had previously passed for a strategy of military defense. Because of his system, Vauban came to be accepted as a judge: it was taken for granted that he knew what should or should not be done. Vauban's peers in the arts set standards that, despite constant efforts to usurp their authority, were dominant throughout the eighteenth century. In like manner, his work ushered in the Classical century of military engineering during which the authority of his codes was contested, but never overthrown.

Like the great artists of Classicism, Vauban has been characterized as typically, essentially French. For example, such a demonstration is the central goal of Rebelliau's authoritative study: "[Les traits] de son caractère ne sont pas difficiles à résumer. Ils ne sont pas autres, en somme, qu'à un degré éminent les éléments essentiels de l'intelligence française. . . . Les contemporains le comprirent et reconnurent en sa manière de procéder la marque du meilleur esprit français" (pp. 293, 296). Vauban's fortifications have continued to be judged, as he himself judged them, according to standards that are also applied to the artistic masterpieces of Classicism. Evaluating his work on Maubeuge for Louvois, Vauban reflected that "s'il y a quelque chose dans la fortification qui mérite l'admiration des hommes, on peut dire qu'il se trouve dans cette place plus que dans aucune autre du Royaume." He praises it for two reasons: the beauty of its symmetry, and its grandeur ("on n'y trouvera rien que de grand"). Approving Vauban's own criteria, Rebelliau notes: "Maubeuge est donc le chef d'oeuvre de la forteresse rationnelle et le reflet de la pensée classique du Grand Siècle" (pp. 81-82).

The language of fortifications is the foundation of a literary topos frequently encountered in the Classical age: for writers as dissimilar as the *précieuses,* Bussy-Rabutin, and Laclos's libertine correspondents, the woman's body is a fortress to which her lover lays siege. Quite distinct from such imprecise and cliché-ridden usage are the descriptions of fortresses and the art of siegecraft made by some of the greatest writers of the Golden Age—Lafayette, for example, in her *Mémoires de la cour de France pour les années 1688 et 1689,* or Racine in the fragments he composed for the never completed royal history. Texts such as these demonstrate that literature and fortifications were frequently coupled in seventeenth-century France: the founders of Classicism were well-versed in the strategies of siegecraft and, furthermore, considered Vauban the key figure in the development of that military art.[8]

In his *Histoire de la sexualité,* Foucault argues that war and military strategy provide the principal model for the functioning of political power in Western society.[9] His analogy may be extended to describe not only the political structure

[8] Seventeenth-century writers could assume that their readers would be equally well-versed in the language of defensive military strategy. Blomfield asserts that "by the middle of the seventeenth century, the art of fortifications was no longer a mystery to the general public. They were familiar with all its technical terms." To support this view, he quotes a poem (1652) about the Parisians' conduct during the *Fronde,* which contains a long enumeration of terms of fortifications, from "demi-lune" to "courtine" (p. 39). He might also have cited the example of Furetière's *Nouvelle allégorique* (1658), a vision of rhetoric as siegecraft.

[9] Foucault, *La Volonté du savoir* (Gallimard, 1976), p. 135.

developed by Louis XIV, but also the Classical art nourished by that political structure. In what could be considered a parallel investigation, a recent school of French architects has attempted to show the relationship between defensive military architecture, in particular the bunker, and the definition or repartition of territory.[10] Their comparison suggests an additional relationship, between military architecture and the structure of mental territory. Freud calls fantasies "psychical outworks constructed in order to bar the way to the memories [of primal scenes]." Lacan characterizes the "structure" of "obsessional neurosis" as "si comparable en ses principes à celle qu'illustrent le redan et la chicane, que nous avons entendu plusieurs de nos patients user à leur propre sujet d'une référence métaphorique à des 'fortifications à la Vauban.' "[11] The Vaubanian fortifications Lacan describes are designed to "camouflage" and "displace" patients' aggressiveness. The structure of the actual defensive constructs that are the source of their metaphor may, I contend, have a great deal to teach us about the obsessions and the repressed violence of the Golden Age, may even reveal the shape of its (monarch's) primal fantasies.

The Vaubanian fortress is an appropriate representation of the disposition of territory during France's Golden Age. Versailles, intended to stand as the ultimate symbol of Louis XIV's reign, is the product of a struggle to tame nature and thereby prove that no forces could resist the Sun King's vision. French critics have characteristically understood, and approved, this struggle. Witness Corpechot's account of the creation of Versailles's park: "C'est dans la création du parc de Versailles qu'éclate avec le plus d'évidence le drame de la pensée aux prises avec les phénomènes naturels. . . . La guerre est déclarée

[10] See, for example, Paul Virilio's *Bunker archéologie* (Centre Pompidou, 1975) and his *Essai sur l'insécurité du territoire* (Stock, 1976).

[11] Freud, draft of letter to Fliess, 2 May 1897, *The Origins of Psychoanalysis* (New York: Basic Books, 1954), p. 197; Lacan, *Ecrits* (Seuil, 1966), p. 108.

à la nature dans ce qu'elle a d'ennemi, d'impénétrable à la pensée. Il la faut dompter."[12] A similar need to control and systematize instinctive, irrational forces is persistently recurrent in the artistic productions of the Classical age. Constant uneasiness, even paranoia, and insistent attempts at self-protection constitute the recurrent themes of many of the literary masterpieces of the period, from the *Princesse de Clèves* to *Bérénice*.[13] Its masterworks paint the portrait of Classicism as an extended state of siege during which Vauban's description of siege mentality seems perpetually applicable: "Dans ce temps les murailles parlent . . . et tout le monde est aux écoutes."

Perhaps the most persistent (and surely the most frequently chronicled) political anxiety of the *Grand siècle* involved the existence of hidden siblings of Louis XIV. Saint-Simon notes rumors of a sister locked away in a convent because of her mysterious blackness of skin. The best-known variant of this threat is the story of *l'homme au masque de fer*, allegedly a twin brother who threatened Louis's right to the throne, a natural force he kept under control with the aid of every kind of geometry possible. For Versailles's maker, Vauban came to represent still another incarnation of the *frère ennemi*.

Vauban enjoyed a particular "walking" relationship with his monarch, one paralleled only by Louis's relationship with the other great shaper of nature in his employ, Le Nôtre. Together, king and soldier walked through the sites of projected sieges, as Vauban explained his projects *in situ*. They quite literally walked (and rode) through entire campaigns together. It was no secret that the king could not have become a great conqueror without Vauban's advice—Saint-Simon, for example, described him as "le célèbre Vauban, l'âme de tous

[12] Corpechot, *Les Jardins de l'intelligence* (Plon, 1937), pp. 74, 81.

[13] The most convincing study of the presence of anxiety in Classical literature is Lionel Gossman's *Men and Masks: A Study of Molière* (Baltimore: Johns Hopkins Univ. Press, 1963).

les sièges que le Roi a faits."¹⁴ The same Saint-Simon was later to hint that Vauban was the soul of more than Louis's sieges.

He described the ceremony when the king made Vauban a *maréchal de France*: "Le Roi, sous lequel en personne [Vauban] en avait tant fait d'éclatants [sièges], crut se faire maréchal de France lui-même et couronner ses propres lauriers par le bâton qu'il lui donna avec complaisance" (Rochas d'Aiglun, vol. 2, p. 518). Saint-Simon's hand, as usual, is on the pulse of his century, for he may be revealing one of the best-hidden skeletons in Versailles's closets. Vauban could be called the soul of more than just the king's sieges: he was the soul of the king and his century as well.

In seventeenth-century Europe, the art of war was essentially synonymous with the art of siegecraft. Field battles would later become the foundation of Napoleon's gloriously romantic legend and inspire the most memorable images of war in nineteenth-century literature from Stendhal to Tolstoy, but they were rarely fought in the century of Louis XIV. The period that translated its literary vitality into Classicism channeled its military energy into the attack and defense of fortified places. There is a particular explanation for the domination of siege warfare in France: like every other ruling structure of the day, it best served the Sun King's personal needs. As the most reliable of Vauban's editors phrases it: "Le Roi, qui tenait avant tout à ne pas compromettre son prestige par un échec, préférait les sièges, où tout peut être réglé à l'avance, aux batailles rangées où l'imprévu joue un si grand rôle. Aussi n'en livra-t-il jamais aucune."¹⁵

¹⁴ Saint-Simon, *Mémoires*, ed. G. Truc (Gallimard, 1953), vol. 1, p. 20.
¹⁵ Colonel de Rochas d'Aiglun, *Vauban, sa famille et ses écrits. Ses oisivetés, sa correspondance*, vol. 2, p. 136 n.2. Rebelliau's evaluation of Louis XIV coincides with Rochas d'Aiglun's: "Ce sont bien les préoccupations que l'histoire civile et militaire de son règne a eu de bonne heure l'occasion de relever chez lui: la haine de la surprise et du hasard; le goût de la police assurée, de l'organisation complète et correcte, de la 'maison bien réglée,' comme on disait alors" (pp. 53-54).
    Racine confirms that the king came to consider Vauban's advice a guarantee of victory. On one occasion when he failed to adopt the strategy proposed

Dangeau notes in his *Journal* that Louis XIV never forgot the one occasion when he failed to conquer his fear of military failure. According to this Versailles insider, the king was obsessed all his life about Bouchain, near Valenciennes, a unique situation where victory was almost guaranteed, but where, nevertheless, he refused to do battle with the prince of Orange. Twenty-three years later, during a stroll through the Classical perfection of the Marly gardens, Louis whispered to his companions "que c'était le jour de sa vie où il avait fait le plus de fautes . . . qu'il y rêvait quelquefois la nuit et se réveillait toujours en colère" (Rochas d'Aiglun, vol. 2, p. 136). The fact that he missed his one chance for nearly risk-free victory in an arena where hazard is normally impossible to avoid may have given the monarch a recurrent nightmare, but his experiences with siege warfare were undoubtedly relatively free of anxiety. Credit for his feeling of control was due not only to the nature of this type of military encounter, but also to the specific modifications for which Vauban was responsible. The man destined to supervise the construction of fortifications during the period of Louis XIV's military expansion had the good fortune to begin his career just at the point when the art of siegecraft was ripe for elevation to the status of a science. Italian engineers of the fifteenth and sixteenth centuries had developed the elements essential to classical methods of fortifying—a systematizer of genius was all that was missing.

All authorities on military history agree that Vauban changed the course of that history, but just how he did so remains a subject of controversy. In any attempt to assess Vauban's contribution to the evolution of siegecraft, two distinctions must be maintained. In the first place, the two interrelated functions he fulfilled—offensive strategist ("le preneur de villes," as he was frequently called) and defensive strategist

---

by the maréchal and the outcome of the siege upheld the wisdom of the master fortifier's counsel, the royal historiographer contends that "le roi lui promit qu'une autre fois il le laisserait faire" ("Fragments historiques," *O.c.*, p. 377).

(the master fortifier)—must be considered separately. Secondly, Vauban the practitioner and man of action must be distinguished from Vauban the theoretician. After a brief summary of some of the facts of Vauban's impressive career, I will attempt to demonstrate the importance of these two distinctions first by examining the publication history of his treatises and then by considering the relationship between Vauban's evolution and that of the monarch he served.

At the time when Vauban began his career, those involved with fortifications could be divided into two almost completely independent classes, the theoreticians and the practitioners. The pedagogical side of the field—from the actual teaching of the subject in schools to the writing of treatises— was almost entirely in the hands of individuals with no field experience whatsoever. Prior to Vauban's time, architects— Leonardo, for example—directed the actual design and construction of defensive systems. The seventeenth century witnessed the transferral of the practical aspects of fortifications to the members of a newly created profession, military engineers. The first of this breed, like Vauban, were essentially self-taught men. They had no formal training other than an apprenticeship. With the proliferation of treatises on fortification during the century (Bar-le-Duc, de Ville, Pagan), reading began to supplement the apprenticeship, eventually to replace it.

Vauban's own career was indisputably marked by practical rather than textual experience. He was equally active as builder and as destroyer of fortifications. He was present at forty-eight sieges and directed all but six of them. He took part in or supervised all but two of the military operations during all of those sieges (and he only missed those two because he was wounded). He designed fortifications for more than a hundred and sixty places, and he directed the construction or the reconstruction of the fortifications of between ninety-two places (Blomfield's estimate) and a hundred and fifty places (Voltaire's estimate). His energy during nearly fifty years of military service appears to have been inexhaustible, and his devotion

33

to his monarch and his country's interests almost fanatical (he spent less than a year with his wife during nearly fifty years of marriage). During the reign of France's most powerful monarch, siegecraft was war, and during the greater part of that reign, Vauban almost literally was siegecraft. Many would-be fortifiers, such as Laclos, never had the chance to put their ideas into practice, but, because he was in the service of a war-loving king, Vauban had the opportunity, as Fontenelle phrased it, "beaucoup v[oir] et avec de bons yeux."[16]

For reasons that will be considered shortly, at various points in his active career the practitioner turned theoretician and attempted to systematize his strategies. In his correspondence, Vauban explained that he did so only to increase and prolong his monarch's invulnerability. Since he could not simultaneously direct all the sieges or all the defenses in a campaign and, furthermore, since he could not know how long he would be able to serve his country, he felt obliged to record the secrets of his success. Yet—and this is one of the most curious aspects of the Vauban story and the factor that, perhaps more than any other, explains the mystique that came to surround his name—Vauban felt obliged to teach but wanted to control the transmission of his ideas. In a section of his treatise on defense entitled "De la necessité de tenir secret ce livre," Vauban defines the particular type of limited public his work required:

Ce livre . . . mériterait bien que sa Majesté le fît imprimer à ses dépens; après quoi retirant tous les exemplaires, elle en pourra donner à ses principaux officiers et au gouverneur de chaque place qui en demeureront chargés: à condition de le tenir dans un coffre fait exprès et de ne laisser lire que chez lui . . . à l'ingénieur et à celui qui commandera l'artillerie. . . . Et le cas arrivant que le Gouverneur meurt, le lieutenant de Roi se saisissant du livre avec son coffre, le devra renvoyer au Roi, sans

---

[16] Fontenelle, "Eloge de M. le Maréchal de Vauban," *Oeuvres*, 9 vols. (Amsterdam: François Changuion, 1764), vol. 5, p. 96.

permettre à qui que ce puisse être d'en prendre des copies. . . . Car de tenir cet ouvrage absolument secret, il ne nous servirait de rien, et si on le rendrait public, il passerait en peu de temps chez les étrangers qui pourraient en faire de mauvais usage contre nous.
(Rochas d'Aiglun, vol. 1, pp. 261-62)

Practical reasons determined Vauban's recourse to an extreme variant of his master's strategy of secrecy: his strategic superiority could only continue to protect France if the written key to its functioning were unique, like Louis's emblematic bird, the phoenix. However, his use of secrecy worked just as if it had been employed for tactical rather than practical reasons, for it helped to establish Vauban's authority. During Louis's lifetime, the treatises were known only by hearsay, but soon after his death what Vauban most feared happened very quickly: his work was made public when several pirated editions appeared. The compiler of one of them explained in a preface the difficulties he had encountered in penetrating the intricate precautions designed to guard Vauban's secret:

Son livre . . . était depuis un grand nombre d'années, en manuscrit, au fond de la bibliothèque du Roi Très-Chrétien: en vain on avait fait des démarches pour engager à le donner au public; il avait été impossible de l'obtenir. . . . L'on ne sait comment il en était échappé des copies, qui, d'abord rares, s'étaient beaucoup multipliées, et commençaient à être portées dans les pays étrangers.

He goes on to add that copies are so expensive that only "Princes, ambassadeurs, et autres seigneurs" could afford them, but that he had spared no expense to bring his edition to the public's attention.[17] By the time the treatises became available, Vauban's early readers must have been ready to believe that the text finally being made public did in fact contain incredible military secrets and have the power to make nations invincible.

[17] *De l'attaque et de la défense des places* (La Haye: Pierre de Hondt, 1737).

35

No other treatise of siegecraft had been surrounded by such secrecy. However, if the readers of the majority of the early editions had examined them closely, they would surely have been a bit baffled by their contents.

While Vauban's programs for the attack of fortified places were reproduced correctly and essentially in their entirety, his rules for their defense did not fare as well. The 1704 *Traité de l'attaque des places* (written for the Duke of Burgundy) was made public in 1737. This edition included a *Traité de la défense des places*, also said to be by Vauban, but actually written by the engineer Deshoulières. The *Mémoire sur la conduite des sièges*, composed at Louvois's request in 1669, was published in 1740. With it was published a treatise on defense alleged to have been composed by Vauban but actually written by an unidentified eighteenth-century author (who seems simply to have reworked the Deshoulières treatise, which he must have believed to have been written by Vauban). These early treatises bear little resemblance to Vauban's defensive texts. Though inspired by Vaubanian strategy, the ersatz compositions lack all the strategic elements that were to form the basis of Vauban's authority. The first of the master fortifier's works on defense published in France appeared only in 1769, but it was in fact a collage of fragments of Vauban's original text, completed with fragments of the Deshoulières treatise that were passed off as the master's work. The first accurate editions of Vauban's treatise on defense were finally published in 1795 and 1829.[18]

Thus even though his early readers may have believed they had first-hand knowledge of his work on defense, for the entire Classical age Vauban's defensive strategy was actually no more than a legend. Yet the market for texts on defense would seem to have been as great as that for texts on attack, since editors consistently felt the need to attribute someone else's treatise

[18] Vauban, *Mémoire sur la conduite des sièges* (Leyden: Jean and Hermon Verbeek, 1740); *De la défense des places* (Jombert, 1769); ed. Foissac (Magimel, 1795); and ed. Valazé (Anselin, 1829).

to Vauban. Those close to the French monarchy in charge of protecting Vauban's treasure must have considered his work on defensive strategies to be the most crucial part of his legacy, for the treatises on defense were obviously more closely guarded than those on attack. The greater scarcity of manuscripts of the treatise on defense is noted by several of Vauban's early editors (see, for example, the Jombert and Magimel editions). Throughout the eighteenth century, Vauban's defensive heritage was ardently desired yet never attainable. His Classical status as hollow presence provoked a dual reaction. On the one hand, Vauban's supporters attributed to him total authority and often almost magical powers for national defense: they claimed that his work had to be kept hidden to guarantee the continued functioning of Louis's *machina*. On the other, his detractors struggled to have the maréchal exposed as a fraud by proving that, far from having invented the perfect system of defense, Vauban had in fact created no system at all: they alleged that his legacy was kept secret so that no one would realize that the emperor had no clothes, that France was not invulnerable. Both reactions enhanced Vauban's legendary status and made the myth of the perfect system of defenses still more powerful.

For nearly a century, all those who wrote on Vauban took sides in this quarrel. Ironically, his supporters provided his detractors with the basis for their attacks. The maréchal's longtime secretary, Thomassin, declared that Vauban had written nothing on the art of fortification. In the eulogy he pronounced upon Vauban's death, Fontenelle stated: "Il a fait voir par sa pratique, qu'il n'avait point de manière, chaque place différente lui en fournissait une nouvelle" (vol. 5, p. 100). His defenders were echoing Vauban's own self-portrait and were seeking to prove that his was a higher type of genius—in Fontenelle's words, a "génie heureux," gifted with "les ressources naturelles et imprévues" that enabled him to invent repeatedly and with spontaneity, rather than applying in a "narrow" manner a limited number of "fixed rules" (vol. 5, p. 100). For them, Vauban's concrete legacy, the complex of fortifications he had created, was the unique foundation of his authority. Throughout the eighteenth century, the shape Louis and his master fortifier had fashioned for France was perceived militarily as a perfect entity. Even Vauban's detractors were thus willing to accord him the title of offensive genius, as Laclos does in his public letter to the French Academy on Vauban's contributions. At stake in the battle for the maréchal's authority was the permanent title to the domain of defense. Vauban was a threatening presence for his critics not because of his reputation for practical, spontaneous genius, but because of his status as a theoretical, systematic, machinating genius. Vauban's detractors sought to prove first of all that the fortifications he had built were not able to stand up under fire, and secondly, that his treatises on defense fell far short of systematic perfection—an accusation that was certainly corroborated by the insubstantial texts published under Vauban's name in the eighteenth century. The great military dream—shared by Laclos, his mentor Montalembert, and many other engineers—was to perfect the system that would make the territory Vauban had won for France invulnerable.[19] Laclos, for example, contended that to continue to proclaim Vauban's authority would ensure that this perfect territorial structure would be eroded, whereas the members of the *corps royal du génie* conversely proclaimed that only the violation of his authority would make France territorially insecure.[20] For the Enlightenment, the body of Vauban's de-

---

[19] The author of the *Encyclopédie* article "fortification," François Quesnay—appropriately, since the *Encyclopédie* is a monument to the belief in flawless systems—is so attracted to the legend that Vauban had turned the art of fortification into a foolproof code that he first denies that the maréchal had a system and then proceeds to describe in detail the three systems allegedly of his invention.

[20] Several "officiers du corps royal du génie" jointly published *Mémoires sur la fortification perpendiculaire* (Nyon, 1786), a defense of Vauban against Montalembert's attacks, because they were afraid that his detractors might be heeded "au préjudice direct des intérêts de l'Etat, relativement à ses Frontières" (p. 6). They did not mention Montalembert by name, a strategy that Montalembert himself used against Vauban in his own treatise on *fortification perpendiculaire*.

fensive work was considered either a stumbling block on the way to France's invulnerability or the ultimate guarantee of its security; in either event, his textual body was synonymous with the country's territorial body.

=== ✳ ===

Mieux Vaut Engin Que Force

A fortress is taken by skill and not by violence alone.
Arthur Conan Doyle, *The British Campaign in France
and Flanders*

The privileged position granted defense over offense by all those involved in the battle for Vauban's authority is also the cornerstone of the maréchal's military activity. In the first edition of the Académie française dictionary (1694), "engin" is defined as an archaic term that survives only in the "old" proverb, "mieux vaut engin que force." The dictionary's authors fail to point out that the proverb is based on an inverted application of the term they seek to define. In military practice, an "engin" was an offensive aid in siegecraft, anything used in the assault of a fortified place. In the proverb, however, the term refers to passive rather than active aggression, to a force that could be considered defensive rather than offensive, especially in terms of Vaubanian strategy. A fortress, like an "engin" in the sense of ruse or stratagem, is an obstacle that forces the enemy to take action and predetermines his battle plan.[21] In seventeenth-century French, this semantic veering is doubled by the evolution of "ingénieur," which no longer refers primarily to the maker of offensive machines, but to

[21] In English, "ruse" first meant the avoidance of an obstacle, rather than the obstacle itself; it referred to the "doubling or turning of a hunted animal to elude the dogs" (*Oxford English Dictionary,* hereafter *OED*). This instinctive avoidance of danger may be related to the original meaning of *bricoler* and to the Lucretian notion of the *clinamen,* both of which are discussed in chapter 3, "The Oblique Way: Defensive Swerves."

the designer, the tracer, of fortified places, a linguistic shift corroborated by the shape of Vauban's career.

Historians usually reach what seems to be a logical conclusion concerning the maréchal's military activities: they assume that he functioned solely as an instrument of his monarch's desires. However, Vauban's writings reveal that this is true only at first, during the years that mark Vauban's reign as "preneur de villes" and strategist of the Sun King's conquests. Throughout his career, Vauban continues to besiege and capture fortified places, but increasingly he does so against his will, for as a theoretician he begins to work against Louis's foreign policy long before the ill-fated *Dîme royale*. During the second war of Louis's reign, the war of the Netherlands (1672-1678), Vauban acquires a new reputation as fortifier of newly conquered places. This reputation is officially recognized at the end of this war in 1678, when he receives the title *Commissaire Général des Fortifications*.

The new commissioner's writings of the period establish that until this point, like many of Louis's subjects, as Ferrier-Caverivière's study documents, he had been deceived by the king's dazzling and convincing façades. After 1678, Vauban came to realize that the Sun King was no longer "Dieu-donné," a hero and a humane, peace-seeking monarch. Vauban had believed that his military genius was serving the interests of a king who was conquering only in order to establish a new *pax romana*. However, the much heralded peace of Nimwegen in 1678 was followed by what Parent terms a "cold war" or a "paix armée" (p. 52). The year 1679 begins a period of frenetic activity for the new commissioner; incessantly he crisscrosses France, in his words, "tout de biais," trying to fortify all the recent conquests. Yet his monarch's account of that period in his private memoirs reveals that Louis intended to use this defense not as an end in itself but to further his offensive goals. The king discloses that he made peace only to "dissip[er] dès sa naissance" the league that was about to coalesce in opposition to his conquests:

[M]es nouvelles conquêtes bien affermies m'ouvriraient une entrée plus sûre dans le reste des Pays-Bas; . . . la paix me donnerait le loisir de me fortifier chaque jour de finances, de vaisseaux, d'intelligences et de tout ce que peuvent ménager les soins d'un prince appliqué dans un état puissant et riche.[22]

The immense machine being traced by his military genius gave a dangerous license to the Sun King's ego: Vauban's fortresses gave him the sensation of security that allowed him to exercise his offensive ambitions without fear of reprisals or loss of control. Furthermore, he saw Vauban's protective shield as a smokescreen, still another dazzling façade intended to maintain the fiction of his concern for protection of his country and his subjects. Thus the account of 1678 that Racine began to prepare for public consumption reads: "Toutefois, comme il voit sa gloire au point de ne plus croître, ses frontières entièrement assurées, son empire accru de tous côtés, il songe au repos et à la félicité de ses peuples" ("Des Campagnes de Louis XIV," *O.c.*, p. 397).

Ironically, the official history actually corresponds more closely to Vauban's plan for his monarch and his country as revealed in his writings on fortification than it does to Louis's conduct. The commissioner first shifts from practitioner to theoretician of defensive strategy immediately after the peace of Nimwegen in November 1678 with a short *Mémoire sur les places frontières de Flandre*. His sole full-scale work on fortification, the *Traité de la défense des places,* was begun only in 1706, but it was a direct response to the consequences of the Sun King's version of the *pax romana,* as its first sentence makes clear:

Quand je fis le Traité de l'*Attaque des Places,* je ne m'attendais à rien moins qu'à en devoir faire un de leur dé-

---

[22] *Mémoires de Louis XIV,* ed. J. Longnon (Tallandier, 1927), p. 278. The paternity of these memoirs is doubtful. But if they were ghostwritten by a contemporary author, this makes them of even greater interest as evidence of the fabrication of a royal fiction and the fictionalization of its hero, "Louis."

fense, ne croyant pas qu'elle nous pût être nécessaire, vu
l'état florissant de nos affaires . . . , qui paraissait fort
éloigné de ce qui pouvait le troubler; mais ce qui nous
est arrivé depuis peu m'ayant . . . fait comprendre qu'il
n'y a point de bonheur dans le monde sur la durée duquel
on puisse compter, . . . je me suis résolu à faire ce Traité.
(Rochas d'Aiglun, vol. 1, p. 248)

In the 1678 memoir, Vauban lists the measures to be taken
in order to "régler promptement une nouvelle [frontière] et
la si bien fortifier qu'elle ferme les entrées de notre pays à
l'ennemi" (Rochas d'Aiglun, vol. 1, p. 189). By 1706, this
message had acquired a new urgency, for during the quarter-
century that separates the two texts, Louis's offensive displays,
fueled by his apparent sense of invulnerability, had succeeded
in uniting nearly all of Europe against him. Defense had become the imperative concern it would continue to be for the
century in the shadow of the Sun King's fortifications.

At the time of the peace of Nimwegen, France was far less
vulnerable; on the contrary, Louis's/Vauban's offensive successes made the country seem invincible. From this position
of strength, Vauban, unlike his master, imagines not more
conquests, but a defensive nirvana. Indeed it is in the 1678
memoir that Vauban first gives shape to what is ultimately
his most compelling and suggestive contribution to the literature of defense, his notion of the *pré carré*. In this text and
in subsequent correspondence, Vauban makes it clear that all
the work that guaranteed his long-term authority—the building of fortifications and the writing of treatises—was accomplished in the service of his one great dream and his dominant
obsession, the establishment of a perfectly defendable shape
for France. He believed that if the country could be helped to
find its best limits and were therefore "naturally" fortified as
well as protected by a system of fortifications, it would become
"impénétrable à l'ennemi par terre et par mer."[23]

[23] Letter to Le Peletier de Souzy, 15 Feb. 1693, cited by Lazard, p. 239.
For other quotations from Vauban's correspondence, I will refer to the second

During his years in Louis's service, Vauban became increasingly aware that his monarch did not share his belief in the existence of a predestined frontier. Whereas in other domains the king was always in favor of having a house he could keep in order and of keeping it well-policed, in this case Louis was never able to accept the fact that if he did not set limits to his conquests, he would eventually be unable to maintain order. As his reign and his wars continued, the king found himself locked in a battle with his military surrogate, in which he stood on the side of prodigality and Vauban on that of restraint and caution. As early as 1673, Vauban was trying to open his master's eyes to the idea that France would soon be a finished, completed entity. He wrote to Louvois, *Secrétaire d'Etat de la guerre*: "Le Roi devrait un peu songer à faire son pré carré. . . . C'est une belle et bonne chose que de pouvoir tenir son fait des deux mains" (vol. 2, p. 89). From this point to the end of his career, Vauban's defensive strategies were dominated by this idea of the "pré carré." He more and more insistently warned Versailles's master that he should cut back on his projects and think of defending what he had already won, as in this letter from 1675: "Il semble que le Roi n'a que trop de places avancées. . . . Si nous voulons durer longtemps contre tant d'ennemis, il faut songer à se resserrer" (vol. 2, pp. 131-32). In the 1678 memoir, he cautioned the king that he could not maintain all the fortified places he had taken and that some must be destroyed in the interest of global security.

The expression "faire son pré carré" both denotes the essence of Vaubanian military strategy and indicates the distance that separates it from his monarch's foreign policy. Although he does not actually define the phrase, in his letters Vauban makes his usage of it quite clear. Yet the formula seems to be of his own invention; no Classical dictionary lists it, and the Littré is the only modern dictionary to include it—and the

---

volume of the Rochas d'Aiglun edition and give the page number in parentheses.

unique reference given for it there is to Vauban's letter of 1673. Moreover, the Littré's definition—"s'arrondir, en parlant d'un propriétaire qui accroît son domaine, d'un prince qui gagne des territoires"—is an inversion of the sense Louis's master fortifier intended to convey and closer to the type of misreading the Sun King himself might have proposed. In fact, the Littré misinterprets the two key elements of Vauban's concept. To begin with, the choice of "s'arrondir" is inaccurate; for reasons that will be discussed shortly, Vauban consistently placed the figure he chose as a geometric representation of France's geography, the *pré*, in opposition to the circle and always spoke of "squaring off" rather than "rounding off." "Prêchez toujours la quadrature, non pas du cercle, mais du pré," he advises in the same letter to Louvois. More importantly, the fortifier's message to his master is not one of expansion ("accroître," "gagner"), but of putting an end to acquisition.

The keystone of Vauban's military strategy may be characterized as an attempt to mythicize geography, to exploit the psychological connotations of a territorial entity for the advancement of a nationalistic utopia. Fontenelle called Vauban "un Romain qu'il semblait que notre siècle eût dérobé aux plus heureux temps de la République" (*Eloge*, p. 105). To Saint-Simon, he was a "patriote" in the modern sense of the term. And to Voltaire, he was "le meilleur des citoyens" (*Le Siècle de Louis XIV*, chap. 21). According to the terms of Vauban's vision, the saying associated with his master, "l'état, c'est moi," would have taken on new meaning. For him, true territorial security would be achieved when France had been transformed into an invincible fortress, a *pré carré*, secured by the chain-link fence of its monarch's hands: "C'est une belle et bonne chose que de pouvoir tenir son fait des deux mains." The syntax of the sentence in which he describes the consequences of the fall of Charleroi (1693) makes it clear that, for Vauban, king and country share predestined territorial limits defined by flawless (Vaubanian) fortifications: "La prise de cette place est une des plus nécessaires conquêtes

44

que le Roi ait faites de son règne et qui achève de lui faire la plus belle frontière que la France ait eue depuis mille ans" (vol. 2, p. 398).

"For the first time, the defence of the kingdom of France was treated as a whole," Blomfield declares in his commentary on the *pré carré* (p. 127). Vauban was the first to define France as a territorial unit to be protected and to mark off the limits of that territory according to their defensive potential, thereby making the nation coextensive with the fortress. The frontiers he chose for France were boundaries that the master fortifier could render invulnerable. Blomfield contends that the mark of Vauban's genius was "his eye for ground" (p. 60). Louis's commissioner took the soil of France and made it into ramparts, literally wrapping the country around itself to seal it off against invasion. His fortifications seem camouflaged, for they blend into the surrounding landscape. What are sometimes called France's "natural" frontiers are in fact almost exactly the borders Vauban thought could be perfectly defended—nature fortified by Vauban's machines. Vauban believed that his ramparts were buttressed with the authority of history, of a millennial territorial destiny.[24] Furthermore, the protected and protectable space he chose as the limit of expansion was to mark France's definitive, completed shape, long after the territories of his king's last conquests were lost. In their exceptional recent study, Michel Parent and Jacques Verroust have extended Vauban's millennial historical vision to include the past three hundred years:

A travers les dix-huitième et dix-neuvième siècles, et en dépit . . . des revers occasionnels d'un certain Napoléon, cette "ligne Vauban" s'est à peu près perpétuée à travers les traités et à travers les consciences. . . . Ainsi est-il peu probable qu'aucun homme politique ait finalement con-

---

[24] Modern commentators such as Daniel Halévy confirm Vauban's sense of having returned France to territorial completion: "La Gaule de Vercingétorix et de César, après quinze siècles de dissidences, retrouve sa forme parfaite" (*Vauban* [Grasset, 1923], p. 204).

45

tribué à définir la France autant que cet ingénieur militaire. Il lui est revenu d'avoir "marqué" ce territoire à la façon dont un animal marque et borne le sien: par des signes de reconnaissance. (p. 6)

=== ✳ ===

Squaring the Circle

> Je compris que mes contemporains n'étaient par rapport à moi que des êtres mécaniques qui n'agissaient que par impulsions et dont je ne pouvais calculer l'action que par les lois du mouvement.
>
> Jean-Jacques Rousseau, *Les Rêveries du promeneur solitaire*

"Prêchez toujours la quadrature, non pas du cercle, mais du pré": Vauban maintained that his prescription for territorial security was mathematically viable, a plan for actual, rather than fantastic, castle building. He would never try to do the impossible, to square the circle, for he was, in Fontenelle's words, a "happy genius," a practical man concerned with concrete realities rather than a theoretician driven by the need to observe his perfect system in operation. Thus Vauban always dismissed his writings on siegecraft as the casual scribbling of a man of action whom others had forced into a role for which he had neither inclination nor preparation. He gave the title "mes oisivetés" to several volumes of his most important manuscripts and maintained that treatises on fortification had little value. When he was finally "obliged" to put his practical experience into a systematic form, the maréchal insisted that he was only laying down a few rules to help French fortified places hold out to a "reasonable" degree. He denied any fantasy of omnipotence: "Par ce discours il semble que je veuille rendre les places imprenables. . . . Ce n'est pas mon sentiment, puisque je suis persuadé qu'une armée qui attaque une place, doit, avec le temps, malgré toute la résistance de l'assiégé, demeurer victorieuse" (1795 ed., p. 226). Yet in his denial, he pronounces the key term, "invulnerable," laying, as it were, the foundation for the legend of Vauban as systematic genius. Vauban promises that he will not try "to square the circle," disavows any pretension to invincibility, but the very shape of his denials indicates the utopian nature of his project, the dream of invulnerability he shares with his monarch.

Vauban begins his *Traité de la défense des places* with basic calculations: if the size of a fortified place is given, then the number of days it should be able to hold out can be determined—providing, that is, that the besieged have followed all Vauban's instructions. He then includes such unassailable tables that it is easy to understand why they were accepted as guarantees of victory. As an early editor said: "A force d'étude et d'expérience, on a réduit l'art à des règles certaines" (1737 ed., p. 5). Vauban breaks down into parts the central activity of warfare in his day and then assigns a number of days to each step of laying siege to a fortified place with matter-of-fact simplicity. Like Robinson Crusoe engaged in what has been termed spiritual bookkeeping—balancing off the good and evil in his life as debits and credits—Vauban tabulates such seemingly incalculable factors as "l'attaque et la prise du chemin-couvert" (four days) and "la descente et le passage du fossé de la demi-lune" (three days). He gives no explanation other than experience for the origin of his estimations: "[J]e mets à peu près le temps qu'il nous a fallu pour ces opérations" (1795 ed., p. 192). Any hesitation that the reader may initially experience when dealing with life and death matters calculated in terms of "à peu près" and solely on the basis of one man's practical knowledge gradually disappears in the face of the accumulated weight of the calculations and their definitive air. Vauban has seemingly thought of everything and has reduced each otherwise unmanageable factor to an easily apprehensible number of days. The end result of this calculation is that, according to Vauban's estimations, a regular, six-bastioned fortified place in good condition can "reasonably" be expected to hold out under siege for forty-eight days.

This is only the beginning of Vauban's calculations for this regular, six-bastioned fortified place in good condition. Like Robinson Crusoe's, his bookkeeping is endless, and he goes on first to calculate the number of men necessary for the defense of his hypothetical fortified place, then to compute the quantities of various supplies these men would require during the siege. The spectrum of provisions Vauban includes in his tables ranges from such standard items as gunpowder, to less predictable ones, such as three kinds of paper and six kinds of nails, to somewhat less basic commodities, such as cloves and nutmeg, herring prepared in two ways, and two kinds of sheets (to bury the dead and to cover the beds of the living). He first makes "model" computations for his representative fortified place. (And it should be noted that the figures he gives take the form of precise calculations rather than rough estimates.) For example, the 48 days of siege would require 67,000 rations of biscuit ("pour les besoins pressans et imprevus"), 65 baskets of eggs, and 132 sacks of peas, beans and lentils (1795 ed., p. 131). He then adds pages of tables that give the figures on quantities of staples (13 pages with upwards of 30 items per page in the 1795 edition) for fortified places with four to eighteen bastions. At the end of these more than copious calculations, Vauban even includes a final remark on one of the commodities he found most essential for maintaining morale, tobacco: "Une livre de tabac contient 112 pipes, d'expérience faite, que nous passerons ici pour 100 à cause du déchet. Supposons donc quatre pipes le jour par homme" (1795 ed., p. 139, table xiii).

Vauban apparently found "leisure" time to plan for much more than the common soldier's smoking needs. He used calculations and tables for an extraordinarily wide range of subjects, from the number of canals needed in a region to the potential for growth of the French colonies. Perhaps the most unexpected of these subjects was discussed in a memoir entitled "De la Cochonnerie ou calcul estimatif pour connaître

jusqu'où peut aller la production d'une truie pendant dix années de temps" (Rochas d'Aiglun, vol. I, pp. 402-9). Vauban
allegedly composed this treatise to demonstrate what an effective food resource the pig could be, and to this end, he
calculated ten generations of a sow's productivity. However,
his ever expanding computations eventually take on an unsettling air, because of the disparity between the prosaic subject matter and the grandiose vision it inspires in him. By the
tenth generation, the descendants of the original sow will be
enough to feed France; only two generations later "toute l'Europe en pourrait nourrir," and by the sixteenth generation,
"il est certain qu'il y aurait de quoi en peupler toute la terre
abondamment" (vol. I, p. 408). Vauban attributes this hypothetical success to the "providence divine" that made the
animal so wildly fertile. Because of his never ending foresight,
because it is he who understands and controls the animal's
potential and shapes the vision of its multiplication, Vauban
portrays himself as a God-figure, "peopling" the earth (if only
with pigs), rather than feeding its inhabitants. "De la Cochonnerie" reveals more clearly than Vauban's other predictive statistics the utopian side of the defensive enterprise and
its divine aspirations.

Among Vauban's commentators, only Duffy has called attention to the excessive nature of his foresight: "Vauban went
into almost obsessive detail on the matter of provisions"
(p. 82). In fact, this central kernel of the *Défense des places*
brings to mind Barthes's description of the obsessiveness shared
by Sade, Fourier, and Loyola: "même volupté de classification,
même rage de découper . . . même obsession numérative.[25]
Barthes's description of this obsessive bookkeeping stresses a
factor essential to an understanding of the power Vauban's
system possessed over subsequent generations:

> Dès qu'un objet paraît, . . . il est brisé, divisé, dénombré.
> La comptabilité est obsessionnelle non seulement parce

[25] Barthes, *Sade, Fourier, Loyola* (Seuil, 1971), p. 7.

CHAPTER I

qu'elle est infinie, mais surtout parce qu'elle engendre
ses propres fautes. . . . Le fait de mal compter deviendra
à son tour une faute qui devra s'ajouter à la liste origi-
nelle; cette liste est ainsi frappée d'infinité. . . . C'est en
effet le propre névrotique de l'obsession que de mettre
en place une machine qui s'entretient toute seule.
(pp. 74-75)

Barthes's remarks on the infinity of this accounting shed
light on what is perhaps the most interesting recurrent factor
in all Vauban's systems, the final accounting for error. The
last figure in every table of calculations is always an attempt
to account for error and thereby make the final tally appear
even more convincing. Any such predictive statistics contain
of necessity an attempt to compensate for possible error.
Throughout his treatise, tension is evident between Vauban
the theoretician and Vauban the man of experience—the desire to establish the existence of a foolproof system undoubtedly caused him on occasion to overstep the bounds of practical
knowledge. But nowhere is this tension more apparent than
in the "squaring off" that allegedly brings the perfect defensive
machine to a halt. For example, in the computation of the
tenth generation of the sow's multiplication, 434,874 pigs are
subtracted "pour les accidents, les maladies, et la part des
loups." The calculation of the model fortress's resistance ends
with an equivalent note: "[J]'aurois dû compter la durée du
siège plus longue, mais j'ai pensé que les peres d'hommes, les
blessés et les gens épars ou cachés, feront un équivalent de
huit ou dix jours, capable de suppléer au défaut, si les con-
sommations sont ménagées" (1795 ed., pp. 65-66). The "last"
figures take the reader by surprise, because, like the final element in the catalogues to which Flaubert so often had recourse, they belong to a different order from the previous
elements.

The ultimate entry in Vauban's calculations appears to be
a mark of prudence, but in reality it puts the entire enterprise
into question by pointing out the role of chance and the in-

calculable. It seems possible to assign a limit to such positive actions as the capture of a covered way or a ditch, but much less so to set up an equivalence between a certain number of days and a negative entity such as the number of pigs eaten by wolves or the number of dead, wounded, and deserting soldiers, especially when the dead are taken into account as a "supplement" to compensate for a "lack" of eight to ten days' provisions. Defensive military architecture may be the greatest modern funerary monument, as Paul Virilio has recently suggested.[26] When that architecture's most illustrious codifier attempts to square off his protective machine by setting limits to death, it becomes evident both that his defensive system can never be completely controlled, never be finished, and that it does not merely protect against violence, but engenders it as well.

In all editions of Vauban's works, the treatises on attack are lengthier and more detailed than those on defense. At the end of the section on defense in the 1795 edition, the editor Foissac explains that "Vauban annonce en quelque sorte lui-même que son ouvrage sur la défense des places n'est point achevé" (p. 298). The note is a tribute to the success of Vauban's efforts at systematization. He inspires his students to go on and on, to continue making systems. His calculations for the length of the ultimate siege end in a supplement. His students like Foissac, men of the age of dictionaries and encyclopedias, understand that any system that purports to be flawless is driven by the force of accounting and engenders its own supplement. They accept the last tallies as a challenge: "Et en effet, il ne parle pas de la distinction des bastions pleins et des bastions vides. . . . Nous répétons ici qu'une théorie complète de l'art fortifiant est un ouvrage à faire" (p. 298).

---

[26] Virilio speaks of "les mastabas, les tombes étrusques, les structures aztèques . . . comme si cet ouvrage d'artillerie légère [the bunker] s'identifiait aux rites funéraires" (*Bunker archéologie,* p. 8). The terminology of fortifications in the seventeenth century also suggests that it possesses ritual aspects, for the apprentice is referred to as a "diacre": "Pendant que j'étais diacre de M. de Clerville . . . ," Vauban writes Louvois (vol. 2, p. 13)

The conclusion demonstrates that the student responsible for continuing his teacher's work had not grasped the other sense in which it was incomplete. The second, more fundamental incompleteness is inherent in Vauban's enterprise and is betrayed by every one of his last, negative calculations. Vauban's accounting is doomed to continue ad infinitum, for the perfect defensive work can never be complete. The defensive strategist always sees the possibility of one more attack, and therefore the necessity of an additional, "ultimate" defense.

His system engenders an imaginary violent supplement that dooms it to continuous functioning. The goal of Vauban's perfect defensive system, the "reasonable" end he prescribes for the commanding officer of a fortified place, reveals that his defensive nirvana leads to a holocaust. Once the outworks have been destroyed, the *gouverneur* must retire to his fortress within a fortress, "les autres retranchemens qu'il aura fait de nouveau au-dedans de la place" (1795 ed., p. 272). He will hold out there until those fortifications, too, have fallen, at which point "il pourra alors consentir avec honneur à une capitulation qui ne peut être que glorieuse pour lui et pour les troupes qui auront été sous ses ordres, puisqu'il n'abandonne aux ennemis qu'une place démolie, dont les ruines serviront de monument à sa gloire" (p. 273). Like the Sun King's emblem, the phoenix, the perfect defensive machine "ends" in its own "glorious" (self-)destruction under, if not in, fire. Vauban's treatise reverses the order of Sade's *120 Journées de Sodome* by leaving its reader with the narrative of smoking ruins rather than the tables that compute the extent of the destruction. Yet even this apparently airtight closure cannot erase the memory of the final tally for error that remains as a loophole in Vauban's system just as in Sade's. If there have been no mistakes and if provisions have been carefully husbanded, the besieged might hold out still longer, drawing ever nearer the (denied) dream of invulnerability.

In addition to the last figure, a second computational aberrance undermines Vauban's system from within. Vauban owes much of his acknowledged superiority as a defensive strategist to the fact that he never conceived of defense as possessing an existence independent from offense. He only systematized defensive codes after he had had the opportunity to see defensive structures perform under attack. Furthermore, even as a codifier, Vauban continued to view defense as coexistent with attack. He composed twin treatises, so that rules governing attack were always coupled with codes of defense. This pairing inevitably leads to such paradoxical formulations of Vauban's work as the editor's description of the contents in the preface of the 1737 edition: "des règles sures à assiégeant et assiégié pour conduire avec art et sagesse leurs travaux et leurs manoeuvres, et d'opposer une opiniâtre et formidable défense à l'attaque la plus rigoureuse et la mieux concertée." To pit the perfect attack against the perfect defense is to put into operation a military machine that will function until not a single combatant remains. Vauban's system demonstrates that defense and offense are interdependent, intertwined, and ultimately so intimately related as to be sometimes indistinguishable one from the other.

The ultimate danger of the attempted accounting for violence that produces such perfectly matched offensive and defensive systems as those Vauban created—or the more recent theory of the so-called balance of powers—is that it forces the master of the system to imagine himself simultaneously in the roles of attacker and defender of the fortress. This is the situation of the rulers of Sade's libertine utopia, Silling—locked in an arrangement that leads to a gloriously explosive end as surely as its "rational" accounting veers into numerology, generating an unforeseen form of secrecy. We may still be living in the shadow of such systems of accounting today. Vauban's *pré carré* is the ancestor of the Maginot line, the last defense against a visible, calculable enemy. The silos of our massive, hidden present-day system of "defense" are constructed against the invasion of an invisible enemy, an enemy whose attack we, like Sade's quatrumvirate and Laclos on the île d'Aix, simultaneously dread and fantasize—if only to test our defenses. Like Vauban's, our accounting ends in impossible equations. Today's perfect defense is truly a perfect offense in the eyes of the enemy threatened by what is contained in the silos. Yet we continue to balance one MIG against one F-16, one MX against one of "their" latest deterrent weapons, as though we believed, as Vauban so "rationally" explained it, that oblique strategy had to be perfected in order to foster a utopia of peace and plenty, and that, this goal achieved, the defensive machine could simply be maintained and not allowed to proliferate.[27]

Yet the notion of defensive proliferation is nowhere more evident than in the very groundplans or traces that Vauban designed for the places he fortified. By the end of his career, in his so-called third system, Vauban multiplied almost endlessly the outworks, the elements of the fortified place in front of the main rampart. A Vaubanian fortified place bristles with layer after layer of the demi-lunes, ravelins, tenailles, and hornworks that would later be so dear to my uncle Toby's heart. (See figs. 1-3.) To Sterne, this proliferation of outworks seemed ridiculous, but the object of his mockery provides an important clue to the origin of Vauban's success. Vauban's traces, or groundplans, seem in a sense "alive" because, like works of baroque art, they are based on a wild multiplication of elements. However, unlike the baroque artist, who multiplied so-called natural or vegetal elements, Vauban took geometric fragments and proliferated them. As a result, his traces have an unsettling quality, as though the lifeless had come alive in them and geometry had gone wild. His fortified places are immense inorganic monsters that become progressively more disturbing as the observer takes stock of their elements.

[27] The most recent variant of this violence of accounting may be seen in our newest calculating aid, the computer. The sole subject of an ever proliferating series of computer "games" is the destruction and the devouring of one's enemies and the absorption of their territory. These strategic contests could be seen as a foreshadowing of what seems to be the ultimate role for the computer, that of commemorator of our defensive holocaust; the latest underground fortresses are now being constructed to protect computer data banks in the event of a nuclear disaster.

Trace of the fortified place at Ath, as shown in the 1795 (Magimel) edition of Vauban's *Traité de la défense des places*, Planche 1. Reprinted by permission of the University of Michigan library.

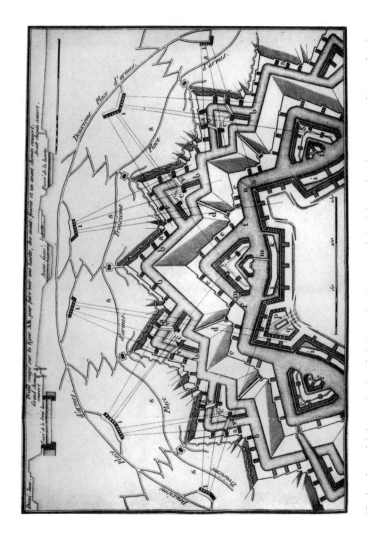

The last line of defense of a fortified place (detail). *Traité de la défense des places* (1795 edition), Planche 2. Reprinted by permission of the University of Michigan library.

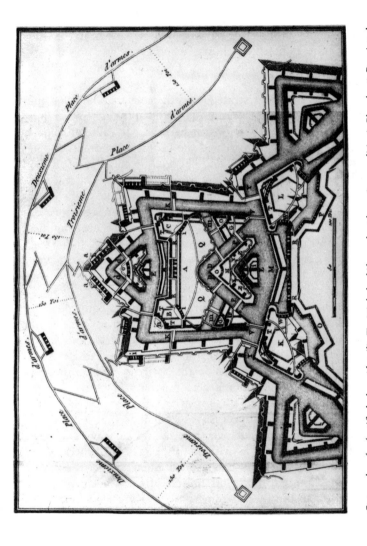

Outworks of a fortified place (detail). *Traité de la défense des places* (1795 edition), Planche 6. Reprinted by permission of the University of Michigan library.

Like a Busby Berkeley production number, they eventually seem simultaneously controlled and out-of-control. The trace of a Vaubanian fortress seems driven by a demon of defense. This systematization gone haywire makes Vauban in the true spirit of the eighteenth century, when every attempt at perfecting codification leads, like the *Encyclopédie*, to a nonstop accounting machine.

Vauban's defensive strategy was the cornerstone of his authority and his monarch's offensive audacity. Yet he was blind to the unforeseen deviations in his allegedly all-controlling system. He consistently denied the geometric monstrosity in his traces and his treatises and believed he could turn off the machine created by his ingenuity as soon as nirvana was reached. The period during which Vauban composed the *Traité de la défense des places* was also devoted to the final revisions of his most controversial and in the long run his most famous work, the *Projet d'une dîme royale* (begun 1697, published just weeks before his death in March 1707). The two major products of Vauban's last years are also, more or less overtly, works of rebellion.

The *Dîme* is for Louis's entire kingdom the equivalent of the *Défense* for fortified places. In it, Vauban uses tables of predictive statistics similar to those in the treatise on defense to demonstrate his economic model for France as fortress utopia, his plan for life inside the fortress.[28] The resulting prescription made Vauban a hero for the progressive economists of the Enlightenment, for it revealed that he had kept his eyes open during the fortifying missions that led him to crisscross France during over forty years of travels. In the *Dîme*, Vauban stands as witness to the misery of the French people whose resources had been drained to fuel the royal (war) machine. He takes his notion of the *pré carré* to its logical conclusion by providing the Sun King with a plan to carry out his servant's vision of using perfect defenses, and

---

[28] His tables also include a similar accounting for error. Vauban, *Projet d'une dîme royale*, ed. Coornaert (Alcan, 1933). See, for example, p. 178.

perfect attacks, as a prelude to peace, liberation, prosperity, and plenitude for all those inside the fortress. For Vauban, territorial security would bring cultural and political security. Safe inside the chain-link fence of Louis's *pré carré*, France was to know a true golden age. His wall would keep out the barbarians, like the Great Wall of China, but his fortifications were so perfect that they would ensure that what was for Borges the threatening aspect of the wall be avoided, that books inside need not be burned. The master fortifier believed that he could leave his mark, his fortifications, on territory and thereby make that territory French. It was his wish to fill the center of the national fortress, and he refused to believe that his king wanted to keep it hollow. His blindness was a costly mistake. The Sun King, who ignored similar implications in Vauban's works on defense because their strategic lessons were so useful to him, suppressed Vauban's last book and tried to suppress his authority. At the time of Vauban's death, Fontenelle's eulogy was the only public tribute he received.

In a preface to the *Dîme royale* indirectly addressed to the king, Vauban explains his text as intended to safeguard "la sûreté de son Royaume, . . . l'augmentation de sa gloire et de ses revenus, et . . . [le] bonheur de ses Peuples" (p. 6). He tried to make his utopian vision palatable to his ruler by linking the two kinds of defense his strategies had buttressed—Louis's glorious magnificence and national security—to his dream of ripeness and plenitude. But Louis, like the emperor of China, saw things differently. He wanted to build the wall *and* burn the books. He had no interest in the *pré carré* or the utopia it was to protect as completed entities; he only used them as façades to disguise his thirst for conquest and to enhance his image as "God-given" monarch. Vauban maintained that his own genius was instinctive, practical, nonsystematic, but the Sun King realized that it was also calculating and mechanistic. He saw what Vauban himself persistently denied, even though his accounting consistently reveals it—that is, that this war machine could not be brought to a halt and that fortification is an endless project.

The policies the Sun King did adopt demonstrate that he had mastered the maréchal's strategies. He applied the model of the Vaubanian fortress to his own person. He made himself into a scale model of the *pré carré* and used the variant of Vaubanian outworks he developed to camouflage his attempts to find loopholes in others' fortifications. In a defense of respecting sacred mysteries that can be read as a justification for royal secrecy, Guez de Balzac describes a kingdom where "mille barrières, mille grilles, et mille rideaux séparent [le Roy] de ceux mesmes qui viennent traiter avec luy." He warns that these fortifications should not be besieged: "Arrêtons-nous à ses Dehors et à ses Remparts, sans la poursuivre jusque dans son Fort et dans ses retranchements."[29] Like the medieval kings Bloch describes in *Les Rois thaumaturges,* the Sun King decided to "fortifier [son] prestige" by appropriating divine rights; he chose to be seen, not as miracle worker, but as divinely inscrutable.[30]

But Louis did more than re-create the defensive strategies Vauban explicitly prescribed. He also read between the lines of the master fortifier's treatises; he understood their implicit message and translated that, too, into policy. Vauban imagined that the fortress was necessary as protection only against the enemy positioned outside its walls, the foreign Other. His is a seductive, optimistic vision: the *pré carré* as a realization of territorial destiny would serve as the basis for nationalism, since all those inside its walls would be seen as the same (French). His monarch, however, understood that Vauban's calculations could never be perfectly squared off, that is, that

[29] Balzac, *Le Socrate chrétien, Oeuvres,* 2 vols., ed. Moreau (Lecoffre, 1854), vol. 2, p. 37.

[30] In *Les Rois thaumaturges: Essai sur le caractère surnaturel attribué à la puissance royale* (Strasbourg: Istra, 1924), Bloch examines the origin of the medieval vision of the king as miracle worker: "Certains souverains, dans la France capétienne et l'Angleterre normande, imaginèrent un jour—, afin de fortifier leur prestige un peu fragile, de s'essayer au rôle de thaumaturges" (p. 17).

the enemy within may be more dangerous than the foreign, barbarian Other. "On attaque le coeur d'un prince comme une place," Louis admonishes his son. "Le premier soin est de s'emparer de tous les postes par où on en peut approcher" (*Mémoires*, p. 258). Territorial security of any kind must never be allowed, and the fortress must be doubly defended with outer and inner shields.

The ruler of Versailles saw accounting as the foundation of his glory. In his memoirs, he explains how he personally balances his books, discusses the innovative nature of this strategy, and justifies its importance: "[C]e soin et ce détail sont le plus assuré fondement [de la] splendeur et [de la] magnificence [d'un prince]" (p. 93). From his perspective, the result of Vauban's defensive accounting is a logical conclusion: at the end of the *Défense des places,* the commanding officer of the fortified place, after the fall of both its outworks and the inner protective barrier, gives up to his enemies "une place démolie, dont les ruines serviront de monument à sa gloire" (1795 ed., p. 273). The Sun King's calculated Classical magnificence could only culminate in just this kind of fiery devastation. His personal and foreign policies had set France on the course charted by his master fortifier's machine. Vauban always emphasized that he could never make a fortress invulnerable. His monarch realized that if the price of a siege were high enough, this goal would have been approached—and the charred ruins would remain as a monument to the systematic glory of the master of the defense.

=== ✳ ===

Conquering Nature with Art

Dans ce temps les murailles parlent . . . et tout le monde est aux écoutes.

Sébastien Le Prestre de Vauban,
*Mémoire pour servir d'instruction
dans la conduite des sièges*

Ces murs mêmes, Seigneur, peuvent avoir des yeux.
Racine, *Britannicus*

In *Abstraction and Empathy,* Wilhelm Worringer criticizes "subjective" or "behavioristic" aesthetic theory, that is, aesthetic theory based on the premise that the viewer's or reader's instinctive response to artistic creation is a movement of identification and projection—a type of sympathetic, emotional reaction. He calls for a broadening of aesthetic theory to take into account, in addition to works of art directed toward man's desire for empathy, artistic production that responds to a desire for abstraction. Worringer contrasts the types of beauty privileged by the two desires (which he calls "urges"): "Just as the urge to empathy as a preassumption of aesthetic experience finds its gratification in the beauty of the organic, so the urge to abstraction finds its beauty in the life-denying inorganic, in the crystalline, or, in general terms, in all abstract law and necessity."[31] When dealing with creations inspired by the need for abstraction, "it is not the life of an organism which we see before us, but that of a mechanism" (pp. 114-15). In Worringer's characterization of the "climates" that generate these opposing artistic drives, he theorizes that the art of empathy is born of "a happy pantheistic relationship of confidence between man and the phenomena of the outside world," whereas the art of abstraction "is the outcome of a great inner unrest inspired in man by the phenomena of the outside world," "an immense spiritual dread of space." The viewers of the former type of artistic creation seek in it "the possibility of projecting themselves into the things of the outer world." The public for an art of abstraction, on the other hand, driven by a need for tranquillity, seeks "to wrest the object of the external world out of its natural context, out of the unending flux of being, to purify it of all its dependence

[31] Worringer, *Abstraction and Empathy* (New York: International Universities Press, 1953), p. 4.

upon life, of everything about it that is arbitrary, to render it necessary" (pp. 15-17). Worringer sets chronological limits to the urge to abstraction, associating it with relatively primitive artistic creations. However, his explanations for the origin of abstraction can be applied to the Versailles era, and perhaps as well to subsequent periods that have produced what is now called modernist art. Worringer creates a variant of what today would be termed reader-response theory. Yet his explanation for the public's need for an art that makes nature correspond to geometric progression seems more applicable to the creators of French Classical art.

In 1678, the year that marked the major turning point in Vauban's relationship to his king, the newly appointed Commissioner of Fortifications began an important project, the fortification of Dunkerque. He was so proud of the new harbor he designed there and of the canals, dams, and sluices he had constructed in order to keep it free of sand—according to Blomfield, his system is essentially still in use (p. 82)—that he asked the Baron de Woerden to provide a Latin inscription that would commemorate his stratagem. The text selected to inscribe the nature of the king's (Vauban's) accomplishments credits Louis le Grand (Ludovicus Magnus) with having surpassed his predecessor, Caesar Augustus, the conqueror of Britain. Caesar was able to "conquer the world," but he was defeated when he tried to turn Britain into a fortress that would control the ocean ("structa arce Britannico / injicere oceano claustrum"), while Louis has tamed both land and sea "with an art that conquers nature" ("Arte Naturam superante").

Vauban, working in—or "under," in Laclos's description of a similar phenomenon—the name of Louis le Grand, uses engineering to tame nature. His land reforms foreshadow those to which Goethe's Faust devoted his last energies. The commissioner built a new physical contour for Dunkerque in the form of a reconstructed harbor. The "scandal," as Virilio terms it, of this man-made nature is that, like Julie and Wolmar's work on the Elysée, it fuses structures for defense and control into the landscape without a trace of artifice.[32] The ebb and flow of all forces can be perfectly monitored and channels will never be obstructed by sand or any other obstacle. According to the portrait Vauban had painted of him, France's new Caesar used victories on the two great natural frontiers, land and sea, to turn nature into a fortified machine.

A similar battle against land and water was waged at Louis's residential re-creation of the *pré carré,* Versailles. In *Les Jardins de l'intelligence,* Corpechot contends that the Sun King's palatial hall of mirrors represents "un spectacle vraiment nouveau" in the domain of landscape architecture. Previously, gardens had been designed to appeal to their viewers on an emotional level by "charming" them with their "grâces" and "voluptés." Unlike such examples of an art of empathy, Versailles presents its public, in Corpechot's description, with "un ensemble de masses sévères ou de lignes sobres qui *subjuguent, imposent* leur majesté, parlent à l'intelligence qu'elles entraînent . . . exaltent au-dessus de toute sensibilité" (p. 29, emphasis mine). Once order is imposed on natural disorder, nature becomes "intelligible, logique, facile." Nature geometrized is made accountable. This calculated nature allegedly has a calming effect on its viewer. After a day spent in Versailles's park, he leaves "l'esprit tranquille." He experiences the same "quiétude sans égale" that is produced by the spectacle of perfectly trained troops passing in review (p. 34).

Corpechot, like Worringer, assumes that the "tranquillity" that results from what he realizes is a militaristic tabulation of nature is the effect Le Nôtre intended to produce on all spectators. Yet there is little evidence that the creators of the monuments of French Classicism had any viewers but the royal spectator in mind. The Sun King is seen as somehow simultaneously creator and viewer of his creation—thus Vau-

---

[32] Virilio describes how bunkers blend into the landscape around them: "Le profil courbé apportait, dans les quartiers portuaires, comme une trace de la courbure des dunes et des collines avoisinantes, et c'est surtout cette naturalité qui faisait scandale, . . . le scandale du bunker" (*Bunker archéologie,* p. 10).

ban engineers France's second nature for the king and at the same time has Louis portrayed as the controller of land and sea, the builder of the wall. The tranquillity of that supreme viewer was always ensured by providing him with foolproof systems. When the Classical artists and builders considered other viewers, they sought to usurp their critical freedom, to keep them on the path already traced for their response by the royal spectator. Thus the Sun King personally provided guided tours of the marvels of Versailles for important—and potentially creative or uncontrollable—visitors like Lafayette. To guarantee that future viewers would not stray from the assigned itinerary, Louis composed the *Manière de montrer les jardins de Versailles,* in which the visitor is given a series of commands, is ordered to turn first left, then right, to advance five paces, and so forth, so that he can file through the park in proper military fashion and make the uniquely perfect visit to Versailles.[33] Moreover, as his title indicates, Louis had a precise audience in mind for his tour. He composed a "manière de montrer," not a "manière de visiter," a training manual for future Louis, future authors of these gardens, authors who will share the Sun King's indifference to the desires of the spectator.

The writers responsible for the creation of French Classicism often echo their monarch's concern for order and for the elimination of the unpredictable. In *Les Amours de Psyché et de Cupidon,* La Fontaine addresses precisely this question of whether the spectator of an artistic creation should be granted interpretive freedom. He evokes the possibility that spectators might not always be willing to follow the itinerary prescribed for them, that they might try instead to peek behind the curtain that conceals other perspectives and thereby unmask the work's creator. La Fontaine's fable of reader response, like Louis's garden manual, teaches its lesson from the point of view of the creator rather than the observer. The

---

[33] *Manière de montrer les jardins de Versailles* (Editions de la Réunion des Musées Nationaux, 1982).

visitor's desire for inside information is portrayed as a threat to the master artist. The consequences of one spectator's refusal to confine her role to the passive pleasures of contemplation may serve as a warning to all those who choose to contemplate the outworks of the fortress of Classicism. Although La Fontaine's work dates from the beginning of the Versailles era (1669), his reflections on the place reserved for the reception of a work of art constitute a foreshadowing of the intended effect of Louis's later efforts at landscape architecture and thus merit our close attention here.

In the preface to *Psyché*, La Fontaine pledges that "mon principal but est toujours de plaire." This apparent invitation for the reader's projection is tempered by La Fontaine's assertion that his version of *Psyché* conforms to what he calls "le goût du siècle," a code which does not reject a strong emotional involvement ("non que l'on méprise les passions . . .") in a work "plein de merveilleux," but which clearly indicates a preference "au galant et à la plaisanterie."[34] Yet the tale he tells—"merveilleux" and "galant" though it may be—issues a warning about the dangers of "the urge to empathy" and depicts the reader's pleasure—defined in the text as the freedom to identify with a character and participate vicariously in the unfolding of his or her story—as a threat to the creative artist's all-consuming desire for control.

For his version of this tale of a wife punished because she dares to look her dazzling royal husband in the face, La Fontaine uses a more complex version of the narrative situation that his monarch would adopt for his guide to the royal gardens. In the opening frame narrative, four friends are entertained by a visit to Versailles, the masterpiece of a king identified only as "notre monarque" (p. 127). The main body of the text illustrates two additional moments when a work of art is put before its public. In one, Polyphile entertains the three other friends with his version of Psyché's adventures. In his

[34] La Fontaine, *Les Amours de Psyché et de Cupidon*, in *Oeuvres diverses*, 2 vols., ed. Clarac (Gallimard, 1954), vol. 2, p. 121.

tale, he describes a second visit to a pleasure dome, Psyché's inspection of Cupidon's palace. The three moments of contemplation inscribed in the text imply a fourth moment of artistic transmission: the text's mirror structure invites La Fontaine's reader to consider her own reception of *Psyché* in light of these descriptions of artistic reception. In the conversation that "frames" these guided tours, Cupidon is identified with Louis XIV and with *Psyché*'s author, and the tale's heroine with all curious, undisciplined spectators of both Versailles and La Fontaine's fictional re-creation of the Sun King's palace.

Psyché incurs her husband's wrath as a result of a "defect" "accoutumé de nuire aux personnes de [son] sexe, la curiosité" (p. 159). She wants to see her husband and have access to the text of his life. Cupidon seeks to control the transmission of knowledge, to present only as much of his story as he wants. He attempts to keep his bride in the dark about the most interesting part of his story, his identity. He wants her to be satisfied with "forme" rather than "matière," with what she can touch but not see (know). Cupidon asks to be treated as a Sun King, like the sovereign of the mythical kingdom Balzac describes where "c'est crime de leze-majesté de regarder le Roy au visage." Cupidon would have Psyché follow Balzac's advice to the subjects of such a kingdom: "Puis que [cette Majesté] habite une lumière inaccessible, ne faisons point de dessein sur le lieu de sa demeure. N'essayons point de la surprendre par la subtilité de nos Questions, de la forcer par la violence de nos Argumens" (*Le Socrate Chrétien*, vol. 2, p. 37). When Psyché is punished because of her desire to uncover what is hidden from her, the less docile of La Fontaine's readers may identify with her plight. Cupidon characterizes curiosity as a defect particular to women. However, inquisitiveness is an instinct also habitually associated with intellectuals, long referred to as "les curieux." In *Psyché*, La Fontaine tells the tale of a woman punished for a crime common to readers, being inquisitive enough about a good story to want to know more.

Psyché, logically enough, believes that her husband would have no reason to limit her to the trace of a presence, were he not the monster the oracle had predicted. Indeed, the only definition of monstrosity proposed by the tale is related to his desire to remain invisible. In *Psyché*, he who hides is a monster: "tout invisible et tout monstre qu'il voulait être" (p.149). In one passage, Polyphile makes this notion more explicit:

Il se peut trouver des personnes laides qui affectent de se montrer: la rencontre n'en est pas rare; mais que ceux qui sont beaux se cachent, c'est un prodige dans la nature; et peut-être n'y avait-il que cela de monstrueux en la personne de notre époux. (p. 150)

La Fontaine's tale teaches that monstrosity is wanting to hide when there is no reason to hide, a definition that seems unrelated to any accepted usage of the term. However, the pleasures afforded Cupidon by his unnatural secrecy are far from innocent. By remaining inscrutable, he gains access to the psyche, or life principle, of the object of his contemplation: "[O]utre le plaisir de la voir, il avait celui d'apprendre ses plus secrètes pensées" (p. 146). The fictive Sun King's voyeurism is a source of great satisfaction, satisfaction which, as he admits to his wife, is overtly sadistic: "Je prends un plaisir extrême à vous voir en peine" (p. 151).

The god of love is not the only one of Psyché's admirers to relish her suffering. In his transmission of her story, Polyphile can be accused of a type of narrative sadism. He speaks frequently of pity in his meta- and extranarrative commentary, but rather than showing involvement with the characters whose lives he is unfolding, the term is indicative of narrative distancing and of a desire to keep his audience's response within predetermined limits. When Polyphile speaks of how he "pities" the lovers, Gélaste calls his bluff: "Vu l'intérêt que vous prenez à la satisfaction de ces deux époux, et la pitié que vous avez d'eux, vous ne vous hâtez guère de les tirer de ce misérable état où vous les avez laissés" (p. 155). Just at the moment when Psyché awakens Cupidon, Polyphile breaks off both his story and any possibility of identification with Psyché's plight: "Dispensez-moi de vous raconter le reste: vous seriez touchés de trop de pitié au récit que je vous ferais" (p. 172). He then suspends his narrative to include a long parenthesis (pp. 172-86) on the merits of the comic and serious styles. Clearly, Polyphile, like Cupidon, wants to give his readers a brilliant style instead of psychological complexity.

In the course of the digression on styles that temporarily puts Psyché's fate in a parenthesis, Ariste calls pity "le mouvement le plus agréable de tous" (p. 181). He repeats his stand on this issue (and thereby his implicit criticism of Polyphile's narrative methods) at *Psyché*'s conclusion, when he tries to force Acante to admit that he preferred the moments when Polyphile was trying to arouse compassion to his narrative playfulness. Acante's evasive reply ends both the discussion and the tale: "Ce que vous dîtes est fort vrai . . . mais je vous prie de considérer ce gris de lin, ce couleur d'aurore, cet orangé, et surtout ce pourpre, qui environnent le roi des astres." The primary narrator then intervenes to side with Acante and wrap things up: "En effet, il y avait très longtemps que le soir ne s'était trouvé si beau" (pp. 256-57).

Like other discussions in *Psyché*, the debate over pity is cut short, and no final opinion, whether that of the author or a consensus among his characters, is established. Just what is the reader to think of Ariste's eulogy of pity, when pity is an emotion consistently denied all the participants in Psyché's perils? The ending acts as a clear repudiation of Ariste, the member of Polyphile's audience who defends emotions traditionally ascribed to the reader, and therefore as an indirect repudiation of those of *Psyché*'s readers who share his desires and who, like Psyché herself, want more than the mere contours of a presence: "Tous vos palais, tous vos meubles, tous vos jardins, ne sauraient me récompenser d'un moment de votre présence" (p. 151). *Psyché*'s ending informs its readers that they should exchange active participation in the story—the charms of pity and identification—for the passive pleasures of admiration and contemplation. "Arrêtons-nous à . . . ses

Remparts. . . . Adorons les voiles . . . qui sont entre nous et elle" (*Le Socrate chrétien*, p. 37). Those who venture into La Fontaine's literary *galerie des glaces* should be prepared to heed Balzac's warning: the reader is ordered to do no more than move around the textual outworks, admiring their dazzling perfection.

In their efforts to use visual seduction to control a situation, La Fontaine and Cupidon borrow the tactics developed by the master artist whose presence is in filigree throughout this work—Louis XIV. Versailles's master built a pleasure palace remarkable for its dazzling interplay of surfaces. When Cupidon's bride wakes after her wedding night, "au lieu d'un jeune mari, la pauvre Psyché ne voya[it] en cette chambre que des dorures" (p. 142). Those who contemplate the artistic manifestations described in *Psyché* see, like the tale's heroine, only "dorures." Cupidon wants his wife to be content with a gilded cage; Louis XIV used dazzling façades to control his subjects. La Fontaine, the re-creator of both palaces, imitates this technique. Psyché sees only gold in the palace and finds it empty of life. The same could be said of La Fontaine's version of her story, if "life" represents the reader's involvement in the characters' psychology, what Worringer calls empathy. *Psyché* can be described as a *mise en abyme* of the functioning and goals of the art of abstraction known as French Classicism. The dazzling surfaces of the artistic creations that serve as models for the Sun King's age constitute a brilliant machine for controlling all readers, for keeping them in the dark, for discouraging them from asking questions about the identity of the master artist who surrounds them with "dorures" to protect his own monstrous invisibility.

The reading suggested by La Fontaine's metatextual commentary in *Psyché* makes plain a tension already present in his acknowledged model, Appuleius, a tension between allegory and fairy tale or love story—or in the context of French seventeenth-century literature, one might say between allegory and novel, a genre to which *Psyché* has often been related.[35] As an allegory for La Fontaine's age, the tale represents the struggle of a superhuman monarch to create fortifications invincible enough to protect against all natural forces outside the fortress, against spectators who must be taught the charms of "tranquil" contemplation so that they will never interfere with the machine's smooth functioning, and, even more important, against the psyche or instinctual energies inside the fortress. "Il faut se garder contre soi-même," the Sun King warns, "prendre garde à son inclination et être toujours en garde contre son naturel" (*Mémoires,* p. 281). Any movement not absolutely systematic and mechanical must be suppressed. Empathic projection is never permitted—there is no Same, only Other—in the endless Classical war against nature. The Classical psyche is locked up and kept in the dark, is treated, like La Fontaine's heroine, as an object for commentary rather than for emotional response.[36] In an exclusively literary context, *Psyché* may also stand as a warning to practitioners of the literary form then being given its modern expression in France, the novel, the genre most intimately associated in the course of its history with the question of reader empathy. *Psyché* demonstrates to the novelist that the foundation of his authority should be a system of accounting whose flawless

[35] Henri Coulet compares *Psyché* to various types of contemporary novels; see *Le Roman jusqu'à la révolution,* 2 vols. (Colin, 1968), vol. 1, pp. 284-85. H. J. Rose summarizes allegorical readings of Appuleius in *A Handbook of Greek Mythology* (New York: Dutton, 1959), p. 287.

[36] It is appropriate that La Fontaine's inquisitive, threatening reader figure be female. When Louis warns against those who seek to "attaque[r] le coeur d'un prince comme une place," the only example he gives of an emotional besieger is that of a "femme adroite," who will always manage to violate the royal fortifications of secrecy: "Dès lors que vous donnez la liberté à une femme de vous parler de choses importantes, il est impossible qu'elles ne nous fassent faillir" (*Mémoires,* pp. 258-59). The conclusion of Rousseau's *Julie* may be seen as a reenactment of this Classical struggle to suppress the female threat to perfect defenses.

operation will be considered beautiful and will serve as a deterrent force to secure his territory.

The concluding lines of one of the literary monuments of the Golden Age, Boileau's *Art poétique*, delimit the territory in the realm of letters that the Classical authors, on the model of their monarch, designated for their literary production. Boileau's final message confirms the lesson of *Psyché*. His prescription for Classical literature closes with a coda celebrating Louis XIV's (and Vauban's) military successes. The writer traditionally known as the arbiter of Classicism glorifies France's offensive might, as he evokes Louis's ever spreading conquests: "Que de rempars détruits! Que de villes forcées! / Que de moissons de gloire en courant amassées!" (p. 185). According to the *Art poétique*, military success seems to be synonymous with offensive action, with conquest, with the destruction of defenses, and the glory of Classicism is described as a purely aggressive glory. Thus Boileau's Malherbe is a worthy counterpart of the "Vainqueur rapide" to whom the poem's coda is dedicated, a literary "preneur de villes": "Les Stances avec grace apprirent à tomber / ... Tout reconnut ses loix" (p. 160).

Yet in the *Art poétique*, the primary demand Boileau makes of writers is that they seek control over the shape of literature. He reserves his highest praise for Malherbe because he sees him as the first French poet able to keep both the individual word and the line of poetry in place: "D'un mot mis en sa place enseigna le pouvoir"; "Et le vers sur le vers n'osa plus enjamber" (p. 160). Boileau's characterization of Malherbe makes clear that the so-called arbiter of Classicism believed that literature and language have a preordained shape, dictated by "les regles du devoir." He admires the poet he adopts as a model for classical authors, not because Malherbe invented or conquered a new space for literature, but because he knew how to serve as a "guide fidele" in the task of "repairing" ("la Langue reparée) literature and language, of bringing them back within boundaries that had already been traced for them. For Boileau, the model writer is the tracer of a literary fortress and a systematizer of preexistent elements. In order to establish their authority in the French tradition, future authors should square off a *pré carré*, a perfectly defended strategic space that could be seen as an original, predestined one. Such a space would predetermine subsequent literary strategies just as in siege warfare the structure of the fortress decides the structure of any attack. The fortress's enclosure constitutes the original obstacle, generating all subsequent offensive attempts to encircle and destroy its space. In siege warfare, the defensive space is both definable and defined. By contrast, the attack, although by no means uncontrolled, is dependent on a form, on laws, and on strategies that predate its conception.

Boileau's *Art poétique* shows those who live in the shadow of the Classical literary fortress that only the builder of the perfect wall can know territorial security. Boileau's authoritative code was not intended to police the territory of the novel, then considered the most unruly and undefinable of literary forms. But subsequent practitioners of the genre whose modern demarcation in 1678 coincided with the Sun King's self-transformation into a gilded fortress sought to re-create, as La Fontaine had, that monarch's Vaubanian strategies.

The eighteenth-century authors considered here saw themselves as both inside and outside the Classical fortress. They were threatened by its menace, by the obstacle of its greatness. Thus, like Vauban, they were critics of the official regime and promised to liberate those who would live inside the new enclosures they were constructing, to create for them a territorially secure utopia. They completed La Fontaine's promise of pleasing with Vauban's goal of instructing. But the pedagogical systems put into operation in their *pré carré* by Rousseau, Laclos, and Sade repeat the accounting that leads to the violence at the heart of the Vaubanian defensive project. Boileau contends that Malherbe's authority is imperiously pedagogical: "[D]'un mot mis en sa place [il] enseigna le pouvoir" (p. 160). The aggressively defensive strategists considered here all demonstrate that the *pré carré* can function successfully only if everything is in its proper place. They use teaching as a form of control through placement and teach thereby a lesson about the power of teaching and the teaching of power: "enseigna le pouvoir." As much as La Fontaine, the novelists of the Enlightenment were cultural insiders: they enjoyed the benefits of the *pré carré*, the status, the invincibility, guaranteed French literature by the belief in the existence of a literary patrimony.[37] Speaking of *Psyché*, La Fontaine declared: "Apulée me fournissait la matière; il ne restait que la forme, c'est-à-dire les paroles" (p. 121). The mark of the novelists who follow his lead, their inherently Classical genius, is their ability to use already carved building blocks to make ever more invincible fortifications. Their "parole" or discourse bears the trace of this aggressive defensiveness; pastiche and parody make the verbal fabric of their texts a vocal battleground.

From a man of offense, a "preneur de villes"—what the marquise de Merteuil considers a facile, "risk-free" military position—Vauban in the course of his career became the central defensive genius of the neoclassical age of the fortress. As a result of his monarch's reliance on protected aggression, the defense of territory became the keystone of Vaubanian strategy. Vauban understood the notion of territory in both a literal and a metaphoric sense. He knew that the fortifications he was building along France's "natural" borders provided the perfect image for his dream of a nation-state. He understood the psychological import of geography and sensed the power that would come from the realization of his goal of impenetrable frontiers. His vision of the *pré carré*—along with the magnificently panoptic reading of it proposed by his monarch—proved to be a remarkably seductive one. In the novels

[37] In 1693, just before the publication of the Académie française's first dictionary, the academician Charpentier, already convinced of the merits of the *pré carré* for the status of French literature, claimed that only Louis's patronage would make the dictionary possible and spoke of "cette fatalité qui joint ordinairement ensemble l'excellence des armes et celle des lettres" (cited by Ferrier-Caverivière, p. 172).

examined in the following pages, it is repeatedly realized when fictional engineers seek to protect their territory, establish secure borders, and bring everyone and everything inside their *pré carré*—be it a garden utopia, a pedagogical enclave, or a libertine fortress—under their absolute domination.

La Fontaine's Crafty Parable:
The Pedagogical Trap

> Les génies lisent peu, pratiquent beaucoup, et se font
> d'eux mêmes. Voyez César, Turenne, Vauban. . . . C'est
> la nature qui forme ces hommes rares-là.
>
> Diderot, *Le Neveu de Rameau*

In the beginning of the last book of the *Confessions,* Rousseau describes the attacks on him from all sides when he was exiled from France after the publication of *Emile:* "J'étois un impie, un athée, un forcené, un enragé, une bête féroce, un loup. Le continuateur du journal de Trévoux fit sur ma prétendue Lycantropie un écart qui montrait assez bien la sienne."[1] Rousseau attempts to deflect this attack by turning it against his aggressor—"un écart qui montrait assez bien la sienne." He uses what is perhaps his favorite defensive strategy—one to which Freud often refers in his case studies—the *tu quoque* argument. Freud associates this defense with "the process of delusion formation" in paranoia and contends that the model for the *tu quoque* argument is to be found in children's behavior. Thus, he suggests that this is an instinctive, primitive technique for self-protection.[2] Furthermore, Freud argues that this type of defense can be considered a form of admission, or at least fear, of guilt: "A string of reproaches against other

---

[1] Rousseau, *Oeuvres complètes,* vol. 1, p. 591.

[2] Freud, *Dora: An Analysis of a Case of Hysteria* (New York: Collier Books, 1963), p. 51. Lacan makes specific the relationship Freud suggests between paranoia and primitive thought: "Les chercheurs italiens modernes . . . attendent la clef des structures mentales de la paranoïa d'un rapprochement avec les *formes,* définies par les sociologues, de la *pensée primitive,* dite encore *pensée prélogique.*" Lacan cites Tanzi and Lugaro: "Les paranoïaques sont des anachronismes vivants" (*De la Psychose paranoïaque dans ses rapports avec la personnalité,* 1932 thesis [Seuil, 1975], pp. 288, 26).

people leads one to suspect the existence of a string of self-reproaches with the same content" (p. 51). Thus it would seem that the name calling engaged in by Rousseau and the editor of the *Journal de Trévoux* was actually a complicated round of a "game" that might be called "it takes a wolf to know one." If Freud's explanation is adopted, the initial attack can be understood as an outgrowth of the editor's desire to camouflage his own wolflike ferocity. And by the same token, Rousseau's response was so heated because he sensed that he was not entirely a lamb, according to the traditional division La Fontaine adopts between two types of behavior in the struggle for power to which the fabulist devotes so much attention.

A note in the Pléiade edition of Rousseau's works defines *lycanthropie* according to eighteenth-century sources as a mental disease in which the patient believes he has been changed into a wolf, but adds "mais ici ce serait plutôt l'état mental d'un homme qui est hargneux, cruel, enragé comme un loup." To document this point, the editor quotes the entry from the *Journal de Trévoux*, November 1762, that provoked Rousseau's wrath: "Quoique vous rangiez tous les Européens dans la classe des *bêtes féroces,* il n'en est pas moins vrai qu'ils sont amis de l'humanité: ils ne se croyent point en droit d'user de représailles en insultant à l'espèce de Lycanthropie qui vous arme contre eux" (1: 1566). The citation demonstrates that in adopting the *tu quoque* defense, Rousseau is only mimicking editorial strategy. The anonymous Trévoux continuator claims to trace the accusations of wolflike ferocity to their origin in *Emile*. There, in his words, Rousseau levels a charge of lupine behavior against all mankind. Because the editor feels himself to be included in Rousseau's choice of target, his account of *Emile* is not the attack Rousseau would consider it, but really a defense, a *tu quoque* defense. Just as Rousseau would later argue, the editor asserts that *Emile*'s author sees the wolf in others because he has only to recognize what is in himself; he is able to attack because he is so well defended by "l'espèce de Lycanthropie qui vous arme contre eux."

A reviewer claimed that Rousseau found humanity lupine because he suffered from lycanthropy; Rousseau himself argued in return that only a lycanthrope could find his philosophy lycanthropic—their convoluted exchange is a perfect illustration of the interdependence of attack and defense that Vauban came to realize. The exchange originates in Rousseau's characterization of mankind in *Emile,* but this "origin" is a problematic one, since Rousseau's position can be interpreted as a self-defensive gesture to protect himself from those who wished him ill, or as a gratuitous attack, or as an attack that also serves to defend him against a self-reproach. Their exchange also exemplifies the complex and intertwined relationship between wolf and lamb, attacker and defender, aggressor and victim. In terms of these traditional dichotomies, Rousseau never doubted that he himself was a sacrificial lamb— certainly not a wolf in sheep's clothing. His bestial self-image influences his readings of literary works that portray couples locked in power plays, struggling for influence. Thus he takes the side of Alceste over Philinte in his interpretation of the *Misanthrope* and the side of the *corbeau* over the *renard.* Rousseau's reading of La Fontaine's fable serves as a *mise en abyme* of his relationship both to his literary predecessors and to the pedagogical act.

Rousseau's encounter with La Fontaine occupies a privileged position in *Emile.* It is one of the first imaginary lessons (what Rousseau calls "la pratique" [4: 316]) of this "treatise." Furthermore, it is unique in its class, for all the other lessons take the form of pedagogical scenarios through which the child encounters either an individual or a problem. The purpose of these encounters is either to introduce the child to an abstract concept (for example, personal property) or to make him acquire a practical skill (such as telling directions). The lesson involving La Fontaine's fable is closer to what a modern teacher of literature would identify as a classroom encounter, albeit a rather idiosyncratic one, organized around the discussion of a literary text. It is, of course, easy to explain why the fictive teacher and his fictive pupil[3] do not together study other works of fiction in *Emile*: one of the most frequently discussed aspects of Rousseau's philosophy of education is its violent attack on reading and all other forms of "study" normally included in a child's education. In fact, as if to point up its exceptional status, the La Fontaine passage is framed by two illustrations of this attack: it is preceded by Rousseau's rejection of what he calls "science de mots" (the study of facts, as opposed to practical experience: "il n'y a point d'étude propre aux enfants" [4: 350]), and followed by a repudiation of books ("j'ôte les instrumens de leur plus grande misére savoir les livres" [4: 357]).

Given its context and its uniqueness, Rousseau's confrontation with La Fontaine would seem to be a logical starting point for an investigation of the implications of Rousseau's pedagogical theories. This study of a literary work framed by attacks on both study and literary works reveals a great deal about the nature of teaching—and not only for Rousseau. Rousseau's most comprehensive confrontation with his twin pedagogical enemies, books and study (especially memorization, an educational concept with which the *Fables* were already associated in Rousseau's day), apparently serves to justify his generalized enmity. However, Rousseau's choice of author and text is particularly instructive: to illustrate the dangers of exposing children to literature, he proposes a "reading" of a text that is doubly associated with pedagogy (because it was already used as a pedagogical tool in the French educational system and because it is a representative of an overtly didactic literary genre). Furthermore, the author of this text is his most illustrious predecessor in the teaching of French children.

Rousseau's resentment of representative figures from the Golden Age of French literature and his scandalized rejection

---

[3] The problem of the (shifting) identities of teacher and student will be discussed in the chapter on Rousseau. In this section, I will refer to the pedagogical voice as "Jean-Jacques," one of the names used to identify that voice in *Emile*.

of the pedagogical role generally accorded Classical literature in his day are recurrent features of his works (an especially striking example is the attack on Molière in the *Lettre à d'A-lembert*). In *Emile*, Rousseau had intended to make a broader rejection of Classical literature's pedagogical function, for his reading of La Fontaine originally contained the phrase: "Il est très simple qu'un père qui tire sa morale des pièces de Molière tire des fables de La Fontaine celle qu'il donne à ses enfans" (4: 1380). The seventeenth-century fabulist undoubtedly merited his position as a target in *Emile* by virtue of his preeminent role in the tradition of pedagogical literature in France. Rousseau implicitly aspires to overthrow La Fontaine, to take over his position as the arbiter of "la morale des enfans" (4: 352). Rousseau's resentment of the predecessor who casts too long a shadow is apparent in the myopic pettiness that characterizes his treatment of "Le Corbeau et le Renard," a treatment that is closer to a dissection than a reading.

The method Rousseau adopts (and perhaps deforms) to deconstruct the fable does not fail to baffle and eventually irritate contemporary readers. Rousseau's lesson on La Fontaine's lesson takes roughly the form of what has come to constitute the basic tool of literary training in the French pedagogical system, the *explication de texte*. He cites "Le Corbeau et le Renard" line by line. As if to cast himself as a victim of the educational practice he denounces, he quotes from memory, rendering the line in La Fontaine's original "Que vous êtes joli!" as "Que vous êtes charmant."[4] He reacts to each line, largely by means of a series of questions. These are meant, apparently, to simulate the questions of the "average" child, presumably Emile, if the fable were read to him or if he were asked to memorize it. Rousseau is more than usually imprecise about the pedagogical status of this vignette,

---

[4] Because he quotes from memory, Rousseau misquotes several other lines. "Monsieur du Corbeau," becomes "Monsieur le Corbeau," "se rapporte" (line 8) becomes "répondoit," and "êtes" (line 9) is given as "seriez."

but in *La Nouvelle Héloïse*, Julie encounters a parallel instinctive resistance on the part of her eldest child when she recites the same fable to him: "J'avois dessein de lui dire de tems en tems quelque fable de La Fontaine pour l'amuser, et j'avois déjà commencé, quand il me demanda si les corbeaux parloient?" (5: 3: 581). Julie's son's question prefigures one of those (re)imagined by Jean-Jacques for the child reacting to the fable in *Emile*. Other questions include "On ment donc quelquefois?" and the one that Rousseau's readers today find most surprising, "Etoit-ce un fromage de Suisse, de Brie, ou de Hollande?" (4: 354, 353).

Modern theoreticians commenting on the reception of fairy tales and fables would contend that children would never question whether crows can talk and that only an adult would be so literal and fact-conscious. But this behavioral issue is ultimately less interesting than the psychology of Rousseau's (over)reaction. Just as with his reading of *Le Misanthrope*, it is evident that something about this fable makes him angry. Rousseau attacks Molière because he believes that Alceste, with whom he identifies, is wronged by his fellow characters, by the playwright, and by readers. Such a desire to right wrongs also motivates his impassioned attempt to undermine the authority of "Le Corbeau et le Renard." Rousseau's quibbling about the unsuitability of poetic inversions and mythological references for children is not central to his sweeping condemnation of La Fontaine as a children's author. That condemnation is prompted by Rousseau's conviction that the fable deludes its (young) readers by secretly seducing them into an identification with the side of evil, by prompting, in other words, the wrong *tu quoque* defense. Rousseau contends that Classical educators have children commit the fable to memory in the belief that they will identify with the crow's plight and, from that self-projection, learn to avoid finding themselves in his situation ("se corriger sur la dupe"). What actually happens, in his reconstruction of the child's reaction, is that the pupil learns the opposite lesson and hopes to model himself on the fox ("se former . . . sur le fripon"). He explains that standard pedagogical technique backfires because it fails to account for a basic fact of human nature: "On n'aime point à s'humilier; ils prendront toujours le beau rolle, c'est le choix de l'amour-propre, c'est un choix très naturel" (4: 356). According to Rousseau, this pedagogical miscalculation represents a danger only for children. Adults, like Jean-Jacques the teacher, are not tricked into the wrong projection, for they see through the foxy flattery to the fable's lesson: "Je promets quant à moi de vous lire avec choix, de vous aimer, de m'instruire dans vos fables; car j'espère ne pas me tromper sur leur objet" (4: 357). However, in his reconstruction of the fable's functioning, he fails to take into account two factors that influence his classification of its readers. First, Rousseau assumes that Jean-Jacques's position can be considered representative of that of all adult readers—he refuses to admit the idiosyncratic nature of interpretive projection. Second, he does not consider the fact that his reasoning about the child's position with regard to the fable's two characters—"on n'aime point à s'humilier"—is perhaps not an exclusively childish perspective. Identifying with "le beau rolle" is certainly an impulse common to adult readers as well as to children; in Rousseau's words, "c'est un choix très natural." Jean-Jacques is correct in pointing out the foxiness of La Fontaine's fable, but its dangerous implications for teaching are more widespread still. It is of course also possible that Rousseau's resentment of La Fontaine was inspired by his recognition, in La Fontaine's fable on teaching, of unsettling implications for all pedagogical systems, even his own.

Elsewhere, *Emile* has aspects of a pedagogical treatise. While its teaching vignettes are not necessarily intended to serve as literal models for future pedagogues, Rousseau does at least include commentary on how his dream could be realized, and on possible modifications for other teaching situations. However, he makes no place in his reading of La Fontaine's fable for any discussion of its pedagogical value. Granted, this is a negative demonstration; Rousseau is showing what *not* to do. But even in view of this premise, it is surprising that he draws

no conclusion about the nature and functioning of the pedagogical act from his illustration. Just as Laclos would later
try to show that Vauban was a master of offense rather than
defense, Rousseau is primarily concerned with proving his
seventeenth-century precursor to be a teacher of adults rather
than of children, and this concern blinds him to the broader
issue of what all types of teaching have in common.

Rousseau explicates "Le Corbeau et le Renard" in order
to show that those who would use the fable for the instruction
of children, including implicitly La Fontaine himself, do not
understand the child's mind because they have been unable
to "analyser toutes les idées de cette fable, et les réduire aux
idées simples et élémentaires dont chacune d'elles est com-
posée" (4: 355). Throughout his analysis, Rousseau implies
that because he is able to formulate ideas, and therefore a
moral, on a child's level, he is a superior pedagogue, one who
projects himself outside of himself and into the mind of his
pupil. The implied definition of conscientious, morally enlightened teaching established by this section of *Emile* is a
form of projection or identification parallel to that which
inspires Rousseau's interpretation of literary works or, for
that matter, to that which he claims inspired his writing of
literature—witness the account in the *Confessions* of the composition of *Julie*. According to this vision, in order to teach
children properly, in order to produce an appropriately child-
like reading, it is necessary to *become* the child.

But then, at the end of his *explication de texte,* Rousseau
abruptly rejects the type of analysis he has just provided at
such length and the possibility of knowing the pupil/Other
well enough to be able to become him for the space of the
lesson: "Nul de nous n'est assés philosophe pour savoir se
mettre à la place d'un enfant" (4: 355). By situating his rejection of the teacher's perfect identification with his student
in a passage that had previously seemed premised on just such
a total projection, Rousseau may actually be defining by implication the space of teaching. In so doing, he repeats the
definition already proposed by the fable. The fox teaches the

crow (a lesson at least) by successfully predicting his desires (becoming the crow) while never losing touch with his own identity (remaining the fox). According to the fable's somewhat ambiguous moral, in the process he presumably shows the crow how to repeat this movement, how to step outside of himself and become a bit wiser, foxier, closer to the teacher/ Other.[5] His commentary on the fable and on its pedagogical effect reveals Rousseau's awareness of this double transformation: "se corriger sur," "se former sur."

Both the fable and Rousseau's *explication de texte* present teaching as a borderline activity, as an interchange between self and Other, between inside and outside. The teacher builds a barrier around himself to define the limits of this loss of self and to protect his territory from the encroachment of the student/Other. The space of teaching in this vision may be compared to the "position in space" Freud assigns to the conscious ego (the system "Pcpt.-Cs.," the perception-consciousness system) in the fourth section of *Beyond the Pleasure Principle*.[6] Freud resorts to a surprising image to convey his sense of the spatial configuration of this system that "lies on the borderline between outside and inside; it must be turned towards the external world and must envelop the other psychical systems" (p. 18). He describes it as an amoeba-like creature, a "little fragment of living substance which is suspended in the middle of an external world charged with the most powerful energies." At some (impossible to imagine) origin, the "living vesicle" is defenseless: its external surface is receptive to the stimuli from the intense forces surrounding it, and "it would be killed by the stimulation emanating from these if it were not provided with a protective shield against

[5] This act of self-transformation in order to provoke the transformation of the student corresponds to the definition of teaching recently proposed by the president of Yale University, Bartlett Giamatti: "The act of teaching is an exemplary act of self-fashioning on behalf of knowledge that teaches others how to fashion the self" (*Annual Report of the President*, 1979-80).

[6] Freud, *Beyond the Pleasure Principle* (New York: Liveright, 1961), p. 18.

stimuli." In order to prevent its destruction, it undergoes a partial death: "Its outermost surface ceases to have the structure proper to living matter, becomes to some degree inorganic and thenceforth functions as a special envelope or membrane resistant to stimuli" (p. 21). This "natural" fortification serves to protect the ego against external dangers. Threats from within are warded off by a system of defenses that strives to mimic the functioning of the outworks: "When faced with internally troubling 'excitations,' there is a tendency to treat them as though they were acting, not from the inside, but from the outside, so that it may be possible to bring the shield against stimuli into operation as a means of defence against them. This is the origin of projection" (p. 23).

Freud's analogy can help elucidate the intersection of Rousseau and La Fontaine in several ways. The most evident application results from its description of a space that is both inside and outside, a space that facilitates the passage between outside and inside, first by "deadening" external stimulants so that they can be received by and as internal elements, then by reevaluating and refocusing internal forces that threaten to disrupt the process of assimilation so that they can be viewed and acted upon as though they were external. Freud's vignette illustrates the primacy of the defensive instinct. The formation of the shield or fortification around the ego is not provoked by an original attack; that barrier is always already there, and it is protective only in that it is designed to be preventative. The treatment of internal as external that Freud describes—already discussed here in reference to one variant of projection, the *tu quoque* defense—further blurs, if not the distinction between attack and defense, at least any notion of a chronological dependency of defense on attack. In his description of the ego's struggle to maintain control over its exterior and interior environments, Freud stresses the primacy of what might seem the most primitive of all defenses, the external or fortification defensive model.

At the end of his commentary on La Fontaine's fable, Rousseau finally admits that it is impossible for a teacher to put himself in his pupil's place, when by putting himself in his pupil's place he means predicting all the pupil's problems and reactions. He does not comment on the presence of this same desire in the teaching couple depicted by La Fontaine, although it is this projection of teacher into student that reveals the true nature of their interchange. The teacher-fox tricks the crow into giving up his prize possession by correctly interpreting his desire to be Other, his desire to be transformed, his desire, in other words, to be taught, since in teaching the pupil is reshaped by the teacher. The crow's desire to be Other is simply a desire to be beautiful, and the fox's promise conforms perfectly to his desire: "Vous seriez le Phénix." Commenting on his flattery Rousseau refers to "la menteuse antiquité" (4: 354), yet the lie is not in mythology but in the nonconformity of this promise not only with the crow's nature, but also with the nature of teaching. The fox promises his student a transformation worthy of the Sun King's Vaubanian dream. The phoenix is unique, as the definite article in the fox's guarantee (accidentally) implies: there is only one such bird at a time. As a necessary result of his uniqueness, the phoenix is self-sufficient and self-regenerating. His machine of perfection is autonomous and destined to function eternally. The phoenix shapes himself and cannot be shaped by another. No one can be made into *the* phoenix, even by the wiliest of teachers.

The fox's promise is fallacious, but the status of the moral he delivers after his act of deception is more difficult to establish. As Louis Marin has pointed out, it is customary at the end of a fable for the narrator to assume final responsibility for the pedagogical value of his tale by reciting its moral: "L'auteur . . . nous ordonne à la règle et à la norme, nous engage à la juste conduite."[7] Here the fox not only makes the crow eat crow, but has the responsibility, normally reserved by La Fontaine for his narrator, of explaining what his actions

[7] Marin, "La Bête, l'animal parlant, et l'homme, ou la rencontre du renard et du corbeau," *Traverses* 8 (May 1977):47.

mean. His commentary is far stranger than even Rousseau's scrutiny reveals:

> Apprenez que tout flateur
> Vit aux dépends de celui qui l'écoute.
> Cette leçon vaut bien un fromage, sans doute.[8]

The fox's moral, unlike La Fontaine's usual ones, is difficult to analyze in pedagogical terms. It represents a type of "negative" teaching very different from the one Rousseau advocated. In his analysis of the fable, Rousseau camouflages its uniqueness by comparing it with "la fable qui suit," "La Cigale et la Fourmi." Yet the morals of the two fables are quite different because, whereas a teacher can show a pupil how to repeat a gesture (putting away for the winter) and to be *like* someone (the ant), it is far more difficult to learn *not* to repeat an action, especially if the action is a nonaction, a passive reception of another's intention.[9] Learning to avoid listening to someone who can predict your desires is a more complex lesson than learning to avoid consuming your provisions too quickly. The moral reveals the limits of the vulpine educator's identification with his pupil, for its lesson really concerns the teacher. "Tout flateur" is its subject, and the moral "teaches" the crow more about his instructor than about himself. It also represents a final deformation of the pupil's desire to be Other and beautiful, for, in order to carry out the moral's lesson, the crow would have to become Other and foxy. He would need his teacher's wiles in order to unmask future flatterers. In the moral, the fox actually teaches the crow that, in order to learn from his loss, he has to become the teacher. The fox

---

[8] I follow Rousseau's orthography.

[9] Barbara Johnson has analyzed a related attempt at negative pedagogy in the work of the other seventeenth-century moralist resented by Rousseau, Molière: "The teaching of ignorance . . . may be a structurally impossible task. For how can a teacher teach a student not to know, without at the same time informing him of what it is he is supposed to be ignorant of?" ("Teaching Ignorance: *L'Ecole des femmes*," *Yale French Studies,* hereafter *YFS,* 63: 165).

ultimately reverses his initial identification with his student and completely internalizes the external. He, too, eats crow for he submerges and eliminates the identity of his partner in the fable's power play much as his cousin does in a similar fable, "Le Loup et l'Agneau." This can explain the predator's strange lack of interest in his prize, the cheese. If he had really been out to seduce the crow in order to win his cheese, he might have been expected to run off with it immediately, instead of remaining to teach his victim a second, verbal lesson.

La Fontaine never depicts the fox eating the cheese. It is clear that the fox has been chosen to represent the fabulist here because, like the fabulist himself, he is primarily interested in teaching, which he sees as an act of mastery. In the fable, only the crafty teacher possesses the power of speech. He first uses his power to trick his unrealistic student out of the only treasure he possesses, and he dupes him by means of an eminently professorial technique: repeat after me; follow my example. The crow believes that he can use his "ramage" because he witnesses the prowess of his teacher's. However, as soon as he opens his mouth to participate, as a good student should, the vulpine professor silences him with more of his own "ramage": "mon bon monsieur, / Apprenez . . ." Rousseau was incensed by the fox's power of speech ("Les Renards parlent donc?"). The talking animal, Marin contends, represents a vision of a problematic central to Rousseau's thought, for he is "la figure d'une origine du langage à partir de l'entredévoration bestiale des corps." "Cette origine du langage," Marin continues, "est également indiscernable d'une origine du pouvoir dont l'entredévoration des corps est à son tour la figure. Pouvoir du langage, langage du pouvoir" (p. 37).

The fox's final gesture of mastery, the sign of his *prise de pouvoir*, takes the form of a rather devious formulation: "Cette leçon vaut bien un fromage, sans doute." He makes teaching enter into a system of exchange, turns pedagogy into a kind of money. Rousseau is critical of the fox's bartering because he finds it beyond a child's comprehension: "Il y aura encore bien peu d'enfans qui sachent comparer une leçon à un fro-mage" (p. 355). But the message of the formulation can be analyzed in more general terms. In his commentary on his pedagogical technique in the *explication de texte,* Rousseau gives a definition of the philosopher: "Nul de nous n'est assés philosophe pour savoir se mettre à la place d'un enfant." He establishes an equivalence between the philosopher and the teacher, and the talent he feels both should share is one pos-sessed to an exemplary degree by the archetypal philosopher-teacher, Socrates. In Rousseau's definition, the philosopher has the ability to rediscover a Socratic naiveté that enables him to arrive by analysis at the simple ideas of a text.

In *The Economy of Literature,* Marc Shell paraphrases Marx's aphorism "logic is the money of the mind" to provide an explanation for Plato's critique of his teacher Socrates: "Socratic thought, feared Plato, is the money of the mind."[10] Socratic thought and logic can be described as mental money because they transform reality into abstractions and replace it with concepts, thereby making it invisible. But Shell also describes the process by which money, in the hands of a tyrant, was used to subjugate the tyrant's reality, his kingdom, by making it too visible. He recounts the story of Deioces the Mede "who became invisible to his subjects by establishing one of the first great bureaucracies in Western civilization" (p. 17). The tyrant instituted his despotism by remaining him-self invisible behind the fortifications of the concentric circles of his walled city while dealing with his subjects via the media of exchange on which his bureaucracy was premised, writing and money. A network of spies kept his subjects as visible, and therefore as controlled, as possible.[11]

[10] Shell, *The Economy of Literature* (Baltimore: Johns Hopkins Univ. Press, 1978), p. 48.

[11] Deioces the tyrant hid behind "ring-walls" (p. 19), thereby preferring the fortification of the circle to the Vaubanian "pré-carré." Shell's description of the tyrant who depends on fortifications to protect his power (and ulti-mately as a source of power) is one of the most frequently encountered models in the study of defensive systems. This is, of course, the Sun King's ideal (the

A system of exchange enabled the tyrant to remain invisible and ensured his supremacy. For Plato, his teacher's philosophy was not only mental money, but also the master's (tyrant's) thought. The teacher shares the tyrant's invisibility because the (presumed) enlightenment of his superior knowledge puts him beyond interrogation and shelters him from any attempt on the part of the student to see through him. At the same time, the pedagogue can use his protected position to make the student supremely visible. He can use his illumination to make the student transparent to his gaze. When, like the Socratic teacher and the tyrant, the fox replaces reality with a concept, he gains complete mastery over his pupil. He has forced the crow to enter into a system of exchange that ultimately functions to protect his wiliness and to ensure, not that his student will be able to avoid falling victim to it in the future, but rather that he who has already mastered it will be able to continue to flourish behind the walls of his tyranny.

Thus far, this discussion of vulpine tyranny implies that the crow is purely a victim, that he is innocent of complicity in his predator's crafty plot, but this is obviously not the case. The crow is not without knowledge of the strategies of power (plays). "Le Corbeau et le Renard" does not tell the story of the birth or origin of power, but of a transfer of power. That the fox needs the crow is obvious, but the crow shares his need for his opposite in the struggle for supremacy. "Que n'a-t-il en fin de compte," Marin comments, "mangé son fromage dans quelque recoin de la forêt et montré ensuite sa belle voix, tout son saoûl? Mais Maître Renard n'aurait pas été par l'odeur du fromage alléché; il n'aurait pas non plus donné la fallacieuse occasion à son propriétaire de chanter" (p. 44). The crow tempts the fox and then seduces him into repeating his seduction, because of their mutual attraction. He, too, does not eat his cheese in hiding, because, like the fox, he is

---

sun is that which can never be looked at directly, can never be seen). It is also a crucial model for the functioning of the Sadean system, and it remains familiar to readers of modern literature from such works as *The Castle*.

more interested in their pedagogical relationship, in the *leçon*, than in the cheese.

From his child's eye view of the fable, Rousseau concludes that children would never understand the system of exchange accepted by the fox and the crow: "Il y aura encore bien peu d'enfans . . . qui ne préférassent le fromage à la leçon" (4: 355). As an adult, he himself is able to comprehend their exchange ("Ceci s'entend et la pensée est très bonne"), but as a teacher, he condemns the fable's so-called moral as immoral and its fabulist for his child abuse ("l'apologue en les amusant les abuse"). The fable is immoral because the pupils who memorize its words are being tricked into an erroneous self-projection. The fable's youthful readers all see themselves as would-be foxes: "[I]ls s'affectionnent tous au Renard. . . . [I]ls prendront toujours le beau rolle" (4: 356). But in reality "séduits par le mensonge ils laissent échapper la vérité" (4: 352), and they therefore fail to demonstrate "cet esprit de critique judicieuse qui ne s'en laisse imposer qu'à bonnes enseignes, et sait discerner la vérité du mensonge dans les narrations d'autrui" (4: 353). The children, in other words, are seduced by flattery into thinking they could be Other (clever as a fox), when the character in the fable they most closely resemble is fiction's dupe, the crow. They leave themselves open to the fabulist's crafty seductions because of their desire to feel superior to the crow: "les enfans se moquent du corbeau" (4: 356).

The vicious circle that links mocker to mocked is one to which Rousseau is particularly sensitive. In the rewriting of the *Misanthrope* he proposes, the relationship between Alceste and Philinte would be reversed, so that Alceste would become less ridiculous at the same time as the *raisonneur* "dont les maximes ressemblent beaucoup à celles des fripons" would become subject to the mockery of others.[12] Rousseau would

---

[12] Rousseau, *Lettre à Mr. d'Alembert sur les spectacles*, ed. M. Fuchs (Geneva: Droz, 1948), p. 51. My reading of Rousseau's reading of "Le Corbeau et le Renard" privileges Rousseau's reaction to a pedagogical threat. English Showalter has reminded me that other biographical and psychological

invert the pedagogical relationship between the two characters and deprive Philinte of his position as representative of wisdom ("le sage de la Pièce") and Alceste's teacher in the ways of the world. He reads Molière's play essentially as another illustration of the link between the student/teacher relationship and ridicule.

Rousseau relives in his critical readings a relationship that, according to his testimony in the *Confessions,* he traced in his own life. His understanding of the exchange between *corbeau* and *renard* is undoubtedly colored by his relationship to the phenomenon of *persiflage.* In the *Confessions,* Rousseau describes one of his first projects in the French literary community, a project that took shape in the context of his weekly dinners with Diderot and Condillac: "Je formai là le projet d'une feuille périodique intitulée *le Persiffleur,* que nous devions faire alternativement Diderot et moi" (1: 347). *Persiflage,* the art of ridiculing someone by means of bantering irony, was certainly an appropriate focus for a journalistic enterprise. But it is hard to reconcile the notion of Rousseau as master *persifleur* with the image he habitually paints of himself as the eternal victim, so the reader of the *Confessions* is hardly surprised to learn that the project of *persiflage* did not have a glorious existence: "Des évenemens imprévus nous barrèrent, et ce projet en demeura-là."

But the concept of *persiflage* does not disappear from the Rousseau saga along with the projected *feuille.* The rite of power that constitutes *persiflage* recurs frequently in Rousseau's account of his life, although never does Rousseau himself come close to fulfilling his dream of excelling at its practice. Not surprisingly, the would-be *persifleur* is soon, and frequently, *persiflé.* In fact, most of the central relationships in his life end with Rousseau the victim of the Other's *persiflage:* Sophie d'Houdetot's and St. Lambert's, for example (1: 442),

---

factors helped determine Rousseau's outraged response to the fable. For example, in the fable the "courtier" is victorious in his confrontation with the "bourgeois."

and Voltaire's, whose *persiflage* takes the form of *Candide*— "je voulois philosopher avec lui; en réponse, il m'a persifflé."[13] The drama of the *persifleur persiflé* that Rousseau acted out is projected onto his critical vision. Thus the *raisonneur* becomes an incarnation of the *persifleur* for him, as does La Fontaine's foxy pedagogue. Rousseau, the would-be *renard* who finds himself more often the victim of other *renards*, understands the position of the *corbeau persiflé*. In his analysis of the fable's moral, he even uses the telltale word: "On pourroit . . . leur apprendre qu'il y a des railleurs qui persifflent les petits garçons, et se moquent en secret de leur sote vanité" (4: 356). Rousseau identifies his own fate with that of his student(s): "les enfans se moquent du corbeau," and in turn "[l]es railleurs persifflent les petits garçons."

Throughout his reading of "Le Corbeau et le Renard," Rousseau implies that bad teachers, following the model of La Fontaine, seduce their pupils into a crowlike state of ignorance of moral questions. He thereby prefigures the insight of recent critics, Marin for example, by viewing the fox as a figure of the fabulist-(bad) teacher (in his personal vocabulary, the *persifleur*). Rousseau warns his readers—who, since they are readers of *Emile*, are potential teachers—against the danger presented by pedagogues blind to the power of their own seductions. He takes us into his confidence and teaches us how to avoid being the dupe of La Fontaine's *persiflage*. In so doing, he flatters us by making us think that he considers us somehow his equals, able to understand, in addition to the *science de mots* that is beyond the child's comprehension, a lesson in wiliness that generations of our predecessors in pedagogy have failed to grasp.

What the fox and La Fontaine have in common is the fact that they are both talking animals—"l'animal parlant" is the title of Marin's article on the fable in a collection appropriately entitled *Le Récit est un piège*. The fox talks in order to flatter,

[13] Rousseau, *Correspondance générale*, ed. T. Dufour (A. Colin, 1924– 1934), vol. 10, p. 347.

to weave a fiction of the phoenix that makes the crow forget the reality of his situation. La Fontaine's fictional web, in Rousseau's interpretation, seems to help its reader avoid the foxes of this world, but is really a trap for trusting child and trusting pedagogue alike. According to the law, if not precisely of the jungle, at least of "ces bois," by helping us avoid La Fontaine's *persiflage,* Rousseau must surely be making us victims of his own *persiflage,* must be at last the *persifleur* of his youthful ambition. After all, foxes and wolves belong to the same animal family, and, as the continuator of the *Journal de Trévoux* claimed after *Emile* was published, it takes a wolf/ fox to know one. The *persifleur,* like the *trompeur* who is proverbially *trompé,* can only be *persiflé* if he has been a *persifleur* in the first place.

It is appropriate that the attacks Rousseau reserved for La Fontaine's pedagogical enterprise would later be directed against the educational model he himself was creating in *Emile.* Rousseau's attempted exorcism of his Classical precursor reveals both his proximity to La Fontaine and the Classicism of his own pedagogical system. His reading of La Fontaine indicates that a deferred, defensive violence is the cornerstone of literary interpretation: not only the origin of language but also the origin of Classical French literary analysis (*l'explication de texte*) can be traced to what Marin terms "l'entredévoration bestiale des corps." In *Emile* and *Julie,* Rousseau theorizes about the liberating potential of the educational enterprise, yet the teaching vignettes he creates to illustrate his theories consistently echo the defensive aggressiveness of pedagogical projection found in "Le Corbeau et le Renard." Rousseau's fictional pedagogues are inherently Classical, for, like the Sun King and La Fontaine's vulpine educator, they put in place elaborate outworks, allegedly to enlighten their students, but in reality designed to protect the teacher's own territory and to enlarge it by swallowing up the student's space. The Classical pedagogue promises his student that he will make him into a Sun Bird, but he does so only to guarantee his own omnipotence and unique status. Classical pedagogy is inherently negative; its only creative goal is the regeneration of the teacher-phoenix who, like the libertine heroes of Sade's *120*, the marquise de Merteuil, and the "new Julie," Claire's daughter Henriette, is reborn from the ashes of the educational debacle.

III

The Oblique Way:
Defensive Swerves

The origin and the rise of Fortifications is undoubtedly
due to the degeneracy of mankind.

J. Muller, Professor of Fortification
Royal Military Academy, Woolwich (1746)

Jacques Lacan frequently uses elements of fortification as metaphors for the structures of defense. On at least one occasion,
he makes explicit the almost automatic association (for a
Frenchman) between fortifications and Vauban:

> Ces noeuds sont plus difficiles à rompre, on le sait, dans
> la névrose obsessionnelle, justement en raison de ce fait
> bien connu de nous que sa structure est particulièrement
> destinée à camoufler, à déplacer, à nier, à diviser et à
> amortir l'intention agressive, et cela selon une décom-
> position défensive, si comparable en ses principes à celle
> qu'illustrent le redan et la chicane, que nous avons en-
> tendu plusieurs de nos patients user à leur propre sujet
> d'une référence métaphorique à des "fortifications à la
> Vauban."[1]

The terms Lacan (and his patients) borrow from defensive
military architecture, *redan* and *chicane,* have in common a
zigzag structure, a structure that eludes the parallel and the
perpendicular. In reasoning, "chicane" refers to the opposite
of straightforwardness, to a persistently tangential mode of
argumentation that attempts to distract attention from the
central question. The "redans" (etymologically derived from
"dent") were laid out in a serrated line, forming a structural

[1] Lacan, "L'Agressivité en psychanalyse," in *Ecrits* (Editions du Seuil, 1966),
p. 108.

96

and defensive chevron around a fortification that, by virtue of its divergence from the habitual directness of geometry, seems the most overtly threatening element in the defensive arsenal. (See figs. 1-3.)

The terminology Lacan appropriates is linked to geometrical deviousness in a second manner. The serration of the *redans* is built into a sloping wall, and it is thereby an integral part of the obliqueness that serves as the outermost defense of a Vaubanian fortified place (the military equivalent therefore of what Freud describes as the ego's protective shield against stimuli). Recently, Parent and Verroust have stressed the exceptional status during the Versailles era of Vauban's use of obliquity:

> Le besoin de s'enclore par des moyens relevant à la fois de la mécanique balistique, de la commodité de la circulation et des services des pièces et de la psychologie fait autour des citadelles de Vauban régner l'oblicité, à une époque où le classicisme l'a exclue de ce qui est considéré comme le seul domaine digne de la formulation de l'architecture, l'ordre des palais et des hôtels résidentiels. (p. 162)

Vauban's defensive military architecture privileged slanting forms at a time when such forms were considered deviant. Lacanian psychoanalytic theory admits the aptness of the vocabulary of Vaubanian obliqueness to characterize the defensive displacements of obsessional neurotics. The military and psychoanalytic theories of defense intersect at a particularly elusive crossroads: the territory they both privilege is a space of indirection, of swerves, of divergence, of deviation. This oblique space is also a central continuum for the three writers studied in the following pages. The writings of Rousseau, Laclos, and Sade portray to an exceptional extent the swerves and zigzags of defensive deviousness. In the domain of textual obliquity they share, a number of recurrent patterns can be detected in the deflections traced in their works.

Perhaps the most prominent swerve enacted by the texts of

these authors is the movement Harold Bloom has described
as the anxiety of influence. Bloom defines poetic history as
poetic influence, which is in turn defined as poetic misreading.
A writer creates a space for himself by distorting the work of
the writer or writers who seem to him to have prior claim to
some part of the territory where he wants to establish his
greatness. His distortion always originates in a sense that his
predecessor was on the right track but did not go far enough,
that he stopped short of gaining mastery over the territory of
his exploration, of perfectly fortifying it and making it his
own. It is this gap in his precursor's fortifications that justifies,
and even necessitates, the inheritor's work. In characterizing
these poetic misreadings, Bloom consistently turns to a vocabulary of devious movement; he sees poetic history, not in
terms of a straight line of "progress," but as a sort of curved
zigzag formed by a series of swerves.

The key term in this process is "clinamen," which Bloom
uses to define poetic veering away from the straight line of
the predecessor's course. For Bloom, the history of writers'
interaction follows an oblique and devious pattern:

> "Perverse" literally means "to be turned the wrong way";
> but to be turned the right way in regard to the precursor
> means not to swerve at all, so any bias or inclination
> perforce must be perverse *in relation to the precur-
> sor....* To swerve (Anglo-Saxon *sweorfan*) has a root
> meaning of "to wipe off, file down, or polish," and, in
> usage, "to deviate, to leave the straight line, to turn aside
> (from law, duty, custom)."[2]

According to Bloom's theory, the writer (or the "strong" writer
at least) is always on the defensive, always obliged to chart a
devious course of self-protection.

[2] Bloom, *The Anxiety of Influence* (New York: Oxford Univ. Press, 1973),
p. 85. See also pp. 5, 14, 30, 88. I follow Bloom's practice and refer to "the
writer" as "he." I do not share his male-centered view of poetic history, but
see no reason to alter Bloom's usage in a book on three male authors.

One of the central terms Bloom uses to characterize this devious history is borrowed from Lucretius' *De Rerum natura*. In the Lucretian system, the *clinamen* denotes the declination that defines the natural movement of elemental particles of matter:

> While the first bodies are being carried downwards by their own weight in a straight line through the void, at times quite uncertain and uncertain places, they swerve a little from their course, just so much as you might call a change of motion. For if they were not apt to incline, all would fall downwards like raindrops through the profound void, no collision would take place and no blow would be caused among the first-beginnings: thus nature would never have produced anything.[3]

Lucretius posits that deviation from a straight course is the essence of natural formation: without the *clinamen,* there would be no progress.

For Lucretius, genesis follows a zigzag course. But it would seem impossible to compare matter's obliquity with poetic deviousness, because, whereas the first is a result of chance ("at times quite uncertain and uncertain places"), the second is an instinctive movement of self-protection. However, the Lucretian system also applies the original swerve to human behavior. A note by W.H.D. Rouse to his translation of *De Rerum natura* comments on the origin of the *clinamen.* What Lucretius calls the *clinamen* "is no part of the theory of Democritus, but was added by Epicurus in order to use it later in his explanation of human freewill" (p. 112). In the Lucretian system, the *clinamen* is not only the swerve that takes place "at times quite uncertain and uncertain places" during the free fall through the void made by particles of matter. The

---

[3] Lucretius, *De Rerum natura*, tr. W.H.D. Rouse (Cambridge: Harvard Univ. Press, 1975), p. 113. The Lucretian notion of the *clinamen* has recently been discussed by Michel Serres. See his *La Naissance de la physique dans le texte de Lucrèce* (Editions de Minuit, 1977).

term also applies to movements of human will, the will Lucretius calls "wrested from the fates": "Don't we also swerve at no fixed time or place, but where our mind directs us?" (p. 115). The examples he gives of free will portray it as a defensive power used, for instance, to resist a foreign will in conflict with one's own. A blow from an external force may drive the matter in a body in one direction, but that undesired movement lasts only until "our will has curbed it [the matter of the body] back through the limbs." An individual's will impels him to swerve and thus defend himself against foreign control. In this exceptional description of free will, Lucretius characterizes it as the human *clinamen*, an instinctive self-defensive veering. Like the divergences Bloom posits, this use of the *clinamen* makes of it a tool for the self-assertion of the theoretically weaker partner in a struggle, a means by which he can appropriate the power of his aggressor.

Everything about Lucretius' characterization of the human *clinamen* suggests that it is among the most elemental and basic drives. He uses the same term for the essential original inclination of matter and for the human will's resistance to a conflicting will. The *clinamen*, the declination Bloom theorizes as the anxiety of influence, traces a movement similar to and as instinctive as the *tu quoque* defense. Lacan refers to paranoiacs as "des anachronismes vivants" and cites efforts to learn about the structure of paranoia by comparing it with "la pensée primitive" or "pensée prélogique."[4] Worringer specifies that the art he calls abstract, that is, art that protects its viewer from his anxious dread of space, appeals to primitive peoples. Such diverse speculations indicate that a model of primal divergence is necessary for the comprehension of the swerves of defensive art.

One of the basic distinctions stressed by Lévi-Strauss in *La Pensée sauvage* presupposes just such a collusion between obliquity and what he calls the "savage mind." Lévi-Strauss contrasts modern and primitive (or "prior") ways of ap-

---

[4] On Lacan, see n. 2 in chap. 2 above.

proaching the unknown or a problem to be solved: the scientist faced with a challenge "cherche toujours à s'ouvrir un passage et à se situer *au delà*; tandis que le bricoleur, de gré ou de force, demeure *en deçà*."[5] The scientist is a man of abstractions and concepts, one who invents new tools for each new job. The *bricoleur*, firmly anchored in origins and the past, is less an inventor than a remodeler. "La règle de son jeu est de toujours s'arranger avec les 'moyens du bord,' c'est-à-dire un ensemble à chaque instant fini d'outils et de matériaux" (p. 26). From his already formed stock of materials, the *bricoleur* chooses those appropriate for the job at hand. His means are always already there, while the scientist is constantly forced to create his. The *bricoleur* manipulates a stock of secondhand remnants, fragments with a past that he deconstructs, reconstructs, and reshuffles. Even when he shapes these borrowed fragments into new formations, the *bricoleur* does not sever them completely from the context of their origin. This creature of memory never forgets that his reality is shrouded in what Lévi-Strauss terms "une certaine épaisseur d'humanité" (p. 30).

Bricolage, as Lévi-Strauss reminds us, has its roots in deviation and surprise, rather than in predictable success:

Dans son sens ancien, le verbe bricoler s'applique au jeu de balle et de billard, à la chasse et à l'équitation, mais toujours pour évoquer un mouvement incident: celui de la balle qui rebondit, du chien qui divague, du cheval qui s'écarte de la ligne droite pour éviter un obstacle. (p. 26)

Today, the remains of the deviousness initially linked to *bricolage* are in the realm of technique: "Et, de nos jours, le

[5] Lévi-Strauss, *La Pensée Sauvage* (Plon, 1962), p. 30. Lévi-Strauss uses the engineer as the example of the modern scientist whose approach he contrasts to the *bricoleur's* "prior" speculative activity. I replace his "engineer" with "scientist" because I hope to demonstrate the close proximity between the techniques of early military and textual engineers and *bricolage,* to stress the origin of engineering and of (devious) art in *bricolage.*

bricoleur reste celui qui oeuvre de ses mains, en utilisant des moyens détournés par comparaison avec ceux de l'homme de l'art" (p. 26).[6] Lévi-Strauss fails to note, however, a crucial shift in deviousness. Originally, the deviation of *bricoler* seems accidental and unconscious, made by either an animal or an inanimate object. The movement might be self-protective (the horse avoiding the obstacle), and it is always "natural" and beyond the control of either the sportsman riding the horse or the player hitting the ball. In the case of the modern-day *bricoleur,* however, the deviation is no longer "natural," but rather a conscious choice of technique. Furthermore, it has shifted its association from the so-called object (the horse or the ball) to the subject (the man manipulating the objects). In the case of the original meaning of "bricoler," the deviation could be considered a movement toward subjectivization, a form of self-assertion, albeit unconscious or instinctive, on the part of the animal allegedly in the sportsman's or gamesman's control. When it swerves, it momentarily escapes the ruling hand and the preconceived plan. (*Bricolage* could be the essence of sport; without it, perfect control would guarantee victory.) However, the deviousness of the modern *bricoleur* shows no lack of control, but is the code governing his technical arsenal.

The shift in deviousness traced by the semantic evolution of *bricolage* repeats in part the relationship between Lucretius' two uses of *clinamen* in *De rerum natura*. In both cases, the original swerve is the random swerve of an inanimate object (or the protective deviation of an animal). When this term is

---

[6] The original deviation in *bricolage* today plays a crucial role in the realm of theoretical physics. Subatomic particles are detected by slamming nuclei apart. The smallest particles are never seen, only inferred from their *clinamena*: "The nature of such particles can only be learned by inference, like the nature of a ball or boomerang that you cannot see but which is being thrown between two boats. You study the angles and speeds at which the boats recoil after each throw, and from that you deduce the properties of the object itself and how the boats interact with it and each other" (Dr. Leon Lederman, *New York Times,* 2 Sept. 1979, p. 28).

applied to human behavior, it is seen on the one hand as the equivalent of a self-defensive reaction on the part of the human body, and on the other as a consciously chosen technique. In the first instance, the deviator is the victim of outside aggression, swerving after having been struck. In the case of *bricolage* as technique, the defensiveness seems to result from a fear of lack of control. Lévi-Strauss describes the *bricoleur* as a paragon of prudence, as an individual who avoids risk and is comfortable with a finite set of tools, already tried and tested (albeit for other purposes), tools that can be manipulated to handle any task imaginable.

When Bloom applies Lucretian theory to the world of textual struggle, he portrays the writer as a victim of an aggression that is all the more threatening because the aggressor is invisible. When a writer moves to establish his textual territory, he generally does so in the absence of direct contact with the precursor with whom he feels a special bond. (While the term is not found in Bloom, the precursor might be called a teacher.) The fledgling writer can only imagine what must be for him the ultimate act of judgment, his teacher's. The teacher's judgment is imagined as an act of aggression, either to confirm the student writer's anxiety, or to facilitate his rejection of his precursor's position. Bloom does not re-create this hypothetical original attack and begins his history with the writer's initial, self-assertive swerve. He thereby places the writer's defensiveness, like the *bricoleur*'s, outside a chronological situation, and makes his defensiveness less a response to aggression than a stance. This stance, in turn, can be viewed as a provocation that renders other defensive veerings necessary, those of the writers who follow in the defensive writer's wake.

The obliquity of *bricolage* and that of the anxiety about influence share an important similarity in technique: in both cases, defensive strength results from a "dismemberment" and reuse of structures of power from the past. Both the writer in his struggle to establish his position and the *bricoleur* in his attempt to fabricate new implements are cannibals. The writer

fears the dead ancestor's power and is conscious of his in-
debtedness to him. He conquers that fear and overcomes his
debt by "consuming" the inhibiting prior work and appropriating the ancestor's power. Like Rousseau in the case of
"Le Corbeau et le Renard," by taking the threatening text
apart, he first settles the score in what is for him an arithmetic
of persecution. He then ultimately proves his superiority when
his precursor's power is added to his own. In similar fashion,
the *bricoleur* owes his strength to his ability to see the usefulness in disparate objects and to reshuffle those objects until
he has made them his.

Rousseau's favorite character in literature, Robinson Crusoe, an instinctive and obsessive fortifier, provides what is
perhaps the most striking literary illustration of the cannibalistic urge that is the essence of *bricolage*. Robinson could
be called the ultimate *bricoleur,* and the principal source he
exploits in the development of his creativity is the ship that
brought him to the island. The two concerns that from the
very beginning dominate his solitary life are self-defense and
the dismemberment of the ship with the intention of trans-
lating the ship's "wealth" into personal treasure. His journal
entries over the period of a month show him returning over
and over again to the vessel and stripping it of items whose
immediate usefulness becomes less and less apparent: "By this
Time I had gotten Timber, and Plank, and Iron-Work enough,
to have builded a good Boat, *if I had known how.*"[7] He strips
and strips until he reduces the wreck to a skeleton—prefig-
uring thereby the treatment of their victims by the cannibals
on the island, a treatment that will later so disgust him. In
the course of his stay on the island, Robinson's fear of cannibalism becomes obsessive. (Indeed the obsession continues
even after his return to Europe and surfaces at the time of the
attack by man-eating wolves in the Pyrenees.) If this obsession
is viewed in the light of the solitary *bricoleur*'s initial under-

[7] Daniel Defoe, *Robinson Crusoe,* ed. M. Shinagel (New York: Norton,
1975), p.69, emphasis mine.

taking, however, it can be argued that Robinson's fear, like Rousseau's use of the *tu quoque* defense, is a projection of his own cannibalistic instincts. It takes a wolf to know one, applies to him as it does to Rousseau, or to the continuator of the *Journal de Trévoux,* or to La Fontaine. Lycanthropy may be the disease of the writer, or of the teacher, or of any would-be possessor of knowledge. "For Plato and a tradition which lasted throughout the Classical age," Michel Serres has argued in a commentary on another "cannibalistic" fable by La Fontaine, "knowledge is a hunt. To know is to put to death—to kill the lamb, deep in the woods, in order to eat it."[8] Aggression lies at the origin of these various models of obliquity and oblique technique.

Any choice of devious technique is also a choice of protective technique, and protective techniques are by nature devious techniques. Fortification is obliged to follow an oblique course in its evolution. Witness this definition of his branch of study by a nineteenth-century professor at the Royal Military Academy: "[F]ortification is peculiarly dependent upon other arts. It is the making of armour to protect men from the weapons of others while allowing them to use their own, and must adopt itself therefore to all the changes of weapons, instead of taking its own course."[9] Fortification is forced to deviate, and it is doubly devious. All fortifications impede the traditional way of progress, the straight line. "Créer un enclos," Claude Parent has argued in *Vivre à l'oblique,* "implique la détermination d'un obstacle au parcours. Le tracé de la circulation directe tirant une ligne droite de A à B est perturbé par l'interposition de l'enclos C. L'espace privatif C doit être contourné pour se rendre de A en B."[10]

---

[8] Serres, "The Algebra of Literature: The Wolf's Game," in *Textual Strategies,* ed. J. Harari (Ithaca, New York: Cornell Univ. Press, 1979), p.276.
[9] E. M. Lloyd, *Vauban, Montalembert, Carnot* (London: Chapman and Hall, 1887), p. 1.
[10] Parent, *Vivre à l'oblique* (n.p., 1970), p. 11. This work is a prophetic manifesto for what Parent calls the *fonction oblique.*

Defensive declination constitutes itself as a *clinamen,* and it also necessitates future *clinamena;* anyone in the path of a defensive system is obliged to repeat the swerve of its defensiveness. Defensiveness generates defensiveness, as all the theoreticians of histories of obliquity—from Lucretius to La Fontaine to Bloom—resoundingly demonstrate. Because of this most elementary rule of the protective enterprise, all distinctions between attacker and defender, wolf and lamb, collapse. The members of this couple are united by their similar stance. It is this similarity that makes it possible to discover common ground between theories of obliquity that differ as fundamentally on the issue of intentionality as do those of Lévi-Strauss and Bloom. The veering object or victim and the defensive strategist whose defenses constitute the obstacle that provokes its divergence are finally united by strategic similarities parallel to those that bind defense to attack.

Once the (protective) gesture of victimizing others by making them swerve to avoid the fortifications of the "master's" defense is accepted as similar in essence to the (self-protective) deviation on the part of the being forced from its chosen (and presumably straight) path by an obstacle, then other oblique movements frequently encountered in the universes of Rousseau, Laclos, and Sade can be shown to be related to declinations already examined here. Two of these veerings are consistently intertwined in these works: seduction and education. Seduction, aptly defined by Georges Blin as *dévoiement,*[11] means etymologically "to draw away from the right and intended course of action into a wrong one" (*OED*). The act or scene of seduction includes two paths ("voies"), both of which are presumably straight and correct ("droite"). The intended path undertaken but not completed by the victim of seduction swerves or zigzags when it is barred by the obstacle formed by the scandal the seducer has manipulated. *Scandal*

[11] Cited by P. Brooks, *The Novel of Worldliness* (Princeton, N.J.: Princeton Univ. Press, 1969), p. 190.

comes from the Greek *skandalon*, "obstacle, stumbling block," and in religious terms signifies an "occasion de péché créée par la personne qui incite les autres à se détourner de Dieu" (Robert). Scandal, as Laclos's master seducers comprehend perfectly, can be manipulated to serve as a form of fortification that protects the libertine and his/her path while causing the victim to change course—and generally to adopt the course chosen for him by his debaucher. The second *voie* of the paths that cross in the scene of seduction is the seducer's path. This course is not usually thought of in terms of direction, but the Vicomte de Valmont demonstrates his certainty that the master's way is always straight: "Vous jugez qu'ainsi remis sur la voie, je ne la quittai plus; c'etait réellement la bonne, et peut-être la seule."[12]

Seduction can thus be viewed as a crossing of paths that necessitates a switching of paths, that induces a *clinamen* on the part of the victim that is less self-defensive than self-destructive. In this description, it seems closely related to the veering illustrated in "Le Corbeau et le Renard," education. Etymologically, of course, the two concepts are intimately connected, both related to the Latin *ducere*. Educate is derived from *educare*, to rear, bring up, but it is also affiliated with *educere*, to lead forth, to take away. The etymological bond between *seducere* and *educere* is one that is consistently reinforced by the oblique fictions of Rousseau, Laclos, and Sade. However, the *clinamen* of the student victim of *educare* may differ in one important respect from that imposed by the action of *seducere*: the student, as in the case of Cécile in *Les Liaisons dangereuses* or in those of the best known Sadean pupils, may swerve and then follow the master's course, but the student's *clinamen* may equally well be an unconscious, self-defensive veering, an act of protection from the control of the outside will, of which there are many examples in Rousseau's pedagogical vignettes.

[12] Laclos, *Les Liaisons dangereuses*, letter 125, p. 303.

The seducer causes his victim to swerve, the writer veers from the path that appears charted out for him by influence, particles of matter react to collisions and against blows, *bricoleurs* turn to an arsenal of devious techniques to protect themselves and establish their mastery. The reader of the oblique text is faced with a surface of narrative quicksand, a surface that will inevitably trouble the course of his reading. In *Kabbalah and Criticism,* Harold Bloom has argued that all reading is a defense.[13] If this is so, then the reader of a text that is already a deviational zigzag must surely find the task doubly deflective. By retracing the declination of the oblique text, the reader also defines the space of reading as, somehow, oblique. Such a space of reading is not only biased and devious, it is also ill-defined. Perhaps because this reading of necessity follows a zigzag pattern, it is difficult to conceive of a theoretical model to guide the reader-critic in dealings with the oblique text. To begin with, the reader must be aware of the stakes involved in such a critical enterprise. Will the *clinamen* of interpretation be entirely self-defensive, or will the critic be seduced by the master debauchers into switching paths, and thereby simply imitating the course of their deviations?

In *Dora: An Analysis of a Case of Hysteria,* Freud proposes what he alleges to be a foolproof means of detecting hysterical narrative and a framework for the reading of such narrative. Freud describes his request to the patient for "the whole story of his life and illness." He compares the information he receives to "an unnavigable river whose stream is at one moment choked by masses of rock and at another divided and lost among shallows and sandbanks" (p. 30). Freud goes on to describe so-called hysterical narrative as "leaving gaps unfilled, and riddles unanswered" (p. 30). A smooth, ordered "reading" of such material can be traced neither by the hys-

---

[13] Bloom, "The Necessity of Misreading," in *Kabbalah and Criticism:* "To interpret is to revise is to defend against influence. . . . [A]ll reading . . . constitute[s] a kind of defensive warfare" (p. 64).

teric—Freud speaks of "the patients' inability to give an ordered history of their life" (p. 31)—nor by "the medical observer": "I cannot help wondering how it is that the authorities can produce such smooth and exact histories in cases of hysteria" (p. 30). In such cases, the river of narrative cannot flow freely and must make its course in zigzag fashion, swerving around obstacles and shallows. The goal of psychoanalytic treatment is to clear away the obstacles and make it possible for the stream once more to rush smoothly in a straight course to the sea. The aim of Freud's work is to make the river of narrative navigable again, that is, to make it easily decipherable by its would-be reader. "It is only towards the end of the treatment that we have before us an intelligible, consistent, and unbroken case history. Whereas the practical aim of the treatment is to remove all possible symptoms and to replace them by conscious thoughts, we may regard it as a second and theoretical aim to repair all the damages to the patient's memory" (p. 32).

Confronted with a narrative characterized by its obstacles and its gaps, a narrative that can be termed defensive or hysterical, the Freudian reader makes it his task to "unbend" that narrative, to remove its obliquity, to put it back on a straight path. This model suggests that the reader of defensive narrative should eliminate its ambiguities, eliminate its swerves, eliminate, in short, its defensiveness. In his *Histoire de la folie à l'âge classique,* Foucault explains the etymology of *délire*: "Ce mot est dérivé de *lira,* un sillon; de sorte que *deliro* signifie proprement s'écarter du sillon, du droit chemin de la raison."[14] The Freudian reading proposed in *Dora* would take the *délire* out of hysterical narrative, would put this narrative back in reason's furrow. Such a reading is only possible, however, if the reader remains unaffected by the swerves of narrative obliqueness, straightens out a tale without either repeating its deviations or adding supplemental deviations.

Dora portrays Freud as Sherlock Holmes and this is in fact

[14] Foucault, *Histoire de la folie* (Gallimard, 1972), pp. 287-88.

only one, and perhaps the least problematic, of the roles he adopts in struggling with the interpretation of narrative.[15] But his image of unchoking the river of narrative constitutes an undeniable temptation for all readers dealing in his wake with texts whose flow is biased and deviated. Recent critical thought may be acutely aware of textual *clinamena*, but surely no critic, not even among those most conscious of declinations, is a stranger to Freud's dream of an obstacle-free, "straight" reading, a reading so perfect that no deviation is necessary or possible, a reading that would not be already a deviation. For example, Michel Serres's *La Naissance de la physique dans le texte de Lucrèce* is an explosive study of Lucretian physics, a book whose enormous energy is devoted to retracing the swerves and deflections of the *clinamen* and other Lucretian declivities. Yet, even at the heart of such a devious work, as Shoshana Felman has remarked: "La joie même de la découverte . . . est constamment marquée par le désir d'un système sans reste, d'un modèle ou d'une métaphore sans écart. Or, dans ce désir consiste, justement, le paradoxe du livre: tout l'effort du chercheur est pour articuler, *sans écart,* une *théorie de l'écart.*"[16]

Felman's commentary on Serres leads us into an apparently total impasse. If one of the wiliest critics currently writing, interpreting some of the most devious issues concerning one of the most oblique authors—if even this critic is unable to erase his desire for a critical discourse without *écart,* without *redans,* how are other critics to trace a more authentically devious path in their readings of oblique texts? This problem is further complicated if the critic is dealing with authors such as Rousseau, Laclos, and Sade, all of whose works, even as they remain intimately related to swerves of all kinds, transmit

[15] Elsewhere, in the *Interpretation of Dreams* for example, Freud advocates other, more supple, models of reading, but his treatment of defensive narrative in *Dora* is representative of an important tradition of dealing with oblique narrative. The Wolfman's memoirs record Freud's admiration for Dr. Holmes.

[16] Felman, "De la nature des choses ou de l'écart à l'équilibre," *Critique* (Jan. 1979): 10.

a belief in the possibility of a nondeviant reading. Rousseau, for example, is convinced that, through enlightened pedagogy, mankind can somehow right the original *clinamen* of civilization, and find again the straight path of nature. Such a "utopian" drive can only reinforce the critic's desire for a reading without *écart* and is perhaps the ultimate narrative trap laid by the oblique text for its reader.

Julie and *Emile:*
"Studia la Matematica"

Many great gaps were left, which were only filled in
gradually and bit by bit, some, indeed, not until after
the official announcement that the wall was finished. In
fact it is said that there are gaps which have never been
filled at all. . . . How can a wall protect if it is not a
continuous structure?

> Franz Kafka, "The Great Wall of China"

===== ✳ =====

The Arithmetic of Persecution

Je sais que toutes nos grandes fortifications sont la chose
du monde la plus inutile, et que, quand nous aurions
assés de troupes pour les défendre, cela seroit fort inutile
encore: car sûrement on ne viendra pas nous assiéger.
Mais, pour n'avoir point de siège à craindre, nous n'en
devons pas moins veiller à nous garantir de toute surprise: rien n'est si facile que d'assembler des gens de
guerre à notre voisinage. Nous avons trop appris l'usage
qu'on en peut faire, et nous devons songer que les plus
mauvais droits hors d'une place se trouvent excellens
quand on est dedans.

> Rousseau, *Lettre à d'Alembert*

"*Zanetto, lascia le Donne, e studia la matematica*" (1: 322).
Rousseau never comments on the words with which the Venetian courtesan Zulietta dismissed him after his vision of what
he calls a "téton borgne" made it impossible for him to continue his appreciation of her charms. ("Me voila cherchant
dans ma tête comment on peut avoir un téton borgne . . . ,"
1: 321.) Apparently Zulietta's target for once did not consider

an insult insightful or menacing enough to feel threatened by it. However, had Rousseau considered her words more closely, he might have realized that Zulietta's carefully meditated formula[1] could be understood as a description of some of the essential structures governing his relationships with others as he characterizes them in his autobiography and the fictive interactions among characters in his novels, *Julie* and *Emile*, including the bond between teacher and student to which Rousseau grants such a high priority.[2]

Rousseau's discourse can be read as an attempt to counteract Classicism's rigidity, its fascination with geometric structures, its refusal to make a space for the reader. Yet Rousseau's reaction against the defensiveness of Classicism replaced Classicism as a threatening summit of perfection for many of the eighteenth-century writers who worked in his wake, in particular Laclos and Sade. Furthermore, his reaction itself takes a defensive shape: Rousseau puts into operation what is arguably the most remarkable defensive machine in literature.[3] In the *Confessions,* Rousseau praises the solid and

[handwritten margin note: Counteracting rigidity of classicism]

---

[1] Zulietta's words take the form of a predictive evaluation rather than a hasty attack/defense. In Rousseau's description of the scene, Zulietta hesitates at great length before making her enigmatic final statement: "Elle prit d'abord la chose en plaisantant. . . . Mais . . . je la vis enfin rougir, se rajuster, se redresser, et sans dire un seul mot s'aller mettre à sa fenêtre. . . . [E]lle . . . fut s'asseoir sur un lit de repos, se leva le moment d'après, et se promenant par la chambre en s'éventant, me dit d'un ton froid et dédaigneux: Zanetto, lascia, etc." (1: 322).

[2] I will return to the problem of *Emile*'s classification shortly, but for now will refer to it as though it were generically identical to *Julie.*

[3] In the *Confessions,* Rousseau offers an explanation for the fact that the most appreciative readers of *Julie* were the Parisian courtiers: "Il faut, à travers tant de préjugés et de passions factices savoir bien analyser le coeur humain pour y démêler les vrais sentimens de la nature. Il faut une délicatesse de tact qui ne s'acquiert que dans l'éducation du grand monde, pour sentir, si j'ose ainsi dire, les finesses de coeur dont cet ouvrage est rempli. Je mets sans crainte sa quatriéme partie à côté de la Princesse de Cleves. . . . Il ne faut donc pas s'étonner si le plus grand succés de ce Livre fut à la Cour. Il abonde en traits vifs mais voilés qui doivent y plaire, parce qu'on est plus exercé à les pénétrer" (1: 546). Rousseau compares his novel to the master-

tenacious foundation of his mathematical knowledge: "j'achettai des livres d'arithmetique et je l'appris bien, car je l'appris seul. . . . [E]t maintenant que tout ce que j'ai su s'efface journellement de ma mémoire, cet acquis y demeure encore" (1: 179). Hans Wolpe has described Rousseau as "in irrationality, the most rigorous of logicians."[4] While on the surface the mathematical permutations in Rousseau's work hardly seem rigorous when compared to those of Laclos and Sade, the patterns of Rousseau's so-called irrational logic are repeated with an inevitability whose cruelty rivals that of the more overtly depersonalizing geometry practiced by his followers in defensiveness.

It may be that Rousseau's logic has been referred to as irrational because of the impossibly utopian formulae that are the foundation of his arithmetic. Three permutations that defy the basic premises of mathematical logic recur persistently in Rousseau's works. The first impossible equation serves to justify Rousseau's belief in the spontaneous generation of the "murs de tenebres" within which his enemies try, ever more effectively, to isolate him (1: 493, 706, 752). In Rousseau's arithmetic, one plus one equals not two, but the origin of a plot: "[S]itôt que j'ai rapproché l'un de l'autre deux amis que j'avois séparément, ils n'ont jamais manqué de s'unir contre moi" (1: 397). This equation could also be read as one plus one equals zero in that the addition serves to exclude Rousseau from any potential union. This reading is confirmed by the second equation forming the basis of Rousseau's persecution. Jean-Jacques does not equal one, but zero: "Seul j'étois pres-

---

piece of Classical fiction; he stresses the veiled nature of both novels' psychological portrayals; and he declares that his best readers are those whose defenses make it possible for them to "penetrate" his characters' defensiveness. His description here of his novel's psychology and of the appeal it has for its public contradicts the statements on *Julie* in which he praises the novel's transparency, but it is more insightful than those statements about the true nature of *Julie*'s power.

[4] Wolpe, "Psychological Ambiguity in *La Nouvelle Héloïse*," *The Toronto Quarterly* (Apr. 1959): 287.

que toujours compté pour rien en toute chose" (1: 411). Like the first, this reduction is the result of the desire of those with whom he is intimate to use their power against him: "[I]l [Grimm] me regardoit comme nul" (1: 466).[5] When others turn against him and build a wall of darkness around him, Rousseau is reduced to a cipher, to invisibility.

The third formula of Rousseau's mathematics defines the basic strategy of his struggle against this reduction. This formula is the translation of an impossible, utopian dream. As Saint-Preux demonstrates by using economic reasoning, solitude is bad business: "Les ames humaines veulent être accouplées pour valoir tout leur prix, et la force unie des amis . . . est incomparablement plus grande que la somme de leurs forces particulieres" (2: 13: 228). By means of the union Rousseau would use to fight the conspiracy's reductive mathematics, one plus one would equal, not two, but one. "Le premier de mes besoins, le plus grand, le plus fort, le plus inextinguible, étoit tout entier dans mon coeur: c'étoit le besoin d'une societé intime et aussi intime qu'elle pouvoit l'être. . . . [I]l m'auroit fallu deux ames dans le même corps; sans cela je sentois toujours du vide" (1: 414). "Deux ames dans le même corps": one and one equals one. Rousseau feels that, had he been able to put this utopian defensive equation into operation, he would have been able to people his solitude and make it productive and thereby fight the alienation sought by those who plotted against him. However, he is never able to reach this arithmetical nirvana, so that with Thérèse, for example, "de quelque façon que je m'y sois pu prendre, nous ayons toujours continué d'être deux" (1: 415).

Because this equation continually eludes him, Rousseau resorts to the incalculable mathematical element that has fascinated recent critics, *le supplément*. The supplement is situated in an arithmetical no man's land, for it belongs neither to

---

[5] The power to make someone invisible is one that Julie de Wolmar shares with her literary predecessor, Clarissa Harlowe. Thus a faculty of the heroines Rousseau allegedly admired is used against him in the *Confessions*.

attacker nor to defender. Rousseau explains that he knows only two states, perfect union (one) and total solitude (zero). He denies the existence of a scale from zero to one—"il n'y eut jamais pour moi d'intermédiaire entre tout [one] et rien [zero]" (1: 332)—yet his denial is immediately followed by the explanation that "je trouvois dans Therese le supplement dont j'avois besoin." The supplement is therefore doubly impossible, doubly incalculable, for it has no place on the scale that situates the already impossible configurations that Rousseau uses to tell the story of his persecution. Moreover, the supplement is multiple, not only in theory but also in practice. Thus Thérèse functions as a supplement, as do Diderot, Grimm, and others. Only a multitude can begin to fill the emptiness caused by the absence of the fortified one: "Faute d'*un* ami qui fut à moi tout entier, il me falloit *des* amis dont l'impulsion surmontat mon inertie" (1: 416, emphasis mine). The supplement can also be inanimate. As a result of his attempts to fill the emptiness, Rousseau finds himself "rejetté sans y songer dans la litterature dont je me croyois sorti pour toujours" (1: 416). Finally, the supplement is no more successful at counteracting reductive mathematical operations than is the equation whose failure provokes its genesis. Rather than having a cumulative effect, the literary supplement marks a loss of ground—"je me trouvai . . . rejetté . . . dans la litterature." Rousseau describes his creation of fictive "intimate societies" to replace the one that could never be found in real life as a descent, literally a *mise en abyme* "dans la litterature dont je me croyois *sorti* pour toujours." Ultimately, all the supplements bring only new unhappiness; this makeshift plurality, too, is equivalent to zero. In Rousseau's universe, the only successful mathematical operation is subtraction.[6]

When Rousseau follows Zulietta's advice and gives up women

---

[6] Because he is able to carry out only reductive arithmetic, Rousseau is never able to forgive Thérèse's mother for her talent at multiplication: "Cette femme possedoit au suprême degré l'art de tirer d'un sac dix moutures" (1: 419). (The saying normally goes "tirer d'un sac deux moutures," so Rousseau exaggerates her inflating ability.)

in order to devote himself to the study of mathematics, he uncovers persecution's arithmetic. The equations of this arithmetic are constructed on the dual basis of an always frustrated desire for a union to be found through multiplication[7] and a fear of the perfect subtraction that always results in a reduction to zero. Rousseau constantly senses the equations of this arithmetic in operation around him, and he passes on this conviction to the principal characters in his fictions, whose *modi vivendi* are founded on the belief that there is no intermediary stage between total, seamless union and annihilation. The mathematical model in which Rousseau and his characters believe is based on the isolating geometry of fortifications. In Rousseau's life and in his fiction, the arithmetic of persecution leads to the construction of walled enclosures. The *Confessions* and *Rousseau Juge de Jean Jaques* describe the erection by Rousseau's enemies of a multi-layered *enceinte*— "triples murs de ténébres qu'on élève avec tant d'efforts autour de lui" (1: 752)—designed to complete and protect their subtraction of his being. They also record Rousseau's efforts at creating an internal shield designed to keep his identity hidden and thereby to annihilate it. (Rousseau's last self-portrait bears an uncanny resemblance to the amoeba-figure Freud imagines in *Beyond the Pleasure Principle*.) This ultimate self-protection is also the final response to the frustrated search for union: "[A]près avoir cherché longtems sans succés un homme, [il] éteignit sa lanterne et se referma tout à fait au dedans de lui" (1: 792). The inner *enceinte* is a primitive space since, like Robinson Crusoe's island, it is closed to all but a nonhuman supplement: "[J]e me suis retiré au dedans de moi, . . . vivant entre moi et la nature" (1: 727).

It can be argued that the fortification model becomes so pervasive in Rousseau's last autobiographical writings because it is one with which he was familiar from his early childhood.

---

[7] Like Vauban's predictive statistics, Rousseau's dream of controlled multiplication reveals divine aspirations, for such a union is based on the same principle as the Trinity. I will return to this idea later in conjunction with *Emile* and *Julie*.

After his father's exile, "je restai sous la tutelle de mon Oncle Bernard, alors employé aux fortifications de Genève" (1: 12).[8] Rousseau's uncle later became director of Geneva's fortifications, and his nephew evidently felt he had been marked in some special way by this exposure to the mysteries of the fortifying art. For example, he borrows from the vocabulary of fortifications the metaphors he uses to describe what would become a topos for the nineteenth-century French novel, the dreams of glory and conquest of the young provincial on his way to Paris:

> J'allois m'attacher à un militaire et devenir militaire moi-même; car on avoit arrangé que je commencerois par être cadet. . . . J'avois quelque teinture de geometrie et de fortifications; j'avois un oncle ingénieur; j'étois en quelque sorte enfant de la balle. . . . Je m'échauffois tellement sur ces folies que je ne voyois plus que trouppes, remparts, gabions, batteries, et moi au milieu du feu et de la fumée donnant tranquillement mes ordres. (1: 158-59)

Rousseau's interest in the "paternal" profession ("enfant de la balle") does not disappear with his youthful dreams of military conquest, for the second dialogue describes Rousseau watching Jean-Jacques "longtems arrêté devant une gravure" that turns out to be "le plan des attaques du fort de Kehl" (1: 817).[9]

Rousseau's sense of being a child of fortifications casts new light on his choice of metaphor to characterize both the form of his persecution and his defense against it. His predilection

[8] In *Jean-Jacques Rousseau: sa philosophie de l'éducation* (Vrin, 1962), Jean Château contends that Rousseau's memory of his early education can be used to explain the fact that Emile grows up in isolation. He bases his argument both on Rousseau's uncle's profession and on the fact that Rousseau was first raised with no companions (p. 74).

[9] The anecdote is cited as another illustration of Rousseau's widespread persecution. Jean-Jacques is also watched by "de jeunes gens inquiets de savoir ce qui l'occupoit si fort," who, once they learn the subject of the engraving, "fatigoient leur Minerve à chercher quel crime on pouvoit méditer en regardant le plan des attaques du fort de Kehl" (1: 817).

for the imagery of walls and enclosures is instinctive. Rousseau's usage of this imagery is colored by a sense of personal investment unheard of in either writing on fortifications or defensive literature. There is no place inside the Classical, Vaubanian fortress for any involvement more intimate than straightforward professionalism. Laclos and Sade follow this policy and erase from their fiction any impression of emotional commitment on the part of author or principal characters. Rousseau, on the other hand, internalizes even the normally depersonalized geometry of fortifications to such an extent that each enclosure seems paradoxically further to expose rather than to camouflage the self for whose protection the ramparts have been constructed. Like the Sun King, Laclos and Sade erect barriers that guarantee that the personal will not be revealed to prying eyes. As Jean Starobinski has brilliantly argued, Rousseau's works pay tribute to the unmasking power of the *regard* with a force unequalled except, perhaps, by Lafayette.[10]

However, Rousseau's use of the protective shield parallels that of Laclos and Sade in one important way. In all three cases, the walls of the enclosure inspire in the individual hiding behind them feelings of omnipotence with regard to those outside the fortress. Although the strength of those feelings increases sharply from Rousseau to Sade, the extent of Rousseau's sadistic sense of superiority should not be underestimated. For example, the drama of *persiflage,* analyzed in conjunction with Rousseau's reading of La Fontaine, bears interpretation in this light: Rousseau portrays himself as increasingly engaged in a struggle to expose others before they expose him (for example, 1: 162, 417, 625-26). In the last books of the *Confessions,* Rousseau has recourse to increasingly sadistic imagery to convey a sense of the *solitaire*'s scornful superiority to those unaware of society's vices: "Le mépris que mes profondes méditations m'avoient inspiré pour les

[10] Starobinski, *L'Oeil vivant* (Gallimard, 1961). See p. 93 especially, for his analysis of "le mangeur mangé" and the question of *gourmandise.*

moeurs, les maximes et les préjugés de mon siécle me rendoit insensible aux railleries de ceux qui les avoient, et j'écrasois leurs petits bons-mots avec mes sentences, comme j'écraserois un insecte entre mes doigts" (1: 417). The aggressiveness of what Starobinski has termed Rousseau's "extrémisme vertueux," the sense of divine right inspired by this virtue, and the cruelty reserved for those outside the virtuous enclosure merit close examination. The characters in Rousseau's fiction share his belief in the mathematics of persecution, and the fortifications behind which they carry out what their creator affirmed to be virtuous activities, the *enceinte* of Emile's education and the "natural" barriers of Julie's garden, camouflage activities as disquieting as the desire Rousseau professed in the *Confessions* to crush his enemies like insects. Rousseau's main characters are not military engineers, but they are engineers in the other sense of the term: "One who contrives, designs . . . a plotter, a layer of snares" (*OED*). Rather than use their genius to build military machines, Emile's tutor, Julie, and Wolmar scheme to lay snares, to entrap their students, to build teaching machines.

Narrative Patchworks

> Quoi donc l'attaque et la deffense ne sont elles pas des loix de la nature?
>
> Rousseau, *Lettres morales*

According to the *Confessions,* the one period of Rousseau's life during which he successfully manipulated cumulative mathematics was marked by the composition of two masterworks of what he considered literature as supplement, *Julie* and *Emile* (1: 427-28). The writing of Rousseau's novel was so closely entwined with that of his work on education that he was able to indulge in self-citation in the second work: part of Julie's pedagogical system (5: 3: 580-81) reappears with only minor changes in *Emile* (4: 3 5 1). Critics have conversely argued that *Julie* leads into *Emile* (Burgelin, introduction to *Emile* [4: cvii]) or, paradoxically, that "l'*Emile* ... débouche ... sur la *Julie*, ... car c'est la *Julie* qui nous fait le mieux comprendre quel doit être l'aboutissement réel de l'*Emile,* par la création de ces petits centres sociaux que gouvernera un sage" (Château, p. 92).

If, after completing Rousseau's novel, the reader thinks back to its title page, *Julie*'s second subtitle seems curiously inappropriate: "Lettres de deux amans, habitans d'une petite ville au pied des Alpes" (this was the only subtitle on the copy Rousseau made for the maréchale de Luxembourg—*Julie ou lettres de deux amans*—and it is used as the work's sole title in the *avertissement* that introduces the second preface). The subtitle indicates that the correspondence between Julie and Saint-Preux forms the center of the novel's story, and even that *Julie* is most specifically concerned with the love letters they exchange. "Lettres de deux amans" creates a misleading image of Rousseau's novel, for *Julie* is anything but an "average" novel, that is, principally a story of love and the adventures and misadventures of young lovers. By the end of the novel, the initial love story lies buried under the far greater narrative mass of the adult lives and philosophies of the work's four central characters.

In the most comprehensive contemporary attack on Rousseau's works, *Anti-Emile,* Formey argued that "*la nouvelle Héloïse* et *Emile* en se suivant de près, ont mis a nud l'âme de leur Auteur, et ne laissent plus aucun doute sur ses intentions."[11] Formey is able to make such a statement based on a joint study of *Julie* and *Emile* because he, like most modern readers of Rousseau's epistolary novel, virtually ignores its preliminary correspondence and is primarily interested in the philosophy developed from the utopia created at Clarens. Initiating a *parti pris* that has been echoed in many recent readings, Formey considers *Julie* much less as a novel than as a

[11] Jean-Henri-Samuel Formey, *Anti-Emile* (Berlin: J. Pauli, 1763), p. 17.

philosophical treatise. The title with which he chooses to refer to the work, *la nouvelle Héloïse* (also the title generally adopted by the current tradition of Rousseau criticism), is an appropriate choice, given this critical bias. A critic who refers to Julie's story not by the name Rousseau created for his heroine but by the title that identifies her as a fictive reincarnation of an historical figure indicates that he privileges a reading of the novel that stresses its larger implications and its moralizing-pedagogical value at the expense of its love story and the individuality of its characters' psychology. Such a reading may not run contrary to Rousseau's intentions, for many crucial aspects of *Julie*'s structure and content encourage its readers to consider it principally as a work of moral literature, a work whose framework is supple enough to contain both vignettes that could be read as parables or fables and digressions on philosophical or ethical topics.

Teaching is a, if not the, central activity of the novel's principal characters. Like his predecessor Abelard, Saint-Preux makes a carefully calculated use of his pedagogical authority to seduce his pupil. However, in this aspect as in others, the novel's initial stage differs quite markedly from its later developments. During Saint-Preux's reign as teacher, teaching serves almost exclusively as a (rather banal) metaphor for seduction.[12] The classroom is never used as anything but a pretext for the young lovers' forbidden games. In fact, the only time Saint-Preux really sounds like a teacher is when he gives a brief presentation of his pedagogical system for his "écolière" (1: 12: 57-61), but the passage seems so out-of-character that it does not invite serious consideration. However, after Julie's conversion, the novel becomes what Burgelin has called a "traité pratique de l'éducation" (4: cvii). Lessons of all kinds take place all day long, and the educational system

---

[12] In Rousseau's day, the seduction of a student by a teacher was common enough, as either an occurrence or an obsession, for a law to exist condemning the guilty teacher to hanging (*Correspondance littéraire* vol. 4, p. 347; quoted in Daniel Mornet's introduction to his edition of *Julie* [Hachette, 1925], vol. 1, p. 252).

that counterbalances Saint-Preux's teaching is laid out at much greater length (5: 3: 561-85) and far more convincingly. Credit for the development of this system is given to Wolmar, but it is explained by Julie, and the scene of her explanation is transcribed by Saint-Preux in a letter to Milord Edouard, so this might be termed a collective educational vision.

After Julie's conversion, the figure of the teacher reappears endowed with new powers and a new image. Saint-Preux is the novel's only "professional" figure of intellectual authority, but the later parts of *Julie* present the reader with a proliferation of pedagogical characters in search of a student. Julie turns into "la prêcheuse."[13] Claire tries to upstage her cousin when she indulges in an occasional round of "prêcher la prêcheuse" (4: 12: 506). Wolmar, with his nonstop lessons in generosity, becomes one of the most powerful influences on the once corrupt pedagogue, Saint-Preux: "il commençoit à prendre une si grande autorité sur moi . . ." (4: 6: 425). Julie "la prêcheuse" is a model for the new type of pedagogue in the novel—she teaches ethical values rather than facts, and she does so in a self-effacing manner for the general moral betterment of the Clarens community. When the novel concludes, the "letters of two lovers" have long since been relegated to the status of youthful error and sometimes troubling memory. Like this young love, fiction with its seductive charms has been largely subjugated to morally justifiable exposition (nonfiction). A powerful rechanneling of energies progressively turns *Julie* into a manual of various types of pedagogical encounters, dressed up for popular consumption in fictionalized garb. Perhaps the work's second subtitle remains as a remnant of an initial conception from which Rousseau gradually detached himself in his urge to redeem his heroine's and his novel's initial corruption, a (forgotten) memorial to the generating potential of fiction without *thèses*.

[13] After her fall, Heloise, like Julie, became a teacher. She was prioress at the convent of Argenteuil, and one of her duties in that capacity was the education of nuns, novices, and the children brought up there.

Julie seems to bear traces of a shift in focus. There can be no doubt about the existence of such an evolution in *Emile*. Because Rousseau radically changed his conception of the work in the course of its composition, *Emile* is riddled with strange, Ur-passages where the narrative flow is as troubled as in the hysterical narrative Freud describes. As Peter Jimack has painstakingly demonstrated from a study of *Emile*'s manuscripts, "l'idée de créer ce personnage [Emile], ainsi que l'identité de l'auteur avec le gouverneur, ne s'est présentée à Rousseau qu'à mesure que la rédaction avançait."[14] In the first version, the Favre manuscript, *Emile* is recognizably a treatise on education. The fictionalizing/autobiographicizing of the central couple has not yet occurred in this account of methodological principles in which the *gouverneur* (tutor) does not speak in the first person. For example, in the initial version of *Emile*, the description of the ideal tutor begins: "mais supposons ce prodige trouvé. C'est en considérant ce qu'il doit faire que nous verrons ce qu'il doit être" (4: 71). In the Favre manuscript, it is evident that Rousseau had already begun to consider the possibility of merging the tutor with the work's narrator. Thus he adds to the passage just cited, "je ne parle point ici des qualités d'un bon gouverneur, je les suppose, et je me suppose moi-même doué de toutes ces qualités" (Book 1, 26R; quoted by Jimack, p. 180; see also 6: 265). This merging—which Jimack believes was originally "unconscious" (p. 185)—eventually leads to the creation of a pupil with a name (Emile) and an increasingly individualized personality, in order to provide a challenge worthy of the powers of the newly identified pedagogue.

The traces of its evolution have not been erased from the final version of *Emile*. The early books sometimes fall into a narrative no man's land between treatise and fictionalized

[14] Jimack, *La Genèse et la rédaction de l'"Emile" de Jean-Jacques Rousseau, Studies on Voltaire and the 18th Century*, hereafter *SVEC*, 13 (1960): 181.

treatise, because Rousseau did not always alter the final text in conformity with the increased presence of the fictional/ autobiographical elements in the later books. Thus in the work's first lesson in dialogue form (a general lesson on moral issues), the two characters are referred to simply as "le maître" and "l'enfant" (4: 317-18). When the second dialogue (on private property) takes place only a few pages later, the central participants have acquired names: "Jean-Jaques" and "Emile" (4: 331-32). The pupil's transformation from anonymity to an increasingly full-fledged character is occasionally confusing at first but it is rarely troubling for the reader. On the other hand, the tutor's shifting status is never clearly resolved, even after the identification between the teacher and the narrator of the treatise has become evident.

In *Emile*, the first-person pronoun "je" masks four separate positions (in a topological sense), and these positions are at best only partially overlapping. The first-person singular is used in turn and/or simultaneously to refer to the tutor, to *Emile*'s narrator, to the man of letters who is *Emile*'s author, and to a biographical individual who makes allusions to his friendships (and more often to friends who betrayed him) and who foreshadows in a sense the author/narrator of the *Confessions*. This fractured narrative identity is far more complex than is the traditional narratological distinction between author and narrator. There is a primordial and troubling confusion at the heart of *Emile,* and this confusion results in part from the shifting identity of the "I" taking responsibility for its narration. At times, this "I" appears to be a genuine narrator, that is, a voice of general knowledge, a voice disembodied from the work's author or from any historical being, in short the type of narrative voice suitable for a treatise. At others, this Everyman becomes a superman ("plus qu'homme" [4: 263]), and the impossible nature of some of his attributes roots him in fiction every bit as much as his imaginary pupil, Emile—"[S]upposons *ce prodige* [le gouverneur] trouvé" (p. 263, emphasis mine). On occasion, "I" indicates an historical individual who, according to the testimony provided by the *Confessions*, can be identified as *Emile*'s author and the future author of his autobiography.

For example, in the fifth book of *Emile*, the tutor explains his decision to force his pupil to see the world shortly after Emile has fallen in love with Sophie. Emile's teacher states that this is not an original idea, but is inspired by a scene he witnessed while in Venice between another tutor and his young English pupil, M. John. The Venetian anecdote allegedly finds a place in *Emile* in order to provide a model for Rousseau's fiction, but, because the reader never sees Emile and his teacher in Venice, the anecdote replaces the primary fiction and becomes integrated into that fiction's chronology. If the reader stops to examine this narrative slippage more closely, she comes to realize that M. John's story is one of the most problematic episodes in *Emile*. The narrator of the anecdote uses "I," as does the voice recounting the passage that surrounds this story and provides a context for it. In both cases, "I" is a teacher or at least someone interested enough in teaching to have paid attention to the scene at the time and remembered it afterwards. But the experience contained in the Venetian anecdote falls outside the identity otherwise assumed by or for Emile's tutor. It is not, however, outside the identity of the individual known to be *Emile*'s author, whose adventures in Venice are described at length in the *Confessions*. Furthermore, the narrator encourages this autobiographical assimilation by explaining why he remembers the story so well: "Le trait de ce jeune homme . . . n'étoit pas propre à ne rien produire dans la tête d'*un rêveur comme moi*" (4: 854, emphasis mine).

The anecdote of M. John serves as an example of the blending between fictional and autobiographical chronologies that is a frequent occurrence in *Emile*. It illustrates the troubling and changing identity of both the narrator and the master teacher. Because of this factor, it is difficult to know how to refer to the "I" in *Emile*. I will say "the narrator," but this is obviously no more comprehensive than the other possibilities: "the author," "the *gouverneur*," "Rousseau." On at least one occasion, even the narrator seems aware of the confusion that can arise from such cleavage. He is recounting his actions as tutor during a lesson (the race for the prize cookies): "Voici comment je m'y pris." Suddenly, he breaks into his narrative to add a precision: "moi, c'est à dire celui qui parle dans cet exemple" (4: 393).

It is hard to imagine this statement on narrative identity in a treatise on education that would correspond to the reader's image of the "average" treatise on education. It is equally hard to imagine that such a treatise would contain, in addition to general remarks on pedagogy, interpolated treatises on religion, government, and other subjects, various anecdotes from the life of an individual never very precisely identified, and the increasingly developed fiction of the life together of the two principal characters, a fiction that culminates in a romantic adventure for one of them, albeit a somewhat bizarre love story. On the one occasion in *Emile* on which the narrator defines what he is writing, he refers to it as a "roman . . . de la nature humaine" (4: 777). He thereby chooses for it the same generic title Rousseau adopted to characterize *Julie.* That Rousseau considered the two works similar in narrative style is confirmed by the first dialogue where they are singled out and referred to as "des romans" (1: 673).

Julie is also marked by an autobiographical intrusion that is either insufficiently camouflaged or insufficiently developed, although to a lesser extent here than in *Emile*.[15] The "I" who takes responsibility for the presentation of the text and who comments on it in footnotes is not to be confused with the race of *éditeurs* and *rédacteurs* familiar to readers of eighteenth-century epistolary fiction. The work's title page and its

---

[15] In the second dialogue of *Rousseau juge de Jean Jaques,* Rousseau compares his identification with Saint-Preux to his identification with Emile's tutor. "Rousseau" says of "Jean Jaques": "Je lui trouve aujourdui les traits du Mentor d'Emile. Peut-être dans sa jeunesse lui aurois-je trouvé ceux de St. Preux" (1: 778).

two prefaces identify the "I" who intervenes in the footnotes as Jean-Jacques Rousseau. Like the narrative voice in *Emile*, this one occupies a range of positions, from an objective and anonymous editorial presence, providing information on terms particular to the novel's Swiss setting, to an overtly subjective presence whose commentary complicates rather than facilitates a reading of the novel by adding long moralizing comments that often reflect a scornful disdain for the characters and their weaknesses. On occasion, these comments leave *Julie* far behind and are more relevant for a discussion of Rousseau the author (for example, 4: 10: 456, the note in which he comments on "ma Lettre à M. d'Alembert sur les spectacles"), or of Rousseau the future author of the *Confessions* (for example, 3: 20: 371, a note of which Bernard Guyon says: "On croirait lire un fragment des *Confessions*" [p. 1556, n. 7]).

What links the two "novels" most closely is the type of narrative construction they share, what could be termed narrative *bricolage*. In the course of its development *Julie* becomes less a novel and more a treatise. The opposite is true of *Emile*, which progresses from what seems plainly a treatise into the novel of Emile and Sophie. In the course of this evolution, the works grow closer together. When I refer to these vast narrative aggregates as the products of literary *bricolage*, it is not in order to suggest that there is anything amateurish or unpolished about their structure. Lévi-Strauss's commentary on the origins and the techniques of the *bricoleur*'s art provokes speculation on the potential for deviousness of all patchwork constructs. Rousseau considered *Julie* and *Emile* "redemptive," morally progressive works. Yet Rousseau's own mathematics of persecution teaches us that all instances of cumulative arithmetic, or addition, culminate, not in the originally predicted utopian situation, but at best in a supplemental *pis aller*, or at worst in a total negation of the original premise. With this caveat in mind, I would like to examine the central redemptive situation highlighted in both *Julie* and *Emile*: the pedagogical act.

======= ✳ =======

Teaching in the Wilderness

> In such a large governmental office as the Count's, it may occasionally happen that one department ordains this, another that; neither knows of the other, and though the supreme control is absolutely efficient, it comes by its nature too late, and so every now and then a trifling miscalculation arises.
>
> Franz Kafka, *The Castle*

By the end of *Julie*, the initially corrupting force of teaching has allegedly been rechanneled, making possible the final vision of purification. "[A]près avoir été ce que nous fumes être ce que nous sommes aujourd'hui, voila le vrai triomphe de la vertu" (6: 6: 664)—so Julie sums it up for Saint-Preux. It is fitting therefore that the first subject on which Julie addresses those gathered around her deathbed is education: "Elle nous parla de ses enfans, des soins assidus qu'exigeoit auprès d'eux la forme d'education qu'elle avoit prise" (6: 11: 704). This is the interpretation of his novel that Rousseau himself consistently supported (by means of *tu quoque* defenses), the interpretation that provided him with a justification for his infraction against his own ban on fiction: "Au reste, je persiste à croire, quoi qu'on en puisse dire, que quiconque après avoir lû la nouvelle Héloïse la peut regarder comme un livre de mauvaises moeurs, n'est pas fait pour aimer les bonnes."[16]

With *Emile*, the case for the redemptive value of teaching is even easier to make, and Rousseau's "roman de la nature humaine" has traditionally been read as one of the greatest contributions to the creation of a humane and enlightened pedagogy. Thus the most influential recent readings of *Emile*, those of Jean Château and Allan Bloom, for example, stress the beneficial effects of Rousseau's method for the pupil: "Eduquer Emile, ce sera donc le garder des chaînes de l'opi-

---

[16] Rousseau, 13 Feb. 1761, in *Correspondance générale*, vol. 6, p. 21.

nion, de la société, l'entourer, le protéger" (Château, p. 174). Such an interpretation is based on the fact that *Emile* was responsible for a revolution in pedagogy whose long-term effects continue to be felt. Rousseau called for the child's liberation from a wide range of constraints. His professed goal was all the more remarkable because he wrote at a time when prevailing educational thought sought only to impose new restrictions, perhaps because, as Philippe Ariès has suggested, childhood's separate status was only beginning to be recognized during the eighteenth century.[17]

Yet even educators who profess that their own pedagogical practice was influenced by Rousseau's method admit on occasion that the psychological relationship between tutor and Emile is marked by a certain strangeness. For example, a note of hesitation creeps into the last pages of Robert Dottrens' eulogy of Rousseau's educational theories: "Rousseau, partisan déclaré d'une éducation à la liberté par la liberté, étonne quand on le voit ne jamais quitter son élève. . . . Il faut reconnaître, enfin, Rousseau n'a pas compris la petite enfance." In his evaluation of the teacher/student relationship, Jean Starobinski makes a far more drastic claim: "Le précepteur trouve un secret plaisir aux larmes qu'il fait couler: mais nous n'avons pas eu à attendre le cinquième livre de l'*Emile* pour découvrir le sadisme du précepteur."[18]

Even Rousseau's own descriptions of his master teacher are not free of ambiguous comparisons that hint at a darker view of the pedagogical experience. For example, the engraving he chose to introduce Book 2 in the first edition represents "Chiron exercant le petit Achille à la Course" (4: 869, "Explications des Figures"). Rousseau evokes a mythical precursor of his tutor in conjunction with a pedagogical vignette in which the teacher uses a child's (not Emile) love of cakes to turn

---

[17] Bloom, introduction to *Emile* (New York: Basic Books, 1979), esp. p. 13. Ariès, *L'Enfant et la vie familiale sous l'Ancien Régime* (Plon, 1960).
[18] Dottrens, *Colloque Rousseau* (Neuchâtel: La Baconnière, 1962), p. 121. Starobinski, *Jean-Jacques Rousseau: La Transparence et l'obstacle* (Gallimard, 1971), p. 155.

him into an avid runner.[19] When telling the story of how the child learned to run, *Emile*'s narrator seems to distance himself from the methods of his mythological predecessor in pedagogy: "Courir moi-même eut été un moyen peu sur et sujet à inconvénient" (4: 393). Yet Rousseau's choice of engraving elevates Chiron to the status of model, not only for this episode, but for all Book 2, the book richest in "practical" pedagogical examples. All the subjects Rousseau selected for the engravings in *Emile* are surprising because they are borrowed from what he refers to in his critique of La Fontaine as "la menteuse antiquité" (4: 354). For example, the engraving for Book 5 represents the enchantress Circe, who changed people into different shapes, yielding to someone who resisted her: "Circé se donnant à Ulysse, qu'elle n'a pu transformer" (4: 869). But Chiron is the most disturbing subject of all, for this predecessor in the pedagogical art was a centaur—for all his wisdom only half human. Rousseau's choice of model could be read as an emblem for the existence of monstrosity, of bestiality, at the origin he chooses for his pedagogy.

Similarly, many readers do not find *Julie*'s last pages as unproblematic as Rousseau's theory of perfect redemption presents them. Christie McDonald Vance affirms that there is "something confusing about the end of *La Nouvelle Héloïse*." According to Jean Starobinski, happiness at Clarens "reste . . . menacé par le retour désastreux du désir charnel."[20] The figure of the teacher remains a disturbing presence throughout *Julie,* and the pedagogical presence in the novel

[19] In the vignette, the pupil is identified as "un enfant indolent et paresseux" (4: 393), but subsequently Emile seems to subsume the identity of the lazy child (pp. 410, 806). The story of the race, as Burgelin points out, "reste étrange" (4: 1396, n. 1 to p. 394), for it is also at this point that Rousseau seems to detach the narrator's "I" from the tutor and identify it exclusively with a moment from his own past: "[M]oi, c'est à dire celui qui parle dans cet exemple."

[20] McDonald Vance, *The Extravagant Shepherd: A Study of the Pastoral Vision in Rousseau's "La Nouvelle Héloïse,"* SVEC 105 (1973): 179. Starobinski, "L'Ecart romanesque," *Sept essais sur Rousseau,* in *La Transparence et l'obstacle,* p. 413.

ultimately teaches a lesson about teaching that, like the shadow Chiron casts over *Emile*, hints at a monstrosity at the heart of the pedagogical enterprise. It becomes clear from an examination of pedagogy's role at *Julie*'s conclusion that the initial placement of the novel's relationship to teaching under the sign of Abelard, and indeed the entire corruption/redemption schema that this placement permits, constitute an elaborate and complex *fausse piste*. Just as Julie's education serves as a smoke screen for the lovers' trysts, so the apparently utilitarian goals of the novel's other acts of teaching distract attention from their far more problematic seductions and power plays. What we learn about the Rousseauian conception of the teacher/student involvement in *Julie* is far less "classic" than the initial relationship between Saint-Preux and Julie allows us to realize. Rousseau revolutionized pedagogical theory, and he upset the traditional structures of pedagogical seduction as well. If the reader looks beyond Rousseau's theories of education to the results of their practical application, if she reads both *Julie* and *Emile* as fictions (as Rousseau invites us to do), it becomes evident that Rousseau's essential protective strategy, the persecuted victim's *tu quoque* attacks, camouflages a type of defensive behavior that serves as a striking prefiguration of Sade's fortress mentality.

In *Emile* and *Julie*, the educational enterprise is developed within the boundaries of man-made enclosures in order to protect the pupil and the educational experience as much as possible from contact with the outside world. This barrier is necessary to keep the pupil in contact with nature's ways and therefore on the straight path it lays out—"Observez la nature, et suivez la route qu'elle vous trace" (4: 259)—and away from the deviation of man's war against nature. A vocabulary associated with fortifications recurs frequently in the first two books of *Emile*, indicating the tutor's goal of progressively turning the child's body into a miniature armed camp: "[J]e fais son bien dans l'avenir en l'armant contre les maux qu'il doit supporter" (4: 313). All those within the confines of the educational *enceinte* are, as much as Robinson Crusoe on his island, "solitaires." On occasion, Rousseau uses "sauvage" as a synonym for "solitaire" (4: 456). If the rules he sets down for the education of "solitaires" are examined, important parallels become evident between what might be termed "la pensée solitaire" and Lévi-Strauss's "pensée sauvage."

Both Rousseau's philosophy of education and the end results he hopes to achieve have marked affinities with the strategies Lévi-Strauss attributes to the savage mind, the techniques of *bricolage*. The model Rousseau terms "éducation négative," "éducation" or "méthode" "inactive," or "éducation solitaire" is past-oriented, conservative, retrograde, and prudent (anti-risk). It is a system that makes wasting time, rather than gaining it, its most important rule. "Oserai-je exposer ici la plus grande, la plus importante, la plus utile régle de toute l'éducation? Ce n'est pas de gagner du tems, c'est d'en perdre" (4: 323). The entire educational process is to take place in slow motion. Certain forms of ignorance are valorized. "Si vous pouviez ne rien faire et ne rien laisser faire; si vous pouviez amener votre éléve sain et robuste à l'age de douze ans sans qu'il sut distinguer sa main droite de sa main gauche. . . ." (p. 323). Above all, the educator is told to efface himself whenever possible and simply let nature take its course, for less is more: "Peu lire et beaucoup mediter nos lectures," Saint-Preux suggests to Julie (1: 12: 57). Erudition is less valuable than a well-formed head. Once again according to Saint-Preux: "[I]l vaut toujours mieux trouver de soi-même les choses qu'on trouveroit dans les livres: c'est le vrai secret de les bien mouler à sa tête et de se les approprier" (p. 58). And as Julie later points out to Saint-Preux, the well-formed head should be nothing more than a head shaped according to nature's laws and a head made receptive to nature's lessons. A child is impressionable: "pour que toutes les idees . . . qui se raportent à son bonheur et l'éclairent sur ses devoirs s'y tracent de bonne heure en caracteres inéfaçables, et lui servent à se conduire pendant sa vie d'une manière convenable à son être et à ses facultés" (5: 3: 580).

Both the Rousseauian educator and the *bricoleur* proceed

slowly and with all due caution, avoiding risk and the unknown. The child is never a mystery for the tutor, because "je lus avant lui dans sa pensée" (4: 394). The *bricoleur* manipulates a limited number of tools whose usage he has thoroughly mastered. The educator's role seemingly involves even fewer risks: to form a mind, he has only to engrave upon it laws that, because they are natural, must already be there in some preformed state. Neither "system" contains provisions for failure. It is the nature of the *bricoleur*'s genius to be able to fix anything with what is at hand. All of the master teacher's educational experiments are successful: the child, however recalcitrant, never fails to come around in the end, and consequently no provision is made for the possibility of his refusal to "learn." The tutor constantly flaunts his self-confidence: "j'étois à peu pres le maitre de lui faire perdre ou gagner . . . à ma volonte" (4: 395).

Lévi-Strauss devotes particular attention to what is perhaps the most prudent technique of *bricolage,* reduction in size or miniaturization, "le modèle réduit." He investigates miniaturization in order to define the *bricoleur*'s relationship to the artist. He contends that this technique is precisely what the artist has in common with (borrows from?) the *bricoleur*. ("La question se pose de savoir si le modèle réduit . . . n'offre pas . . . le type même de l'oeuvre d'art," he queries, and his question delimits precisely the status of Vauban's scale models at the court of Louis XIV.) Lévi-Strauss's remarks on the psychology of reduction in size are relevant to an understanding of both the *bricoleur* and the Rousseauian teacher:

> Quelle vertu s'attache à la réduction . . . ? Elle résulte, semble-t-il, d'une sorte de renversement du procès de la connaissance: pour connaître l'objet réel dans sa totalité, nous avons toujours tendance à opérer depuis ses parties. La résistance qu'il nous oppose est surmontée en la divisant. La réduction d'échelle renverse cette situation:

plus petite, la totalité de l'objet paraît moins redoutable.
(pp. 34-35)

Miniaturization, it seems, is adopted as a result of the *bri-coleur*'s attempted rejection of risk and failure. Such excessive prudence must stem from a fear that the object being controlled could somehow step out of line (and out of control)— from a fear of the original swerve of *bricoler*. ("Dans son sens ancien, le verbe bricoler . . . évoque . . . un mouvement incident: celui de la balle qui rebondit, du chien qui divague, du cheval qui s'écarte de la ligne droite pour éviter un obstacle" [p. 26]). Reduction in size therefore means also reduction in fearfulness: the miniature is more easily knowable, more easily controllable. With a miniature, the anxiety caused by its potential for deviation can be put aside.

The Rousseauian pedagogue and the *bricoleur* share such fundamental aspects of a common stance as the desire for success without risk, the rejection of failure, and the belief in the existence of a finite number of tools, materials, laws, or possibilities. All these positions attempt to deny the *clinamen* that is at the genesis of *bricolage*, the *clinamen* that makes *bricolage* originally a devious and oblique strategy. Thus in his conception of teaching Rousseau attempts to deny the veering that takes place when man enters history and starts to work against nature. In the microcosms that shelter the pedagogical act in *Emile* and *Julie,* Rousseau hopes to make what he believed impossible, possible: teaching here can straighten out the path of man's entry into the world, can make man at one with the straight path of nature's ways. "[L]'âme . . . suivant mollement l'impulsion de la nature, se détourne au choc d'un obstacle comme une boule prend l'angle de la réflexion; au lieu que celle qui suit plus vigoureusement sa course ne se détourne point, mais comme un boulet de canon, force l'obstacle ou s'amortit et tombe à sa rencontre" (1: 669). As a result of the power of pedagogy, the pupil's instinctive swerves ("comme une boule prend l'angle de la réflexion") are transformed into the crushing, un-deviating force of an offensive weapon ("comme un boulet de canon").[21]

In Rousseau's pedagogical system, miniaturization is used to eliminate deviation and control not only man, but nature as well.[22] Like the *bricoleur*, Rousseau's pedagogues make reduction in size an essential element in their technical arsenal. Young pupils are dominated by the wills of their teachers until they become miniature projections of the adults who control them—the tutor lives through Emile; Claire's daughter Henriette is turned into a "nouvelle Julie." Adult pupils like Saint-Preux are made infantile. The pedagogical vignettes in *Emile* and *Julie* reveal an obsession with the control of the student that has as its goal the erasure of every *écart*. As we have seen, however, none of Rousseau's defensive barriers is ever unassailable. The fate of teaching foreshadows the story of the failure of self-protection told by the *Confessions*. Despite the pedagogues' vigilance, they are never successful in making the space of teaching safe from deviation, safe from the self-assertive swerve at the origin of *bricolage*. I break with chronological order in order to trace education's battle for control first in *Emile* and then in *Julie*, because I share Château's conviction that *Julie*'s "création de ces petits centres sociaux que gouvernera un sage" (p. 92) marks the logical conclusion of the pedagogical trajectory traced by *Emile*.

---

[21] The sentences that lead up to this one retrace Rousseau's version of man's entry into nature: "Tous les premiers mouvemens de la nature sont bons et droits. Ils tendent le plus directement qu'il est possible à notre conservation et à notre bonheur: mais bientot manquant de force pour suivre à travers tant de resistance leur prémiére direction, ils se laissent défléchir par mille obstacles qui les détournant du vrai but leur font prendre des routes obliques où l'homme oublie sa première destination" (1: 668-69).

[22] *Rousseau juge de Jean Jaques* affirms the attraction of miniaturization for Rousseau when Rousseau describes Jean-Jacques making miniature *herbiers*: "Il employoit un tems et des soins incroyables à dessecher et applatir des rameaux . . . de sorte que, collant avec soin ces fragmens sur des papiers qu'il ornoit de petits cadres, à toute la vérité de la nature il joignoit l'éclat de la miniature et le charme de l'imitation" (1: 794).

=== ✳ ===

Emile: The Fox and the Crow

Le petit mechant ne songeoit guére en faisant un trou
pour planter sa féve, qu'il se creusoit un cachot où sa
science ne tarderoit pas à le faire enfermer.

Rousseau, *Emile*

Near the middle of Book 1 of *Emile*, the narrator defines the
tutor and his relationship to his pupil. In lieu of a description
of the teacher, he gives only the brief paragraph that, according to Jimack's analyses, marks the transition from the anonymous teacher to the tutor as a semi-autobiographical projection
of *Emile*'s author: "Je ne parle point ici des qualités d'un bon
gouverneur, je les suppose, et je me suppose moi-même doué
de toutes ces qualités. En lisant cet ouvrage on verra de quelle
libéralité j'use envers moi" (4: 265).[23] Despite the abruptness
with which the narrator draws the curtain over a subject that
could have occupied him at some length in a treatise on education (a similar abruptness characterizes many of the autobiographical interventions in *Emile*), the narrator does include
one particular central to his conception of the tutor: "Je re-
marquerai seulement . . . que le Gouverneur d'un enfant doit
être jeune, et même aussi jeune que peut l'être un homme sage.
Je voudrois qu'il fut lui-même enfant s'il étoit possible." The
passage is marked by an unmistakable regression—from young,
to as young as a "wise man" can be, to the ideal of childhood.
As he moves back through time, the narrator moves beyond
the possibility of a realistic identification between the tutor
and *Emile*'s author. Indeed, this chronological regression allows for slippage between the initial identification and a second, more problematic one.

In the narrator's description, the teacher identifies more

---

[23] The second sentence ("on verra de quelle libéralité j'use envers moi")
seems to indicate that *Emile*'s author identifies the tutor with an idealized
version of himself, further complicating the question of the character's various
components.

and more strongly with his pupil, until by the end he moves to take over the pupil's space, to *become* the pupil—"qu'il fut lui-même enfant." In the course of the passage, the reader witnesses a shifting of topological formations. Initially, there is a triad (narrator, tutor, pupil). The narrator first occupies the tutor's space, then a second reduction blends the three figures into a single mass. The pedagogical relationship is founded on a drive toward narcissistic engulfment so strong that the goal of impossible union announced in the *Confessions* ("deux âmes dans le même corps") is surpassed: in *Emile,* three souls are meant to share the same "body." The hybrid creature inhabiting *Emile*'s narrative voice reveals through this vision its desire to take over all the principal roles in this pedagogical drama.

"Emile est orphelin. Il n'importe qu'il ait son pére et sa mére. Chargé de leurs devoirs, je succéde à tous leurs droits" (4: 267). The tutor has a utopian union with his pupil because he orchestrates Emile's generation, takes responsibility for it even if he cannot be responsible for it. The tutor "murders" Emile's father for him. He acts as a prefiguration of a complex, when he eliminates the paternal presence before the Oedipal conflict can occur. The master teacher's protean fluidity once again casts him in an impossibly multiple role. He is simultaneously the son killing the father and the father reborn, a pedagogical phoenix strategically related to the Sun Birds evoked by La Fontaine and Louis XIV. In the strangely contrived sexual atmosphere that pervades *Emile,* the tutor even replaces the mother. For, while the mother's physical role is turned over to a nurse, the "duties" and the "rights" of motherhood are appropriated by the tutor.

The union between teacher and student is utopian not only in intensity but in duration as well. Like Julie and Claire, the two are to be "inseparable"—forever: "on ne nous ôtera jamais l'un à l'autre que de notre consentement. . . . je voudrois même que l'élève et le gouverneur se regardassent tellement comme inséparables que le sort de leurs jours fut toujours entre eux un objet commun" (p. 267). They share the same thoughts ("je lus avant lui dans sa pensée" [p. 394]), the same life story. They are not even allowed to think about the separation and distance that could create different, individual stories and therefore a space for interpretive difference.[24] Indeed, the narrator makes this provision as though it were a legal matter: "Cette clause est essentielle." They envisage their fate as "un objet commun." Under the terms of the contract that binds them together, the limits of their lives will be conterminous with those of the pedagogical enterprise. The tutor at least enjoys a certain freedom of choice within the educational fortress—if only the freedom to choose cookies and not tarts to awaken his pupil's *gourmandise*. Emile, on the other hand, is increasingly a prisoner of the pattern through which teaching comes to usurp nature's power, that is, teaching is used to suppress the *clinamen* that threatens the straight path of "natural" movement.

Teaching becomes the instrument of Emile's repression, the means by which his nascent powers are cut short, just as his father's were before him. This conclusion is the inevitable result of any close examination of the only moments of interaction between teacher and pupil, the pedagogical vignettes that occupy a central role in Books 2 and 3 of *Emile*. These anecdotes provide a unique opportunity for the reader to judge what Rousseau presents as the practical aspect of his theorizing, to observe his projection, the tutor, actually acting out his vocation, and to note the effects of his teaching on his pupil. Moreover, since Emile is allowed to speak on these occasions, they alone offer even a limited sense of the pupil's psychology. During these vignettes, *Emile* is farthest removed from the treatise on education and closest to the educational novel.

In early autobiographies and pseudo-autobiographies, teaching is often invoked in defense of the autobiographical impulse: the life story must be told because it is exemplary.

---

[24] This observation was suggested by Luz Nuncio in a graduate seminar I gave at Yale University in 1980.

Thus Rousseau's favorite hero, Robinson Crusoe, offers himself as an "emblem" or "token."[25] In the preamble to the *Confessions,* Rousseau declares his text to be the "prémiére piéce de comparaison pour l'étude des hommes" (1: 3). In *Emile,* the narrative tables have turned: autobiography is presented as coming to the defense of teaching. In general, the autobiographical elements in *Emile* are justified as a confirmation of pedagogical theorizing. The narrator maintains that a particular technique will or will not work either because Jean-Jacques Rousseau has actually had the opportunity to test it out during an episode in his own teaching career, or because Jean-Jacques Rousseau observed a fellow pedagogue successfully or unsuccessfully at work, as in the example of the English tutor in Venice.

In practice, however, the autobiographical passages damage rather than sustain *Emile*'s narrative coherency. As we have seen, when *Emile*'s author indulges in evident self-referentiality, the narrative becomes troubled in its flow, and this trouble does not remain unnoticed: "[M]oi, c'est à dire celui qui parle dans cet exemple." This trouble is perhaps induced by the fact that the examples autobiography furnishes, far from substantiating the tutor's self-portrait as master teacher, portray him on the contrary as an individual endowed with decidedly limited pedagogical insights. For example, in order to illustrate the dangers of teaching history to children, Book 2 recounts a day in the country "chez une bonne mére de famille." Burgelin refers to Rousseau's correspondence to establish the anecdote's autobiographical content (4: 1376, n. 2 to p. 349). The narrator dwells on this account of the pedagogical misuse of the story of Alexander's doctor because he sees it as a confirmation of the tutor's victory over a rival pedagogue and the other guests who marveled at first at the fool's gold of that rival's pedagogical finesse: "[J]'évitai de combattre pour ne pas le décréditer dans l'esprit de son

[25] Defoe, *Robinson Crusoe,* ed. M. Shinagel (New York: Norton, 1975), pp. 13, 14.

élève. . . . [J]e m'en retournai riant en moi-même de la haute sagesse des péres et des maitres qui pensent apprendre l'histoire aux enfans" (4: 348-49, 350).

However, the scene around the dinner table during which the young pupil and all the assembled guests with the exception of Jean-Jacques Rousseau's autobiographical projection allegedly reveal their incomprehension of the real meaning of the historical anecdote is no easier for the readers at *Emile*'s banquet to interpret than was the story of Alexander for the guests at the fictive dinner in the country. The narrator affirms that there is madness in the anecdote, and he claims that the guests came to share this judgment made by his autobiographical double: "Pour moi, leur dis-je, il me paroit que s'il y a le moindre courage, la moindre fermeté dans l'action d'Alexandre elle n'est qu'une extravagance. Alors tout le monde se réunit et convint que c'étoit une extravagance" (p. 349). But *Emile*'s readers have not always been convinced by his reading, and future readers of the Pléiade edition will certainly never be able to take his version at face value, for Burgelin contends that the other guests interpreted the madness as residing in the tutor-to-be rather than in the history lesson. "Il faut entendre que l'auditoire se réunit contre Rousseau et le traita d'extravagant" (p. 1376, n. 2 to p. 349).

Burgelin's reading belongs to the oldest tradition of interpreting the anecdote, one inaugurated by Formey who used the incident's "punch line," "tai-toi, Jean Jaques" (p. 349), as the epigraph for his *Anti-Emile*. According to the narrator, this line marks a sympathetic gesture on the part of the one guest wise enough to have understood the proceedings and to have recognized Jean Jacques's superiority: "[U]ne femme qui étoit à côté de moi et qui n'avoit pas ouvert la bouche se pencha vers mon oreille et me dit tout bas: tai-toi, Jean Jaques, ils ne t'entendront pas." In Formey's reading, the gesture of complicity is really a mark of condescension: Jean Jacques should keep quiet, because his autobiographical reflections only serve to "lay bare" his true nature (p. 17). Here and elsewhere, autobiography provides the best ammunition against

Rousseau's teachers—Formey could lift the perfect epigraph to his attack directly from this scene. Furthermore, the association between Jean Jacques and madness made in Burgelin's final comment on the scene would never have come up, had not the narrator suggested the very word himself in this vignette from one of his pasts. Formey was correct in reading this episode as a *mise en abyme* of *Emile*'s educational enterprise, for the anecdote of the "jeune docteur's" history lesson teaches *Emile*'s reader that any pedagogical example— the narrator's or someone else's—is open to contradictory interpretations. The tutor implicitly invites the reader to reverse his readings of the work's subsequent teaching vignettes.

The narrator is not blind to the possibility of antagonistic readings of this passage: "Quelques lecteurs mécontens du *tai-toi Jean-Jaques* demanderont, je le prévois, ce que je trouve enfin de si beau dans l'action d'Alexandre?" (4: 350). His analysis reveals an awareness that it is precisely the phrase "tai-toi Jean-Jaques" that is crucial to the episode's ambivalence. But in a curious shift, the narrator seems to use this perception against himself when he increases the level of the antagonism in the reader's hypothetical future objections: "Infortunés! S'il faut vous le dire, comment le comprendrez-vous?" By foreseeing the attack, the narrator can be said to provoke it. Then, instead of responding to the imagined attack, he launches an attack of his own. He answers the objection, but only after insulting the moral sensibility of the reader who would be interested in the explanation he provides.

The narrator's offensive defense of his dual interpretation (of the historical anecdote and of the reception of that anecdote in the context of his own educational exemplum) is strategically valid for the fortified pedagogy he advocates. Vauban corroborates his position: "Comme dans les combats et dans les batailles de Troupes, l'avantage demeure le plus souvent à celui qui tire le dernier, le contraire arrive dans les Sieges, où l'Artillerie de celui qui prime a ordinairement l'avantage" (*De l'attaque des places*, 1737 ed., p. 195). In the passage on Rousseau's reading of the historical anecdote, as on all the occasions when the reader of *Emile* is confronted by the hostile dialogue that seems to be the narrator's desired reader response, the discussion is already closed. In such instances, the narrator offers a preview of the situation various critics have analyzed in Rousseau's overtly autobiographical works: the reader's hostility is a foregone conclusion, and the only way of communicating with the reader is to provoke him into attacking *Emile*.[26] In his educational novel's pedagogical vignettes, the use of autobiography goes beyond the initial defensive position, the justification of teaching, in two ways. As in this example, autobiography may be used to provoke a veritable chain reaction of defensive and offensive positioning, to imagine an attack that, if realized, would give Rousseau's narrative representative the opportunity to defend himself against it and feel therefore that his intuitive sense of hostility had been necessary all along.

Not infrequently, the autobiographical interventions in *Emile* are also used defensively to evoke old grievances in order to "settle" them. For example, shortly after the historical lesson, the narrator introduces a teaching vignette that reveals itself to be just such a settling of a score with a former student, presumably a former student of *Emile*'s author.[27] The episode with the "petit tiran" invites the same kind of interpretive

---

[26] For example, the opening pages of Jean Starobinski's "Jean-Jacques Rousseau et le péril de la réflexion" provide a brilliant description of the vicious circle of persecution in the *Confessions*: "La malveillance du témoin n'est pas un risque à courir, mais une certitude qui précède et empoisonne tout mouvement ultérieur. Desormais, les gestes de Rousseau seront moins des initiatives que des ripostes" (*L'Oeil vivant*, pp. 95-96). See also Robert Osmont's introduction to *Rousseau juge de Jean Jaques*, Pléiade edition, vol. 1.

[27] Josué V. Harari has recently reached conclusions about this episode similar to mine. ("Therapeutic Pedagogy: Rousseau's *Emile*," *MLN* 97 [1982]:798-800). Harari's general argument concerning *Emile* runs parallel to my thesis here. Unfortunately, I only discovered his stimulating article after I had completed both this chapter and an earlier version of it ("*La Nouvelle Héloïse*, or the Case for Pedagogical Deviation," *YFS* 63 [1982]:98-116), so my reading does not take his analysis into account.

reversal to which the story of Alexander's doctor exposes the reader. This exemplum is included to illustrate pedagogy's erasure of a type of unnatural *clinamen* to which children are particularly susceptible, capriciousness: "Le caprice des enfans n'est jamais l'ouvrage de la nature mais d'une mauvaise discipline" (4: 364). The narrator tells how he was called in as temporary tutor for a headstrong child who until his arrival had been completely successful at manipulating everyone around him, including his official teacher. The "petit tiran" tries to carry on as usual with the new teacher, and he manages at first to wreak havoc on the patterns of the narrator's life. The score is finally settled between them, and the child learns his lesson, when his temporary tutor refuses to accompany him on an outing. His teacher notes with evident satisfaction how the headstrong child goes out alone for his walk and walks into, not only a trap, but a play:

> Tout étoit préparé d'avance, et comme il s'agissoit d'une espéce de scéne publique, je m'étois muni du consentement du pére. A peine avoit-il fait quelques pas qu'il entend à droite et à gauche différens propos sur son compte. Voisin, le joli Monsieur! où va-t-il ainsi tout seul? Il va se perdre. . . . Un peu plus loin il rencontre des poliçons à peu près de son age, qui l'agacent et se moquent de lui. Plus il avance, plus il trouve d'embarras. Seul et sans protection, il se voit le joüet de tout le monde. (4: 367-68)

The child's perception of the scene is correct, for he is just what he thinks, the plaything of all the falsely innocent passers-by and especially of the author and director of this elaborate vignette who has the pleasure of imagining it all and then controlling it from afar.

In his description of the scene, the narrator at no point mentions his personal motivation for transforming the figure of the pedagogue into a theatrical director. On the contrary, he portrays himself throughout the drama as a detached, scientific observer ("sans m'émouvoir"; "pour moi je le receus sans reproche . . . mais avec un peu de gravité," [pp. 367, 368]). According to his account, the only hostility present was directed at him by his "masters." Because he refused to lie to her like all those around her, the child's mother "[me] prit en haine" (p. 366). Any desire for revenge is projected onto the "tiran": "Voyant l'occasion bonne pour se vanger . . . "; "il voulut . . . se venger" (pp. 365, 366). However, the narrator's extra-professional motivation is betrayed by the expressions he uses to signal the chronological unfolding of his narrative: "Le lendemain ce fut mon tour"; "C'étoit là que je l'attendois" (p. 367). Any coolness in his behavior is only a mask, designed to keep his pupil off his guard so that he may easily be snared— "dans le moment où je l'en vis le plus engoüé j'allai lui pro- poser un tour de promenade" (p. 366)—and to camouflage the sadistic pleasure his victory affords the narrator. In toying with his pedagogical plaything, Emile's future teacher acts in the name of the father, "muni du consentement du pére." And after the "lesson," the biological father prolongs this identi- fication with the pedagogical father, even adding a stronger dose of cruelty than the teacher prescribes: "[L]e pére lui dit plus séchement que je ne m'y serois attendu. . . ." (p. 368).

The lesson the child allegedly learns from the little drama staged for his benefit is to stop indulging in capriciousness by overcoming the dialectic of command and obedience on which such behavior is founded: "Le caprice des enfans n'est jamais l'ouvrage de la nature mais d'une mauvaise discipline. C'est qu'ils ont obéi ou commandé, et j'ai dit cent fois qu'il ne faloit ni l'un ni l'autre" (p. 364). Yet—and this may be the Achilles' heel of the pedagogical enterprise in *Emile* in general just as in "Le Corbeau et le Renard"—the child is taught neither to overcome this opposition nor to create a synthesis from its antithetical terms. He learns to step outside the circle circum- scribed by this movement of authority and simply remain inert. When the former "petit tiran" returns from his walk, he is "souple, confus et n'osant lever les yeux" (p. 368). His will has been broken.

The expression, "to teach someone a lesson," combines the

CHAPTER IV

language of pedagogy with the aggressiveness of a desire for revenge. The story of the little tyrant is a perfect illustration of this combination, and this can only be explained by supplementing the motivations proposed by the story itself with an additional interpretation of the all too evident hostility. The narrator/teacher perceives the *clinamena* caused by the child's will as a threat to his well-being, a threat he is determined to suppress. Even the appellation with which he refers to the child, "le petit tiran," reflects his desire to keep him under control. The diminutive stresses the child's status as a miniature man, as do the eighteenth-century paintings by Van Loo and others depicting the "little musician," the "little painter," and other such reductions in size. By the end of the moral tale, the tables have quite literally turned, and the teacher has assumed all the menacing force the child initially represented for him. At first, everyone was against the teacher (the fact that the father was on his side is not revealed until the balance of power is already shifting). By the tale's conclusion, everyone is working on his side for the humiliation of his enemy (the mother is absent from the ending). The narrator takes over his pupil's original role by becoming the tyrant the child wanted to be. Like carnival in Bakhtin's definition, the play turns the world upside down, for the former tyrant is left in a position parallel to that originally occupied by his teacher, a position, furthermore, parallel to that occupied by Jean-Jacques Rousseau in the *Confessions* and from time to time by *Emile*'s narrator in his autobiographical incarnation.[28] The lesson the child ultimately receives from his teacher is a lesson in paranoia. Like Jean-Jacques Rousseau in Starobin-

[28] Lionel Gossman has pointed out the parallelism between Rousseau's description of man in society and Rousseau's own experience: "Rousseau's formal sociological reflections on man and society are accompanied, enriched, and in an important sense completed by a concrete personal experience of alienation, isolation, and disharmony. The autobiographical works can in fact be thought of as presenting in the form of an existential self-analysis that which in the political and sociological works is the object of an abstract and theoretical analysis" ("Time and History in Rousseau," *SVEC* [1964]:341).

146

ski's description of the *Confessions,* he becomes "la victime
d'un regard anonyme, d'un spectateur sans identité. Il est, de
la sorte, livré au péril universel" (*L'Oeil vivant,* p. 94). Pedagogy ultimately seems more useful for the pedagogue than
for his pupil: by manipulating the power it puts at his disposal,
the teacher is able to turn the hostile glances of his social
superiors away from him. He is also able to take revenge upon
the "unique héritier de sa famille" by showing him what it
feels like to have all eyes on him—and the humiliation planned
for the heir is all the greater because all those staring at him
are his social inferiors.[29]

In a footnote to this passage in the Pléiade edition, Burgelin
discusses the various identifications that have been proposed
for the "petit tiran": M. de Chenonceaux, an unknown child
in Chambéry (p. 1384, n. 1 to p. 364). The discrepancy among
opinions is indicative of the lack of concrete evidence situating
this incident in the domain of the autobiographical experience
of *Emile*'s author. The autobiographical classification of
the episode has no factual basis and results from the critical
convention that identifies the narrator-tutor in *Emile* with
Jean-Jacques Rousseau. In the case of the little-tyrant story,
Rousseau scholars probably owe their conviction of the autobiographical presence to the air of authenticity that surrounds the episode, an air created by the single-mindedness
of the desire for revenge that animates the vignette. In his
commentary, Burgelin admits that the paranoia play at the
lesson's conclusion could well be fictional: "Il est vraisemblable que cette fin est inventée de toutes pièces." His willingness
to suspect the intermingling of artifice and autobiography is
faithful to the narrator's own suggestions. For example, the
tutor indicates that this particular open-air lesson borrows
both its structure and at least part of its inspiration from the
theatre. One of the narrator's friends follows his student, pro-

---

[29] The tutor works in the name of the father to take implicit revenge on
the mother, since the child's capriciousness is blamed on her. Rousseau's
misogyny comes into play more discreetly here than in his more developed
portrayal of the mother as teacher in *Julie.*

viding commentary from time to time on what is happening to the former tyrant: "Ce rolle qui ressembloit à celui de Sbrigani dans *Pourceaugnac* demandoit un homme d'esprit" (p. 368). The narrator stages a lesson in which he, like the *bricoleur*, uses devious means and indirect action that mimic natural forces while remaining purely artificial. His lesson's success depends on the creation right outside his door of a miniature version of the city with all its dangers, its warnings, and its threats. Rousseau's evocation of Molière is appropriate, for there is as much art in this teaching as in any diversion staged for Louis XIV in the microcosm of Versailles.

Indeed, the tutor puts so much artifice into his own teaching that he suspects its presence in every pedagogical act. The would-be tyrant's undoing is inspired by a play. The narrator follows a preplanned scenario to prevent the young lovers, Emile and Sophie, from enjoying their budding love. As we have already seen, Emile's mentor gives credit for "l'idée de rendre Emile amoureux avant de le faire voyager" (4: 853) to an English tutor "he" met in Venice. While the narrator is visiting with his English counterpart, a letter arrives that the Englishman reads to his pupil. The letter is in English and Emile's teacher "n'y compris rien; mais durant la lecture je vis le jeune homme déchirer de tres belles manchettes de point qu'il portoit, et les jetter au feu l'une aprés l'autre." He asks what this means, and the Englishman explains that his pupil ripped up the cuffs given him by a Venetian lady, because the letter the teacher was reading contained a description of the young English lady to whom M. John is promised, Miss Lucy, working on another pair for him. John leaves the room, and the French teacher, incapable of imagining a lesson that is not the product of artifice, asks his English alter ego if he had set up the whole scene by inventing the letter against the Venetian lady: "Non, me dit-il, la chose est réelle; je n'ai pas mis tant d'art à mes soins; j'y ai mis de la simplicité, . . . et Dieu a béni mon travail" (p. 854).

Emile's tutor fails to heed this call for simplicity. He makes this "natural" lesson "unnatural," when he forces his student's education to follow the model it establishes. In addition, he deforms the meaning of the scene when he transplants it to French soil. His English counterpart does not intend to teach his ward a lesson. The gesture that accidentally results from his reading serves as a reaffirmation of M. John's loyalty to his English fiancée. *Emile*'s narrator admits that he misinterpreted the model teacher's intention, but he does not see that he misreads the context of the pupil's gesture as well. M. John's choice is simply between two women. Emile's tutor acts as if the stakes were much higher when he affirms that he is obliged to bring Emile and Sophie together before he sends his ward off on his world tour to safeguard his pupil's purity during his journey: "[C]ette contagion n'est guére à craindre pour mon Emile. . . . Parmi toutes les précautions que j'ai prises pour cela, je compte pour beaucoup l'attachement qu'il a dans le coeur" (p. 853). He is thus able to justify the ease with which he manipulates both Emile and Sophie and the detachment that characterizes his reference to their relationship as a "précaution."

Perhaps the clearest indication of the extent of the power "natural education" confers on the teacher is provided by the discussion in Book 2 of the one work that escapes the ban on reading proposed by *Emile, Robinson Crusoe*. The narrator's explanation of the qualities that make this book alone beneficial for his pupil exposes the ultimate deviousness inherent in his method. *Robinson Crusoe* is described as "le plus heureux traitté d'éducation naturelle" (4: 454). It is considered worthy of this eulogy because, like the narrator-pedagogue, Robinson is a *bricoleur*, obliged by his isolation to resort to indirection in order to fortify his existence: "Robinson Crusöé dans son isle, seul, dépourvu de l'assistance de ses semblables et des instruments de tous les arts, pourvoyant cependant à sa subsistance, . . . voila un objet . . . qu'on a mille moyens de rendre agréable aux enfans" (p. 455). The narrator stresses the direct correspondence he sees between Robinson's situation and the educational enclosure: "Voila comment nous réalisons l'isle déserte qui me servoit d'abord de comparaison"

(p. 455). But the practical information contained in *Robinson Crusoe* is not alone sufficient to explain the fascination the story exerts on the narrator. Robinson Crusoe is destined to play a central role in Emile's education because of the type of total union his presence makes conceivable. An implicit comparison runs in filigree through the passage: the narrator-pedagogue and Robinson are both examples of "l'homme isolé" (p. 455), both "solitaires" (p. 456). The comparison is founded on the autobiographical projection Jean-Jacques Rousseau-Robinson Crusoe,[30] but the explicit goal of the discussion is to transform Emile into a reincarnation of the hero of "le plus heureux traitté d'éducation naturelle." And through the intermediary of Defoe's character, pedagogue and pupil (and author as well) become temporarily one, in an illustration of the movement prescribed by the definition of the tutor: "Je voudrois qu'il fut lui-même enfant s'il étoit possible" (p. 265). Emile's teacher uses the story of Robinson Crusoe to take over his pupil's thoughts, to fill his mind with his teacher's dreams, and then to use those dreams to drive his pupil literally out of himself, out of his mind.

The tutor instructs Emile to repeat Robinson's practical education and gives him lessons in the techniques of *bricolage*. His instruction aims at creating a fundamental confusion in the child's head: "Je veux que la tête lui en tourne, qu'il s'occupe sans cesse de son château, de ses chèvres, de ses plantations, . . . qu'il pense être Robinson lui-même, qu'il se voye habillé de peaux, portant un grand bonnet, un grand sabre, tout le grotesque équipage de la figure" (p. 455). After studying Defoe's novel as an educational treatise, Emile will come to believe that he is Defoe's hero. As happens to Don Quixote and to all previous fictional readers of fiction who try to live as though they were a part of that fiction, the experience of

[30] G. Pire has attempted to find biographical explanations for Rousseau's attraction to Defoe's hero: both Rousseau's and Robinson's brothers disappeared; both their families were "d'origine étrangère" ("Jean-Jacques Rousseau et Robinson Crusoé," *Revue de littérature comparée* [Oct.-Dec. 1957]:479-96).

this total projection will drive him mad ("que la tête lui en tourne"). Furthermore, Emile's progressive alienation from himself is not described as an accidental by-product of his immersion in practical education. It is ardently desired by the tutor who orders its development. "Je veux" inaugurates each sentence that recounts a stage of this process. Of course, at the end of his pedagogical fantasy, the tutor makes it appear quite innocent: "L'enfant pressé de se faire un magazin pour son isle sera plus ardent pour apprendre que le maitre pour enseigner" (pp. 455-56).

But the unfolding of this educational play belies the simplicity of its declared goals. The "little tyrant" is taught to be paranoid; the "little Robinson" learns to be obsessive: "Je veux que la tête lui en tourne, qu'il s'occupe sans cesse de . . . ; qu'il pense être Robinson lui-même. . . . Je veux qu'il s'inquiette. . . ." For once, the tutor draws the obvious conclusion about the goal of his teaching: "Quelle ressource que cette folie pour un homme habile qui n'a su la faire naitre qu'afin de la mettre a profit" (p. 455). In his system of natural education, madness is a "resource" at the disposal of the pedagogue or "homme habile." When his head is turning after the sight of the footprint in the sand, Robinson Crusoe says he is "out of my self" (p. 121). The narrator-pedagogue wants Emile to come to share in this awareness as an essential part of the pedagogical process.

In the *Confessions,* Rousseau describes his dream of reenacting Crusoe's drama on an island in the lake of Bienne. He goes so far as to people the island with rabbits (1: 644). From his description, it becomes clear that this particular dream has such a powerful attraction for him because, like Vauban populating the earth with imaginary pigs, this fantasy allows him to feel omnipotent. When he sees himself as Robinson Crusoe, he sees himself as a godlike figure with complete power over his kingdom and its inhabitants. This vision of omnipotence becomes even more pronounced when *Robinson* is revisited in *Emile.* When the narrator-pedagogue acts out his creator's fantasy through his pupil, he uses the fiction of the castaway against the pupil. He revels in his power to make the human animal repeat not only the swerve of *bricolage,* but the *écart* of the literary *bricoleur,* Robinson's madness. Within the enclosure, his powers are so great that he feels safe from the Other's self-defensive *clinamen.*

The Rousseauian pedagogue is not always perfectly successsful at keeping all potentially threatening forces under his control. The madness Wolmar encourages gets out of hand in a crucial scene of *Julie* that we will examine shortly, and one of the most developed pedagogical vignettes in *Emile* contains a slip in the narrator's domination that even an elaborate defense cannot explain away. The episode I have in mind is the story in Book 2 of Emile's encounter at a fair with a mountebank ("bateleur") who uses a magnet to manipulate little wax ducks. The episode initially follows the pattern established by most of the other educational vignettes: under his teacher's simultaneously watchful and covert supervision, Emile becomes acquainted with a phenomenon for which he has no explanation. Emile, who has been learning about magnetism and magnets, happens onto a "joueur de gobelets" who uses a magnet to work his sleight of hand. The mountebank camouflages the magnet in the duck's bill and hides a bit of metal in a piece of bread.[31] Consequently, an artificial duck appears to follow real food. Characteristically, the tutor takes charge of his pupil's response: "Fort surpris, nous ne disons pourtant pas: c'est un sorcier, car nous ne savons ce que c'est qu'un sorcier" (4: 437). Also characteristically, he moves from the outset to cancel his pupil's identity both by adopting the pronoun "we" and by his choice of explanation. The evocation of sorcery startles the reader because it is extraneous to the context of this pedagogical scene. Emile (or "nous") does not know what a sorcerer is. Even if he did, it seems unlikely that, given his training, he would resort to

---

[31] This initial situation is reversed on the third day, thereby causing Emile's humiliation. For a divergent reading of this passage, see Robert Ellrich, *Rousseau and His Reader: The Rhetorical Situation of the Major Works* (Chapel Hill, N.C.: Univ. of North Carolina Press, 1969), p. 52.

witchcraft to explain the phenomenon of the wax ducks following a piece of bread. The evocation of sorcery at the outset of this episode is more than a psychological *fausse piste:* it serves to inscribe the encounter with the mountebank under the sign of a power just as uncontrollable as Robinson's ultimately "profitable" madness.

This episode is also similar to other teaching vignettes in that it parcels out its revelations. The lesson follows a binary structure: confrontation with problem, acquisition of knowledge that seems to resolve its practical aspect; new mystification by problem, second and final moment of enlightenment in which the moral lesson is more important than the technical one. The progression of this deferred and hesitant acquisition of knowledge can be traced by following the evolution in the pronouns adopted by the narrator. Initially he employs the first person plural suggesting a solidarity between teacher and student (although in the evocation of sorcery just discussed, his usage is artificial, since "nous" evidently refers only to Emile). The pedagogical team goes to the fair and watches the mysterious ducks; the pair returns home, discovers the ducks' secret, and prepares the bread designed to upstage the professional trickster—all in the congenial atmosphere of the first-person plural. However, once teacher and student return to the fair, they go their separate ways, as a "split" in pronouns indicates. For the description of his moment of victory when he uses his bread to seduce the ducks away from their master, Emile is returned to third-person status—"mon petit docteur"; "il est pris au mot" (pp. 437, 438). A form of narrative solidarity returns for parts of the account of the following day's return match between novice *trompeur* and experienced *trompeur* recently *trompé*, but "nous" has been replaced by the less precisely encompassing "on" (p. 438). At the novice's downfall, when the tables have turned for a second time and the *joueur de gobelets* is back in control of the situation after Emile's magnetized bread failed to reproduce the desired effect of bringing the ducks to him, his narrative isolation is once again complete: "[I]l s'éloigne enfin tout confus et n'ose plus s'exposer aux huées" (p. 438). After this temporary humiliation has passed, narrative solidarity again becomes dominant through the account of the final return home, the visit of the *bateleur* who comes to reveal his secret and lecture them for having tried to take away his livelihood: "[N]ous nous évadons sans être apperçus . . . "; "nous voulons lui faire un présent . . ." (pp. 439-40). "I" only intervenes in the ending first in a gesture of self-recrimination—"Je me blâme de ma molle facilité"—and then to explain the pedagogical usefulness of the lesson (p. 440).

It might seem from this description that a correlation exists on the one hand between the narrative union of teacher and student and the success of their pedagogical enterprise and on the other between their narrative dissociation and the failure of their experiment—in other words, that the teacher is one with his student in prosperity, but abandons him to learn his lesson alone. While this schema is roughly borne out by the text, it is not sufficient to account for its pattern of union and rupture. For the narrator-pedagogue does not completely divorce himself from his other half when the pupil becomes "le joüet de tout le monde." Had he done so, he would have provided *Emile*'s author with better ammunition for his defense of the passage against its first critique.

In his *Anti-Emile*, Formey points out the bizarreness of the mountebank's apotheosis as teacher when he appears at the pedagogical domicile in order to lecture teacher and student on their misconduct: "Ce Joueur de Gobelets, qui se pique d'emulation contre un enfant, qui va lui faire des reproches amers, et sermonne gravement son Instituteur, est un individu du monde des Emiles, qui n'est certainement pas le nôtre" (p. 104). Formey finds the omnipresence of the pedagogical vocation farfetched; he cannot accept that a minor confidence man is now putting "sinners" to shame with a lecture on their moral legerdemain. He is also incredulous at the vehemence with which the mountebank-turned-preacher blames and humiliates both teacher and student. Recently, Robert Ellrich has acknowledged that Formey generally has some justification, but has explained his objections as the result of intellectual myopia: "How many of Rousseau's contemporaries were capable of accepting as valid and useful the self-avowed imaginings of a visionary?" (p. 52).

It is hardly surprising that Rousseau was not as generous in the face of Formey's criticism. However, his self-defensive attack on Formey's interpretation of the passage is of interest not for its vehemence but for what it reveals about Rousseau's reading of Formey's text. In a copy of the original edition of *Emile* that he annotated in preparation for a new edition, Rousseau added near the beginning and near the end of the episode scornful rebuttals of Formey's objections.[32] Rousseau does not mention the implications of Formey's critique for an interpretation of either the theoretical or the practical value of his work on education. The only point in his adversary's argument to which he is sensitive is the implication that the scene reveals a momentary lack of control on the part of his sometime double, Emile's tutor. His defensive obsession is called into action by one phrase in the commentary, "[Ce Joueur de Gobelets] sermonne gravement son Instituteur," a phrase that implies that the tutor shared in Emile's humiliation. Although he does not say so, Formey clearly believes that the teacher for once had not staged the little play, or at least not all of it. Rousseau's critic takes the *bateleur*'s lecture at face value, and feels that the tutor was just as surprised as his student by the mountebank's sudden apparition. In his defense, it should be noted that this vignette does not explain the extent of the pedagogue's control over the experiment—unlike, for example, the story of the "petit tiran," which is studded with such comments as "tout étoit preparé d'avance" (p. 367). However, it is evident from its context that the episode serves a premeditated pedagogical purpose and that its occurrence at precisely this point in the development of

[32] Rousseau's responses to Formey's *Anti-Emile* are included in the footnotes to the Pléiade edition, and they are reprinted in the main body of the text in many editions.

Emile is not accidental. The vignette is prefaced by four sentences describing teacher and student's ongoing experimentation with magnets, and its conclusion is signaled by a transitional passage explaining how everything learned from the mountebank's act can contribute to Emile's education. The passage begins "le tout pour nous faire une boussole qui nous tienne lieu de méridienne" (p. 440).

Yet during the episode's peripetia the tutor genuinely seems to share in his pupil's disappointments—his narrative detachment, as we have seen, is far from complete. And he appears truly a victim of the turn of events Formey finds most problematic, the *bateleur*'s reprimand of the pair. Indeed, the confidence man reserves his harshest criticism for the teacher: "En sortant il m'addresse à moi nommément et tout haut une réprimande. J'excuse volontiers, me dit-il, cet enfant; il n'a péché que par ignorance. Mais vous, Monsieur, qui deviez connoître sa faute, pourquoi la lui avoir laissé faire?" (p. 440). The tutor even seems genuinely distraught after the lecture: "Il part et nous laisse tous deux très-confus" (p. 440). He therefore uses to characterize his own reaction the adjective he always evokes at moments of pedagogical humiliation: the "petit tiran," for example, returns home "confus" (p. 368). In fact, the only phrase that could be seen as hinting at the narrator-pedagogue's complicity in all aspects of the elaborate scenario is found near the end as part of his apostrophe on the utility of the episode to a "jeune maître": "Que d'apprets, direz-vous!" (p. 440). In his discussion of the passage, Ellrich provides evidence to support Formey's reading. He affirms that all the readers of *Emile* whose opinions he had solicited confirmed the premise on which Formey based his commentary (pp. 53-54). None of them felt that the tutor had arranged for the episode's outcome, a reaction my own pedagogical experience substantiates. Rousseau's vehement rebuttal, if integrated into the main body of the text as in many editions, actually renders parts of the passage almost incomprehensible.

Rousseau takes on his adversary Formey with the same tone of aggressive mockery he introduces into his addresses to the future reader of *Emile:*[33] "Je n'ai pu m'empêcher de rire en lisant une fine critique de M. de Formey sur ce petit conte" (4: 1420, variant *a* to p. 437). He then attacks this reader on exactly the same grounds on which he always bases his angry dismissal of the imaginary reader—Formey is not competent to judge this text, because he evidently needs everything spelled out for him and is incapable of interpreting narrative subtleties:

> Le spirituel M. de Formey n'a pu supposer que cette petite scene étoit arrangée et que le bâteleur étoit instruit du rolle qu'il avoit à faire; car c'est en effet ce que je n'ai point dit. Mais combien de fois, en revanche, ai-je déclaré que je n'écrivois point pour les gens à qui il faloit tout dire? (p. 1420)

The addendum Rousseau prepared for the end of the episode continues this argument:

> Ai-je dû supposer quelque lecteur assez stupide pour ne pas sentir dans cette reprimande un discours dicté mot-à-mot par le Gouverneur pour aller à ses vues? A-t-on dû me supposer assez stupide moi-même pour donner naturellement ce langage à un bâteleur? Je croyois avoir fait preuve au moins du talent assez médiocre de faire parler les gens dans l'esprit de leur état. Voyez encore la fin de l'alinea suivant. N'étoit-ce pas tout dire pour tout autre que M. Formey? (p. 1421, variant *a* to p. 440)

For Rousseau, this affirmation that the *joueur de gobelets*'s role was a fiction and that the mountebank was an actor repeating a part composed for him by the tutor is a revelation that invalidates Formey's objections. He understands the cri-

---

[33] The hostile dialogue Rousseau develops with his reader-to-be repudiates the reader either on the grounds of hypothetical literal-mindedness or incompetence, or because of equally hypothetical differences of opinion with regard to *Emile:* "S'il faut tout vous dire, ne me lisez point . . ."; "[J]e sens bien que vous et moi ne verrons jamais mon Emile sous les mêmes traits. . . ."(4: 387, 637).

CHAPTER IV

tique as pertinent only to the passage's mimetic value. Furthermore, he feels he can dismiss it by insisting that the charlatan cannot be judged as an unrealistic confidence man, since the confidence man was acting as the tutor's representative. Any related moral issue, such as the function of such pronounced humiliation in "le monde des Emiles," is submerged by what is for Rousseau the only annoying question, that of the precise determination of humiliation's genealogy, including the central distinction between perpetrator and victim of the humiliation. "Cette humiliation, ces disgraces, sont donc de ma façon et non pas de celle du Bâteleur" (p. 1421 , variant *b* to p. 440). Humiliation, like madness, is pedagogically profitable and therefore pedagogically admissible, as long as it is under the control of "un homme habile," or the ideal pedagogue. This observation is confirmed by "la fin de l'alinea suivant" that Rousseau evokes as a proof of Formey's misreading. The paragraph in question leads to a remark about the future evolution of the relationship between the tutor and Emile that concludes "il faut tout prévoir, et tout prévoir de fort loin" (p. 440). Rousseau's ideal reader, seeing this, would realize that the phrase was intended to "tout dire." He would see that this pedagogue would never allow any situation to get out of control, that the power of the teacher's vision was such that he saw everything, and saw it "de fort loin."

In the face of such myopic dissections of a (mis)reading, it may seem excessive to point out that Rousseau actually answered not Formey's critique but his own interpretation of that critique, that he reacted so violently to Formey's critique because he projected into it his fears of the most threatening objection possible. Rousseau's interpretation of Formey's interpretation reveals that his dominant concern in these pedagogical vignettes was to stress his tutor's (and therefore by implication Rousseau's own) control over all rival forces, whether a rebellious child or a pedagogically inclined charlatan. Furthermore, the stridency of Rousseau's self-defense does not manage to erase the possibility that the *joueur de gobelets*'s intervention is actually a *clinamen* illustrative of the

158

uncontrollable forces at work within the pedagogical enterprise.

In my own readings of *Emile*, I have tried to stay as close to the text as possible, even at the risk of seeming interested only in criticizing Rousseau (through his narrator) because of his cruel manipulations of a fictive pupil. I have stressed the tutor's obsession with keeping his student in line because of the light his compulsion throws on Rousseau's conception of the pedagogical act. At the time of its publication, *Emile* was widely condemned as a dangerous work. This censure was almost exclusively inspired by the presence in it of the Vicaire savoyard's profession of faith, a passage whose theological implications were considered immensely threatening. Of course, this condemnation has not stood the test of time, any more than the criticism of *La Nouvelle Héloïse* because of the initially illicit relationship between Julie and Saint-Preux. However, I would argue that, like Julie's seduction, the Vicaire's religious pronouncements serve to camouflage the implications of *Emile* that today could be considered far more unsettling. The lessons of practical pedagogy in *Emile* illustrate the defensiveness of the tutor-Rousseau's pedagogical vision. In *Emile*, the pedagogue teaches through humiliation, sudden reversals, table turning. The pupil learns only after he has been put on the spot, for teaching is always teaching a lesson and, implicitly if not explicitly, an act of revenge, as if every pupil deserved punishment to atone for the original rebellion of a nameless prototype of the "petit tiran." This teaching is a response to a fear of the loss of control, a loss of control that could put the teacher in danger of humiliation in the presence of the tyrant he had intended to subjugate. Like every defensive construction, the pedagogical act thus conceived stands as an obstacle for all those who come into its path, both students who will be taught according to its rules and would-be teachers who are inspired by its model: it is at the origin of their future deviations.

In the anecdote just discussed, the tutor chooses the mountebank as a pedagogical model: "Nous abordons avec un profond respect nôtre bâteleur-Socrate" (p. 440). Thus in the play's last act, he makes its star a reincarnation of the archetypal teacher, a teacher who, like the tutor, employed devious means to turn the tables on his interlocutor-pupil at the end of the lesson. Prior to this moment, the narrator uses a series of names to refer to the future Socrates figure: *joueur de gobelets, sorcier* (by implication only, the word not being in Emile's vocabulary), and *bateleur*. The master of the shell game has the opportunity to become a master teacher and perhaps even to teach Emile's teacher a lesson because he has followed the tutor's (Socratic) practice of keeping his best tricks in reserve: "Si je ne vous ai pas d'abord montré mes coups de maitre, c'est qu'il ne faut pas se presser d'étaler étourdiment ce qu'on sait; j'ai toujours soin de conserver mes meilleurs tours pour l'occasion" (p. 439). The decision to make a charlatan a model pedagogue (even if he is only acting the part) might seem scandalous. When the implications of this gesture are considered, the reader realizes that Formey accidentally put his finger on the pulse of this work. He called the *bateleur* "un individu du monde des Emiles." The confidence man could in fact be seen as the figure who best represents *Emile*'s truest implications. He plays the "bâteleur-Socrate" to the tutor's pedagogue-*escamoteur*. Both depend for their success on feats of legerdemain. Both make a regular use of red herrings: there is not always a pea under every shell lifted in the course of *Emile*'s lessons. Above all, both are masters of camouflage: like the *joueur de gobelets* who hides his magnet in a piece of bread and the metal in a wax duck, the tutor disguises his motives and intentions.

The confidence man's ultimate secret weapon, the means by which he (apparently) puts the tutor and his pupil to shame ("ce secret qui vous a tant embarrassés," [p. 439]), is a secret Emile's teacher should have been able to uncover, because it is the perfect fulfillment of all the technical deviousness they have in common. "Alors il nous montre sa machine, et nous voyons avec la derniere surprise qu'elle ne consiste qu'en un aimant fort et bien armé, qu'un enfant caché sous la table faisoit mouvoir sans qu'on s'en apperçut" (p. 439). In the anecdote, each master teacher has a child. The tutor leaves the miniature of himself out in the open, lets his hand show and does not keep his forces in reserve. The professional *escamoteur* keeps the scale model of himself hidden just as Louis XIV guarded Vauban's scale models, and because he keeps his *infans in machina,* he wins the right to deliver the final sermon. The child hidden under the table is an unsettling emblem for *Emile.* He could represent the master teacher's realization of his dependency on both the child's help and his wiles, of the complicity between master and miniature. He could also represent the master's decision to suppress those realizations because they are too threatening to his mastery. If *Emile*'s author allowed his tutor to be outtalked by a confidence man, it was only because the *bateleur*'s legerdemain could be held up as a model for the aspiring pedagogue.

═══ ✳ ═══

Julie: The Well-ordered House

Je suis seule au milieu de tout le monde.
Rousseau, Julie

Formey drove *Emile*'s author to a frenzied defensive aggression by intimating to Rousseau that Emile's tutor temporarily lost control of the educational enterprise. At key moments in *La Nouvelle Héloïse,* the specter of pedagogical impotence casts a long shadow over the story of Julie d'Etange/de Wolmar. Teaching in *Julie* is a form of determination, the means by which characters try to seduce others into accepting the novel's moral universe as a beneficent one. This teaching aims to convert the student by controlling his or her response. However, that goal of nonerotic seduction is rarely, if ever, reached, since the central acts of teaching end in an *écart* veering into madness.

161

The rise and fall of the novel's original and only professional teacher, Saint-Preux, can be used to illustrate one variant of this pedagogical loss of control. Initially, Saint-Preux bears a certain resemblance to a familiar type of hero, the young man whose arrival throws havoc into the calm routine of happy family life, a young man who, à la Lovelace, sets his will in opposition to the father's and fights the paternal plan for the daughter's future. The novel's title establishes Julie as a reincarnation of Heloise and, by implication, the role of Abelard is reserved for Saint-Preux in Rousseau's reenactment of the medieval story of ill-fated love. Saint-Preux may condemn Abelard as vigorously as he pleases—"Abelard ne m'a jamais paru qu'un misérable digne de son sort, et connoissant aussi peu l'amour que la vertu" (1: 24: 85)—but he begins his career in Rousseau's novel by retracing the logician's road to calamity. In the early stages of *Julie*, the teacher is a corrupt figure, condemned by all participants in the drama of seduction, including Julie, who calls him a "vil séducteur" (1: 4: 39), and the "publisher" himself, who describes his hero as falling just short of being a "scelérat" (1: 24: 85).

However, even at the height of his success as a lover, Saint-Preux demonstrates no ability to dominate the situation, as the successful Rousseauian pedagogue always does. In a perceptive recent analysis of Rousseau's novel, Tony Tanner has argued convincingly that the alleged hero of the "Lettres de deux amans," like the "petit tiran," is actually no more than the "joüet de tout le monde": "I will note now that Saint-Preux is never allowed to initiate any meeting, decide any venue, fix on any abode. His life is entirely shaped and directed by others, starting with Julie."[34] In Tanner's view, "if Saint-Preux was not a masochist at the start, he quickly becomes one" (p. 120). There is ample evidence to support his opinion, even in Saint-Preux's early letters. For example, his first letter is essentially a declaration of love and an attempt to learn if

---

[34] Tanner, *Adultery in the Novel: Contract and Transgression* (Baltimore: Johns Hopkins Univ. Press, 1979), p. 117.

his love is reciprocated by Julie. But the letter also reveals a desire for punishment: "[F]aites-moi refuser votre porte; chassez-moi comme il vous plaira" (1: 1: 32). In his second letter, Saint-Preux discloses what he really means by his request, what he wants—and will get time and again—from Julie: "La seule grace que j'attends de vous est de hâter mon supplice. Contentez une juste vengeance. Est-ce être assés malheureux que de me voir réduit à la solliciter moi-même? Punissez-moi, vous le devez" (1: 2: 36). Saint-Preux's discourse cannot be dismissed as a mere topos, for he lives out fully the masochism inherent in the image of the suffering lover.

Saint-Preux is the most ineffective member of the novel's central quartet. All the forces of authority in the novel conspire to weaken his position. Like Emile, he is a virtual orphan. He is not even allowed to use his real name, the name that could provide a link with his past. The "inséparables" decide to take his name away from him so that no one will know that Julie's lover has returned during her illness: "[N]ous l'avons appellé devant nos gens d'un autre nom que le sien" (3: 14: 332). In a note to this letter, the editor informs us that "On voit dans la quatrieme partie que ce nom substitué étoit celui de *St. Preux*." The information he provides is necessary, for his hero's "real" name or names are so little in evidence that it is possible that a reader, familiar with the appellation "Saint-Preux" from commentaries on the novel, might not realize that it is a pseudonym. Indeed, the only clue hinting at the existence of a prior given name is the hero's signature on the note giving Julie her freedom, "S.G." (3: 11: 327). Likewise, there is only one occasion on which another character confers his false name on him: "Cent fois le bien arrivé, cher St. Preux, car je prétends que ce nom vous demeure, au moins dans notre société" (4: 5: 417). With these words, Claire formally baptizes the heretofore nameless pedagogue with the title that makes him officially a child of the Clarens family—and permanently destroys his right to an independent existence.

In his explanation of his rejection of the man his daughter has chosen for her husband, Julie's father scorns her former teacher as a "quidam" (1: 62: 169). Tanner points out that "*quidam* is precisely . . . an unnamed individual" (p. 138). As far as the father is concerned, Saint-Preux's family did not pass on an acceptable name to him. Finally, as though in a gesture of complicity with these efforts to reduce the teacher to onomastic nothingness, the editor identifies Saint-Preux's letters only by the name of his correspondent; they are marked "A Milord Edouard," "De Julie," "Réponse," and so on. Each of the teacher's letters thus reinscribes another character's name into the text, thereby making of that character a greater onomastic presence, while at the same time reiterating "Saint-Preux's" onomastic absence. This treatment is reserved for Saint-Preux's letters alone, with the result that, as the novel progresses, all the other characters' names become increasingly familiar as they acquire the power taken from the gradually fading pedagogical presence.

Julie's principal characters toy with Saint-Preux onomastically by conferring names upon him and taking his real name away from him. This reduction is reaffirmed by the loss, or rather the removal (in accordance with the Abelard model) of the one-time seducer's sexual powers. Saint-Preux himself brings into play in the novel's power struggle the technique that will later be used against him. The fetishistic objects that are introduced during the period just prior to and just following the consummation of his passion for Julie—especially her portrait by "un peintre en miniature" (2: 24: 290)—are forms of reduction in size. Saint-Preux's recourse to them at this pivotal moment in his relationship with Julie could be interpreted as a defensive reaction against his mistress's increasingly awesome power over those around her. However, once Julie d'Etange becomes Julie de Wolmar, it is her former teacher who is increasingly threatened with miniaturization. In the "monde à l'envers" situation that Clarens provides, the fallen "maître" becomes the "child" (and therefore the pupil) of his former students. In Claire's description: "Toute la différence est que je vous aimois comme mon frere, et qu'à présent je vous aime comme mon enfant; car quoique nous soyons toutes

deux plus jeunes que vous et même vos disciples, je vous
regarde un peu comme le notre" (3: 6: 319). The "inséparables" treat Saint-Preux like (their) adult child, as does the
father of teaching in Rousseau's "utopian" society, Wolmar,
who, as Saint-Preux himself explains, "me parla comme un
pere à son enfant" (4: 6: 423). In *Julie,* the menace of the
"classic" model of pedagogical seduction is suppressed when
the once dangerous teacher becomes a student whose sexuality
is redefined, limited, and brought under control by the more
subtle erotic manipulations of a new, Rousseauian pedagogy.
Reeducation at Clarens effectively completes Saint-Preux's reduction to zero as the shifts of power in *Julie*'s central quartet
consistently act out for his benefit the functioning of the first
equation of Rousseau's arithmetic of persecution. When two
members of the Clarens family form a union—Julie and Claire,
Julie and Wolmar—the former seducer is literally eliminated
by their combined forces. Saint-Preux's early dreams of forming a perfect union with Julie are short-lived, and once they
become impossible, he never learns to build supplemental defenses, to be successful at any form of makeshift addition.

Given his education, it is surprising that Julie's lover is the
victim rather than the instigator of the rites of control that
gradually move life in the Elysian garden toward entropy.
When he writes his young friend to sign him up for a trip
around the world, Milord Edouard reveals that teaching was
not Saint-Preux's first vocation: "[V]ous êtes couché sur l'état
en qualité d'Ingénieur des troupes de débarquement; ce qui
vous convient d'autant mieux que le génie étant votre premiere
destination, je sais que vous l'avez appris dès votre enfance"
(3: 25: 395). Saint-Preux was "destined" to be a military man
and work for the "génie" in fortifications. This profession was
presumably chosen for him by his family, so the strategies of
military defenses represent the only direct link with Saint-
Preux's genealogy revealed in the novel. Rousseau originally
intended to leave a reminder of his hero's formation in his
speech. In a passage eliminated from a letter by Claire to Julie
on the use of coquetry as a defense of virtue (6: 5: 661), the

cousin was to have included a citation from Saint-Preux in which Julie's former teacher sounds like a forerunner of Valmont or a successor to the Sun King:

Rien, dit Saint-Preux, ne forme mieux un ingénieur que d'attaquer ou défendre des places fortes où les premieres approches se font de tres loin. Mais qu'apprend-on dans celles qui ne valent pas qu'on y perde son temps, dans celles qu'il ne faut que sommer de se rendre et qu'on enlève ou qu'on laisse du premier moment. Un guerrier doit être plus en garde contre les surprises qu'une jolie femme de bien. (p. 1759, variant *b* to p. 661)

Even if the overt imprint of its origin is ultimately erased from the ex-fortifier's speech, his student is nonetheless sensitive to its defensive slant. Early in their pedagogical relationship, Julie teases Saint-Preux about his use of literature as "rampart" (1: 25: 87). And in the last letter of their correspondence (excepting the deathbed note Wolmar sends for her), Mme de Wolmar still insists that aggression motivates even her former teacher's friendly dialogue:

[V]ous faites avec vos amis dans la dispute comme avec votre adversaire aux échecs, vous attaquez en vous défendant. Vous vous excusez d'être philosophe en m'accusant d'être dévote. (6: 7: 692)

Julie's analysis highlights a pattern recurrent in Saint-Preux's letters. She describes a variant of the *tu quoque* defense in which an individual throws back at his aggressor not the original accusation but a related one. When her former teacher interprets her remark as an attack, he obliges her to return his aggression. Saint-Preux's aggressiveness serves as his only defense against the reduction to zero with which he is threatened.

Saint-Preux must be eliminated as a real force so that two relationships can come to dominate the redemptive part of Rousseau's novel: Julie's and Claire's friendship and Julie's and Wolmar's marriage. In a reversal parallel to that with which Emile's tutor is menaced by the mountebank's intervention, Julie's first pedagogue is supplanted by new teachers. The other main characters can orchestrate this reversal because their defenses are far more efficient than Saint-Preux's haphazard *tu quoque* thrusts. Collectively, Julie, Wolmar, and Claire appear to have life at Clarens under their control to such an extent that the perfect system of defenses has become a reality in their utopia. It is difficult to determine the chain of command in their triumvirate. The manner in which Wolmar exercises his authority may be distinguished from both Julie's and Claire's manipulations, for it is always discreet (camouflaged) and generally oblique. For example, he is credited with the development of the pedagogical system enforced at Clarens, but it is his wife who describes the system and puts it into practice. Despite (or perhaps because of) this devious discretion, Wolmar could be viewed as the ultimate figure of authority in the novel, a hypothesis I will consider shortly. However, before examining Wolmar's role, I want to explore the bond between the "inséparables."

In a well-considered violation of the union this adjective designates, certain critics have insisted on separating Claire from Julie. Their decision to single out the "inséparable" previously left in Julie's shadow has produced some of the most provocative recent interpretations of Rousseau's novel. Hans Wolpe centers his reading of *Julie* on Claire, and the viewing angle he selects for his study has also been adopted to some extent by Tanner. Most recently, Janet Todd has taken this point of view on *Julie* to its logical conclusion. Wolpe's contention that the novel is psychologically "ambiguous" is largely based on his reading of Claire's presence during *Julie*'s key moments—at the scene of the first kiss, for example, during which the cousin's presence becomes more than voyeuristic attendance on the two lovers when it is she, and not the lover Saint-Preux, who supports the fainting Julie in her arms (Wolpe, p. 284). Both Wolpe and Todd interpret Claire's tenacious presence during the lovers' trysts, the obsessive concern she exhibits throughout the novel for perfect knowledge of Julie's whereabouts, the events surrounding Julie's death, and the work's final letter from Claire to Saint-Preux as indications that Julie and Claire were inseparable because they were more than friends. Todd describes Claire as anything but what her name suggests, as *Julie*'s equivalent of the mountebank's hidden child, "a sort of *dea ex machina* of the plot."[35] Wolpe sees the gesture by which Claire brings Julie's story to a close as "the triumph of ambiguity" with Claire as "its protagonist" (p. 287).

The strangeness of what Todd has aptly called Claire's "brooding presence" (p. 137) in Rousseau's novel is undeniable. Her "inseparable" union with her cousin constitutes an obstacle that stands not only between Julie and her lover, but also between Julie and her husband—it is Claire, after all, who removes the mark of Julie and Wolmar's union when she speaks of "Julie d'Etange" in her last letter. Claire's many ambiguous statements complicate the traditional reading of her friendship with Julie. For example, she writes to the enigmatic M. d'Orbe before their marriage: "[J]e suis en femme une espece de monstre, et je ne sais par quelle bizarrerie de la nature l'amitié l'emporte en moi sur l'amour" (1: 64: 179). Claire is "en femme une espece de monstre," although not simply because Julie is dearer to her than her husband. The "inseparable" cousin can be called monstrous because she is constantly lurking in Julie's shadow, as though to vampirize her cousin's strength. Furthermore, she herself is a force that constantly threatens to burst out of control: Claire frequently refers to herself as "folle," and she often reminds her reader of her first teacher, Chaillot's, warnings about her "madness" (1: 7: 45, for example). What is most disturbing about the cousins' "inseparable" relationship is that it is never defined. Janet Todd provides ample evidence to support her view that it cannot be held up as a model of a disinterested, supportive

---

[35] Todd, *Women's Friendship in Literature* (New York: Columbia Univ. Press, 1980), p. 141. See also pp. 133, 137, 143, 167.

women's friendship. And yet that is just what it was apparently taken to be by the legions of women who were allegedly Rousseau's most ardent early readers—and for good reason, since that is just what Rousseau wants it to be taken for. "The whole force of illusion of the characters in *La Nouvelle Héloïse*," Wolpe contends, "is founded on this subtle psychology that appears so straightforward, on this ambiguity that assumes the semblance of clarity" (pp. 289-90).

"Cynical" readings like Tanner's, Todd's, and Wolpe's propose a view of the novel as an Elysium controlled by voyeurism and manipulation. Yet Wolpe and Todd exaggerate the centrality of Claire's manipulative force. Their readings do not take the evidence of the "mad" cousin's weakness into account. Claire suffers the same fate as Saint-Preux after his fall. As she explains it to Julie, her miniaturization is a denial of adult sexuality: "[L]'ame a-t-elle un sexe? En vérité, je ne le sens guere à la mienne. Je puis avoir des fantaisies, mais fort peu d'amour" (2: 5: 206). In the Clarens family, Claire remains a child, capable of having sexual fantasies, and of being their object, but incapable of sexual love. She both perceives herself and is perceived as sexually prepubescent. She even denies her past sexual reproduction by giving her child to another, more rational mother. Claire does indeed, as Todd points out, keep constant watch over Julie's movements, but she does so not in order to control those movements, but in order to serve Julie's supreme authority. She is a self-styled "garde de Sesostris" (4: 2: 410), the first exterior line of defense around what she perceives to be the defensive control center of their paradise. This is a major difference between Claire and Saint-Preux, the two adult children in Elysium. Whereas the former teacher's reduction is beyond his control, Claire is actually an accomplice of the individual who, from the beginning of the novel, rules over the miniaturized adults.

Claire herself is the first to give credit where credit is due and point to Julie as the source of her power. Thus she writes to her cousin:

C'est que ton coeur vivifie tous ceux qui l'environnent et leur donne pour ainsi dire un nouvel être dont ils sont forcés de lui faire hommage, puis-qu'ils ne l'auroient point eu sans lui. . . . Ne sais-tu pas que tout ce qui t'approche est par toi-même armé pour ta deffense, et que je n'ai par dessus les autres que l'avantage des gardes de Sesostris, d'être de ton âge et de ton sexe, et d'avoir été élevée avec toi? (3: 2: 409-10)

Here Claire credits her cousin's example with redemptive force: her influence over those who come into her sphere of influence is so great that she can give them new life ("vivifier") and even a new being, a new self. Claire attributes the origin and the motivation of Julie's powers to "[l]es charmes de la vertu et [l]es douceurs de l'amitié" (p. 410). In the novel's second preface, the "man of letters" with whom the "publisher" dialogues suggests that its heroine, like *Emile*'s mountebank, is a conjuror who can perform feats of sorcery: "Cette Julie, telle qu'elle est, doit être une créature enchanteresse; tout ce qui l'approche doit lui ressembler; tout doit devenir Julie autour d'elle" (p. 28).

Early in the novel, Claire attempts to help Julie understand her influence on those around her, and this formulation of the workings of Julie's power reveals the ambiguity of what Claire later calls her strength of "virtue" and "friendship."

Voila ce qui doit arriver à toutes les ames d'une certaine trempe; elles transforment pour ainsi dire les autres en elles-mêmes; elles ont une sphere d'activité dans laquelle rien ne leur resiste: on ne peut les connoitre sans les vouloir imiter, et de leur sublime élévation elles attirent à elles tout ce qui les environne. C'est pour cela, ma chere, que ni toi ni ton ami ne connoitrez peut-être jamais les hommes; car vous les verrez bien plus comme vous les ferez, que comme ils seront d'eux-mêmes. Vous donnerez le ton à tous ceux qui vivront avec vous; ils vous fuiront ou vous deviendront semblables, et tout ce que vous aurez vu n'aura peut-être rien de pareil dans le reste du monde. (2: 5: 204)

Claire's evaluation provides a perceptive analysis of Julie's role in the novel. This "créature enchanteresse" beguiles all those who come near her and attracts them into her sphere of influence. Within this sphere her charms are nearly irresistible. Julie controls those near her by assimilating them, by submerging their separate identities. More successful than *Emile*'s model, Circe (*Emile*, p. 869), Julie yields to no one's wiles, is able to transform all those around her, and even to transform them all according to the same pattern, making them over in her likeness.

Julie's obsessive need to control the collective sexual life of the Elysium community appears yet more disturbing in light of Claire's remarks. At key moments, she binds herself, Claire, and Saint-Preux together until their union creates a human syzygy, a configuration in which the three characters "lie" in a straight line so that, as when the earth and the moon are in conjunction with the sun, one character obstructs our view of the two others. They act out romantic vignettes that surprise even many readers who are able to take the novel as a whole at face value. Julie stages these passion plays with as much care as the master teacher uses to plan Emile's lessons. For example, her direction of the scene of the first kiss substantiates the tutor's motto: "il faut tout prévoir, et tout prévoir de fort loin" (4: 440). At the end of a letter to her amorous pedagogue, Julie announces that "je destine une petite surprise à mon ami" (1: 14: 63). She then assembles her cast of characters: "je dois vous prévenir que nous n'irons point ensemble dans le bosquet sans l'*inséparable cousine*." Claire's presence at the lovers' tryst is indeed strange, but she cannot be held responsible for it, since Julie orders her to be there. Once the trio is (safe) inside the natural enclosure of the most charming of arbors, a ritualized kissing ceremony takes place. Claire asks for and receives the first kiss, then Julie completes their teacher's consternation by locking him in still another em-

CHAPTER IV

brace. Through all of this, Saint-Preux takes no initiative. He is no more than the cousins' plaything: "Mais que devins-je un moment apres, quand je sentis . . . la bouche de Julie . . . se poser, se presser sur la mienne, et mon corps serré dans tes bras?" (p. 64). At this key moment in the seduction for which he will later be held responsible, Saint-Preux may talk of being "on fire" with passion, but he is so under his student's control that he allows himself to be passively squeezed in her arms rather than violate the line Julie has traced for his conduct. "It is all rather like the kissing games played at children's parties," according to Tanner's apt formulation, "as if Julie wants to defuse sexuality by infantilizing it" (p. 114). The future mistress of Clarens succeeds in making Saint-Preux a very docile seducer indeed.

The interlude comes to an abrupt end when Julie faints (in Claire's arms), a sudden *clinamen* that is difficult to interpret. Her swoon is clearly not to be confused with the usually feigned tactic of submission to seduction that is a cliché of eighteenth-century fiction: Rousseau obviously means this faint to be real. It is hard to imagine that Julie, who normally orchestrates such events so thoroughly, could suddenly lose control of the scene she has been flawlessly directing. Her fainting spell may not represent a real loss of control, since it provides the only easy way out of the situation. Saint-Preux could have been expected to come to life sooner or later and attempt to take a more active role in this seduction. By fainting, Julie ensures that her plaything cannot escape her domination. She maintains to the end her position as the absolute *dea* in the *machina* she has created and she also guarantees her escape from that *machina* at the appropriate time. Of course, Julie's faint can also be viewed as an involuntary reaction to a situation whose complexity has grown beyond her original estimate of its ramifications. This initial loss of control is emblematic of all subsequent moments in Rousseau's novel when the new kind of teacher Julie represents is unable to retain complete mastery over the pedagogical act.

Julie continues to orchestrate the remaining stages of her

involvement with Saint-Preux. Tanner has analyzed the emasculation implicit in the intricate scenario she devises for the key moment of her seduction, the night Saint-Preux spends in her room (pp. 120-23). Throughout their courtship, Julie's conduct with regard to her teacher-become-lover is always marked by the detachment necessary to command him to come and go at will. Saint-Preux qualifies one of the occasions on which she orders him out of her life, acting as cooly as the tutor separating Emile and Sophie, as "un rafinement de cruauté" (1: 16: 66). At no point is her detachment from the affairs of the heart more unsettling than at the moment when Julie de Wolmar decides that she should arrange the marriage of her former lover to her widowed cousin. What she is in fact proposing is an arrangement that would grant her complete and perpetual control over the pair. By offering him Claire, she has finally found a solution whereby she can continue to dominate Saint-Preux's life as completely as if they were still lovers. She is really proposing her cousin to him in name only, for as she points out: "N'est-ce pas aussi Julie que je vous donne?" (6: 6: 670). The mistress of Clarens has so successfully assimilated her cousin that Claire can be offered as a surrogate Julie.

For Julie, it is not enough to dispose of the lives of all the children of Clarens; she reshapes their physical environment as well. Like all utopias (etymologically, "paradise" means "circumvallation," "walled-in park"), Clarens is sealed off from the outside world. Starobinski has studied its self-sufficient economy (*La Transparence et l'obstacle*, especially pp. 134-36). In the micro-society the Wolmars create there, only homemade products are permitted, because everything produced outside their control is viewed with suspicion: "Comme tout ce qui vient de loin est sujet à être déguisé ou falsifié, nous nous bornons, par delicatesse autant que par modération au choix de ce qu'il y a de meilleur aupres de nous et dont la qualité n'est pas suspecte" (5: 2: 550). Wolmar plays an important role in assuring the economic stability of their Elysium, but the tasks that require the most obsessive attention to detail and systematization, from the disposition of the garden to the selection and the distribution of the incredible variety of imitation wines served after their meals, are inevitably assigned to the domain of the mistress of the gynaeceum. Once they enter the magnetic field of Julie's sphere of influence, all problems, however humble, are dissected, ordered, and catalogued in the best Vaubanian spirit. So thorough is Julie in her obsession with keeping her house in order that Clarens has been compared to the fiefs over which Sade's heroes rule with undisputed power (Tanner, note, p. 153). Due to the encyclopedic nature of her labors, Julie can even be said to achieve a degree of omnipotence unequalled by the lords of Silling and Sade's other châteaux. Julie rules over a miniature world of a complexity and sophistication that far surpass those attained by the more savage *bricoleurs,* Robinson Crusoe and Emile.

Julie's garden, the Elysium, is a paradise within a paradise, an enclosure totally under her devious control. An examination of the technical arsenal Julie deploys in her garden reveals that, following the model of the Chinese garden, reduction in size is the basic technique used in Julie's Elisée. Technically, one of the principal ways in which Chinese gardens are different from French and Italian gardens, the alleged enemies of her *locus amoenus,* is precisely by their use of miniaturization. As André Haudricourt points out:

> Si l'on [in Chinese gardens] veut avoir des plantes de petites dimensions, au lieu d'agir directement en les taillant, on agit indirectement, pour obtenir des plantes naines. L'action directe semble donc aboutir à l'artifice, l'action indirecte apparaît comme un retour à la nature.[36]

A garden with the *appearance* of a return to nature—what could be more in the spirit of Julie's horticultural goals? However, Saint-Preux's description of the Chinese gardens he vis-

[36] Haudricourt, "Domestication des animaux, culture des plantes, et traitement d'autrui," *L'Homme* 2 (1962): 42-43.

ited during his travels tends to abolish the possibility of this comparison:

[J]'ai vu à la Chine des jardins . . . faits avec tant d'art que l'art n'y paroissoit point, mais d'une maniere si dispendieuse et entretenus à si grands fraix que cette idée m'ôtoit tout le plaisir que j'aurois pu goûter à les voir. . . . On n'y voyoit à la vérité ni belles allées ni compartimens réguliers; mais on y voyoit entassées avec profusion des merveilles qu'on ne trouve qu'éparses et séparées. La nature s'y présentoit sous mille aspects divers, et le tout ensemble n'étoit point natural. (4: 11: 484)

Saint-Preux's principal criticism of the Chinese garden stems from its miniaturization of nature: all the natural beauties it contains could not be found naturally in one place. Yet even he is surprised by the number and the variety of plants in Julie's "*prétendu* verger"—and how could he help but be, since he notes in it "massifs, grands berceaux, touffes pendantes, bosquets bien ombragés . . . serpolet, baume, thim, marjolaine et d'autres herbes odorantes, *mille* fleurs des champs, quelques unes de jardin" (pp. 472-73, emphasis mine)—and the list is far from complete? With the exception of excessive cost and maintenance, which Julie is careful to avoid, all Saint-Preux's objections to the Chinese garden could be extended to Julie's garden: it, too, is "fait avec tant d'art que l'art n'y paroissoit point," and no more than in the Sun King's lavish floral displays, "le tout ensemble n'étoit point naturel." Chinese gardens are the horticultural equivalent of the Great Wall. When Saint-Preux rejects any resemblance between the Elisée and these fortified gardens, his denial, like Vauban's denial of his desire for invulnerability, only calls attention to Rousseau's gardeners' quest for invincibility. Julie forbids the use of any foreign products at Clarens on the grounds that they can be "suspected" of being "disguised" and "adulterated." Yet the theoretician and builder of the Elysian garden falsifies and camouflages all the elements that compose her "prétendu

CHAPTER IV

verger." What is disguised by her hand is evidently no longer suspicious. Whatever is under Julie's control cannot threaten the stability of her utopia.

On his island, Emile's model, Robinson Crusoe, uses book-keeping to put his mind at ease with regard to the inconsistencies in his spiritual life. Within her more civilized enclosure, Julie also turns to the techniques of bookkeeping to manage nature as she would a general store. The main difference between the way Julie controls nature for her garden and the way it is controlled in the Classical French gardens she attacks so vehemently is that her manipulations are more devious: "L'erreur des prétendus gens de goût est de vouloir de l'art par tout, et de n'être jamais contens que l'art ne paroisse; au lieu que c'est à le cacher que consiste le veritable goût; surtout quand il est question des ouvrages de la nature" (4: 11: 482). Like the gardens of Versailles, the Elysium is calculated to control the viewer's response, but the viewer is more likely to fall victim to its manipulations than to more overt ones, since all traces of management have been eliminated. Robinson Crusoe externalizes internal problems in order to suppress their potential for disturbance. The mistress of Clarens domesticates nature and external forces by bringing them into her personal sphere of influence. As a result, her garden construct is stamped with the trace of a hidden presence that, like the child under the table, signals its mistress's flawless control: Julie's carefully erased fingerprints are invisible on every inch of her domain.

Julie puts her varied domestic activities as landscape architect, wine steward, and so on, at the service of her permanent vocation, pedagogy. Eternally "la prêcheuse," Julie is only too willing to explain to any member of the Clarens community (primarily to Saint-Preux, since he maintains a correspondence with the outside world) the code governing each system and the lesson to be learned from the Elysian model for the general good. However, in the area most directly related to Julie's pedagogical vocation, the reader has only rare glimpses of the application of her authority. Her role as mother of two sons is surprisingly undeveloped. One of the boys even remains nameless. In a novel whose principal characters stress the educational value of all their actions, little is made of the instruction of the Wolmar children. On the rare occasions when the reader does have the opportunity to observe Julie working on her sons' education, it is evident that her pedagogical techniques have much in common with both those of Emile's tutor and the methods of containment Julie herself uses to domesticate foreign elements. For example, Julie describes at some length how she tries to inspire in her eldest son the desire to read (her formulation is more passive than mine: "[C]omment lui est venu le goût d'apprendre à lire" [5: 3: 581]). She writes tales especially tailored to his concerns and uses every means possible to heighten his interest in her readings of them. Then she takes him off guard, just as she did Saint-Preux in the bower: "[Q]uand je le voyois le plus avidement attentif, je me souvenois quelquefois d'un ordre à donner, et je le quittois à l'endroit le plus intéressant en laissant négligemment le livre" (p. 582). All those who could have continued the child's pleasure are in on the plot—everyone he turns to has been instructed to refuse to read to him. At last, someone suggests "secretly" that he should learn to read for himself. He likes this idea, and searches for a teacher, but his troubles are not over yet. His search, too, is transformed into a "nouvelle difficulté qu'on n'a poussée qu'aussi loin qu'il faloit." In Julie's opinion, this complex scenario serves as an illustration of a purely natural educational model:

> C'est ainsi que livrés au penchant de leur coeur, sans que rien le déguise ou l'altere, nos enfans ne reçoivent point une forme extérieure et artificielle, mais conservent exactement celle de leur caractere originel. (p. 584)

Yet the criticism reserved by Saint-Preux for Chinese gardens could also be applied to the teaching methods favored by the mistress of Clarens, for Julie's child is educated, just as a Chinese garden is laid out, by means of indirection that masquerades as a return to nature's ways. He is the plaything of a so-called "natural" method in which there is so much art and so much artifice that, to borrow Saint-Preux's expression, "le tout ensemble n'étoit point naturel."

Throughout Rousseau's narrative of her life, Julie can be observed trying to pull everything she wants or needs from the world outside her being into her sphere of influence. Cousin and ex-lover become infantilized extensions of Julie's defensive system—"tout ce qui t'approche est par toi-même armé pour ta deffense" (p. 410). "This enormous book," Tanner argues convincingly, "is for the greater part concerned with an extensive dream of union whereby the family house can be extended and modified so as to contain within it everyone (and everything) that Julie loves" (p. 178). Julie shares with her creator a belief in the total union of utopian mathematics. Early in their correspondence, she explains to Saint-Preux just how perfect their alliance is, by means of a comparison inspired by a pedagogical experiment common to her education and Emile's: "Le sort pourra bien nous séparer, mais non pas nous désunir. Nous n'aurons plus que les mêmes plaisirs et les mêmes peines; et comme ces aimans dont vous me parliez, qui ont, dit-on, les mêmes mouvements en différens lieux, nous sentirions les mêmes choses aux deux extrémités du monde" (1: 11: 55). Julie paints for her lover a picture of inseparable union and identity, yet the idealism of her vision is belied by the context of its enunciation. Julie d'Etange waxes eloquent about equality, indeed interchangeability, with a man who is still unnamed and whose letters are identified only as "A Julie." In fact, scarcely a paragraph later in the same letter, Julie overtly moves to establish herself as *prima inter pares:* "Je voudrois que vous pussiez sentir combien il est important pour tous deux que vous vous en remettiez à moi du soin de notre destin commun. . . . [J]'ai les mêmes intérêts que vous et un peu plus de raison pour les conduire" (p. 55).

The driving force in Julie's existence is a desire for union even more impossible than the cohabitation of one body by two souls Rousseau yearns for in the *Confessions.* Julie attempts to blend everyone and everything dear to her into one interconnected, indivisible, interchangeable mass. Yet her dream is never realized, if for no other reason than because of her own refusal to undergo the loss of self necessary to make such a blending possible. In the "total" union, Julie's "one" is always dominant. The mistress of Clarens gives up no ground: her partner comes to her. Thus Claire describes the way she yields to her cousin: "Ton empire est le plus absolu que je connoisse. . . . [T]u m'en imposes, tu me subjugues, tu m'atterres, ton génie écrase le mien, et je ne suis rien devant toi" (4: 2: 409). Julie's enforcement of her dream of unity reveals its complicity with the equation of persecution. Ultimately, both mathematical operations perform the same function, the subtraction of one element. Rousseau alleges that the members of any plot reduce their victim to zero. An examination of Julie's empire shows that this is also the inevitable result of her much desired unions. This aspect of Julie is perhaps her most revealing similarity with the heroine whose defenses Rousseau so admired, Clarissa Harlowe. Clarissa's sister Belle accuses her of "devaluing" those who come into contact with her, of reducing them to "cyphers."[37] As Claire points out, Julie acts as her own magnet and attracts people to her. Her influence over them is so great that, for all intents and purposes, they cease to exist thereafter: "[J]e ne suis rien devant toi." The mistress of Rousseau's paradise annihilates those closest to her. She also eliminates chance, innovation, unpredictability, surprise—any factor that could be judged suspicious or seen as a threat to the stability and the total calm of life at Clarens. Indeed, Julie's drive to eliminate difference and reduce friction indicates that her utopian vision is motivated by a desire for omnipotence stronger than that which inspires Robinson Crusoe and Rousseau to people their islands.[38] Like

[37] Samuel Richardson, *Clarissa Harlowe,* ed. Sherburn (New York: Riverside, 1962), p. 64.
[38] Even as ardent a proponent of Rousseau's ideas as Germaine de Staël may have been sensitive to the misogyny that fuels her mentor's insistence

Vauban and Sade, Julie tries to make death accountable to a system. The mistress of Clarens strives for a reduction to zero of all forces; her dream of a microcosm that is a family or of a family that is a world unto itself is no life-creating dream, but a powerful act of homage to the death instinct. The novel's last words are reserved for Julie's/*Julie*'s final destructive surge: "son cercueil ne la [Julie] contient pas toute entiere. . . . il attend le reste de sa proye . . . ," a note all the more disquieting because of the ambiguity of the referent of "sa" (6: 13: 745).

The fourth member of the novel's central quartet, Wolmar, is, like the proverbial good child, seen and talked about but seldom heard. The patriarch of Clarens even has others explain his theories in his place. In the governing of their microcosm Wolmar is Julie's *éminence grise,* the hidden child whose magnet creates her magnetic field. It is Wolmar who oversees the economic stability and self-sufficiency of life at Clarens. Husband and wife have in common a devotion to precisely enacted rituals, but during their life together Wolmar serves as high priest, while Julie often seems a mere handmaiden acting out his will. For example, Julie orchestrates the first kiss in the bower. By the time of the "deprofaning" of that bower, the ceremony that reverses and invalidates the original rite, Wolmar has taken charge. The master of Clarens oversees the ritual of the second kiss, using his wife as an actress in his anti-passion play. Michèle Ansart-Dourlen stresses the cruel detachment with which Wolmar plays with the lives of the members of his artificial family when he creates situations designed to transform the relationships among the principal players at Clarens: "La volonté de créer des situations tendues, de susciter le rappel du passé, apparaît explicitement

---

on the tyranny of the mistress of Clarens. Her *Lettre sur les ouvrages et le caractère de J.-J. Rousseau* (Geneva: Slatkine, 1979) reveals that she was troubled by Julie's systematic choice of strategy over sentiment: "Je ne puis supporter . . . la méthode que Julie met quelquefois dans sa passion; enfin tout ce qui, dans ses lettres, semble prouver qu'elle prend d'avance la résolution d'être coupable" (p. 41).

dans les attitudes de Wolmar; il paraît approprié d'évoquer une dimension sadique du personnage."[39] Starobinski argues that Wolmar rules as an "enlightened despot," that, in Rousseau's eyes, the means he employs are justified by the ends he achieves: "Cet ennemi [Rousseau] ... des masques et des voiles, accepte cependant que le maître dissimule la contrainte qu'il exerce en vue d'instaurer dans sa maison l'ordre et la concorde" (*La Transparence et l'obstacle*, p. 125). Such a justification may be faithful to Rousseau's intentions, but it avoids the issue of the effect of Wolmar's particular psychological equivocalness. Like his wife, the patriarch of Clarens is driven by an immense longing for order. When he brings the former lovers back to the scene of the crime, he offers the following description of himself: "Mon seul principe actif est le goût naturel de l'ordre, et le concours bien combiné du jeu de la fortune et des actions des hommes me plait exactement comme une belle simétrie dans un tableau, ou comme une piece bien conduite au théâtre" (4: 12: 490-91). Like the tutor's reference to *Monsieur de Pourceaugnac*, Wolmar's comparisons reveal his awareness of the artifice in the manner in which he tries to arrange human lives as though they were pawns in a chess game or figures in a painting. Julie's portrait of her husband stresses the detachment that allows him to pass judgment on others: "[O]n diroit qu'il n'aime qu'autant qu'il veut aimer et qu'il ne le veut qu'autant que la raison le permet. ... Le plus grand goût de M. de Wolmar est d'observer. Il aime à juger des caracteres des hommes et des actions qu'il voit faire" (3: 20: 370).

In his speech in the sacred and profaned arbor, Wolmar confirms the accuracy of Julie's observation about his own powers of observation. He reveals in his self-portrait a sense of invulnerability and omnipotence rare even in the obsessive microcosms of Rousseau's fiction and worthy indeed of the epithet Sadean:

[39] Ansart-Dourlen, *Dénaturation et violence dans la pensée de Jean-Jacques Rousseau* (Klincksieck, 1975), p. 199, n. 23.

Si j'ai quelque passion dominante c'est celle de l'observation: J'aime à lire dans les coeurs des hommes; comme
le mien me fait peu d'illusion, . . . je ne me trompe guere
dans mes jugemens. . . . Si je pouvois changer la nature
de mon être et devenir un oeil vivant, je ferois volontiers
cet échange. Ainsi mon indifférence pour les hommes ne
me rend point indépendant d'eux, sans me soucier d'en
être vû j'ai besoin de les voir, et sans m'être chers ils me
sont nécessaires. (4: 12: 491)

Wolmar's self-portrait as a "living eye" could be called the
paranoid ur-fantasy: to see all without being seen is the vision
of omnipotence that can put an end to the reductive powers
of all plots. No mere mortals could ever threaten Wolmar's
rule, for the power of his gaze makes everyone else, even Julie,
transparent. He alone remains invisible, unknowable to anyone but himself. Wolmar's self-portrait as living eye reveals
that he has mastered the essence of Louis XIV's fortifications
of secrecy. He is constantly vigilant, never exposed, always
master of his own absent (hollow) presence, worthy of Madeleine de Scudéry's characterization of the Sun King: "[D]e-
puis que le Roy regne on ne l'a jamais vû absent de luy-
même. . . . [N]ôtre Roy, soit dans les perils de la Guerre, dans
les plaisirs de la Paix, dans la douleur, dans la joye, dans les
accidens imprévûs, dans les affaires les plus difficiles, n'a jamais oublié ce qu'il doit à sa propre gloire."[40] Because he
keeps his own "heart" so perfectly defended, Wolmar is the
sole member of the Clarens family whose being remains intact.
He never speaks of union as Julie does for he sees through to
the meaning of her message. The master of Clarens accepts
no merger: "[I]l n'aime qu'autant qu'il veut aimer." He seeks
total control over others, while all the while adding more links
to the fence he has built around himself, perfecting his *pré
carré*.

Wolmar is generally presented obliquely. Other characters

---

[40] M. de Scudéry, *Conversations nouvelles* (Amsterdam: Wetstein and Desbordes, 1685), p. 99.

relate his thought and actions for him; as is fitting for an individual obsessed with his self-protection, he rarely exposes himself to the risks of direct, "live" self-presentation. For example, despite his capacity as supreme pedagogue during the Clarens epoch, Wolmar is shown only once dealing with a child in an educational situation. The scene I have in mind is actually the novel's culminating action, Wolmar's training of Claire's daughter Henriette. Earlier in the novel, Claire does not wait for Julie to assimilate her daughter, but transfers Henriette completely to her cousin's control: "[S]ois dès aujourd'hui la mere de celle qui doit être ta Bru, et pour me la rendre plus chere encore, fais en s'il se peut une autre Julie. Elle te ressemble déja de visage" (4: 9: 439). In fact, Henriette resembles Julie so closely that, after the transfer, strangers always take Julie for her mother (5: 6: 601-2). After Julie's death, Wolmar briefly takes on Henriette's "instruction." For the space of this lesson, Henriette becomes a "new Julie." In an apparent reversal of Julie's magnetic activities, Wolmar orchestrates Henriette's assimilation of Julie's powers. The scene of this transfer of energy is perhaps the most disturbing and equivocal moment in a novel marked to an extraordinary degree by psychological ambiguity.

As Wolmar explains in a letter to Saint-Preux, he attempts to use Henriette as an instrument in a typical Rousseauian teaching play aimed at consoling Claire after her cousin's death:

> Vous savez que sa fille ressemble beaucoup à Madame de Wolmar. Elle se plaisoit à marquer cette ressemblance par des robes de même étoffe, et elle leur avoit apporté de Genève plusieurs ajustemens semblables, dont elles se paroient les mêmes jours. Je fis donc habiller Henriette le plus à l'imitation de Julie qu'il fut possible, et après l'avoir bien instruite, je lui fis occuper à table le troisieme couvert. (6: 11: 739)

At first, Henriette responds perfectly to his teaching:

Henriette, fiere de représenter sa petite Maman, joua
parfaitement son rolle, et si parfaitement que je vis pleu-
rer les domestiques. Cependant elle donnoit toujours à
sa mere le nom de Maman, et lui parloit avec le respect
convenable. (p. 739)

There is, however, one important departure from the usual
structure in this particular teaching vignette: for once, the
child is not a victim, "le joüet de tout le monde," but an actor
toying with the sensibilities of an adult victim. This may explain the conclusion of Wolmar's lesson:

[E]nhardie par le succès, . . . elle s'avisa de porter la main
sur une cuillere et de dire dans une saillie: Claire, veux-
tu de cela? Le geste et le ton de voix furent imités au
point que sa mere en tresaillit.

Far from consoling Claire, the play drives her to the brink of
madness:

. . . elle se mit à manger avec une avidité qui me surprit.
En la considérant avec attention, je vis de l'égarement
dans ses yeux. . . . Je l'empêchai de manger davantage,
et je fis bien; car une heure après elle eut une violente
indigestion. . . . Dès ce moment, je résolus de supprimer
tous ces jeux, qui pouvoient allumer son imagination au
point qu'on n'en seroit plus maitre. (pp. 739-40)

This scene is recounted only five pages before the end of
Rousseau's immense novel and provides therefore one of its
last images, that of teaching gone haywire, out of control. As
the originator of Julie's pedagogical system, Wolmar is the
archetypal teacher of the "redemptive" part of the novel. He
stages a corrective lesson whose every aspect is subject to his
control, from the costumes ("je fis habiller Henriette le plus
à l'imitation de Julie qu'il fut possible") to the acting ("après
l'avoir bien instruite"). The central figure in his production,
his marionette, is designed to remain completely his creature,
for she is a perfect miniature, and therefore both instantly

knowable in her totality and less threatening. Julie herself controlled all others, and through what Claire calls her refusal to see others for what they were, transformed them into reductions of herself. After her death, Wolmar attempts to rechannel and contain her formidable powers. For once, it is not Julie who turns the child into a miniature projection of her desires, but an outside will that imitates her technique of reduction of size, and in the process attempts to control not so much the child being miniaturized, as the child's model Julie, the chief proponent of teaching as *bricolage*. As Lévi-Strauss explains, "la poupée . . . n'est plus un adversaire" (p. 35).

But here, in *Julie*'s last pedagogical vignette, the devious origin of *bricoler* takes its toll with a double swerve in the planned structure of the lesson. Henriette refuses to be confined to her nonspeaking part. She pits her will against Wolmar's and breaks out of his control, at least momentarily. She refuses to be objectified, and her self-assertion constitutes an unsettling swerve beyond the preimposed limits. Henriette's imitation of Julie's gesture and speech is a *clinamen,* a self-defensive reaction of her will against the will attempting to impose its control. She proves that a doll can still constitute a threat.[41] And in this human billiard game, her swerving ball hits another, causing it to swerve in turn. So Claire, too, breaks out of Wolmar's sphere of influence with her own instinctive *clinamen.* Her "violente indigestion" is a concrete sign of the movement, a deviation from physical equilibrium. Wolmar's mastery was designed to relieve her grief; his loss of control brings her, and all involved in the "lesson," to the brink of madness. In Wolmar's account of the scene, the last sentences are curiously vague. After the phrase "sa mere en tresaillit,"

[41] In conjunction with the Henriette vignette, the disturbing quality of the eighteenth-century "child-miniature" paintings already mentioned here ("the Young Painter," etc.) should be noted. Canvases depicting "The Young Woman," that is, a naked child wearing elaborate makeup and jewelry, present images that are as unsettling as the recent advertisements using child-women as models of sophistication.

he uses no further nouns or proper names to help the reader work her way through the maze of "elle" and "la" in his description of female "égarement." This results in a certain confusion, so that at times it seems that the madwoman he is describing is the new Julie. Wolmar's suppression of proper names reflects his sense of a generalization of female madness, and he feels forced to intervene directly to stamp out this madness that threatens Clarens: "[J]e résolus de supprimer tous ces jeux."

Julie's final action is parallel to the encounter with the mountebank in *Emile*. Henriette's intervention, like that of the confidence man for *Emile*, could be viewed as the emblematic scene of *Julie*. In both cases, the pedagogical situation escapes, or at least threatens to escape, the educator's seemingly all-encompassing control. In both cases, evil genius (chance, the unforeseen) comes disguised as a child. Henriette takes on both the roles confided to children in *Emile*. First she acts out Emile's part and strives to break the force of a magnetic field. Julie is described in Claire's last letter as "cette ame encore aimante" (6: 13: 744). The descriptive adjective she chooses is derived from "aimer," but "aimant" recalls the pedagogical experiments with magnetism to which both *Julie* and *Emile* refer. Wolmar's project of using the new Julie to sever the tie binding Claire to the first Julie is thwarted when Henriette abruptly shifts to the role assigned the second child in *Emile*, that of *infans in machina*. Rousseau was outraged at Formey's suggestion that the ultimate move in this pedagogical vignette had escaped the tutor's control. In *Julie*, it is harder to make such an allegation. Wolmar decides to "supprimer tous ces jeux." He also decides to mail Julie's letter to her former teacher, a missive that sets the stage for a last pedagogical act in *Julie*'s drama. But this time the pedagogue will be endowed with new powers, powers that will enable him to keep both Julies under control.

At the novel's close, Saint-Preux's return is imminent. He is charged with the education of Julie and Wolmar's two sons and, of course, of Henriette.[42] He is coming home to Clarens to resume the duties he was forced to abandon so abruptly, and so long before, by Julie's father. In the episode of the little tyrant in *Emile,* the tutor takes revenge on both the rebellious child and his mother, "muni du consentement du pére," and this structure of authority can also be said to characterize the ending of *Julie.* Although in the course of the novel he is rarely portrayed in a paternal role, in its last letter Wolmar is described not as a grieving husband but as a grieving father: "La douleur d'un pere infortuné se concentre en lui-même" (6: 13: 743). Wolmar is more than the father of Julie's children; he is also Julie's father's best friend, who married his daughter "muni du consentement du pére." Furthermore, at the novel's close, the Baron d'Etange has come to take up residence at Clarens, completing the transformation of what had threatened to turn into a gynaeceum during Julie's reign into a kingdom legitimated by a dual paternal authority. When Saint-Preux is invited back to Clarens to resume his first duties, he is invited to do so this time "armed" with the approval of both of the novel's fathers—Wolmar is careful to point out that, whereas the idea of handing over the children's education to Saint-Preux was formulated by Julie in the letter she left for her husband to mail, the plan was originally of his conception: "[I]l est venu de moi le premier" (6: 11: 740).

When Claire reiterates Wolmar's invitation to Saint-Preux in the novel's final letter, she makes a significant onomastic change in speaking of the former mistress of Elysium: she suppresses the customary "de Wolmar" and speaks of her cousin as "Julie d'Etange." Claire's gesture, while it would seem to run counter to the fathers' plan for Julie, is in fact faithful to its ultimate provision. When Claire replaces the sign of Julie's marriage, and therefore of her maternity, with

[42] In 1764 Louis-Sébastien Mercier composed, for a pastiche of Rousseau, a new last letter for *Julie,* in which Saint-Preux writes Wolmar to tell him that he is coming back to Clarens to raise Julie's children. Cited in G. Genette, *Palimpsestes* (Seuil, 1982), p. 197.

her maiden name, she reveals the primary goal of the new pedagogy for which Saint-Preux will be responsible. Julie's former teacher will work in the name of the father, like the little tyrant's tutor, to take revenge on the mother. When he takes up his new duties, he will find himself in the ideal pedagogical situation decreed by *Emile*'s tutor. Julie dies because of her maternal instinct, but her child survives, fulfilling (half of) the tutor's dream by providing his future teacher with a child without a mother. Furthermore, Henriette corresponds even more closely to *Emile*'s ideal child, since she is, for all intents and purposes, an orphan. At *Julie*'s close, procreation has been thwarted, and Henriette, phoenix-like, represents the perfect instrument for the future of pedagogy, an orphan, and an orphan with a known past. "Il faudrait que le gouverneur eut été élevé pour son élève, que ses domestiques eussent été élevés pour leur maitre, . . . il faudroit d'éducation en éducation remonter jusqu'on ne sait où" (*Emile*, p. 263).

Since Elysium is the mythical home of the blessed dead, the name given Julie's secret garden at first seems a surprising appellation for what purports to be a family utopia. However, when Julie's goals for her paradise are examined, the appropriateness of this onomastic choice becomes apparent. The garden at the center of Clarens is a monument to the inorganic, to its mistress's struggle to contain life's disorder and its surprises: it is a funerary monument. Julie, however, is doubly unfit to govern the Classical microcosm she has helped establish. The joint rule of Wolmar and Saint-Preux at *Julie*'s close represents the victory of the fortifiers over the natural power of woman as mother. (Saint-Preux will finally become an "enfant de la balle," realizing thereby both his and his creator's youthful ambition, acting as *gouverneur* in the sense of director of fortifications and as *gouverneur* in the sense of tutor.) In addition, it signals the pedagogue's revenge against woman as sorcerer, as enchantress. The engraving Rousseau chose to introduce the last book of *Emile* for the first edition represents, in his description, "Circé se donnant à Ulysse, qu'elle n'a pu transformer" (4: 869). His choice would be equally appropriate for the final book of *Julie*, where the Circe-figure, who has seduced and infantilized a representative of pedagogical authority, yields—her powers at least—to clever, wily ("ingénieux"), masculine genius. In his education of the "new Julie," Saint-Preux can be expected to play a more dominating role.

The fortifiers' victory also represents a victory over the literary form so often impugned by Rousseau, the novel. *Julie*'s penultimate footnote is an attack on the novel. Wolmar has explained to Saint-Preux why he kept his sons away from the final educational play: "[L]e spectacle des passions violentes . . . est un des plus dangereux qu'on puisse offrir aux enfans. Ces passions ont toujours . . . quelque chose de puérile qui les amuse, qui les séduit, et leur fait aimer ce qu'ils devroient craindre" (6: 11: 738). The "publisher" then intervenes to comment that "voila pourquoi nous aimons tous le théatre, et plusieurs d'entre nous les romans." Burgelin interprets the note as simply another attempt on Rousseau's part to maintain the fiction that he was only *Julie*'s "publisher" (p. 1810). However, the reiteration of this classic Rousseauian argument at the close of one of the great Classical French novels can also be read as an indication of the place its author intended for his work. *Julie* is in actuality an immense indictment of the novel, an attempt to contain its "violent passions," and a condemnation of the novel as love story ("lettres de deux amans"), the novel as family romance. Rousseau replaces this model with the "roman de la nature humaine," a Classical French version of Robinson Crusoe's story, the struggle to dominate nature and to rewrite genealogy.

Nevertheless, a seemingly unintentional loophole (*meurtrière*) remains in *Julie*'s fortified ending. Like her model, Henriette appears to retain an autonomy that could threaten the perfection of Wolmar and Saint-Preux's pedagogical project. She has already escaped once from Wolmar's paternal control. To have Saint-Preux teach Julie again without reliving the initial pedagogical experience would constitute the novel's final triumph over the rebellious, disorderly forces of sexuality. But this final repetitious configuration may also represent a threat to the law and order of Clarens unforeseen by its rulers. Henriette could live out completely her role as "nouvelle Héloïse/Julie." The impending relationship Julie has arranged (under Wolmar's instigation) for Saint-Preux and Henriette is more disturbing than the union she had planned for Saint-Preux and Claire. Henriette is Julie's foster daughter made into her reincarnation. Saint-Preux is Julie's former lover transformed into her "adopted" child. When their future union is projected by *Julie*'s conclusion, a taboo more threatening than the marginally illicit initial relationship between Julie and Saint-Preux menaces the purity of Clarens's lines: according to the genealogy of the Elysian family, the new Julie who will be Saint-Preux's student is both his sister and his mother. Despite all the Vaubanian strategy of the paternal "living eye," the final outworks around *Julie*'s garden may still contain breaches, breaches that Laclos and Sade would strive to eliminate from their textual fortifications.

══ V ══

Les Liaisons dangereuses:
Writing under the Other's Name

Entre les hommes il n'existe que deux relations: la logique et la guerre.
Valéry, *Monsieur Teste* (posthumous fragments)

══ ✳ ══

The Attack on the Vaubanian Fortress

Nous ne sommes plus au temps de madame de Sévigné.
La Marquise de Merteuil

René Pomeau begins the introduction to his edition of *Les
Liaisons dangereuses* by embroidering the single literary myth
most enticing for a study on literature and defense. He imagines Laclos composing his novel as a replacement for the attack that would not come to test the fortifications this
artilleryman-turned-engineer had at long last been permitted
to build. The setting for this defensive (melo)drama is the *île
d'Aix* where Laclos was assigned to direct the construction of
a system of defenses to protect the military port of Rochefort.
He was preparing for an attack by an English fleet that his
superiors believed would be sent to avenge Louis XVI's support of the American rebels. In order to appreciate the poi-
gnancy of Pomeau's reconstruction, one should know that
Choderlos de Laclos was a professional soldier who spent his
entire life in search of a war in which to demonstrate his
talents, a would-be fortifier in search of someone to attack
his defenses. This is Pomeau's version of the scenario on the
île d'Aix:

Tenait-il enfin, cet obscur, la grande chance de sa car-
rière? Il allait avoir à expérimenter une nouveauté prônée
par l'avant-garde de la recherche militaire: il construisait
un fort "perpendiculaire," et non pas à la Vauban. . . . A
lui, la gloire de démontrer au Ministère, plus que réticent,
l'efficacité de ces innovations. Que la flotte anglaise con-
sente seulement à attaquer!
  Des mois passent. Aucun navire ennemi ne se montre
sur l'horizon. Laclos s'ennuie dans son île, trop myope,
trop géomètre pour s'intéresser au grand spectacle de la
mer et du ciel. Il va tenter une autre vie. Prenant pour
sujet une guerre qui, elle, ne chôme pas, celle de l'homme
et de la femme, il se met à écrire les *Liaisons dangereuses*.[1]

Pomeau does not invent this myth; he simply takes proper
advantage of its potential. And it is easy to understand why
he does so, for this version of the genesis of the *Liaisons* is
not only tantalizing, but highly convenient as well. What could
appear more psychologically convincing than to imagine the
creation of the most diabolically plotted novel, a novel whose
moves seem a glorification of oblique strategy, as a projection
of a desire for actual (oblique) military conflict? Yet, as recent
critics have repeatedly concluded, Laclos successfully resists
such straightforward decoding: in both his personal and
professional lives he appears to have been a master of indirect
tactics. The strategy of his unique literary bombshell is rooted
in the indirection of epistolarity. We never see Laclos's characters in action; the novel's plot consists of their accounts,
often unabashedly distorted, of their activities. Vivienne Mylne
has recently demonstrated that even the discourse of these
accounts testifies to a penchant for indirection, for in the
Liaisons Laclos consistently prefers indirect and narrated speech
to direct discourse.[2] This distanced novelistic stance is echoed

[1] Pomeau, introduction to *Liaisons* (Garnier-Flammarion, 1964), p. 8.
[2] Mylne compares Laclos's practice with that of other epistolary writers
of his century in France and England and concludes that he makes a most
sparing use of direct discourse. She finds the speech pattern in the *Liaisons*
closer to that of a novel like *La Princesse de Clèves*. See "Le Parler des

both by the oblique tactics favored by his libertine heroes and by what might be termed his novel's strategic position, that is, the relationship to authority that fuels Laclos's devious masterpiece. When the *Liaisons* is read in tandem with the only other important texts produced by Laclos, the *Lettre à Messieurs de l'Académie française sur l'éloge de Monsieur le Maréchal de Vauban* (1786) and the three texts on the education of women (1783-?), two central and related issues come to the fore: the "anxious," aggressive relationship of student to master and the complex and profound equivocalness that results from such pedagogical hostility. These issues, far from being only tangentially related to the study of Laclos's novel, are on the contrary of central importance for its interpretation. The *Liaisons* has long been the object of a dual interpretive tradition: the novel is seen either as (diabolic) glorification of libertine intelligence (Laclos as precursor of Sade) or as a critique of the society in which the libertine strategists could flourish (Laclos as follower of Rousseau). All major readings of the novel are at least implicitly, if not explicitly, rooted in critics' perception of Laclos's stand on these two issues, military strategy and the pedagogical imperative. The central configuration in the history of the *Liaisons* has been the triangle of its readers' mediated desire, with Laclos at its apex and Vauban and Rousseau as the two poles between which the artilleryman of letters is positioned.

I contend neither that the *Liaisons* can be read only within a biographical context, nor that the fullest reading possible is one that takes into account the greatest number of elements belonging to the portrait of the biographical individual Laclos. However, a study on defensive strategy, a study that posits an essential collusion between pedagogy and defensiveness, cannot avoid Laclos's manifestoes of defensive and pedagogical tactics. For traditional literary history, the testimony provided by these texts is of dubious value, since all of them

personnages dans *Les Liaisons dangereuses,*" *Revue d'histoire littéraire de la France,* hereafter *RHLF,* 82 (1982): 575-87.

postdate the *Liaisons*. However, these texts are important documents for a study of the literature of defense because of the obsessive repetition that characterizes Laclos's treatment of these twin notions, military defense and pedagogy. In addition, a reading of these texts is essential for a comprehension of the literary artilleryman's double *clinamen*. Laclos's place in this study, *after* Vauban (the master of defensive military strategy) and Rousseau (the master pedagogue), was also the place in which he saw himself. In his work, Laclos is forced onto an oblique course by two "obstacles": Vauban and Rousseau.

When Laclos was assigned to defensive work on the *île d'Aix*, his military superior was one of the strangest figures in the history of fortifications, Marc-René, marquis de Montalembert. The Laclos-Montalembert collaboration was a sustained one and the dominant force in Laclos's military career: the novelist served under Montalembert; he attempted on the *île d'Aix* to provide a concrete illustration of his commanding officer's theories; and he defended those theories in print. The "master's"[3] theories were controversial ones, largely because they were set up in resolute opposition to those of the acknowledged master of French defensive military architecture, Vauban. Nearly a century after the high point of his career, Vauban was considered a founding father by the French military establishment. His theories (or often his followers' interpretation of those theories) had become the bible of defensive military strategy. To attack Vauban at this time was a daring enterprise—and to do so as Montalembert did was foolhardy. Laclos's superior was the first notable detractor whose attack on Vauban was openly motivated by a desire to usurp his authority. The scale on which he deployed his forces is re-

---

[3] Ronald Rosbottom has recently argued that Laclos could only function in relationships of this sort, as an "amanuensis" for a series of "masters": "Montalembert, Orléans, Robespierre, the Jacobins, the Committee on Public Safety, Bonaparte, even Merteuil, Valmont: all of these personages and entities made use of Laclos's talents, directly and indirectly, providing him cover as well" (*Choderlos de Laclos* [Boston: Twayne Publishers, 1978], p. 138).

markable: against the slim, fragmented body of Vauban's writings on defense, Montalembert pitted a formidable, eleven-volume study, *La Fortification perpendiculaire*. For his attack, Montalembert invented the strategy that would be deployed by all those who hoped to appropriate Vauban's glory. He first attempts to demonstrate that Vauban had no system. He then proposes a redefinition of Vauban's status: if Vauban can be considered a genius at all, it is only in the realm of offensive strategy.[4] *La Fortification perpendiculaire* is marked by a displaced relationship to authority and to authorship that Laclos parallels in his own work. Even though it is evident that this series of immense tomes, on whose publication Montalembert squandered his personal fortune, had at its obsessional center the figure whose greatness constituted a perpetual threat to their author, Vauban is almost never mentioned by name in their pages. As if to camouflage this silence, Montalembert theorizes that biography, attribution of authority, even proper names—or at least one proper name—should be eliminated from the study of fortifications. Montalembert asserts that Vauban's authority has been used by his followers to suppress all potential new voices of authority. Vauban's name should therefore be banned from discussions of military theory. Only when theories are evaluated on their own merits and those judging them cannot be influenced by their authors' authority, only then will new theoreticians be allowed to supplement the *lacunae* in the Vaubanian system: "Les arrêts prononcés d'après les examens particuliers, sont très souvent dictés, ou par l'intérêt qu'on prend à l'Auteur, ou par la jalousie qu'il dicte. . . . Il faut . . . qu'on ait, pour ainsi dire, oublié quel en est l'Auteur" (pp. iv-v).

The system for which Montalembert hoped to obtain a hearing as a result of the suppression of authors' names was designed to suppress more than Vauban's authority. Mon-

---

[4] Montalembert, *La Fortification perpendiculaire*, 11 vols. (Philippe-Denys Pierres, 1776-), *Discours préliminaire*, vol. 1, pp. xxxii-xxxiii.

talembert sees himself as the first true genius of the *corps de génie* and feels that the history of fortifications will have to be rewritten to make place for his creation of "une Fortification toute nouvelle, fondée sur les seuls principes qu'il semble qu'on doit suivre dans la Fortification des places" (p. i). His system has two cornerstones. First, there is an increased insistence on interior as well as exterior defense (as though the *place forte* were an exact replica of Freud's "protective shield" with a system of defenses on either side), made possible by "une artillerie toujours supérieure à celle de l'assiégeant." Second, the perpendicular flanking that gives the method its name is created by the substitution of small, detached forts for the proliferation of outworks that was the trademark of Vauban's architecture. Montalembert advocated the addition of a new line of defenses, a second, more supple *enceinte* of protection surrounding the main enclosure. Far from being content with influencing the construction of new fortified places, Montalembert also sought to remodel existing structures by including an enclosure of his construction: "ces places [existantes], par le moyen de changements peu considérables, deviendront infiniment plus fortes" (pp. ii-iii). Thus the true project of Laclos's mentor is to outflank the master fortifier; his perpendicular defenses would protect Vauban's fortifications, would cover up the *courtines* and *bastions* left by Montalembert's great enemy. Vauban's fortifications would be out-fortified, and Vauban's work, like his name, would disappear behind the superior creations of the new master fortifier.[5]

[5] A modern theorist has advanced an interpretation of the *fortification perpendiculaire* that would surely have enraged Montalembert, one that provides an interesting perspective on his desire to suppress Vauban and his name. Henry Guerlac believes that Montalembert's reforms were merely a repetition of Vauban's so-called second system: "Here [i.e., in the second system], Vauban had made an important, even revolutionary improvement: he had freed himself from reliance on the main enceinte and taken the first steps toward a defense in depth. . . . In all previous cases adaptation had been through projecting crown works or horn works that were merely spectacular appendages to the primary enceinte. . . . The second system was rejected by

Laclos's collaboration with Montalembert was an appropriate one. The mentor was no more successful than the disciple in forging a place of glory for himself in contemporary military history; ultimately Montalembert's only claim to fame (or infamy) came from his attempt at desecrating Vauban's memory.[6] For Laclos, the chance to participate in the work of fortification must have been enough of an advancement militarily to offset his mentor's less than brilliant reputation. How could he not be flattered by such an opportunity at a time when the verbal expression linking those involved in the construction of fortifications with the essence of military genius was being forged—the Robert traces to 1759 the use of *génie militaire* as a synonym for "art des fortifications," and by extension for the "service technique chargé de travaux de fortification." Laclos, an artilleryman and therefore a traditional rival of the members of the *génie*, must have been pleased to work for the defense of a system that pledged to maintain "une artillerie toujours superieure à celle de l'assiégeant."[7]

Cormontaigne . . . whose ideas dominated the eighteenth century, and whose schemes of fortification were based squarely upon Vauban's first system. . . . Only late in the eighteenth century do we find a revival of Vauban's second system: the revolt of Montalembert. . . . Montalembert's great revolution . . . was implicit in Vauban's second system, though whether Montalembert was inspired by it may well be doubted" ("Vauban: The Impact of Science on War," in *Makers of Modern Strategy*, ed. E. M. Earle [Princeton, N.J.: Princeton Univ. Press, 1943], p. 41).

[6] In the words of Laclos's biographer, Emile Dard: "Le corps de génie tout entier se souleva contre l'imprudent qui avait osé toucher à Vauban" (*Le Général Choderlos de Laclos, auteur des "Liaisons dangereuses": Un Acteur caché du drame révolutionnaire* [Perrin, 1905], p. 113).

[7] Anne Blanchard discusses the conflict between *artilleurs* and *ingénieurs,* and contends that the *artilleurs* reproached the *ingénieurs* for their "indépendance, leurs idées à système, leur infatuation intellectuelle" (*Les Ingénieurs du roi de Louis XIV à Louis XVI* [thesis, Montpellier, 1979], p. 137). In 1755, the position of "grand-maître de l'Artillerie" was suppressed and the artillery put under the official control of the Inspector of Fortifications. Laclos always hoped to use artillery to increase the fortress's defensive capabilities. Ironically, the leader under whom he finally went to battle, Napoleon, intended a far more "open" use of artillery in field battles.

Furthermore, Montalembert's assertions for *la fortification perpendiculaire* must have had an obvious attraction for an individual as fascinated by defense as Laclos revealed himself to be. Montalembert went so far as to make claims for his system that Vauban would never have made for his: if it is followed, the heretofore mythical perfect defense can become a reality, and not only fortified places but even an entire country can be made impregnable. "La force du nouveau système pourra être augmentée, au point de rendre une place imprenable." "Un Etat, dont les frontières seroient bordées de places imprenables, n'auroit vraisemblablement point de guerre à soutenir" (pp. iii, xxxi).

Laclos took their collaboration seriously, for he continued Montalembert's war on Vauban with a fervor that revealed his personal stakes in the quarrel. It was he who first attempted at the *île d'Aix* to give *la fortification perpendiculaire* a practical application, and he who, in Montalembert's place, pronounced the prohibited, Vauban's name, when he composed the *Lettre à Messieurs de l'Académie française sur l'éloge de Monsieur le Maréchal de Vauban*. Laclos explains the origin of this text as an attempt on his part to put the members of the Académie française on guard against the "dangerous" implications of selecting Vauban as the subject for a prestigious essay prize: "les honneurs rendus à M. le Maréchal de Vauban ne peuvent être exagérés sans être dangereux."[8] In his warning, Laclos retraces the two principal arguments already rehearsed for him by his mentor. In the first place, Vauban's name should bear no guarantee of authority, for he was no inventor, but only one of many plagiarists of "le système bastionné, connu dès la fin du quinzième siècle" (p. 578).[9] Laclos even argues that Vauban's fortifications, like

---

[8] Laclos, *O.c.*, p. 573.

[9] According to Laclos's arguments, his mentor's attack on Vauban was really a type of *tu quoque* defense: Montalembert covered up Vauban's name and reused his elements of fortification in his own defensive system just as Vauban had pillaged previous inventors and thereby effaced their names from military history.

the Académie's praise, not only have not served his country
well, but have even rendered it more vulnerable. Because they
are such weak fortresses, they are easily captured by the enemy,
and, once captured

> cette même place . . . pourra devenir inexpugnable, entre
> les mains de l'ennemi qui s'en sera emparé: surtout s'il
> se décide soit à y faire des retranchements inté-
> rieurs . . . soit à faire de la place même le noyau, ou
> réduit, d'un camp retranché. . . . On voit évidemment que,
> dans ce cas, une telle forteresse ne serait pas seulement
> inutile, mais nuisible; puisque, sans opposer à l'ennemi
> une résistance capable de l'arrêter, elle lui fournirait ce-
> pendant les moyens de former, avec facilité, un établisse-
> ment assez redoutable pour ne pouvoir plus en être
> repoussé que par des forces infiniment supérieures aux
> siennes. (p. 582)

Also like Montalembert, Laclos couples this denial of the originality of his precursor's defensive system with an affirmation
of Vauban's offensive greatness: "C'est dans la partie de l'Attaque des places que M. le Maréchal de Vauban s'est vérita-
blement distingué. En ce genre il a fait plus que perfectionner,
il a créé l'art" (p. 577). All the evidence brought forward by
Laclos in the *Lettre* is used to support this dual central argument: Montalembert's right-hand man is willing to give
Vauban all possible credit for his contribution to offensive
strategy as long as this "generosity" can be counterbalanced
by a blanket rejection of his predecessor's value in the field
of defense.

Because of the virulence of his attacks, Laclos succeeded in
distracting attention from Vauban and the importance of his
strategic contributions and in attracting attention to himself—
although certainly not in the way in which he must have hoped
to do. His adamant refusal to accord Vauban any importance
as a defensive strategist was immediately written off as a manifestation of jealousy: "[L]e prétexte de M. de Laclos . . .

ressemble beaucoup à de l'envie."[10] One competitor for the Académie française's prize even chose to devote his essay to Laclos's attack rather than to Vauban's work: "Impitoyable envie, depuis quand cherches-tu tes victimes parmi les morts?"[11] Vauban's eighteenth-century partisans note only the jealousy that dominates Laclos's reaction to the seventeenth-century's master fortifier. They fail to expose his method of defending himself against Vauban's threatening presence. Laclos sees that Vauban cannot be denied all importance; his *Lettre* constitutes an attempt to reposition Vauban's authority and thereby free the space coveted by Laclos for himself and for his master. Laclos's ultimate goal in this text is to demonstrate that this as yet unfilled space is the primordial and central space of military authority.

At times, Laclos's call for the primacy of defensive strategy bears a marked resemblance to the pronouncements of the authority he is attempting to undermine. He speaks, for example, of "la France dont l'intérêt est plus de conserver que d'acquérir" and contends that world peace can only come about as "le fruit de la supériorité des moyens de défense sur les moyens d'attaque" (pp. 591, 576). Such a deployment of Vaubanian rhetoric is essential to Laclos's diversionary tactics. He hopes to capitalize on the powerful attraction Vauban won for the defensive enterprise, only to sever the seemingly indissoluble link binding fortification to Vauban. Prudently, Laclos does not pronounce the name of the individual he

[10] Pidansat de Mairobert, *Mémoires secrets,* 3 June 1786, cited in the Pléiade edition, p. 1514.

[11] D'Antilly, *officier du génie,* cited in the old Pléiade edition, ed. M. Allem (1959), p. 869. Laclos thus found himself accused of a crime more heinous than lycanthropy. Both Versini and Allem recount in some detail the complex history of the Vauban prize. The members of the Académie française evidently encountered great difficulty in finding someone able to praise Vauban with as much eloquence as Laclos used to attack him. They elected not to award the prize that year, announced the subject again for 1789, once again could not decide on a winner, and only presented the prize in 1790. Vauban was honored as the system he worked to buttress was about to crumble.

would put in his archenemy's place. The *Lettre* is much more than mere propaganda for Montalembert. The text is important because it reveals the extent of Laclos's preoccupation with defensive strategy, his conviction that military strategy could essentially be reduced to defensive strategy, and his feeling that the history of that strategy was still to be written.[12]

The Pedagogical Obsession

> Saint-Preux: "Je n'apperçois aucuns pas d'hommes. Ah! dit M. de Wolmar, c'est qu'on a pris grand soin de les effacer."
>
> Rousseau, *Julie*

Laclos's only other foray into the writing of public letters proves as compelling and as revealing as the text on Vauban. Three times he began to write, and each time left incomplete, a discourse on the question of education for women. Although critics use various titles to distinguish one of the three versions

[12] Perhaps the most poignant detail of the scenario of Laclos's unfortunate military career concerns its climax. The professional soldier was finally able to go to war for the first time during the last three years of his life, but, by then, the type of conflict he had prepared for for so long had been replaced by another for which he was not so well trained. The first editor of Laclos's correspondence during those years describes his dilemma in these terms: "Une seule chose fait ressouvenir en lui des méthodes d'autrefois, son amour inassouvi pour la guerre de siège, que Marengo rend inutile. Un génie a tué l'autre." Thus, Laclos was never able to confront Vauban on his own ground, never able to measure himself against the master whose prestige he so resented. He had not foreseen such a dramatic rewriting of military history as that brought about by Napoleon. See Laclos, *Lettres inédites,* ed. Louis Chauvigny (Mercure de France, 1904), p. 22. In his correspondence during his campaigns under Napoleon, the discomfort and the fatigue that the unfamiliar military life caused Laclos are evident. Thus he writes his wife on 7 June 1800: "A présent, je désire de faire un siège, d'y employer mes boulets creux et puis qu'on fasse une prompte et honorable paix qui me ramène à toi et à mes enfants" (*O.c.,* p. 903).

or to refer to them collectively, Laclos himself left both the first and the third fragments untitled and referred to the second as "Des Femmes et de leur éducation." The very fact that he returned on three occasions to the same topic, yet each time failed to complete his effort, suggests that Laclos did not find it easy to exorcise the fascination women's education exercised over him.[13]

Upon closer examination, the strangeness of the discourses becomes increasingly apparent. Laclos does not really return to the same subject, for he never actually began to fulfill his announced plan. In fact, if the *incipit* of the first fragment were not formulated as a response to the subject of a provincial academy's essay contest, a reader might quite legitimately wonder just what the theme of any of the three was. (Only the third essay seems at all close to a treatise on education; it provides a program of reading designed especially for a young woman.) Laclos's (calculated) hesitation about his purpose is evident from the opening of the first fragment: "Une compagnie de savants et de sages décerne aujourd'hui une couronne littéraire à celui qui dira le mieux *quels seraient les moyens de perfectionner l'éducation des femmes.* La foule des orateurs s'avance. Chacun d'eux vient présenter à ses juges le fruit de son travail et tous espèrent en obtenir le prix. D'autres motifs m'amènent" (p. 389).

The discourses on the education of women originate in a paradox: their author enters a contest but denies that he is doing so. In them, Laclos inaugurates the ambivalent relationship to contests also evident in his public letter to the

[13] Versini contends that the third essay was written much later than the first two and assigns it to the period 1795-1799, or even 1802. In his commentary on the essay fragments, he declares the third one to be "bien complet cette fois" (p. 1415). Although he does not mention it, it is obvious that he is defending the text against the classification made by the previous editor of Laclos's work for the Bibliothèque de la Pléiade, Maurice Allem, who in his edition describes it as an "essai laissé inachevé" (p. 842, n. 14). Neither editor justifies his position in any way, but I am inclined to the latter view because of the general lack of both opening and closing signals in Laclos's text.

French Academy on the subject of the Vauban prize. That letter echoes the aloof and perfectly protected stance with regard to public competitions that Laclos consistently demonstrates. The literary artilleryman takes oblique action and refuses to assume an offensive position that would leave him open to judgment. In the letter on Vauban, Laclos adopts neither a positive nor a negative view of the subject proposed; he simply denies its validity. In the first text on education, Montalembert's disciple takes a similarly radical and hostile stand. He refuses to address the question of *how* to improve women's education, because "il n'est aucun moyen de perfectionner l'éducation des femmes" (p. 389). He begins to elucidate his answer by explaining that women cannot be educated until they are freed from their slavery to men. At this point, the discourse breaks off. It is possible that Laclos was simply hoping to win the contest by outstripping the famous negation of Rousseau's answer to another provincial academy's question in the first discourse, just as he used a Rousseauian denial to deflect attention from Vauban in his letter to the French Academy. If so, his predecessor's awesome presence may have been responsible for Laclos's inability to complete his essay.

The second and longest essay's most remarkable trait is Laclos's avoidance of the topic imposed by the Chalons-sur-Marne Academy. To refer to "Des Femmes et de leur éducation" as a discourse on feminine pedagogy is a complete misnomer, for the text never gets beyond the first of its two announced subjects, "Des Femmes," and thus never broaches the question of their education. In it, Laclos airs his views on "la femme naturelle," woman before the bondage that, according to the first fragment, makes women uneducable. Natural woman leads him to the state of nature and to a long (ten pages out of fifty) defense of his views on this subject against those of Buffon and Voltaire. It is incredible, given its starting point and the title under which it is generally known, that the essay breaks off just after a section on beauty tips and advice on how to be seductive, directed at women in general.

The discourses allegedly on the education of women are problematic and puzzling texts, texts that intrigue more because of their deficiencies, because of what is absent or unspoken in them, than because of the views they actually express. As Laclos himself says, "d'autres motifs m'amènent," and one of these unspoken motives seems to be a complex reckoning with Rousseau, a reckoning that is surely as unfinished as the three essays. "Le traité de l'*Education des femmes*," Jean Rousset has remarked in reference to the second fragment, "s'inscrit en marge de *Julie*, du Livre V de l'*Emile*, dans le prolongement des réflexions de Rousseau sur la femme naturelle et sa perversion dans la civilisation parisienne de son temps."[14] "En marge de" is a particularly appropriate expression to situate the discourses with regard to Rousseau. Laclos's texts are quite evidently marginal. They would not exist without the prior existence of the texts on which they comment and whose deficiencies they hope to remedy. Laclos begins the essays in answer to a provincial academy's question, in a gesture openly reminiscent of Rousseau's early pattern of inspiration. As he elaborates them, his obsession with themes treated by his predecessor and his desire to continue Rousseau's project by providing his own version of the story of Sophie's education in *Emile* are increasingly evident.[15]

In view of the unmistakably symbiotic relationship binding Laclos's work to Rousseau's, it is surprising that the name of *Emile*'s author appears so infrequently in the discourses (only three times, once relegated to marginal status in a footnote).

[14] Rousset, *Forme et signification* (Corti, 1962), p. 94.

[15] In his definition of the term *tessera*, or link, Harold Bloom postulates an essential similarity between the desire to complete the work of a threatening predecessor and the desire to deform that work: "In the *tessera*, the later poet provides what his imagination tells him would complete the otherwise 'truncated' precursor poem and poet, a 'completion' that is as much a misprision as a revisionary swerve is" (*The Anxiety of Influence* [New York: Oxford Univ. Press, 1973], p. 66). The fact that his continuation of Rousseau's educational project is also a transgression of the "master's" authority could explain why Laclos was finally unable to complete his discourses.

On the surface, Rousseau seems a far less important presence in them than either Voltaire or Buffon. Yet anyone writing in Laclos's day on such topics as the state of nature and natural woman could not have avoided the realization that Rousseau's name would be invoked in conjunction with his work, especially if that work followed, as Laclos's does, a recognizably Rousseauian line of reasoning and expressed, as Laclos's does, archetypically Rousseauian views.

Laclos does not mention his illustrious predecessor's name more frequently in the three fragments because he suppresses Rousseau just as his mentor, Montalembert, suppresses Vauban. Then, just as Laclos and Montalembert follow their initial suppression of Vauban by adopting an essentially Vaubanian position and Vaubanian techniques, so in the "discourses" Laclos traces out the same pattern of omission coupled with repetition. Montalembert asks that all names (most importantly, of course, Vauban's) be eliminated, so that new authorities can win recognition. Laclos leaves out the name of the recognized authority on pedagogy, even when its presence would seem inevitable, but he advances no theory to explain his silence. Rousseau's ambiguous role as an absent presence in the fragments on education indicates that Laclos entertained a more problematic relationship to his authority than is generally imagined. In these texts, Laclos writes in Rousseau's margin, but he does not admit his texts' status as marginalia. When, without reference to Rousseau, he defends a Rousseauian position in a debate with Voltaire and Buffon, Laclos may be said to put himself in his predecessor's place. He assumes Rousseau's authority, and he ultimately covers up Rousseau's work with his own, much as Montalembert dreamed of camouflaging Vauban's fortifications with his *fortification perpendiculaire*. In the essays on the education of women, the author's position is resolutely defensive: Laclos is obsessed by an awareness of what Bloom refers to as "belatedness," that is, the fact of his existence in Rousseau's shadow. Laclos adopts a Rousseauian strategy when he puts himself in Rousseau's

CHAPTER V

position. He attempts to engulf his precursor and his threatening power, just as the master teacher engulfs Emile, and Julie overshadows Saint-Preux. All these instances of aggressiveness are self-protective; these "unions" are forged in an attempt to silence a threatening voice.

The inability of Laclos to complete the discourses takes on new importance in light of his assumption of Rousseau's identity. He is unable to conclude when he writes in Rousseau's name and in Rousseau's place; Rousseau's voice stifles his own. And the impotence caused by the master's overshadowing proximity is greater still, for Laclos ultimately finds it impossible to undertake his announced subject. The fragments avoid confronting the question of pedagogy just as they avoid a confrontation with the self-proclaimed master pedagogue. This avoidance, coupled with the strategic similarities that mark Laclos's treatment of Rousseau and Laclos's and Montalembert's treatment of Vauban, points to the complexity of Laclos's relationship to pedagogy. The absences and the silences of the three fragments are signs of a love/hate relationship with Rousseau and of a hesitation with regard to the Rousseauian view of the liberating power of the pedagogical act. In the fragments, Laclos stops short of making this doubt explicit, but the Liaisons expresses a revised view of the power of pedagogy that, not surprisingly, grants education a privileged role in a vision of an improved and more sophisticated defensive strategy.

Paul Hoffman and Ronald Rosbottom have recently argued that the Essais sur l'éducation des femmes should be considered, in Rosbottom's words, "a companion text to the Liaisons." The essays' portrait of female servitude is central to Hoffman's reading of the novel as a reflection on the female condition, a reading previously proposed by Arnaldo Pizzorusso.[16] Such a use of the three fragments on education illu-

[16] Rosbottom, Choderlos de Laclos, p. 31; Hoffman, "Aspects de la condition féminine dans Les Liaisons dangereuses de Choderlos de Laclos," L'Information littéraire 15(1963):47-53; Pizzorusso, "La Struttura delle Liai-

minates both the fragments and the novel and provides important insights into the major female characters in the *Liaisons*. Yet any such reading of Laclos's novel ultimately suggests, implicitly if not explicitly, that both Laclos's relationship to Rousseau and the treatment of moral issues in the *Liaisons* are less problematic than is actually the case.

Attempts to read the *Liaisons* in conjunction with the fragments on education for women follow one of two patterns, depending on the critic's interpretation of Laclos's position with regard to Rousseau in these works. Critics generally assume that the Rousseauian stance of Laclos in the fragments is unproblematic, a sign of solidarity with the master pedagogue. From this starting point, they may proceed, as Versini does, to use that alleged solidarity to buttress their reading of the *Liaisons* as a didactic novel, a novel that puts its elaborate machinery in place in order to teach a moral lesson faithful to Rousseau's position in *Julie*. More often, recent critics have viewed Laclos's stance with regard to Rousseau in these works as incompatible with that in the *Liaisons* and have had recourse to some variant of what Versini terms the theory of the two Laclos, "l'un sensible et l'autre diabolique" (*O.c.*, pp. xvii-xviii) to account for what they see as a discrepancy. However, both these views share a straightforwardness that renders them unequal to the occasion. They take into account only the obviously Rousseauian features of Laclos's work on education and pass over Laclos's silencing of Rousseau. In his notes both to the fragments and to the *Liaisons*, Versini points out various problematic moments when the two texts intersect, but he always writes off the strangeness he uncovers. For example, when he notes that in her autobiographical letter (letter 81) Merteuil "suit à l'avance le plan d'études que Laclos recommandera à une jeune fille de bonne famille" (in the third fragment) (p. 1286, n. 4 to p. 173), Versini comments only that she does so in order to achieve radically different goals.

sons dangereuses," *Studi sulla letteratura dell'età preromantica in Francia* (Pisa: Goliardica, 1956).

Yet, if the libertine anti-heroine, the self-proclaimed new Delilah, and the "jeune fille de bonne famille" have the same
intellectual formation, surely this puts even the third fragment,
apparently the most unhesitatingly Rousseauian and therefore
the least problematic of the three, in an equivocal position?
The three fragments on women's education show us neither
a second face of their author, nor an overtly Rousseauian
stance. It is easy to reconcile the Laclos of the essays with the
Laclos of the *Liaisons;* the difficult task facing the critic is
that of determining the nature of that unified authorial voice's
response to his precursor Rousseau. It is only by stressing the
absolute and unremitting equivocalness of that response that
the parallelism evident between the two main strains in Laclos's *oeuvre*—strategy and sentiment, military technique and
didacticism—can be demonstrated. The stance Laclos repeatedly
adopts is one that defies critical evaluation solely because it
is resolutely undecidable, describable only in its indirection.

=== ✳ ===

Les Liaisons dangereuses:
Putting the Master's Language in Its Place

> [O]ur scholar . . . maintained that the Great Wall alone
> would provide for the first time in the history of mankind
> a secure foundation for the new Tower of Babel. First
> the wall, therefore, and then the tower.
> Franz Kafka, "The Great Wall and the Tower of Babel"

The *Liaisons* has often been called a Classical novel. Georges
May, Roger Laufer, and Peter Brooks, among others, have
compared it both to a Classical tragedy and to the tradition
of the French novel contemporaneous with that tragedy, the
tradition represented by *La Princesse de Clèves.* "L'élégante
sobriété des moyens employés," Laufer argues, "le respect des
unités, le nombre restreint des personnages, . . . bref la rigueur

du donné, font de l'oeuvre un bel exemplaire du roman d'analyse." Laufer's description of the *Liaisons* leads him to claim a status for the novel similar to that often attributed to the masterpieces of Classicism: he characterizes the *Liaisons* as a "triomphe de l'intelligence lucide et de la clarté française." His contention echoes Baudelaire's laconic definition of *his* predecessor's masterwork: "Livre essentiellement français."[17] Comparing *Julie* to *La Princesse de Clèves*, Rousseau stresses the oblique ("voilé") nature of both novels' psychological portraits and maintains that *Julie*'s best readers would themselves be defensive and therefore able to recognize and unveil the defensiveness of literary characters (1: 546). This analogy runs counter to Rousseau's often proclaimed view of his novel's openness and communicative directness. In general, critics who have compared Laclos's novel to the masterpieces of French Classicism have done so in order to convey their sense of the lucidity of the *Liaisons*. Yet if a comparison between the novels of Lafayette and Laclos has any validity, it can only be found by exploring Rousseau's intuitive sense of the deviousness shared by his novel and *La Princesse de Clèves*. Laclos's novel seems to be just what Laufer takes it to be, a "triumph" of lucidity and clarity. But this view is difficult to defend when the critic looks beyond the eminently Classical façade of the *Liaisons*. Georges Daniel has aptly described Laclos's novel as "malgré sa structure si classique et la transparence de son style, un déroutant assemblage d'enceintes enchevêtrées, ironie, équivoque, duplicité, faux-semblant, tout l'arsenal du paraître."[18] The *Liaisons* may provide the key to an assessment of Rousseau's self-proclaimed Classicism, for Laclos's novel

[17] Laufer, *Style rococo, style des "Lumières"* (Corti, 1963), pp. 135-36; Baudelaire, *Oeuvres complètes*, ed. Le Dantec and Pichois (Bibliothèque de la Pléiade, 1961), p. 998. See also May, *Le Dilemme du roman au dix-huitième siècle* (PUF, 1963), p. 253; Brooks, *The Novel of Worldliness* (Princeton, N.J.: Princeton Univ. Press, 1969), p. 187.

[18] Daniel, *Fatalité du secret et fatalité du bavardage au dix-huitième siècle* (Nizet, 1966), p. 32.

is the essence of the archetypal Rousseauian bonding between transparency and obstacle. Furthermore, any evaluation of the *Liaisons* as a "triumph" of characteristically French "lucidity" and "clarity" is openly contradicted by the conflicting readings of the novel proposed again and again in the tradition of Laclos criticism.

The *Liaisons* is that strangest of fictions, a novel about which virtually any secondary issue can be readily interpreted, yet one that in its entirety has never received a generally accepted reading. There simply are no adequately demonstrated answers to the most basic questions that inevitably confront the reader of this novel. Are we to take the *Liaisons* simply for a portrait, as the *éditeur* cavalierly claims in his *avertissement*, of "moeurs qui nous sont si étrangères?" (p. 3). Can this be considered an amoral work, that is, a novel whose author does not take sides and therefore does not ask his readers to take sides in his representation, a novel that invites us to imitate its author's/narrator's detachment? Or is there complicity between Laclos and the *roués* he so vividly portrays? Does the *Liaisons* work to win our sympathy for the strategists of seduction? Is this therefore a willfully immoral text? Or can the *Liaisons* more aptly be described as a critique of what Mme de Volanges calls "ces éclats scandaleux qui deviennent tous les jours plus fréquents" (98: 219)? Does Laclos in the *Liaisons* reiterate Rousseau's position in *Julie* by providing a condemnation of Parisian life that is every bit as violent as his predecessor's, despite the fact that he employs radically different means to that end?

All readings of the *Liaisons* are centered on this unavoidable critical dilemma: Laclos's novel may ultimately resist interpretation, but it nevertheless constantly and insistently asks to be interpreted, asks the reader to interrogate the novel's moral stance. As Irving Wohlfarth has pointed out, the *Liaisons* is born under the sign of critical evaluation.[19] The dual

---

[19] Wohlfarth, "The Irony of Criticism and the Criticism of Irony: A Study of Laclos Criticism," *SVEC* 120 (1974): 269.

[marginalia: just a portrait? an immoral work? complicity Laclos/ personnages?]

[marginalia: just condemning Parisian life?]

prefatory texts that prepare the reader for confrontation with the controversial correspondence (the *éditeur*'s *avertissement* and the *rédacteur*'s preface) plunge the novel's reader *in medias res*. Contrary to general novelistic practice, however, the "things" with which the reader is first surrounded are not events, but questions of interpretation.

Many eighteenth-century novels begin with a preface by the publisher, or the editor, or the (alleged) author. The main function of this preface is generally to request a particular type of reading for the work that follows; the author of the initiatory text often claims historical rather than fictional status for the volume he is presenting. Such prefatory gestures do not invite critical debate. These narrative clichés simply put the reader on familiar fictional ground. Even *Julie*'s more developed second preface presents no unusual interpretive difficulties for the reader familiar with the eighteenth-century tradition of *avertissements,* for this dialogue in the margin of Rousseau's novel creates no confusion about the moral status of the correspondence it introduces.

Laclos endows the *Liaisons* with a double initiatory gesture. By doing so, he subverts both a novelistic cliché and the traditional framework for its interpretation. The publisher (*éditeur*) takes the concept of an *avertissement* quite literally, for he immediately moves to put the reader on guard both against the editor (*rédacteur*) and against the work for which both publisher and editor will refuse responsibility:

> Nous croyons devoir prévenir le Public, que, malgré le titre de cet Ouvrage et ce qu'en dit le Rédacteur dans sa Préface, nous ne garantissons pas l'authenticité de ce Recueil, et que nous avons même de fortes raisons de penser que ce n'est qu'un Roman. (p. 3)

The publisher then proceeds to undermine the prestige of the alleged novel's author. He devotes the remainder of his foreword to a detailed demonstration of the novel's shortcomings, all of which result from its author's unskillful ("maladroit") handling of his material—"nous blâmons beaucoup l'Auteur." The publisher concludes his demonstration with an overt plea for the reader's trust: he proclaims that his opinion on the following correspondence is the only one that cannot be refuted.

> Pour préserver au moins, autant qu'il est en nous, le Lecteur trop crédule de toute surprise à ce sujet, nous appuierons notre opinion d'un raisonnement que nous lui proposons avec confiance, parce qu'il nous paraît victorieux et sans réplique. (pp. 3-4)

The publisher's outburst can be read as a type of *tu quoque* defense against the novel's second preface. In it, the editor initiates the practice of sabotaging the authority of the text he is presenting. He casts doubt first on its character, "cet Ouvrage, ou plutôt ce Recueil" (p. 5). He then dedicates the remainder of his lengthy (5 pages) prefatory text to a second detailed demonstration of the weaknesses of the text that follows. In the editor's somewhat less than humble opinion, the correspondence he has prepared for publication is too long, often grammatically and stylistically defective, almost always insincere, at times simplistic, and generally of dubious moral value (pp. 5-9). It would seem that there is indeed little to recommend the work to any but the most untiring reader. Indeed, the main justification for the editor's preface is a self-defensive gesture. He would have improved the correspondence if those who had control over the letters had given him the freedom to do so, "mais je n'étais pas le maître, et je me suis soumis" (p. 6).

Granted, the texts that initiate the *Liaisons* are extended exercises in irony, amusing plays with novelistic convention that demonstrate an affinity with the techniques of self-consciousness. Yet to see only this aspect of the introduction to Laclos's novel—the text as shifting sand, the text that means the opposite of what it says and therefore perhaps means nothing at all, since it is difficult for readers to decide just what the opposite is—is to fail to confront what the dual prefaces actually do have to say. This is not to say that the message of the double prologue to the *Liaisons* is straightforward; uncomplicated statements apparently have no place in this literary hall of mirrors. In fact, the meaning of the prefaces is a denial, best summed up by the editor's self-justification: "Mais je n'étais pas le maître, et je me suis soumis." Publisher and editor devote their energy to finding fault. They then excuse themselves by refusing to accept fault, to take the blame for the tactical deficiencies of the text they are presenting. As Wohlfarth points out, their avoidance of responsibility foreshadows what is perhaps the most famous phrase in the *Liaisons*, "ce n'est pas ma faute." When Merteuil obliquely suggests that Valmont copy this formulation, she claims it was not of her invention but was part of a story she had heard from an unidentified source about a man who refused to accept the consequences of his acts. Thus, neither *roué* has to take responsibility for the results of the rupture provoked by "ce n'est pas ma faute": the phrase has been so often copied that it is effectively beyond origin.

And so it is with the *Liaisons*. According to established eighteenth-century novelistic practice, the authors of prefaces are not obliged to tell the truth, but they are obliged to attribute responsibility for textual origin. By constantly shifting the blame—onto the editor, onto an implied author, onto "les personnes à qui elle [la correspondance] était parvenue" (p. 5), even onto a nameless "on"—the publisher and the editor make one one point absolutely clear: no one is prepared to take responsibility for this text. This denial of authority goes far beyond the familiar authorial hesitation to accept blame for a (potentially) scandalous work. This reticence is no doubt responsible for the coy set of initials that replaces the author's name on the title page of the original edition, "M.C. . . . . de L. . .". As Laclos's public letters on Vauban and the education of women amply demonstrate, the oblique strategy favored by the author of the *Liaisons* is more than coyly elusive. Laclos repeatedly acts to discredit all accepted voices of authority, then refuses to take responsibility for his action by identifying an individual able to speak in the place of the voices he has silenced. He refuses to name Montalembert as Vauban's successor. He suppresses Rousseau's name and his voice is suppressed in turn by Rousseau's authority. The double prefaces to the *Liaisons* so thoroughly discredit all possible textual origins that the novel is situated for its reader in a novelistic no man's land, a textual space beyond origin and beyond authority. The first image Laclos gives of the *Liaisons* is of an extended novelistic excuse, the textual equivalent of "ce n'est pas ma faute."

As the *Liaisons* begins, the reader is confronted with a polyphonic text that seems to weigh the relative strength of two forces, strategy and sentiment. In the "Eloge de Richardson," Diderot expressed his conviction that he had been manipulated by Richardson, "sans que je m'en aperçoive," until he found himself "associated" with one of the forces in the battle for Clarissa.[20] Readers of the *Liaisons* tend to feel analogous pressures. Their final sense of the balance of power between the forces of sentiment and strategy is generally the determining factor in their critical response. They comb the text for evidence of the presence of authority, of a voice that will take responsibility for this novel in search of an author, of a force that can rescue it from the interpretive no man's land of anonymity and excuses.

There are two schools of thought as regards the answer to this question of textual authority. The critic's Rousseauian or Vaubanian bias is generally revealed in his or her view of character in the *Liaisons,* essentially in the extent to which the critic believes that we can come to know Laclos's characters and can judge them according to what might be termed the rules of sentiment. Many influential recent readings of Laclos's novel have tended to take for granted the truth of a maxim formulated early in the novel by Mme de Volanges for the benefit of the Présidente de Tourvel: "L'humanité n'est

[20] Diderot, *Oeuvres esthétiques* (Garnier, 1965), p. 33.

parfaite dans aucun genre, pas plus dans le mal que dans le bien. Le scélérat a ses vertus, comme l'honnête homme a ses faiblesses" (32: 64). She asserts that "cette vérité me paraît . . . nécessaire à croire" in order to save good people from pride and their evil counterparts from "discouragement." Her assertion may contribute unwittingly to Tourvel's decision to believe that Valmont is capable of making an exception for her. Critics like Rousset, Fabre, and most recently Rosbottom have confirmed Tourvel's interpretation of Mme de Volanges's maxim: even the "scélérat" Valmont has his "virtue," his love for Tourvel.[21] They also believe that Merteuil suffers from an unrequited love for Valmont, a love that causes her to be, in Fabre's words, "jalouse comme une amante de tragédie et quelquefois de comédie." These interpretive convictions may save their adherents from a form of critical "discouragement." Indeed, these axioms form the cornerstone of all "hopeful" readings of the *Liaisons,* that is, readings that present a clear-cut answer to the novel's interpretive dilemma. Thus Brooks, for example, believes it is possible to elucidate the conduct of its principal characters: "We feel . . . that we understand Valmont; we feel a closeness to him, a comprehension of his ideals and weaknesses" (p. 208). Like all the novel's "Rousseauian" readers, Brooks redeems the *Liaisons* by placing it in a moral context. He refers to Merteuil's "piece of cheap and limiting worldliness," to Valmont's "personal tragedy" (p. 206). Underlying such readings is the assumption that from their superior vantage point, readers outside the text can second-guess characters, uncover their motivations, and make sense of their actions: "Valmont . . . has to a degree been taken in by his own travesties" (p. 202).

J "hopeful" readings

=> readers second-guessing chars, judging

Those who take the opposing view of the novel contend, however, as Philip Stewart has recently pointed out, that there simply is no hard evidence to justify these assertions. These critics seem increasingly unwilling to accept what Henri Du-

---

[21] Jean Rousset, *Forme et signification,* p. 96; Jean Fabre, *Le Marquis de Sade* (Colin, 1968), p. 112; Rosbottom, *Choderlos de Laclos,* p. 61.

ranton has called "la thèse romantique du libertin joué par l'amour."[22] The marquise and the vicomte consistently deny any emotional involvement. The critic who interprets their denials as "gaps" in their stories that must be filled in order to re-create "an intelligible, consistent, and unbroken history"[23] is seen as working overtime on their decidedly non-"hysterical" narratives, for Laclos provides us with no means of knowing his libertines' emotions, of deciding if they are or are not in love, are or are not jealous. Stewart and Madeleine Therrien have recently argued that at the heart of this critical dilemma is a linguistic problem. We cannot hope, they maintain, to pronounce on the "reality" of sentiments of characters such as Valmont and Merteuil who only use language in order to "dissimulate" and "trick" and who, furthermore, consistently resort to a potpourri of linguistic clichés when speaking of their feelings. "Il s'ensuit que le critique qui affirme catégoriquement qu'un personnage en aime un autre, présente une interprétation sujette à caution car le concept de l'amour ressortit à nombre de codes ambigus."[24] The warning Stewart and Therrien issue with regard to the novel's libertine heroes should also be heeded with regard to the less self-consciously sentimental characters in the *Liaisons*. It also applies to the role reserved for sentiment in the novel as a whole and thus to the question that subtends all such discussions, that of the moral placement of Laclos's fiction.

"A l'école de Jean-Jacques Rousseau," Versini contends, "Laclos réhabilite le sentiment vrai et l'émotion" (p. 1157). Even on its title page, the *Liaisons* bears the mark of its inscription "à l'école de" Rousseau, but just what that initial

[margin handwritten note: but all dsg= dissimulation to trick]

---

[22] Stewart, review of Rosbottom's *Choderlos de Laclos*, *Eighteenth-Century Studies* 13-14 (1980): 433; Duranton, "*Les Liaisons dangereuses* ou le miroir ennemi," *Revue des sciences humaines* 153 (1974): 130-31. See also Tzvetan Todorov, *Littérature et Signification* (Larousse, 1967), p. 187, and Sylvère Lotringer, "Vice de forme," *Critique* (Mar. 1971): 197.

[23] Freud, *Dora* (New York: Collier Books, 1963), p. 32.

[24] Stewart and Therrien, "Aspects de Texture verbale dans *Les Liaisons dangereuses*," *RHLF* 82 (1982): 555.

inscription of a pedagogical relationship between Laclos and *Julie*'s author means and whether it is intended to signify, as Versini argues, that the *Liaisons* is really "un roman d'amour" seems far less clearly encoded. In the three fragments on education, Laclos speaks with and then is silenced by Rousseau's unnamed voice. In the *Liaisons,* that precursor's voice is once again omnipresent, but this time that presence is more difficult to evaluate. Having observed that Laclos's commentaries on female education are inscribed in Rousseau's margins, Jean Rousset concludes that "*Les Liaisons* apparaissent alors comme une *Héloïse* renversée," thereby confirming Georges May's description of Laclos as a "disciple paradoxal" or "négatif" of Rousseau.[25] It can be argued that the form of Laclos's defense of Rousseauian ideas in the essays is indicative of a desire to feel himself the master's equal, if not his superior. In the *Liaisons,* his relationship to his powerful precursor's authority appears both less and more ambiguous. To begin with, the master teacher is a more active presence in the novel than in the essays. References to Rousseau abound in the *Liaisons;* the editor and Valmont are especially given to citing him. Yet none of their citations can be easily interpreted, and some of them seem almost to defy critical scrutiny.

The initial reference of the *Liaisons* to Rousseau is perhaps both the most critical and the most ambiguous as well. Immediately below a minimally camouflaged version of the *nom d'auteur* ("Par M.C. . . . . de L. . ."), the title page of the original edition contains a citation that serves as the work's epigraph: "J'ai vu les moeurs de mon temps, et j'ai publié ces Lettres." A complete identification of the citation is provided: "J.J. Rousseau, Préf. de *la Nouvelle Héloïse*" (p. 1). This quotation, unlike others in the *Liaisons,* has not been tampered with—or "profaned," according to the editor's description of Valmont's deformations of Rousseau (p. 1331, variant

[25] Rousset, *Forme et signification,* p. 94; May, *The Romanic Review* 40 (Dec. 1949): 290.

i to letter 110).[26] In context, the sentence forms part of the initial paragraph of Rousseau's first preface to his novel: "Il faut dès spectacles dans les grandes villes, et des Romans aux peuples corrompus. J'ai vû les moeurs de mon tems, et j'ai publié ces lettres. Que n'ai-je vécu dans un siècle où je dusse les jetter au feu!" (4: 5). One aspect of Laclos's use of Rousseau here seems clear: by citing a passage from the margin of *Julie*, Laclos places his own novel-to-be under the double sign of his alleged literary mentor and of his mentor's novel, the most famous novel of its day. Beyond this point, the reference is elusive, as elusive as all of what might be termed the moral fiber of the *Liaisons*. To open an epistolary novel by mentioning a celebrated example of epistolary fiction from the preceding literary generation (twenty-one years separate *Julie* and the *Liaisons*) is surely the equivalent of a challenge. One message of the epigraph is that Laclos is guaranteeing that his novel will be able to take on, and even surpass, *Julie*'s fame— allowing its author to move out from under Rousseau's shadow.

Predictably, the epigraph has been interpreted in opposing ways determined by the critic's overall view of the novel's stance. Some contend that Laclos's choice indicates the intentions he shares with Rousseau. Thus Peter Brooks argues, "by this epigraph, Rousseau meant to suggest that his novel constituted a lesson to his contemporaries; Laclos uses it to imply that his novel is an exemplum of contemporary behavior" (p. 212). Others agree with Rosbottom that the citation is intended (eventually) to reveal opposite intentions: "[I]t is an ironic juxtaposition, unclear until reread after the novel has been read" (p. 46). Versini even attempts to reconcile the two positions by arguing that the epigraph is the first signal of Laclos's intention of repeating Rousseau's goals, but of doing so in a more honest, more "realistic" way (p. 1164, n. 2).

[26] Versini's study of the manuscript of the *Liaisons* reveals that Laclos had originally quoted Rousseau from memory (as he has Valmont do for various effects) and had written "j'ai vu les moeurs de ce siècle" (p. 1163, variant *b* to p. 1). On the manuscript's title page, Laclos signs the novel "M. Cxxx D.L.c. ."

While I would disagree with Rosbottom's view that the presence of irony is "clear" and certain for a reader who has completed the novel, the title page nevertheless does bear one possible indication that this use of citation is not exactly what it seems. On the title page of *Julie,* the author is identified by his full name, J. J. Rousseau. On the title page of the *Liaisons,* only a set of initials is given. This camouflage is merely a pseudo-camouflage, since the initials are both correct and easily decipherable. The rejection of the complete name indicates less the author's desire to remain hidden than his wish to appear to need protection. When Laclos half hides his name, he provides a subtle hint of the scandalous content of his novel, but the position he takes with regard to that scandal is obviously different from Rousseau's. The presence of the *nom d'auteur* on *Julie*'s title page signals its author's detachment from the volume's potentially scandalous content; his position is clearly that of a moralist teaching a lesson and presenting a case for judgment. Laclos half takes responsibility for his fiction with the "signature," not of a moralist, but of a libertine novelist, a playful construct of a signature that bestows on its user a form of complicity with the world of his fiction. Finally, to the reader familiar with the content of the *Liaisons,* the presence of the sentence from *Julie*'s margin in the margin of Laclos's novel seems more than simply "ironic." The epigraph is dissonant, reminiscent of ironic citation, yet the intention governing this use of the master's voice is not clearly mocking, only profoundly ambiguous.

This inconsonance continues to rupture the narrative surface of the *Liaisons* at regular intervals, most frequently in the form of Valmont's problematic citations from Rousseau. For example, letter 110 from Valmont to Merteuil opens with a citation whose status as citation is signaled by the use of italics: *"Puissances du Ciel, j'avais une âme pour la douleur; donnez m'en une pour la félicité!"* (p. 253). In a strange gesture of pedantic overkill, both the editor and Valmont rush to identify the reference. The editor wins the contest, since the asterisk indicating his footnote with its information, *Nouvelle*

Héloïse, or the source of the citation, immediately follows "félicité." Valmont's second sentence, "C'est, je crois, le tendre Saint-Preux qui s'exprime ainsi," is thus rendered partially redundant for the reader outside the text. Valmont explains his use of the reference as an effort to demonstrate to his partner in vice his strategic superiority to the "tendre" Saint-Preux. His predecessor was only capable of experiencing either sadness or happiness, but Valmont can paradoxically know the two emotions simultaneously: "mieux partagé que lui, je possède à la fois les deux existences. Oui, mon amie, je suis, en même temps, très heureux et très malheureux" (p. 253).

In this instance, the editor does nothing to mediate the impact of Valmont's denigrating vision of his famous recent rival in novelistic heroism, but elsewhere he does intervene in the Valmont-Rousseau struggle, and his interventions inevitably act to complicate the interpretation of such passages. On at least one occasion, Laclos decided in the final version to suppress the signs of what appears to be a three-way conflict. Letter 110 contains a second citation from *Julie:* "Non, elle n'aura pas *les plaisirs du vice et les honneurs de la vertu*" (p. 254). This time, Valmont, although he uses punctuation to designate the phrase as quotation, does not identify it. In a characteristically laconic footnote, the editor provides the source of the borrowing. The manuscript reveals that Laclos had originally intended to follow his identification with a commentary: "Ce M. de Valmont paraît aimer à citer J.-J. Rousseau, et toujours en le profanant par l'abus qu'il en fait" (p. 1331, variant *i* to letter 110). He chooses a forceful term to characterize Valmont's use of Rousseau. However, what exactly he means by "profanation" in this context is difficult to determine. Valmont's persistent, though slight, misquotations evidently constitute what could be termed his first "abuse." In this case, for "l'honneur de la vertu" (1: 9: 49), he substitutes "les honneurs de la vertu." Versini dismisses the change as simply "encore une citation de mémoire" (p. 1332, n. 5), but in this instance, consciously or unconsciously, Laclos is having Valmont vulgarize the moral code of Rousseau's *Julie.*

A second "abuse" is perhaps closer to "profanation," for here Valmont is making mocking use, not of the words of his rival hero, but of those of the one character in Rousseau's novel close enough to "divinity" to be "profaned"—Julie. Valmont's true deformation is not his small mistranslation, but his complete change of meaning. Julie intends the phrase as part of a counterreproach to Saint-Preux's reproach (1: 8: 48) that he is bearing the sole responsibility for their virtue. She is trying to make him realize that "les plaisirs du vice et l'honneur de la vertu" would constitute a "fate" less "agréable" than their present one. Valmont deforms Julie's intentions and uses the phrase as a synonym for the seduction of a woman "à la Lovelace" ("en faire une nouvelle Clarisse"), for possession without consent, or for rape. In the process, "honor" is demoted from a moral quality to the trappings to which that moral quality is reduced by society ("les honneurs").

In a footnote to letter 58, this time addressed by Valmont to Tourvel,[27] the editor goes beyond condemnation to raise questions about the meaning and the consequences of such "profanation." On this occasion, Valmont is not attempting to (re)produce anything like an accurate citation, for he uses no punctuation to signal his borrowing, which he presents instead as paraphrase: "Un Sage a dit que pour dissiper ses craintes il suffisait presque toujours d'en approfondir la cause" (pp. 117-18). He does not name the "Sage," so the editor intervenes with a note that constitutes the most puzzling of his commentaries on Valmont's penchant for citation: "On croit que c'est Rousseau dans *Emile:* mais la citation n'est pas exacte, et l'application qu'en fait Valmont est bien fausse; et puis, Madame de Tourvel avait-elle lu *Emile?*" (p. 118). In *his* footnote, Versini confirms the editor's tentative identifi-

---

[27] I break with accepted practice in referring to the Présidente de Tourvel as "Tourvel," rather than "Madame de Tourvel" or "the Présidente." I see no reason why an onomastic distinction should be maintained between the virtuous character and the two *roués,* generally called simply "Merteuil" and "Valmont," especially since the editor makes no such distinction, but grants all characters their proper titles.

cation and gives as the source a passage in the second book of *Emile* in which Rousseau contends that most nocturnal fears are dissipated when their origin is made known (4: 382-88). In this instance, Valmont "abuses" Rousseau's text more than anywhere else. His "profane" citations are usually included in letters to Merteuil, the ideal *archi-lectrice* for the irony in his usage. In those cases, he deforms the original meaning but, since his addressee is aware of his deformation, he may be said to be more concerned with emptying Rousseau's phrases of meaning than with giving them a new one. When he writes to Tourvel, the foundation of the communication has, of course, shifted. As Versini points out, this "citation approximative" teaches us only about Valmont's intellectual formation, since Roussseau's text could have played no role in Tourvel's education (p. 1248, n. 1). In addition, unlike Merteuil, Tourvel cannot decipher the double-entendres in her correspondent's discourse. When he addresses Rousseau's formula to her, Valmont gives it new meaning, for he transfers the maxim from the realm of children's fear of the dark to a woman's fear of illicit love.

"Madame de Tourvel avait-elle lu *Emile?*" the editor queries, and his question can be read as a commentary both on the functioning and the danger of citation. A citation that is intentionally misquoted, misinterpreted, and delivered without identification for the benefit of an audience ignorant of the original cannot be expected to function as citation—but its malfunctioning is part of Valmont's plan. His "pleasure" results from quoting without being understood, from secret citing. Valmont demonstrates in this letter his ability to speak with another's voice and to appropriate another's discourse while altering the intended purpose of that discourse. He proves that Rousseau's venerated words can be used for any end, that a call to higher virtue can be turned into a mockery of virtue, and that a pedagogical maxim can be used as an instrument of seduction—and the seduction in question is, of course, that of the novel's "Rousseauian" heroine. For Valmont, his paraphrase of *Emile* constitutes a humiliation of

Rousseau: he twists a passage from *Emile,* turns it from its intended route of communication, makes it a tool of seduction. In the three fragments on education, Laclos appropriates Rousseau's discourse and re-creates Rousseau's intentions as well. In his novel, he creates a self-proclaimed libertine who goes one step farther. Valmont reduces Rousseau's words to the corrupt status of the literary works that Laclos's predecessor condemned so violently in the preface to *Julie* and elsewhere. The editor allegedly criticizes Valmont's "profanation," but his very criticisms draw attention to deformations that might otherwise have gone unnoticed. In addition, his use of "profaner" to characterize Valmont's activity is both hyperbolic and too perceptive. The verb seems ridiculously inflated, and, every bit as much as Valmont's mockery, invites laughter—laughter that ultimately is directed at the only voice closed to double-entendres, Rousseau's. With his ironic, worldly tone, the editor seems to take sides with Valmont in his "abuse." It would seem a logical next step to argue that, in doing so, he is only following his creator's lead. For a writer intimidated by his predecessor's power, such a "profanation" would constitute the ultimate defense against an unsettling greatness.

This problem becomes more complicated still when one considers the fact that Rousseau's presence in the *Liaisons* is limited neither to direct, or at least identified, citations, nor to the ironic and twisted style of its libertine heroes and editor. The type of "profanation" just analyzed in Valmont's letters is not confined to quotations that are presented as such. In his letters to Tourvel, Valmont "creates" what might be termed a self-conscious pastiche of Saint-Preux's correspondence with Julie. These letters contain passages that are destined to reach simultaneously two different publics (Tourvel, with her seduction in view; those who share Valmont's secret—Merteuil, eventually all readers of the novel—with their amusement in view). Valmont is at his best when what he says can be read two ways; the most striking example of this is the letter written on Emilie's back. When the pastiche is not tongue-in-cheek, these "love" letters are perhaps the most boring in the novel.

[handwritten margin note: Valmont's pastiche of SP's letters to J]

Valmont never succeeds in captivating the readers of the *Liaisons* when he echoes Saint-Preux. When he imitates without being playful, his discourse, Rousseauian or not, falls flat and is not even successful as pastiche.

For her seductions, Merteuil frequently has recourse to formulations, even strategies, that are obviously Rousseauian. However, she, unlike Valmont, never identifies the source of her borrowings, and the editor always respects her citatory silences.[28] Any reader familiar with Rousseau's work, especially with *Julie*, cannot avoid the sensation that, when she seeks to seduce, Merteuil often speaks with a Rousseauian voice, and any reader with access to Versini's edition of the *Liaisons* has only to consult his notes to find confirmation of such suspicions. For example, Merteuil silently "profanes" (to quote Versini) Rousseau for her seduction of the Chevalier: "O mon ami . . . je me reproche . . . d'avoir pu un instant voiler mon coeur à tes regards" (10: 30; p. 1192, n. 7). Once again according to Versini, she "parodies" Julie's declaration of love (10: 30), Rousseau's thoughts on marriage (105: 238), and even Rousseau's definition of virtue (121: 279), to cite but a few examples (p. 1347, n. 3). Furthermore, just as the editor echoes Valmont's deformations of Saint-Preux, so the libertine Delilah's profanation of the voice of sentiment is often mirrored by the role Laclos assigns her in the novel's structure. Thus Versini compares the place at the center of the *Liaisons* accorded Merteuil's autobiographical letter (letter 81) to that given Julie's homologous missive (3: 18: 340-365): "A la lettre de la fidélité fait pendant la lettre du mensonge" (p. 1279, n. 2). In addition, Laclos couples this elevation of Merteuil to Julie's place with a demotion of "Julie"/Julie through the role he assigns the "new Julie" in the *Liaisons*: Tourvel's *femme de chambre* is named Julie. Laclos displaces the name of Rousseau's heroine, thereby linking his own sentimental heroine

---

[28] That Merteuil's usage is more indirect than Valmont's only confirms her sense of the difference between male and female strategy, a point to which I will return later in this chapter.

metonymically to her predecessor in sentimentality. Laclos's Julie conspires with Valmont to bring about her mistress's seduction and even hands over her mistress's Rousseauian missives; this onomastic reversal constitutes a profanation far more devious than any his creator allowed Valmont to imagine.[29]

In these cases, the reader outside the text finds herself in a position somewhere between Merteuil's and Tourvel's when they act as recipients of Valmont's recycled collages of Saint-Preux's missives to Julie. At times, the extrafictional reader is closer to Merteuil. She can identify the two voices in the double-voiced profanation and is therefore able to join in the textual game along with its master strategists. At times, however, even the most knowledgeable extratextual readers must find themselves approaching the rather more uncomfortable position represented in the novel by Tourvel—the citation is not exact, Merteuil/Valmont is twisting Rousseau's purpose—and they have either not read or cannot identify the relevant passage from *Emile/Julie*.

Versini comments only evasively on the function, parodic or otherwise, of the structural parallels that can frequently be noted between the *Liaisons* and *Julie*. He says only that Laclos's irony is the mark of his "originality," of his liberation from "servitude" to the master's voice and to the type of "poetic novel" Rousseau forged from his "lyricism" (p. 1149). Yet the already complicated question of the presence of these negative citations from the master's texts is complicated still further by the fact that these (parodic) borrowings from Rousseau coexist in Laclos's novel with other interventions of unmistakably Rousseauian voices that are stylistically similar to the "profanations" but diametrically opposed to them in intention. Merteuil's and Valmont's pastiches of *Julie* for the purposes of seduction are in a way counterbalanced by the

---

[29] In similar fashion, Laclos also demotes (and degrades) the name of the title character of Rousseau's *Emile* when he calls the courtesan on whose back Valmont writes his appropriately lyrical (Rousseauian) missive to Tourvel "Emilie."

other Rousseauian voice in the novel, that of Tourvel. From her pen flow the only passages that are reminiscent of Laclos's precursor in both style *and* intention. Valmont acts (and mocks) the art of Saint-Preux, but in the Présidente he finds a true successor to Julie, or at least to the interpretation of his heroine Rousseau advocated. Critics have contended that Tourvel is the strongest character in the *Liaisons,* the character whom the reader admires most and with whom our sympathies lie, and for Versini her Rousseauian voice is the unmistakable sign of Laclos's solidarity with his teacher (p. 1148). "We are closer to the Présidente than are any of the other characters in the novel," Peter Brooks argues; "unhampered by strict allegiance to any system, without ulterior motive, we listen to her letters . . . and we understand her instinctively and sympathetically, as we do the Julie to whom her conception owes so much" (p. 212). In Brooks's vision of the novel, the fact that Laclos "patently admires" Merteuil and Valmont is counterbalanced by the fact that "their system is made to seem limited," and Laclos, writing under "the mark of Rousseau," shares his advocacy of the "inherent morality of real passion." Even if Tourvel falls victim to the *roués,* "she is nevertheless probably happier, and freer, than her torturers" (pp. 213-15). Furthermore, Tourvel is not alone in speaking both with Rousseau's voice and in Rousseau's wake. In Danceny's letters to Merteuil, one can note still more Rousseauian echoes, and on one occasion Versini even hears Rousseau *avant la lettre,* suggesting that Laclos not only could copy the master's voice but even possessed the uncanny ability to predict it.[30]

In one of his letters to his wife from prison, Laclos compares his writing to Rousseau's:

> Tu trouves que Rousseau et moi, écrivons de même! Tu me fais, assurément, beaucoup d'honneur, et à toi, beaucoup d'illusions; mais il a écrit presque tout ce que tu m'as inspiré, et ce que tu m'inspires encore; et tu prends

---

[30] "Danceny . . . se permet ici une cadence très heureuse, qui *malgré les apparences ne doit rien aux 'Rêveries du promeneur solitaire'* parues en 1782" (Versini, p. 388, n. 3 to p. 345, emphasis mine).

la ressemblance du sentiment pour celle de l'expression. . . . [P]eut-être, lui et moi, étions-nous les seuls êtres capables de parler à ton coeur le langage qui lui convient, et que tu sais si bien entendre et apprécier. (*O.c.*, p. 825)

Here Laclos suggests both that his own wife was seduced not by him but by Rousseau (speaking through him?) and concomitantly that he himself was also seduced by *Julie*'s author, that he was programmed stylistically and emotionally by his precursor—"il a écrit presque tout ce que tu m'as inspiré." His letter provides a flawless illustration of triangular desire (as well as an extended application of the strategies of displacement evident in Rousseau's work): Laclos feels that both he and his wife have been driven out of their places by Rousseau. The reader of Laclos's letters to his wife who shares Merteuil's and Valmont's familiarity with Rousseau's work comes to understand what must have inspired this exchange, for his letters provide almost a *mise en abyme* of the unsettling use of Rousseau in the *Liaisons*. They are overtly Rousseauian in tone like Tourvel's letters, but they are punctuated at regular intervals with approximate citations (citations from memory) from Rousseau's work, as though Laclos, when writing in his own name, were a combination of Tourvel and Valmont/ Merteuil, a ventriloquist practicing the various ways of projecting Rousseau's voice through his own.

That same reader of Laclos who approximates his (and Merteuil/Valmont's) knowledge of Rousseau's work—and Versini in his copious notes to the new Pléiade edition seems to represent the *archi-lecteur* for this class of readers—eventually reaches the conclusion that much of the *Liaisons*, like Valmont's letters, is a collage of fragments of Rousseau's voice.[31] This realization leads in turn to a series of interrelated interpretive questions. Did Laclos expect his readers to be Mer-

---

[31] In privileging the presence of Rousseau's voice in the *Liaisons*, I am neglecting numerous citations in Laclos's novel from a wide variety of other sources. Laclos obviously had a broad repertory of authors to put in his characters' mouths, but with no other author does he practice the complex and uncanny ventriloquism that characterizes his relationship with Rousseau.

teuils or Tourvels? In other words, how many of these echoes and direct and indirect borrowings are we intended to notice and identify? Secondly, on the simplest level, Merteuil and Valmont cite Rousseau to victimize those who do not share their knowledge of the master of sentiment. Danceny, a young Valmont schooled by Valmont in the use of Rousseau's voice, also echoes the master's discourse of sentiment. Because he and Tourvel are presumably speaking sincerely, their Rousseauian discourse is the perfect vehicle for the self-exposure that leads to their victimization at the hands of the libertines. The editor of their correspondence outdoes Valmont at his own game by pointing out his citatory deficiencies. If a victim is defined in the *Liaisons* as a person with inferior knowledge of Rousseau, are we then to see Valmont as the editor's plaything? Does the fact that Tourvel and Danceny borrow from Rousseau unwittingly (sincerely) spare them from this ritual of disparagement at the hands of the editor? Behind all these questions lies, of course, the unavoidable, central question: what role is Laclos assigning his precursor when he has Rousseau's voice echo with seemingly every possible interpretive nuance in all the voices of this apparently most polyphonic of epistolary novels, ultimately (re)defining polyphony as a series of variations on one voice?

Versini is representative of the majority of Laclos critics who believe that it is possible to assign an interpretive value to each borrowing from Rousseau. Thus, some are signs of "sincere" admiration, others function as parodies ("profanations"), and the sum of the various parts can be evaluated as possessing either a positive or a negative charge. However, such a reading fails to take into account the multi-layered process of evaluation portrayed in the *Liaisons;* for example, Tourvel is the avowed recipient of certain of Valmont's letters to which she responds, but these are also read and commented on by Merteuil and in turn by the editor, and the author repeats this process in a less direct manner. It also omits the complex interpretive difficulties posed by a text in which repeated copying of discourse serves to place the very notions of responsibility and sincerity in question. Stewart and Therrien's suggestion that the libertines' extended use of cliché makes it impossible to determine their "true" sentiments may be applied to the *Liaisons* as a whole. The complicated and multifaceted proliferation of Rousseau's voice in the echo chamber of Laclos's novel creates a sensation of total equivocalness and thereby places the idea of sincerity in suspension, *sous rature.*

Foucault contends that Sade's entire *oeuvre* is a "gigantesque pastiche de Rousseau."[32] His statement is more obviously applicable in the case of Laclos. Indeed, the effect of Rousseau's voice in Laclos's corresponds perfectly to the three main conditions governing the use of pastiche described by Gérard Genette in *Palimpsestes.* Rousseau's presence is evident, pedagogical, and ambiguous. In the first place, Laclos plainly offers his reader a "contrat de pastiche" when he repeatedly inscribes Rousseau's name in his text, most evidently on the title page of the *Liaisons* where the name of *Julie*'s author has equal, if not superior, billing to that of the novel's author, since his name is written out in full, while that of Laclos is limited to his initials. Secondly, Genette stresses that pastiche has traditionally been associated with a student-teacher relationship: the student imitates the style of the writer he sees as his master. Finally, Genette points out that this pedagogical bond is the only hint the creator of a pastiche gives of his attitude toward the style he copies: pastiche is equivocal, a stylistic transformation or transposition, a process that does not necessarily reveal a semantic attitude.[33]

Genette stresses still another aspect of pastiche, an aspect also noted in all the earliest definitions of the term in French and English dictionaries: pastiche is a form of *bricolage.*

[32] Foucault, *Histoire de la folie à l'âge classique* (Gallimard, 1972), p. 552.
[33] Genette, *Palimpsestes* (Seuil, 1982), pp. 32, 35, 141.

L'art de "faire du neuf avec du vieux" a l'avantage de produire des objets plus complexes et plus savoureux que les produits "faits exprès": une fonction nouvelle se superpose et s'enchevêtre à une structure ancienne, et la dissonance entre ces deux éléments coprésents donne sa saveur à l'ensemble. (p. 451)

The culinary metaphor Genette hints at to give a sense of the "savory dissonance" of pastiche was at the basis of its first definitions. Thus the earliest use of the term in English (1744, according to the *OED*) compares a painter's pastiche of master painters to a pasty "because as the several things that season a pasty are reduc'd to one taste," so the various styles copied blend into one.[34] It seems likely that the culinary comparison is persistently recurrent in order to suggest the simultaneity of the heterogeneous blending that is essential to pastiche. In all forms of pastiche, the components are mixed together, but the resulting "hotchpotch" or "potpourri" (*OED*) is an example of the type of impossible mathematical plenitude Rousseau dreamed of, a total somehow greater than the sum of its parts, a polyphonic creation in which the preexisting voices that compose it can be heard both separately (thereby retaining resonances of the contexts of their former existence) and simultaneously (thereby resonating with an *intentional* dissonance).

The first definitions of pastiche all maintain that, because of their peculiar juxtaposition of elements, pastiches are neither originals nor copies (see, for example, the *OED* or the *Dictionnaire de Trévoux*). In the case of the *Liaisons*, however, it is precisely the type of incompletely processed blending practiced by Laclos that constitutes the greatest mark of the novel's originality. In the *Liaisons*, Laclos seems constantly

---

[34] The term enters English in a translation of Roger de Piles's *Connoissance des Tableaux* (1677), so the *terminus a quo* of the notion of this artistic "pâté" or "stew" art in France corresponds to that of the literary tradition examined here.

to be asking his reader to take sides in the struggle between virtue and vice so vividly portrayed. Many readers decide that the language of sentiment wins, favoring a Rousseauian view of the novel that follows the pattern established by Diderot's reading of Richardson: the reader believes that the author wants him to "associate" himself with those who suffer ("Eloge de Richardson," p. 33). Others choose the opposite course and speak of Laclos's creation of a mythology of intelligence. The mark of the defensiveness of Laclos's novel is that these contradictory readings are both invited. Yet neither interpretation of the *Liaisons* takes into account Laclos's consistent ambivalence toward Rousseau's authority. When, in the fragments on the education of women, Laclos erased Rousseau's name in order to assume his authority, he was made impotent. At the same time, the letter to his wife demonstrates that he needs Rousseau in order to make love to her (a problem characters in the *Liaisons* have occasion to discover). Rousseau's name figures so prominently in the *Liaisons,* and Laclos's characters are influenced by Rousseau's language in so many ways because the novel succeeds in putting both the master's authority and the master's language in what Laclos considered their proper place. In the *Liaisons,* Rousseau's language is no longer threatening. It can be copied (and miscopied, pastiched, profaned, even mocked by the *archi-lectrice* of Tourvel's letters, Merteuil). "Je ne suis point amoureux; et ce n'est pas ma faute, si les circonstances me forcent d'en jouer le rôle" (138: 320)—Valmont excuses himself to Merteuil for his use of Rousseau's language, but his defense is unnecessary. The rhetoric of sentiment belongs to the common domain—Tourvel, after all, consults *Clarissa* just as *Julie*'s author did. Anyone who uses this rhetoric is simply copying, and therefore is no more responsible for the consequences of his text than Valmont is when he copies Merteuil's ready-made excuse, or than the editor is for copying the letters. In the *Liaisons,* the rhetoric of sentiment, the language of Laclos's literary "master," is given authorless status, is made anonymous.

======== ✳ ========

Delilah's Siegecraft: The Mathematics of Seduction

> Que n'aurai-je pas fait pour ce Danceny? J'aurai été à
> la fois son ami, son confident, son rival et sa maîtresse!
> Le Vicomte de Valmont

Julie's last word belongs to its "editor" who devotes a long footnote to a particular aspect of the question of authorial morality, a footnote which has an enigmatic formulation at its center:

> Je ne saurois concevoir quel plaisir on peut prendre à imaginer et composer le personnage d'un Scélérat, à se mettre à sa place tandis qu'on le représente, à lui prêter l'éclat le plus imposant. Je plains beaucoup les auteurs de tant de tragédies pleines d'horreurs, lesquels passent leur vie à faire agir et parler des gens qu'on ne peut écouter ni voir sans souffrir. Il me semble qu'on devroit gémir d'être condanné à un travail si cruel. (2: 745)

"Le traité de l'*Education des femmes*," Jean Rousset contends, "s'inscrit en marge de *Julie*" (*Forme et signification*, p. 94). His argument could easily be applied to the *Liaisons*, with slight alterations. The *Liaisons* stands in a position with regard to Rousseau's novel that is doubly marginal: Laclos inscribes his novel, not only in *Julie*'s margin, but in the margin of *Julie*'s marginalia. *Julie*'s concluding remark apparently has no direct link to the novel that precedes it: Rousseau seems to be indulging in totally gratuitous pity of writers "condemned" to literary endeavors more painful than his. But *Julie*'s conclusion can easily be read as a challenge, and it may be that Laclos decided to take up that challenge by writing the *Liaisons*, and that the epigraph is intended to convey that message to his reader. As an examination of the prefaces to the *Liaisons* reveals, Laclos reserved an important function for his own marginalia: he realized the potential of this oblique position.

In the *Liaisons*, Laclos "imagined" and "composed" two *scélérats*, endowing them with what Rousseau termed "l'éclat le plus imposant." Merteuil and Valmont merit the epithet "scélérats" because they govern themselves, not on the basis of emotions or conscience, but according to the principles of strategy, primarily military strategy. They are representatives of the force that stands in opposition to the Rousseauian language of sentiment. Critics who interpret the *Liaisons* as an affirmation of the power of strategy, who see Laclos as an accomplice of his *roués,* those who admire the rigor and the lucidity of Laclos's novel, read it as an implicit reversal of the views Laclos explicitly expressed in his correspondence with Riccoboni. They see in the novel an obsessive fascination with strategy that overshadows any form of commitment to ideals traditionally considered Rousseauian. That strategy that has so fascinated readers of the *Liaisons* can be termed Vaubanian. Merteuil and Valmont can be read, not only in Vaubanian terms, but even in light of Laclos's placement of Vauban's genius and his attempted rewriting of defensive military strategy. Laclos's *roués,* like Classicism's heroes, seem concerned only with offensive action; they deserve the title "preneur de villes" every bit as much as Vauban or Louis XIV. Yet, like their predecessors, the central characters of the *Liaisons* never forget that the great conqueror can only dazzle offensively if his defenses are airtight. Faithful to their creator's revision of Vauban's claims for defensive systems, Merteuil and Valmont are convinced that the myth of a perfect system of defenses is not only a reality, but a reality that they have mastered.

Valmont revels in his self-portrait as a military conqueror: "Jugez-moi donc comme Turenne ou Frédéric," he boasts to Merteuil (125: 293). But the strategy he so proudly sets out in the same passage reveals itself on closer examination to be less appropriate for a "pure" offensive genius than for a military strategist always mindful of defensive considerations. In general, Valmont devotes less time to questions of technique than does Merteuil, but in this instance he expounds at some length on the strategic intricacies of his conduct. He begins with a moment of self-praise that derives from his fidelity to the cornerstone of their pact: "[V]ous me trouverez, je crois, une pureté de méthode qui vous fera plaisir; et vous verrez que je ne me suis écarté en rien des vrais principes de cette guerre, que nous avons remarqué souvent être si semblable à l'autre." Valmont goes on to explain how the expression, the war between the sexes, can be understood literally. His version of this private war is characterized by Vaubanian prudence: "J'ai forcé à combattre l'ennemi qui ne voulait que temporiser; je me suis donné, par de savantes manoeuvres, le choix du terrain et celui des dispositions. . . . [J]e n'ai rien mis au hasard." Valmont's offensive strategies are never undertaken without regard for defensive security: "[J]e n'ai engagé l'action qu'avec une retraite assurée, par où je pusse couvrir et conserver tout ce que j'avais conquis précédemment."

In their exploits, the *roués* repeatedly demonstrate that defensive strength must be the invisible, unsuspected foundation of libertine conduct. Merteuil explains to Valmont why this is particularly crucial for a woman who would attempt to join in libertine combat when she complains about Cécile's inability to learn a defensive stance:

> . . . de sorte que, tandis que nous nous occuperions à former cette petite fille pour l'intrigue, nous n'en ferions qu'une femme facile. Or, je ne connais rien de si plat que cette facilité de bêtise, qui se rend sans savoir ni comment ni pourquoi, uniquement parce qu'on l'attaque et qu'elle ne sait pas résister. Ces sortes de femmes ne sont absolument que des machines à plaisir. (106: 244)

Merteuil thus reserves one of her purest expressions of scorn and cruelty for a potential "intrigante subalterne" who proves incapable of doing battle because of what she terms "une faiblesse de caractère presque toujours incurable," that is, an incapacity for the defensive obsession. It must be stressed that the female defenses to which Merteuil is referring here are not to be confused with the traditional protection of virtue. What she has in mind is closer to a second line of defenses that functions on the model of Montalembert's *fortification perpendiculaire.* This system of "resistance" surrounds the original protective shield, the culturally inspired defense, and puts it at the service of a stronger and more individualistic line of protection. Montalembert's "detached forts" were designed to permit the adaptation of his system to any terrain. Unlike the traditional rules of female behavior that employ the same "arms" to oppose different attacks, Merteuil's resistance is tailored to fit each situation. When she advises Cécile that "quand vous écrivez à quelqu'un, c'est pour lui et non pas pour vous: vous devez donc moins chercher à lui dire ce que vous pensez, que ce qui lui plaît davantage" (105: 242-43), she outlines the basic principle of all her defensive strategies. To the traditional bastions constructed for the protection of female virtue, Merteuil adds a more protean system of defenses put into operation to safeguard not virtue, but its lack.

The construction of a complex, often multi-layered defensive apparatus around an empty center is an enterprise to which Merteuil and Valmont often refer.[35] As an epistolary novel, the *Liaisons* by nature is a work of deferred communication—in Daniel's words, "un manuel de l'action oblique" (p. 38). Through the libertines' manipulations, the reader observes the transformation of the letter into a diabolical means of double communication. When Merteuil explains to Cécile that her writing should be governed by the idea that she should not seek to express what she is thinking but what her correspondent wants to hear, she lays down the foundation of libertine defensive strategy. Almost the entire correspondence of Merteuil and Valmont with other characters, and a major part of their letters to each other as well, is composed of an accumulation of rhetorical figures that may be read in at least

saying what correspondent wants to hear

[35] The last section of this chapter discusses the importance of this configuration—building a shell around an empty center—in Laclos's military career.

two different ways by different publics—and often, like the novel's double prefaces, seem ultimately emptied of meaning.[36]

The most sustained example of double-entendre in the novel is letter 48, the (in)famous text written by Valmont on the courtesan Emilie's back. Valmont arranges to have the letter mailed twice so that each of its intended recipients can appreciate the original. (The second, "enlightened" *destinataire* generally receives only copies of the missives to whose irony she can pay fitting tribute.) He sends the letter to Merteuil asking her to forward it to its explicit recipient, Tourvel, thereby reversing the usual order of transmission according to which the naive reception precedes the ironic one. As the result of Valmont's manipulations, the letter, like the novel, lends itself to two sustained and contradictory readings, "sincerely" as an outpouring of a lover's torment, and ironically as a self-conscious commentary on the triteness of such outpourings. What the text ultimately communicates to Laclos's reader is an awareness of its stylistic brilliance, a sense of its "author's" pride in maintaining the appearance of communication while in fact revealing nothing of himself beyond his appreciation of the joys of technique. In the average epistolary novel, a (love) letter gives the reader a greater understanding of its author's psychology, but such a letter in the *Liaisons* in most cases provides only a demonstration of the perfection of its author's system of self-protection. Double communication ensures the writer's complete protection from his correspondent's inquiring gaze. Each of Valmont's correspondents receives the original of this letter, yet the letter itself, faithful to the origin of "pastiche," ultimately puts into question the very notion of originality. This letter, of which Valmont is so proud, shows that for its author the mark of genius is not an original creation but the ability to "create" a credible pastiche of a

---

[36] Todorov has provided a thorough treatment of this type of linguistic deformation, to which he refers as "la parole inadéquate," "une parole qui ne désigne pas correctement son référent" (*Littérature et Signification*, pp. 14ff.).

foreign style (the language of sentiment) and then to turn his creation into a joke, meaningless in and of itself and signifying only what is never said, that its (hidden) author intends to subjugate all his readers.

One of the best-known texts in the *Liaisons*, Merteuil's autobiographical letter (letter 81), stands as testimony to the prolonged struggle that results in mastery of such a system of self-protection. The marquise tells a story of self-formation—"je puis dire que je suis mon ouvrage" (p. 170)—whose ultimate goal is to render the creation "invincible" (p. 175). Like Valmont, Merteuil praises her own originality—"j'avais su me créer des moyens inconnus jusqu'à moi" (p. 170)—and, like Valmont, she defines originality as the annihilation of center (a spontaneous, uncontrollable, "sentimental" self) and the construction around that hollow, and therefore unknowable, center of fortifications that are a pastiche of other women's spontaneous behavior. Her self-education has as its primary objective a progressive destruction of instinctive responses and their replacement with learned responses:

[J]e m'amusai à me montrer sous des formes différentes; sûre de mes gestes, j'observais mes discours; je reglais les uns et les autres, suivant les circonstances, ou même seulement suivant mes fantaisies: dès ce moment, ma façon de penser fut pour moi seule, et je ne montrai plus que celle qu'il m'était utile de laisser voir. (p. 171)

Merteuil's ideal of total control is the foundation for her perfect system of self-defense. Like Vauban obsessively planning for the state of siege and Rousseau's master teacher exercising multiple levels of control over the educational vignettes he orchestrates, Merteuil is driven by an all-consuming desire to destroy chance. How many times does she cry out that she has never deviated, never swerved from the path she has prescribed for herself, a path that leads to her victims' seduction and her own feigned seduction—"quand m'avez-vous vue m'écarter des règles que je me suis prescrites, et manquer à mes principes?" (p. 170). Valmont may seem to be echoing her sentiment when he praises his own flawless execution of maneuvers, but his tone is simply self-congratulatory. Merteuil's strident affirmations of her perfect fidelity to a system she has prearranged are the closest thing to emotional release, to self-revelation, that she permits herself, as though the other's recognition of her fidelity would finally bring about the long-desired death of chance.

The protean fluidity Merteuil achieves as a result of her eternal self-vigilance is essential to the operation of the double system of defenses that is the trademark of her success. She "fortifies" (p. 173) herself through reading until she is able to simulate the traditional *redans* and *chicanes* of virtuous behavior: "je m'assurais ainsi de ce qu'on pouvait faire, de ce qu'on devait penser, et de ce qu'il fallait paraître" (p. 173). This line of protection blinds her potential enemies to the existence of a complex defensive machine tailored to fit each occasion on which she decides to "[se] défendre ou à céder" (p. 169). Because she has taken care to "[se] procurer les honneurs de la résistance," she is able to "[se] livr[er] sans crainte à l'Amant préféré" (p. 175). Merteuil's use of "se livrer" is ironic: she never yields, only conquers. Thus she inaugurates her description of her victory over Prévan "nous commençames notre attaque réciproque" (85: 185).[37] Camouflage constitutes the essence of Merteuil's strength. Her attack passes for defense, so she can take by surprise, proving thereby the strategic superiority of an (aggressive) defense over attack. Merteuil's aggressiveness is so well disguised that she can actually "prime la première," giving her the advantage according to Vaubanian strategy. Laclos's heroine practices only offense informed by defensive strategy, and, more importantly, she puts offense to work for defense. Vauban laid

---

[37] As Daniel so aptly points out, "sous la plume de Madame de Merteuil, une certaine identité entre le symbole érotique et la terminologie militaire si caractéristique du dix-huitième siècle, ne se réclame pas seulement d'une mode, mais d'une attitude philosophique qui engage la totalité de l'être. Les clichés les plus usés du langage précieux, sans cesser de traduire l'antagonisme des sexes, deviennent des images de la condition humaine" (pp. 70-71).

siege in order to create a perfect frontier; Merteuil's primary goal is always the protection of her "ouvrage," her fortified self. Merteuil is so proud of the functioning of her "principles" that she uses her self-portrait to characterize herself as the ultimate defensive genius. In her desire to have her superiority recognized, she systematically aims to demolish her rivals, just as her creator worked to wrest Vauban's title from him.

This autobiographical letter marks the first clear illustration of what Merteuil views as the irresolvable difference between female and male defensive strategy. Until this point, and on many subsequent occasions as well, it seems as if the libertine identity Merteuil and Valmont share in the private war they are waging against their inferiors constitutes a bond of similarity more important than their antagonistic position in the war between the sexes. However, Merteuil makes it apparent here that only a woman can become a true master of self-defense; she demotes Valmont's tactics to the realm of offensive technique, the same realm chosen for Vauban by Laclos. In her view, men are never driven to defensive greatness because their stakes in sexual combat are so much lower than women's: "Combattant sans risque, vous devez agir sans précaution" (p. 168).[38] Furthermore, this risk-free position does not encourage tactical creativity. Echoing Laclos's attack on

[38] It may be that Julie and Merteuil, the heroines who attempt to master defensive strategies in the novels of Rousseau and Laclos, suffer such harsh fates because their creators shared Merteuil's assessment of women's natural superiority as engineers of sentiment. In his *Traité de l'origine des romans* (Claude Barbin, 1670), the first major theoretical statement on the French novel, Huet contends that the superiority of the modern French novel can be explained by French women's mastery of verbal defenses. "In order to lay siege to their ramparts," French men have been obliged to follow their strategic lead and learn the language of "politesse" and "galanterie" invented by women to defend their virtue. Their common mastery of this "art" of defense "distingue les Romans François des autres Romans, et . . . en a rendu la lecture si délicieuse" (p. 92). Through Julie and Merteuil, Rousseau and Laclos could be said to take revenge on women (novelists) because of what they felt to be women's prior claim to the language of literary defense, as well as their claim to the territory of the novel—Huet's treatise was published as a preface to Lafayette's *Zayde.*

Vauban, Merteuil denies Valmont any claim to originality and criticizes his lack of flexibility: "C'est que réellement vous n'avez pas le génie de votre état; vous n'en savez que ce que vous en avez appris, et vous n'inventez rien" (106: 243). Indeed, the example of Valmont's attack on Tourvel's virtue serves to confirm his accomplice's opinion of his strategic inferiority: the vicomte, à la Merteuil, simply tries to pass off his offensive action as self-defense (see letter 52, for example). Merteuil's evaluation of Valmont parallels Laclos's evaluation of Vauban: Valmont and Vauban are inferior minds, incapable of defensive creativity. The marquise is jealous of the vicomte because he can work in the open and be recognized as a conqueror, whereas she must hide her successes. Her attitude once again parallels her creator's: Laclos felt that his genius was eclipsed by Vauban only because Vauban had had the opportunity to gain easy recognition as a *preneur de villes*.

On occasion, Merteuil's commentary on the male lack of creativity and defensive talent leads her to trace the origin of her conduct to a defense of the female condition. The clearest formulation of this explanation for her character rings out like a battle cry: "[N]ée pour venger mon sexe et maîtriser le vôtre, j'avais su me créer des moyens inconnus jusqu'à moi" (p. 170). However, this image of Merteuil as a practical and theoretical feminist stands in open contradiction to the attitude she generally expresses toward other members of her sex. There is never a hint of solidarity in her conduct toward fellow women. Indeed, she generally refers to them with total contempt—in the passage about Cécile already discussed, for example, or in this same letter in such expressions as "ces femmes à delire, et qui se disent *à sentiment*" (p. 170).

Perhaps the most remarkable aspect of Merteuil's autobiographical letter is the conviction it expresses that the origin of defense can in most cases be established. "Descendue dans mon coeur, j'y ai étudié celui des autres. J'y ai vu qu'il n'est personne qui n'y conserve un secret qu'il lui importe qui ne soit point dévoilé" (p. 175). Merteuil theorizes that concern for self-protection is an instinctive obsession because everyone, regardless of sex, has something to hide. She attributes her sense of personal invulnerability to the use she makes of this "vérité que l'antiquité paraît avoir mieux connue que nous, et dont l'histoire de Samson pourrait n'être qu'un ingénieux emblème. Nouvelle Dalila, j'ai toujours, comme elle, employé ma puissance à surprendre ce secret important." An element of offensive skill is essential to her flawless self-fortification; Merteuil puts "la chevelure" of all her potential enemies "sous le ciseau," and renders their defensive systems inoperative by unmasking a primordial weakness. As she implies here (p. 175) and elsewhere (152: 348), she holds even Valmont by his "chevelure." Yet the marquise never reveals the nature of his secret, and the editor claims either to have been unable to learn it or to be unable to reveal it ("le Lecteur sentira qu'on n'a pas pu l'éclaircir davantage sur cet objet," footnote, p. 176). Despite her threats, Merteuil protects her companion's secret from their most dangerous enemies, all the readers outside their texts. Her silence suggests that the genealogy of self-defense should not be oversimplified.

Merteuil's letters to Valmont contain other important reflections on the technical arsenal she has created for her protection. In one of the most revealing of these passages (letter 33), she develops a theory of narrative. The marquise describes one of the greatest obstacles she has to overcome in applying her double defensive system to the weapon she and Valmont employ most frequently, the letter: "il n'y a rien de si difficile en amour, que d'écrire ce qu'on ne sent pas. Je dis écrire d'une façon vraisemblable" (p. 68). It is particularly difficult for the dealer in double-entendres to transmit the first or naive meaning in a love letter because he encounters a complex problem of narrative organization. "[C]e n'est pas qu'on ne se serve des mêmes mots; mais on ne les arrange pas de même, ou plutôt on les arrange, et cela suffit." Merteuil argues that when the libertine wishes to seduce a victim into believing in his (nonexistent) love, any semblance of order betrays his true intentions—"Relisez votre Lettre: il y regne un ordre qui vous décèle à chaque phrase." For the letter to succeed in its attack on the victim's sensibilities without ceasing to protect its author's true position, it must be stamped with a paradox: the supreme manifestation of authorial control takes the form of an apparent absence of control. The author must feign a *clinamen* in order to produce one. The libertine can protect himself by appearing to be out of control, engaged in a struggle in which his defensive mechanisms have gone haywire, thereby producing gaps in his account of his passion, apparent breaches in his fortifications.[39] The surest way to defend against passion, to protect oneself against its power, is to strive for mastery over its manifestations. The well-defended writer is immune to love's loss of control because she/he understands too well the nonstructure of its structure.

Merteuil's warning to Valmont creates an opposition between two types of narrative in the way that Freud does in his discussion of "hysterical" narrative in *Dora*: she distinguishes a controlled, orderly narrative without gaps or puzzling passages (the master's narrative) from a narrative dominated by a lack of control (the victim's narrative). The gap-free writing she criticizes in Valmont's letter has much in common with the story Freud hopes to obtain through psychoanalysis, "an intelligible, consistent, and unbroken case history" (*Dora*, p. 32). Merteuil's and Valmont's letters to each other, like the novel as a whole, would presumably be considered representatives of unbroken, "smooth" narratives. Merteuil's reflections on the narrative inscription of emotional struggle belong to a long tradition of criticism of the novel. Her position in the debate is clear: "C'est le défaut des Romans; l'Auteur se bat les flancs pour s'échauffer, et le Lecteur reste froid. *Héloïse* est le seul qu'on en puisse excepter; et malgré le talent de l'Auteur, cette observation m'a toujours fait croire que le fond en était vrai." On the basis of her opinion that only true passion can convince the reader and that any imitation of passion always betrays the novel's fic-

[39] For a discussion of the role played by the illusion of chinks in the protective wall of Sade's narrative fortifications, see pp. 324-25.

tionality, the marquise reasons that in the case of *Julie* "le fond en était vrai." Rousseau was aware that his novel's power had its source in its apparent narrative disorder, in its appearance of weakness. In the second preface to *Julie* he gives a description reminiscent of Merteuil's of the lover's discourse, a discourse that is "toujours figuré": "ces figures sont sans justesse et sans suite; son éloquence est dans son désordre; il prouve d'autant plus qu'il raisonne moins" (2: 15). *Julie*'s author would undoubtedly have explained away the fact that the theory of love's narrative he shares with Laclos's marquise leads her into error on the question of his novel's fictionality on the basis of her sex. This was the reasoning he used to decide that the *Lettres portugaises* were really a novel. Only a man can write such works because "ce feu celeste qui échauffe et embrase l'âme, ce génie qui consume et dévore, ... ces transports sublimes qui portent leur ravissements jusqu'au fond des coeurs, manqueront toujours aux écrits des femmes."[40]

From the clash of positions on this subject, a lesson can be learned about Merteuil's defensive strategy. In her opinion, the simulation of emotion is a dangerous game, and only the best defended (probably only Merteuil herself) can run the risk of appearing to be conquered by love, put themselves in the victim's position, even imitate "hysterical" narrative—all in order to win the supreme victory and turn their correspondent into the victim they only pretended to be. Rousseau accepts the rules Merteuil sets to the task of feigning love, but argues that only a man has the emotional strength to (re)create the necessary "trouble et désordre." In his commentary on the problem of hysterical narrative, Freud takes a more extreme position: he argues that a true hysteric reveals himself/herself through narrative signs and that it is impossible for anyone to feign such disorder successfully (*Dora*, note, p. 31). Behind all these discussions lies the assumption that a lying

[40] Rousseau, *Lettre à Mr. d'Alembert sur les spectacles,* ed. M. Fuchs (Geneva: Droz, 1948), footnote on p. 139.

narrative will always be detected by an *archi-lecteur* just waiting to point out its surplus order, that any listener could turn out to have Merteuil's (or Rousseau's, or Freud's) powers of detection. The marquise is lucid enough to realize that the présidente lacks such powers: "Je veux croire que votre Présidente est assez peu formée pour ne s'en pas apercevoir." Yet as she herself reveals, the obsessive desire for defensive perfection is stronger than any momentary lucidity: "Mais qu'importe? l'effet n'en est pas moins manqué" (p. 68). Because her concern with questions of defensive strategy is so all-consuming, Merteuil insists on technical perfection for its own sake.

After warning Valmont of the risks involved in manipulating a weapon over which he does not have complete control, Merteuil closes the letter on a more reassuring note by explaining what she views as a crucial advantage of epistolary seduction. "Ce qui me paraît encore devoir vous rassurer sur le succès, c'est qu'elle [Tourvel] use trop de forces à la fois; je prévois qu'elle les épuisera pour la défense du mot, et qu'il ne lui en restera plus pour celle de la chose" (p. 68). Her distinction shares more than a terminological similarity with the dichotomy Rousseau establishes in *Emile* between a "science de mots" and a "science de choses," for both systems stress the danger of the word. Writing works for the libertine when it becomes more important for the victim than the reality of lived experience, and when it wears down the victim's resistance by calling defenses into operation against the simple *idea* of seduction. Indeed the *Liaisons* proposes a vision of the relationship between education and seduction that makes clear the implications suggested by La Fontaine and Rousseau. Merteuil and Valmont use pedagogy as the ultimate weapon in their struggle to take revenge on their enemies. They become teachers in order to demonstrate their mastery over those they refer to as *espèces*. The editor passes rather rapidly over the origin of their union: "Pour entendre ce passage, il faut savoir que le Comte de Gercourt avait quitté la Marquise de Merteuil pour l'Intendante de ***, qui lui avait sacrifié le Vicomte de Valmont, et que c'est alors que la Marquise et le Vicomte

s'attachèrent l'un à l'autre" (note, p. 14).[41] A shared humiliation, a shared experience of what they allegedly perceived as
victimization, led the two *roués* to reveal their secrets to each
other, to put each other in the position of playing Delilah to
their Samson. The comte and the intendante having refused
to recognize their strategic importance, the *roués* turned to
each other both to further their revenge and to find recognition
for their talents. The origin of their pact is also in a sense the
origin of their exaltation of the myth of defensive perfection:
a strategic defeat reveals the existence of breaches in their
system of protection, breaches they resolve to close permanently. The marquise determines that a fitting revenge against
the individual held responsible for their unique defeat would
involve the corruption of Gercourt's carefully selected bride-
to-be. Thus the libertines turn pedagogues with Cécile de Volanges as their pupil. In the course of her education, it becomes
apparent that their pedagogical "methods" project a vision
of the student-teacher relationship that forms a bridge between Rousseauian manipulations and Sade's vision of *les
instituteurs immoraux*.

When Merteuil and Valmont use traditional pedagogical
vocabulary, they make its aggressive implications come alive.
Both speak of their project as the process by which Valmont
will "form" Cécile (2: 14; 20: 44, etc.). By this, they mean
nothing less than her complete "reconstruction" according to
their prearranged plan and for their purposes. (Given the use
to which she puts education, it is easy to understand why
Merteuil was, like Rousseau, so careful to remain self-taught.)
However, as is the case with all the maneuvers they undertake
jointly, neither is ever satisfied with any of the other's initiatives. Their project quickly degenerates into a battle for the

---

[41] If it is intended as an explanation for the origin of their desire for revenge,
this story of double betrayal is neither entirely convincing nor without literary
precedent. For example, Richardson's diabolic seducer, Lovelace, also traces
his desire for conquest to a deception in love. The alleged origin of the libertine
conspiracy provides another example of a hollow center protected by a shell
of clichés.

control of Cécile—thus Valmont describes her to Merteuil as "votre pupille, à présent devenue la mienne" (96: 210). They even come to act like parents who, faced with a child's misbehavior, deny responsibility for his conduct by referring to him as the other parent's child: shortly after Valmont takes over the formation of "their" student, he is ready to push her off on Merteuil again when "votre pupille recule" (99: 219).

The manipulation of their student by the *roués* is indicative of the goal of all the defensive strategies deployed in the *Liaisons*. They only "form" Cécile according to the principles of a type of negative education that "profanes" Rousseau's expressed intentions. *Emile* is allegedly an attempt to educate a child to self-sufficiency. The marquise and the vicomte use their pupil to "write" an anti-*Emile*. They train Cécile to be ignorant, dependent, and defenseless. For example, rather than instructing her in the rhetoric of duplicity with which they protect themselves from discovery, Valmont delights in limiting Cécile's vocabulary to terms that do not allow for double-entendres: "Je m'amuse à n'y rien nommer que par le mot technique. . . . Rien n'est plus plaisant que l'ingénuité avec laquelle elle se sert déjà du peu qu'elle sait de cette langue! elle n'imagine pas qu'on puisse parler autrement" (110: 256-57).

The goal of women's education in the *Liaisons* is to mold the pupil into an instrument of her professors' will, a plaything lacking even the energy necessary for a defensive *clinamen*.[42] In the *Liaisons* and in the subsequent fragments on education, Laclos repeatedly writes himself into a paradoxical situation: while he returns obsessively to the theme of women's education, he cannot break his fundamental resistance to this subject. He is able to theorize about a "natural" woman and her behavior. He is able to formulate a utopian (Rousseauian) defense of pedagogy: in the first fragment, he evokes "[le]

---

[42] Male pupils would undoubtedly suffer the same fate, although Merteuil does not have the time to finish the chapter devoted to Danceny in "l'éducation des enfants" (113: 264). The *Liaisons* reverses the pattern of *Emile* in which it is Sophie's education that is less detailed.

développement des facultés de l'individu qu'on élève et . . . la direction de ces facultés vers l'utilité sociale" (p.390). But he is never able to illustrate his theories with the narration of a "model" education. The only story of female instruction the would-be theoretician ever depicts is Cécile's. In her case, education uses up the pupil and exhausts her possibilities, until she is ultimately discarded by her professors. She is so completely finished off by her education that the reader has difficulty imagining what "la suite des aventures de Mademoiselle de Volanges" announced by the publisher in the footnote that ends the novel (p. 386) could possibly contain.

Critics who describe Laclos as a disciple of Rousseau generally have in mind Rousseau's own version of the purpose of his *oeuvre*. It is possible, however, that Laclos did not take Rousseau's novels at face value and looked beyond Rousseau's proclamations on the moral value of his fiction to the implications of *Julie*'s "utopian" vision. In that event, the Rousseauian heroine in the *Liaisons* would be, not Tourvel, but Merteuil, a "nouvelle, nouvelle Héloïse" who is more honest than her predecessor about her goals and her desires. Indeed, Merteuil makes a calculated use of what I have described as Rousseauian mathematics, for example, when she writes to Valmont to inform him that Tourvel is not worthy of his tactical energy:

> [N]'en espérez aucun plaisir. En est-il avec les prudes? . . . réservées au sein même du plaisir, elles ne vous offrent que des demi-jouissances. Cet entier abandon de soi-même, ce délire de la volupté où le plaisir s'épure par son excès, ces biens de l'amour, ne sont pas connus d'elles. . . . [V]otre Présidente croira avoir tout fait pour vous en vous traitant comme son mari, et dans le tête-à-tête conjugal le plus tendre, on reste toujours deux." (5: 19)

"Dans le tête-à-tête conjugal," 1 + 1 always equals 2: Valmont will never forge a perfect, seamless union with Tourvel. Merteuil's evaluation clearly implies that this total union, which she alleges is impossible with prudes, can in fact exist with the right partner—with herself, for example. The marquise's goal, like Julie's, is to forge such a union, her desire being all the more intense because she is aware of the operation of this reductive mathematics.

Emile's tutor hoped to use *Robinson Crusoe* to make his pupil mad; like him, Merteuil dreams of making her partner's head turn. She would like to use her power to produce the same effect, to produce "ce délire de la volupté." Merteuil may speak of "l'entier abandon de soi-même," but she is certainly not referring to any loss of herself. The marquise announces in the letter that inaugurates her correspondence with Valmont: "Vous voyez que l'amour ne m'aveugle pas" (2: 15). When she speaks of perfect union, as Emile's tutor does and as Julie does, it is always the other who experiences a loss of self. Danceny neatly sums up the result of Merteuil's arithmetic of seduction: "[C]e n'est pas nous deux qui ne sommes qu'un, c'est toi qui es nous deux" (150: 344). As a result of the divine marquise's seductions, her partner has been obliterated. Laclos's heroine acts out the fantasy of Emile's teacher with truly Sadean energy; she plays all the roles, takes over all the spaces, completely invades the other's being, and succeeds in driving him out of himself.

Merteuil bases her sense of self-mastery on her conviction that the autobiographical search reveals in the end not a Rousseauian transparency, but the other pole of the duality whose relationship Jean Starobinski has so convincingly traced, an obstacle. According to Merteuil, every individual hides in his or her heart a secret he struggles to keep hidden, a sort of original lie. Her self-mastery leads her to this discovery, then she puts it to use to expose others' secrets and perfect her defense of her own. Her awareness of the duplicity of those around her allows her to reduce them to "ciphers," a reduction that is far more disturbing than any project undertaken by Julie de Wolmar or Clarissa Harlowe. Merteuil is confident that with her knowledge comes total power: the right to destroy those she can control, literally to reduce them to nothingness. Thus her moments of supreme linguistic cruelty are not coded for a double reading. When Merteuil speaks of women like Cécile as "*machines* à plaisir" (106: 244, emphasis mine), or when she distinguishes the *scélérat* from the *espèces* (141: 326), her words for once are meant to be taken at face value. Only the *scélérat* rises above the status of object, machine, thing. The *espèces* can be dealt with as casually as if they truly were inanimate objects: "n'oublions pas que de ces machines-là, tout le monde parvient bientôt à en connaître les ressorts et les moteurs; ainsi, que pour se servir de celle-ci sans danger, il faut se dépêcher, s'arrêter de bonne heure, et la briser ensuite" (p. 245). "Et la briser ensuite"—Merteuil believes that her strategic superiority gives her the right to destroy those unable to defend themselves.

The ultimate goal of Merteuil's obsession with tactical superiority seems to be total mastery over all movement. She desires to function as a sort of supreme military commander with the power to move both attacker and defender at will, truly to act out Valmont's Vaubanian boast: "J'ai forcé à combattre l'ennemi qui ne voulait que temporiser; je me suis donné, par de savantes manoeuvres, le choix du terrain et celui des dispositions; ... je n'ai rien mis au hasard" (125: 293). She is confident of the superiority of her system—"mais qu'est-ce donc qu'elle prouve pour votre système, ou contre le mien?" (141: 326).[43] She is certain she has accounted for everything. She uses her system to trick her victims into thinking she is moving (swerving with emotion) and that her movements are provoked by the power of her desire, whereas in reality all her *clinamena* are feigned. She aims to seduce all those around her, to engage them in wild veerings, while her-

---

[43] Laclos had originally intended to have Merteuil compare herself to one of the conquerors Valmont chooses as an example for his self-portrait, the maréchal de Saxe, but he eliminated the comparison from the final version, perhaps because he realized how inappropriate this image of offensive force would be for a practitioner of the art of defense (p. 1251, variant *a* to p. 123).

self remaining immobile. Even when disaster begins to strike, Merteuil remains frozen in her position. In Mme de Volanges's narration of the scene of the marquise's public disgrace and Prévan's rehabilitation at the *Comédie Italienne,* she describes with disbelief ("mais je crois ce fait exagéré") the rigidity of Merteuil's last stand in the novel: "On assure que celle-ci a conservé l'air de ne rien voir et de ne rien entendre, et qu'elle n'a pas changé de figure!" (173: 382). Near the end of the novel, Mme de Rosemonde writes to Danceny in an attempt to guarantee his discretion and admonishes him that "celui qui le premier tente de séduire un coeur encore honnête et simple se rend par là même le premier fauteur de sa corruption, et doit être à jamais comptable des excès et des égarements qui la suivent" (171: 378). Her description is intended to convey her sense of the wild disorder of Cécile's conduct, but it also provides a valid characterization of the swerves that constitute the novel's climax. The last scenes of the *Liaisons* are played out in the absence of Merteuil's control, and each of the final letters gives an account of new swerves that signal the crumbling of her fortifications.

In answer to Valmont's persistent demands for a (re)union, Merteuil finally explains why their partnership can no longer exist: "qui de nous deux se chargera de tromper l'autre?" (131: 305). How could they pretend to believe in a perfect union when both would be in possession of the secret of reductive mathematics? There is nothing haphazard about Merteuil's behavior during the last act of the *Liaisons.* She may praise herself as the "nouvelle Dalila," but, up until this point, she has only threatened to put her accomplices "sous le ciseau" while never actually doing so. The marquise knows that when she makes a Samson out of Valmont, she will bring herself down with him. She could not fail to remember that in the Biblical story she adopts as her emblem, Samson does not hesitate to bring down the prison house on himself as well as on all the Philistines inside in order to revenge his humiliation at Delilah's hands: "So the dead which he slew at his death were more than they which he slew in his life" (Judges 16:31). Merteuil must also know that Delilah escapes Samson's suicidal holocaust with both her secret and her future intact. Her only loss is that of her seductive but dangerously exposed life in story.

Just what is the secret whose protection allegedly renders Merteuil so ruthless? Daniel contends that she doesn't have one: "Elle cultive l'art de la dissimulation sans nécessité; elle se déguise par vocation" (p. 18). She wears a mask not because she has something to hide, but, paradoxically, because she has nothing to hide. Like the Sun King, she knows the powerful attraction of secrecy and wishes to appear to have something to conceal. While I agree with the essence of Daniel's analysis, it seems to me that the problem is slightly more complex. The means chosen by the marquise to bring the dangerous connections she and Valmont had been plotting to an end teaches a lesson about the power of concealment, and it also establishes a hierarchy of secrecy. Merteuil's crucial last tactical stand implies that her creator understood the devious destructiveness of Rousseau's garden utopia. Like Julie, the marquise works to control the actions of those in her sphere of influence, but she ultimately achieves final domination by literally going beyond Julie/*Julie* and manipulating her partner's use of (Rousseauian) language. For her fundamental first move in the campaign that brings down his fortifications, Merteuil tricks Valmont into exposing his use of pastiche. She has him copy a letter, use, as always in his correspondence with Tourvel, someone else's language. But this time she makes him first of all change styles and secondly, reveal to his reader(s) the nature of all his and of all such activities. "On s'ennuie de tout, mon Ange, c'est une Loi de la Nature" (141: 328). Ironically, the deadly missive with which Valmont "tears the veil" of Tourvel's illusion is the first of his letters to her that resembles his "real" epistolary style, as we have come to know it through his letters to Merteuil. Yet the letter is far from original: more derivative than *his* imitator Julien Sorel, Valmont does not even himself select the text he plagiarizes; he merely copies the words of an anonymous model chosen for him by the marquise. "Ce n'est pas ma faute," Valmont's *billet* repeats eight times, as he proclaims to his readers, fictional and extra-fictional, that they can never know him because there is no one behind the words to take responsibility for them.

We readers outside the text ultimately possess, like Merteuil's *femme de chambre* Victoire, "the secret of [her] actions"—that is, an exterior secret, the genealogy and the trajectory of her diabolical revenge—but we should not rejoice in this apparent victory. No one, as Merteuil herself is careful to point out, knows "le secret de ses sentiments" (83: 176), because Laclos built her without a secret. In Merteuil's discussion of *Julie* (letter 33), she implies that the reason she believes that "le fond en était vrai" is that *Julie*'s center ("le fond") is disorganized, has breaks in its defenses. The language of sentiment, the language of truth, cannot be perfectly controlled and defended. To solve this problem, Laclos destroys the truth (the originality) at the center of his/Rousseau's novel. His language of sentiment is entirely a pastiche, most often feigning (lying) pastiche, endowed with only an ersatz "air de trouble et de désordre" (p. 68)—a construct, like Julie's garden utopia, mimicking natural spontaneity.

The Hollow Presence

Il n'y aura pas de ma faute.
Cécile de Volanges to the Chevalier de Danceny,
dictated by the Vicomte de Valmont

Near the end of his life, Laclos made his only lasting contribution to military strategy with the invention of the *boulet creux,* a hollow shell created to blow holes in protective walls when its inner vacuum shattered its own outer envelope.[44] Both Georges Daniel and Irving Wohlfarth have compared his novel to this *boulet creux*. "To take seriously Daniel's analogy," Wohlfarth argues, "would not be to locate an elusive but secure self behind the concentric fortifications, but to assume that the novel is all the more explosive for having no centre" (Daniel, p. 30; Wohlfarth, p. 301). Both the structural configuration and the functioning of the *boulet creux* have their literary counterpart in the *Liaisons,* where Laclos first worked out the strategy that was to guarantee his reputation for posterity, and to do so by means of a union forged between Rousseauian tactics and Vaubanian strategy. For his novelistic *boulet creux,* Laclos uses a strategic lesson learned from his study of Vauban to fortify Rousseau's language and his own Rousseauian text.

At key points in his novel, Laclos calls attention to the process by which he hollows out the center of his text. For example, we are told that, when the présidente is dying, Valmont writes Mme de Volanges to ask her to act as his go-between with Tourvel. The editor, however, decides to suppress Valmont's letter, even though he includes this speculation on its contents by Mme de Volanges: "Mais que direz-vous de ce désespoir de M. de Valmont? D'abord faut-il y croire, ou veut-il seulement tromper tout le monde, et jusqu'à la fin?" (154: 352). Her query to Mme de Rosemonde is a request for interpretation, a request so pertinent that it might be addressed to extra-fictional readers as well, for the answer to her question would provide at the same time the key to Valmont's character. Laclos, however, fails to supply us with this all important answer. Furthermore, he makes it clear that this absence of motive is intentional, for an editor's note is the only answer Mme de Volanges's query receives: "C'est parce qu'on n'a rien trouvé dans la suite de cette Correspon-

---

[44] Laclos's experiments on the *boulet creux* (which would remain in use with modifications until the twentieth century) date from 1793, during the months immediately preceding his imprisonment in the *Maison de santé* at Picpus where Sade would be his fellow prisoner for seven months.

dance qui pût résoudre ce doute, qu'on a pris le parti de supprimer la Lettre de M. de Valmont" (p. 352). We are denied
access to Valmont's letter precisely so that his character will
remain incomprehensible to us, so that we won't be able to
know for certain if he loved Tourvel, etc. The point is, of
course, as Brooks points out, that such a letter is impossible
in the context of the *Liaisons*: "What would an unfeigning
Valmont sound like?" (p. 208). The very existence of original,
sincere language is put into question by Laclos's novel; in
place of sincerity, Laclos substitutes textual suppression, which
he uses, as Lafayette does in *La Princesse de Clèves*, to create
enigma and to produce an interpretive impasse.

In the final footnote to the *Liaisons,* this elimination of key
information is linked to the all-important question of authorial voice. After all wrongdoers have been punished and
order has been reestablished, just when the novel's moral
framework seems at last firmly in place, a foreign voice in-
terrupts the finality of the *Liaisons*'s closure. The last word
of the *Liaisons* belongs, appropriately, not to a voice from
the center of the text, but to a note in its margins. The footnote
informs the reader that the text she has just completed is not
a finished entity: other letters exist, but these, for reasons that
are deliberately shrouded in mystery, have been withheld. It
is suggested, furthermore, that this has been done at the request of someone personally involved with the individuals in
the story. Hence we are led to believe that the narrated events
actually took place: "Des raisons particulières et des consi-
dérations que nous nous ferons toujours un devoir de respec-
ter, nous forcent de nous arrêter ici" (note, p. 386). Yet only
two sentences later, the concluding note refers to the correspondence as though its fictional status were unquestionable: "Peut-
être quelque jour nous sera-t-il permis de compléter *cet Ouvrage*" (emphasis mine). Curiously, this last word belongs not
to the individual responsible for all the other footnotes, the
editor, but to the publisher. Having announced at the outset
that he had reason to believe we were dealing *only* with a

novel, he is quite consistent in his final insistence on the fictional status of the *Liaisons*. Duranton contends that the return of the publisher at the close of the *Liaisons* demonstrates that the novel is "entraîné dans une circularité parfaite" (p. 130), but the point of departure to which the ending returns is not, perhaps, the one he had in mind. In a footnote to the publisher's footnote, Versini provides information gained from the study of the manuscript that casts doubt on the authenticity of this concluding note (just as the publisher casts doubt on the authenticity of the entire text in his preface): "La note, sans appel dans le texte, n'est pas de l'écriture de Laclos, et est portée sur un papillon blanc, collé au bas du folio 126 V°, de couleur bleue" (p. 1411, variant *f*), he explains, sounding (inevitably) remarkably like the editor chiding Valmont for his misuse of Rousseau. An examination of the manuscript reveals that the last word of the *Liaisons* is unquestionably not Laclos's re-creation of a publisher's voice, unlike the publisher's "warning" that opens the novel, which is in Laclos's hand. Just who is the authorial substitute who takes final responsibility for Laclos's novel, assuring us that it is intentionally incomplete and likely to remain so? To judge from the contract for the printing of the *Liaisons* signed by Laclos and his publisher Durand, included in folio 37 of the *Bibliothèque Nationale* manuscript, it seems possible that the real publisher was the author of the last note, a possibility either diabolic or so prosaic as to be virtually unacceptable as a move in Laclos's game of authorial hide-and-seek.

The manuscript reveals that the novel's last word may well belong to an impostor, someone who has succeeded for two hundred years in passing for Laclos, even though he was not attempting to do so since the editorial seducer tried neither to forge his handwriting nor to match the color of his paper. It is fitting that the last voice we hear at the close of this polyphonic pastiche is not, as Versini and Brooks contend, that of sentiment (that of the présidente and her defenders), but a false voice, that of a counterfeiter posing as Laclos (who wore so many masks to pose as Rousseau) posing as the publisher. The ending of the *Liaisons* takes us back to its beginning in the sense that there is ultimately no one to take responsibility for the text we have just read. Furthermore, the problem of the last voice also shows how this denial of authority hollows out the center of Laclos's discourse and leaves the reader with the impression of having encountered a variety of voices, the majority of which are, somehow, impersonal, and like pastiche in general, neither original nor imitation.

Epistolary novels not infrequently end with the somewhat jarring intervention of a foreign, marginal voice assigned the narration of the work's last act—witness the example of *Delphine*—and critics have generally linked this recourse to a *deus ex machina* to the difficulty of ending epistolary fiction. Yet when the *Liaisons* closes in its own margin, this does not mean that its story is not over, but rather that it ends, as it begins, on a note of interpretive doubt. *Julie* also ends with a footnote, so whoever was responsible for the final marginal commentary to the *Liaisons* may have intended it to stand as the final mark of the novel's settling of scores with Laclos's master teacher. In another footnote (to letter 159), the editor explains that the core of the novel was based on a collection of his correspondence with Merteuil that Valmont had prepared for posterity and handed over to Danceny before his death (p. 374). Valmont had even given the collection a title: "Compte ouvert entre la Marquise de Merteuil et le Vicomte de Valmont" (p. 375). Valmont's title is both novel and more appropriate to characterize the originality of the *Liaisons* than is the hackneyed designation Laclos "created" for the complete *recueil*. Indeed, the novel is just what Valmont calls that part of it for which he served as editor, an accounting, a settling of scores ("compte")—a settling of scores that, like all acts of revenge, as René Girard has taught us and as Vauban's calculations for a state of siege and Rousseau's and Sade's mathematics of revenge also demonstrate, remains eternally "open," even when the tally sheets have been drawn up and put in order.

Accountability was a consistent source of fascination for Laclos. During his imprisonment, he became the teacher of some of his fellow prisoners, with the view of continuing his pedagogical activity upon his release, with the members of his family as pupils. The subject he professed was the recently adopted "new" arithmetic (based on the metric system) and "new" accounting. The accounting that so fascinated Laclos and that he imagined would play an essential role, should the women in his life, his wife and daughter, be forced to earn their livings, was the "comptabilité en partie double," according to which the seller was obliged for each sale to draw up his own account as well as the buyer's (according to the old system of "comptabilité en partie simple," the seller drew up only the buyer's account) (*O.c.*, p. 812 and p. 1616, n. 2; p. 820 and p. 1607, n. 2). Under the terms of the new system, commerce is conceived as a dual operation in which each transaction alters the balance of power between buyer and seller.[45]

It is a similar heightened awareness of the strategic impact of accountability that attracted Laclos to the other pedagogical project he discusses in his letters from prison, the "new" grammar. Like his interest in the new accounting, Laclos's grammatical project was conceived in order to be useful to his family: his daughter was having difficulty learning grammar. Laclos explains to his wife that her trouble would be eliminated if grammar were to be systematized as "honestly" as accounting. "Je prévois que nous allons avoir une foule de grammaires nouvelles," and Laclos, who calls himself a grammarian here ("et je me mets dans cette classe"), plans to join the crowd by writing a "new" grammar (p. 837). Despite the

---

[45] Laclos's conviction of the importance of accounting was shared by Louis XIV who explained to his son in his memoirs that he devoted one of the first days of each month to this task: "[J]e voulus bien me donner la peine de marquer de ma propre main, sur un petit livre que je pusse voir à tous moments, d'un côté les fonds qui devaient me revenir chaque mois, de l'autre toutes les sommes payées par mes ordonnances dans ce mois-là" (*Mémoires de Louis XIV*, ed. J. Longnon [Tallandier, 1927], p. 92).

competition, however, he will not be lost in the crowd; his grammar "n'en sera pas moins un ouvrage absolument neuf, et étranger à tous les autres." Laclos would make the new grammar, like the new accounting, a two-part process, by separating the "mechanical" part of the science (what to say and write) from the true object of study ("pourquoi et comment [chacun] fait ces deux opérations"). The mechanical part of the operation must become "routine," so that "l'attention n'étant plus distraite par l'embarras d'opérer, elle puisse se porter tout entière sur le *compte à se rendre* de l'opération qu'on fait" (p. 837, emphasis mine). Laclos defines his originality (as he had already done in his novel twelve years earlier) as the separation of the mechanical/automatic ("les machines à plaisir") from the true object of study, the rules of the game and the settling of scores, especially the settling of scores with oneself.[46] Laclos's "new" grammar will be "absolument neuf" because it will simultaneously systematize grammar and expose the functioning of the system it develops. Just as in the *Liaisons,* originality is here synonymous with a type of self-honesty, with knowing why and how one does what one does.

The importance of this redefinition of originality as self-honesty for a writer/grammarian conscious of using the same material as a "crowd" of other writers is evident, and it is significant that Laclos proposed a similar refocusing of novelistic creativity when he described his last (and like almost all the textual and pedagogical projects he conceived after the *Liaisons,* never realized) literary vision in a letter to his wife in 1801:

> Depuis assez longtemps l'idée d'un roman germe dans ma tête, et j'ai presque pris hier l'engagement de m'en occuper. . . . Le motif de l'ouvrage est de rendre populaire cetta vérité qu'*il n'existe de bonheur que dans la famille.* Assurément je suis en fonds pour prouver cela,

[46] Sade reaches conclusions about novelistic originality remarkably similar to Laclos's in another text written in prison, "L'Idée sur les romans," conclusions he puts into practice in *Les 120 Journées de Sodome.*

et je ne suis pas embarrassé de savoir où je prendrai le sujet de mes tableaux: mais les événements seront difficiles à arranger, et la difficulté presque insurmontable sera d'intéresser sans rien de romanesque. Il faudrait le style des deux premiers volumes des *Confessions* de J.-J. Rousseau. (p. 1064)

Versini cites this passage as proof of Laclos's definitive commitment to the language of sentiment (p. 1411, n. 4), but the letter actually reveals the concern of the author of the *Liaisons* not with sentiment, but with what might be termed the place of sentiment or the ability to put sentiment in its place. According to this testimony, all that counts for Laclos in the "creation" of a novel is order. The subject matter can be borrowed (presumably from his own life), and the style must be a pastiche of Rousseau, but the arrangement of events is a different matter. The real challenge for the novelist is to keep the novel going, to string the *tableaux* together "sans rien de romanesque," to put the building blocks of narrative together according to Flaubert's dream, without mortar. Originality is a matter of accounting, of keeping everything in order.

Indeed, the *Liaisons* seems to correspond from its inception to the wall-like style to which Flaubert aspired. According to Versini's description, Laclos's manuscript acquires an appearance of solidity because of the manner in which his handwriting fills up the sheets: "'[L]'écriture est petite et serrée"; "l'auteur est avare de ponctuation"; "Laclos ignore, ou presque, les alinéas" (p. 1162). Versini's description does not, however, do justice to the extraordinary sensation of confinement or containment produced by the manuscript. Laclos's handwriting is more than "petite"; it is microscopic. He leaves no margins on the right side of the page, only very small ones on the left. Furthermore, the pages become even more cramped from about letter 78 on, and after letter 96 the manuscript is an editor's nightmare. As his war between the sexes moved toward its final catastrophe, Laclos left less and less space between lines, began to write more extensively in the left margin, and in general to fill up all available spaces. Moreover, individual letters are not even well closed, as though ink had become as precious as paper. The last sections of Laclos's manuscript are a truly claustrophobic document. Laclos was not bound by the same compositional constraints as Sade who, as will be discussed in the next chapter, created *Les 120 Journées de Sodome* while in prison. He nevertheless fortified the pages of his manuscript, as Sade did, by leaving no blanks in his writing or breaches in his textual defenses.

Daniel describes Laclos's genius as that of a fortifier enlightened by the instincts of an artilleryman: he needs to hide behind a wall in order to "atteindre l'objectif sans s'exposer lui-même" (p. 28). He uses this description to explain Laclos's persistent recourse in his political and military careers to the role of *éminence grise*. Laclos addressed to his wife a sentence that seems "predestined" to be quoted and requoted by those critics who agree with Daniel's analysis (although, ironically, they seem to have overlooked it to date): "Tu vois que je suis prédestiné à faire souvent de la besogne sous le nom des autres" (*O.c.*, p. 987). "Self-destined" would seem a more accurate choice than "predestined," since it appears that Laclos repeatedly sought out the particular brand of anonymity that consists of working "under" another's name. Daniel is surely correct in his estimation that this practice has been successful in hiding Laclos's true face forever, but this evaluation is really accurate only as far as Laclos's biography is concerned. In literary terms, Laclos hides behind a name/wall of borrowed discourse, literary *bricolage,* but the "besogne" he was working to accomplish was of his own invention, rather than the work of another.[47] His "work," unlike his face (his biography), can be known, and the task he accomplished under cover provides a crucial link in the development of the French novel.

[47] In "Larvatus Pro Deo," *Glyph* 2 (1977): 14-36, J.-L. Nancy proposes a reading of Descartes's anonymity as masking for constructive ends.

Literary anonymity is a phenomenon that generally might be described as presence wearing the mask of absence: a blank, empty façade camouflages a full center, that is, the author's identity. On the other hand, the anonymity Laclos develops recurrently and on so many levels is a related but opposite phenomenon. He merely toys with authorial secrecy on the title page of the original edition of the *Liaisons*. Laclos is prepared to have his name linked to his creation and to give his novel every impression of textual fullness. But the *Liaisons* is really an absence passing as presence, and that hollow presence is the essence of Laclos's contribution to literary posterity, just as the *boulet creux* guaranteed his place in military history. For his literary *boulet creux,* Laclos adds Vauban to Rousseau. He fortifies the voice of sentiment by erasing the self from Rousseauian discourse. In the *Liaisons,* Rousseau's discourse of sentiment becomes common property. It is neutralized, rendered impersonal, made anonymous. The subject is erased, put *sous rature* behind a wall that corresponds to Laclos's description of Classical Vaubanian fortifications, for it is composed of fragments of borrowed discourse, and its "creator's" only originality consists in his ability to put these borrowed building blocks together. The essence of Vauban's greatness as a systematizer—as Laclos was, if not the first, at least one of the first to point out—was his talent for plagiarism, for the genius of *bricolage.*

"A une composition nouvelle, il faut bien un titre nouveau," Laclos pronounces in the "Observations du général Laclos sur le roman théâtral de M. Lacretelle aîné" (p. 487). Yet for his own "theatrical" novel, Laclos chooses a title that proclaims its sameness rather than its newness. In 1763, Madame de Saint-Aubin published *Le Danger des Liaisons,* which, as the manuscript of the *Liaisons* reveals, was Laclos's own first choice for his novel's title (p. 1163, variant *a*). Versini contends that Laclos did not modify his original option in order to avoid comparison with Saint-Aubin's *Liaisons.* He points out that the title finally chosen "loin de viser l'originalité, offrait au contraire au public une nouvelle occasion de réfléchir sur un thème que romanciers, moralistes et journalistes lui avaient rendu familier" (p. 1163, n. 1).[48] As Daniel observes, Laclos's genius is precisely the genius of a novelistic impostor or counterfeiter. The *Liaisons* is a gigantic pastiche of the conventions of the novel: "Du langage utilisé jusqu'aux noms des personnages, de l'atmosphère jusqu'au titre du roman, rien n'est de l'invention de Laclos . . . . [I]l invente . . . quand il imite" (Daniel, p. 33).

In his public letter to the French Academy, Laclos denigrates what is ultimately the greatest source of his own as well as Vauban's strength. Vauban's system, Laclos proclaims, "n'est autre que le système bastionné, connu dès la fin du quinzième siècle." Furthermore, Laclos contends that after his death Vauban's plagiarized system knew an appropriate fate, "devenu tour à tour le bien de tous" (p. 578). Thus the author of the *Liaisons* unveils the trajectory of discourse whose authority derives precisely from its disposition beyond authority. In the French literary tradition, the *Liaisons* provides an essential link between Classicism and the modernity whose origins are generally traced to Flaubert. Laclos takes Rousseau's (allegedly) spontaneous, self-revealing, self-exploring, self-knowing language and makes it Vaubanian, reduces it to a hollow potpourri of elements borrowed seemingly from all available sources, a wall of clichés—the copied, the already-said—for which no one takes responsibility and no one can be blamed. "Livre essentiellement français," Baudelaire so aptly (and canonically) decreed. Technically flawless *and* impersonal, the *Liaisons* shows us the common bond between Classicism and the Flaubert of *Salammbô*—or even of *Bouvard et Pécuchet*.

[48] For a discussion of other titles of eighteenth-century French novels similar to Laclos's, see Versini's *Laclos et la tradition* (Klincksieck, 1968), pp. 150-58.

══ VI ══

Inside the Sadean Fortress:
Les 120 Journées de Sodome

O la savante, la methodique marche que d'apprendre la
botanique pour se faire empoisonneur! C'est comme si
l'on apprenoit la Géometrie pour se faire assassin.
                    Rousseau, *Rousseau juge de Jean Jaques*

══ ✳ ══

The Space of Cannibalism

Tout le monde sait à quel point la géometrie est atta-
chante: l'exemple d'Archimède tué au siège de Syracuse
sans quitter les yeux de dessus son papier en est une
preuve bien forte.
                    Sade, letter to his wife (4 March 1781)

During seven months in 1794 (27 March-15 October), Sade
and Laclos were fellow prisoners in the *Maison de santé* at
Picpus. Laclos was confined to an *enceinte* just when he was
beginning to achieve a certain military success. He spent the
months prior to his detainment working on his pet invention,
the *boulet creux,* and after his release he went on to serve
Napoleon as a general in the Italian campaign. In contrast,
his fellow prisoner—alumnus of the cavalry school, commis-
sioned in the infantry (the service Napoleon would call "la
reine des batailles")—would never again know active duty of
any kind. For the former lieutenant de Sade, the stay at Picpus
marked just another skirmish in the private war that kept him
under siege inside a series of fortresses nearly all of his adult
life. There is no evidence of a meeting between the eighteenth-
century's two most notorious literary artillerymen during the
months when they were incarcerated in the same enclosure.

And this, despite the fact that the rules of the enclosure were fairly liberal: Sade had frequent visitors, even a last mistress, and it was at Picpus that he collaborated on the theatrical representations that have become an essential part of the legend of the divine marquis. These two inmates with so much in common seem to have been nonpresences for each other at Picpus: their captivity failed to produce, or at least to record, any encounter between the two rival creators of diabolic novels.

Like Laclos's person in Sade's life, Laclos's novel is visible only *sous rature* in Sade's work. Despite the fact that the catalogue established in 1787 reveals that a copy of Laclos's novel was part of Sade's library during his imprisonment in the Bastille, in his historical review of his precursors in the novelistic art from Classical times to contemporary France, "L'Idée sur les romans," Sade remains silent on the subject of *Les Liaisons dangereuses*.[1] His silence is all the more remarkable because of the thoroughness with which he considers contemporary novelistic production in general. The "Idée" cannot be read literally as Sade's honest evaluation of his literary forerunners. In his incursion into the territory of literary criticism, Sade's mood often seems quite playful. For example, his critique of the novel's evolution concludes with a repudiation of *Justine:* "[J]amais je n'ai fait de tels ouvrages" (p. 22). Nevertheless, it is tempting to agree with Gilbert Lely when he calls Sade's silence on the subject of the *Liaisons* "cette étrange omission, dont on ne saurait croire un instant qu'elle n'a pas été volontaire."[2]

Lely offers two related explanations for the omission: either the marquis was simply jealous of the commercial success of his fellow artilleryman's novel, a success that far surpassed

[1] Sade, "Idée sur les romans," *O.c.* (Cercle du livre précieux, 1964), vol. 10, pp. 3-22. The first two volumes of this edition contain Gilbert Lely's monumental *Vie du marquis de Sade.* Information on Sade's library in the Bastille is found in vol. 2, pp. 253-54.
[2] Lely, "Sade a-t-il été jaloux de Laclos?" *NRF* (June 1953): 1125; see also *O.c.,* vol. 2, pp. 627-30.

any obtained by his own fictions, or that hypothetical literary jealousy could have been compounded by some negative personal contact between the two authors at the time of their imprisonment. Lely also offers as additional evidence of Sade's jealousy a fragment from the marquis's notebooks from 1803 and 1804, a "Plan d'un roman en lettres" that contains remarkable similarities with the *Liaisons* in terms of its characters and its plot. Lely contends that Sade felt threatened by what he perceived as an invasion of his personal novelistic territory by his rival. The "Plan d'un roman en lettres" would thus be the trace of Sade's intention to "remake" Laclos's novel and—in what might be considered a novelistic variant of the *tu quoque* defense—thereby to use his rival's own arms against him in order to provide a conclusive demonstration of Sadean superiority (p. 1128).[3] Furthermore, by putting Laclos's fiction in the public domain, Sade may actually have found the only way of turning Laclos's most effective defense against him. The marquis refused to acknowledge the existence of Laclos's novel; he refused to take up the interpretive challenge issued by his predecessor's devious authoritative presence.

Lely provides a convincing reconstruction of this anxiety of influence. According to his theory, Laclos appeared as an "enemy twin" for Sade, a contemporary rival whose greatness threatened his own because it was achieved through a medium so irritatingly close to his own personal style. Laclos was free both to inscribe signs of Rousseau's presence openly in his fiction and to hint at a fundamental ambiguity in his attitude toward his precursor because the territory he intended for himself differed so radically from the space Rousseau had chosen in *Julie*. Laclos mentioned Rousseau openly whereas

---

[3] The "plan d'un roman en lettres" is also cited in the *O.c.,* vol. 15, pp. 29-30. The characters and the plot Sade imagined for his epistolary novel are an exact copy of those of Laclos, with one striking exception: Sade would have eliminated Tourvel's role. Significantly, Sade wanted to attack Laclos on his own territory, rather than echo Laclos's incursion into Rousseau's domain.

Sade was silent on the subject of his predecessor. "[A] aucun moment," Chantal Thomas affirms, "Sade ne connaît la tentation rousseauiste de défense et d'accusation."[4] Instead, he favored another Rousseauian strategy. Like Wolmar in Julie's garden—to whom he compared himself in a letter to his wife in August 1782 (2: 215)—Sade so carefully erased Laclos's footprints that the only remaining hints of his literary anxiety are nonsigns that seem to defy interpretation. As a result, Sade's novels appear more resolutely offensive than the masterpiece of the notorious literary artilleryman. His literary fortifications seem airtight, so perfect in fact that their creator is able to adopt a carefree pose, that of a textual master in such complete control of his literary fortress that he need no longer concern himself with self-defense and is able even to invite attacks on his own outworks.

Thus the introduction to Les 120 Journées de Sodome, the most overtly fortified of Sade's novels, closes with the narrator's apostrophe to the "ami lecteur" in which the reader is explicitly invited to participate in the making of fiction.[5]

C'est ici l'histoire d'un magnifique repas où six cents plats divers s'offrent à ton appétit. Les manges-tu tous? Non, sans doute . . . : choisis et laisse le reste, sans déclamer contre ce reste, uniquement parce qu'il n'a pas le

[4] Thomas, Sade, l'oeil de la lettre (Payot, 1978), p. 108.
[5] Even though the "I" taking responsibility for the narration of the 120 is generally referred to as "Sade," I will maintain a distinction between Sade and his narrator. This distinction is especially useful to mark the separation between the narrator's habitual voice and the voice he adopts in certain clearly autobiographical interventions such as those calculating the number of days devoted to the 120's composition.
Throughout this study, I have referred to "the reader" as "she"; in most instances, "the reader" simply provides the critic with a convenient replacement for "I." Unless the critic believes in a generalized form of "reader response," how can she speak about the exact contours of other readers' readings? However, when speaking of the reader of Sade's fiction, a particular problem occurs: the implied recipient of these stories is unquestionably masculine. So for my discussion of Sade, I will put aside any recognition of my own gender and refer to "the reader" as "he."

talent de te plaire. Songe qu'il plaira à d'autres. . . . [U]n
autre en fera autant; et petit à petit tout aura trouvé sa
place. (13: 61)

On the basis of the contract the narrator offers his reader,
Philippe Roger has called the *120* a "livre, non pas à imiter,
mais à faire." He contends that Sade reverses the Classical
relationship of reader to text by deliberately opening breaches
in his fiction, breaches that enable the reader to enter the
textual fortress.[6] The terms of Sade's invitation to his reader
certainly do suggest that he intends to put an end to the
hostilities and the manipulation that characterize previous defensive texts, and plans to turn his reader into his accomplice rather than his enemy.

The space the *120* leaves for the reader's participation is
much more inviting than the hostile environment promised
within the moralistic confines of Rousseau's novelistic enclosure. Even a brief comparison of passages in which the novelists define the readerships they intend to reach serves to
confirm this impression. Whereas the introduction to Sade's
novel seems an open call for readers, the first preface to *Julie*
sets out to turn away the numerous classes of readers its author
deems unsuitable for it. "Ce livre n'est point fait pour circuler
dans le monde, et convient à très peu de lecteurs. Le stile
rebutera les gens de goût; la matiere allarmera les gens se-
veres. . . . Il doit déplaire aux dévots, aux libertins . . . ; il doit
choquer les femmes galantes, et scandaliser les honnêtes femmes"
(2: 5-6). In his preface to the *Liaisons,* the editor takes a similar
stand: "[I]l me semble toujours que ce Recueil doit plaire à
peu de monde." He follows this discouraging assessment with
a lengthy enumeration of the categories of readers who will
find fault with the work, and he includes in his comprehensive
listing "les hommes et les femmes dépravés," "les Rigoristes,"
"les prétendus esprits forts," and "les personnes d'un gout

---

[6] Roger, *Sade: La Philosophie dans le pressoir* (Grasset, 1976), pp. 79,
119.

délicat," among others (p. 9).[7] These related prefatory gestures could be interpreted as either coyly camouflaged requests for compliments or realistic appraisals of potentially controversial works. Yet both of them, and especially Rousseau's more overtly defensive pronouncements, are also repudiations of hypothetical readers, at least of possibly critical ones. In effect they inform potential readers that the authors do not really need them, and that the readers should therefore be prepared to appraise these texts according to the terms dictated by their authors. Rousseau brings out the ultimate implication of this insinuation with his declaration: "A qui plaira-t-il donc? Peut-être à moi seul" (p. 6). The defensive fictional universe Sade inherits is one in which the reader's/Other's potential for intervention is seen as a threat to be guarded against; only by writing for himself alone can the novelist ensure that the perfection of his narrative fortifications will survive intact the process of his work's reception.

The editors of *Julie* and the *Liaisons* immediately move to create authorial armor to protect themselves and their fictions. In contrast, the narrator of the *120* portrays himself as completely defenseless. He refuses no one willing to participate in his fictive enterprise—all readers uninhibited enough to give themselves without holding back are welcome to take a seat at the *120*'s banquet. In return, he promises to repay this gesture of generosity by offering truths about the human condition that all authors before him have refused to see. The *120* advertises itself as the first work to portray human nature as it really is. The portraits of the libertine heroes who compose the ruling quatrumvirate are painted "non de manière à séduire ou à captiver, mais avec les pinceaux mêmes de la nature, qui malgré tout son désordre est souvent bien sublime, même alors qu'elle se déprave le plus" (p. 7). According to the terms of the pact offered the readers of the *120*, Sade seeks

[7] Even if the editor's preface to the *Liaisons* were written as a parody of *Julie*'s first preface, this does not erase its potential for catching readers off guard.

to portray his novel as radically different from the works previously examined in these pages. Rather than attempting to police his narrative's reception, Sade's narrator professes a desire to give it away, even to hand it over for destruction. The *120*, it would appear, corresponds perfectly to Rousseau's conception of the pedagogical work: it is a generous, totally selfless creative act, a work that asks only to further its reader's education.

What the narrator of the *120* offers his reader in the closing pages of the immense introduction that allegedly prepares him for the "horrors" to come is *not*, however, an invitation to a constructive project, to a cumulative effort in which the reader will join the author in completing his enterprise as Roger contends. Instead, the reader is invited to destroy the *120*, to imitate Robinson Crusoe's work on the ship that brought him to his island, and to take the book apart in order to take away what he wants from it. Before the reader begins his work, the *120* is allegedly a perfect unit, containing all possibilities within its encyclopedic folds: the narrator claims that "nous . . . avions . . . tout dit, tout analysé" (p. 61). The reader is requested to lay siege to the book, to create breaches in its perfect fortifications. Lest he be frightened by the enormity of this task, the narrator reassures him by explaining that he will not be working alone: "C'est ici l'histoire d'un magnifique repas où six cents plats divers s'offrent à ton appétit. Les manges-tu tous? Non, sans doute. . . . Fais de meme ici: choisis et laisse le reste. . . . Songe qu'il plaira à d'autres" (p. 61). The narrator of the *120* imagines a most unusual space for its reader-to-be, a space defined by the basic technique of *bricolage* and the recurrent nightmare of fiction's archetypal *bricoleur*, Robinson Crusoe—cannibalism. The narrator dreams of having his future readers strip his book of its "flesh," pick its bones, and consume it bit by bit. "C'est à toi à le prendre et à laisser le reste; un autre en fera autant; et petit à petit tout aura trouvé sa place" (p. 61).

According to the terms of the banquet pact it proposes, the *120*, in an exceptional gesture for the Classical age, offers to take its reader's desires into account. It asks the reader to do more than passively admire its charms; Sade has his narrator request a type of violently active reading whereby his book would be consumed and its powers assumed. From this cannibalistic process, it seems that each reader would in turn create a personal version of the *120*, in life if not in print. The novel's narrator/author invites his reader to create with him a union through fiction according to which the reader would enjoy seemingly limitless power and the freedom to make of the text what he likes. The narrator surrenders all rights to his creation; he claims not to care how his work will be consumed, as long as it is consumed.

The invitation to a literary feast that Sade has his narrator extend to the reader is representative of just that strain in Sade's work to which recent critics have been most sensitive, Sade's rejection of convention and his invitation to literary liberation. Furthermore, the portrait of Sade as author implicit in these lines also conforms to the image that lies behind recent criticism of his works: Sade as author is the literary equivalent of Sade the liberator of the Bastille. Part of the recent fascination with Sade results from critical admiration for an author so confident of his philosophical and textual superiority that he can invite his reader—just as he invited the crowds that gathered outside the Bastille within earshot of his prison cell— to join him in tearing down the fortress, even when the fortress is his own construction rather than a prison symbolic of the system of authority that had deprived him of his freedom for so many years.

The current vision of Sade has its origin in part in the Surrealist fascination with this *auteur maudit*. One document that testifies eloquently to the power of that fascination, Man Ray's "Portrait imaginaire du marquis de Sade" (1938), also betrays the limits of the legend of Sade the liberating author (see frontispiece). In the Man Ray portrait, the figure of Sade (shown from the shoulders up) dominates the image. The marquis is looking at a fortress in the background. The fortress is under siege; clearly the Bastille is being stormed. Yet the portrait represents far more than the triumph of a revolutionary spirit over the forces of oppression. Man Ray's most striking insight is his representation of the figure of Sade as a construction of stones, of the same stones that compose both the fortress under siege and its protective outworks: the divine marquis is himself a fortress. Man Ray's portrait illustrates above all Sade's paradoxical position, simultaneously inside and outside the fortress. Sade is made of the same material as the Ancien Régime.

The truth of Man Ray's vision is also borne out by Sade's *oeuvre*. The novels of the Ancien Régime's illustrious prisoner are too often viewed as a marginal manifestation of the archetypal Enlightenment drive. They are said to announce our modernity even as they bring down the fortress of Classical literature by throwing light on the dark areas repressed by earlier novelists. While this view is faithful to Sade's self-portrait as author—witness the address of the *120* to the reader—it can account neither for Sade's views of his literary predecessors, including his (alleged) jealousy of Laclos, nor for the shape he chose for at least certain of his fictions, notably the (in)famous *120*. Sade is an essentially equivocal author: he speaks simultaneously with two voices, a voice of liberation and a voice of control. The effect of this second voice on his fiction will be my principal subject here. I will take up Man Ray's suggestion that Sade was made of the same building blocks as the Ancien Régime. From this perspective, it becomes clear that Sade intended his fiction to be viewed not as a rupture with previous literary tradition but as its culminating point. Sade, the great rebel outcast, was trying not to destroy the great tradition of the French novel, but to continue it. The marquis foresaw what has become the prevailing view of the history of the early French novel, with Lafayette's *La Princesse de Clèves* as that novel's origin, and the *Liaisons dangereuses* as its culmination.

Gilbert Lely agrees with Maurice Heine's assessment of the *120* as Sade's literary masterpiece (*Vie du marquis de Sade,* vol. 2, p. 333). Sade himself describes on several occasions the "larmes de sang" he cried when he believed the manuscript lost in the confusion that followed the fall of the Bastille.[8] That bitterly mourned masterpiece suggests both how Sade believed his *oeuvre* should be interpreted and the place in literary history he intended for it, the place already assigned the *Liaisons* in the "great" French tradition of the novel, that of the final masterpiece *prima della rivoluzione*.

=== ✳ ===

The Fortress of the (Ir)rational

> Against whom was the Great Wall to serve as a protec-
> tion? Against the people of the north. . . . We have not
> seen them, and if we remain in our villages we shall
> never see them, even if on their wild horses they should
> ride as hard as they can straight towards us. . . . [T]he
> land is too vast and would not let them reach us, they
> would end their course in the empty air.
>
> Franz Kafka, "The Great Wall of China"

Sade's writing "L'Idée sur les romans" is a perfectly Classical gesture. Like Scudéry's preface to *Ibrahim* (1641), Huet's *Lettre à M. de Segrais sur l'origine des romans* (1670; originally published as a preface to *Zayde*), or Staël's *Essai sur les fictions*

---

[8] See his correspondence for August 1789. I will quote from Sade's *Correspondance*, ed. G. Lely, vol. 12 of the *O.c.* Sade's role in inciting the pre-Revolutionary crowds to storm the Bastille was acknowledged by those in command of the prison—as the marquis himself later never tired of reminding various leaders of the Revolution. Because of the trouble he was stirring up, he was transferred out of the Bastille on 4 July 1789, on such short notice that he had no time to rescue his literary possessions, among them the manuscript of the *120* he had so carefully hidden in the wall of his prison cell. Ironically, the destruction of the fortress Sade had incited as a prisoner also put an end to his authorship of the novel. The manuscript was saved by Arnoux de Saint-Maximin, but its author was mysteriously and inexplicably never to learn that it had survived.

(1795), Sade's "Idée" retraces the history of the novel in order to make place for a new type of fiction as the culmination of the schema he (re)creates.[9] However, Sade's critical effort is marked by a unique slant. Unlike his precursors, Sade is less interested in portraying the French novel as the inheritor of an unbroken tradition with a long and illustrious past, than in presenting his theory of what could be termed the genre's multiple birth: "Il est des modes, des usages, des goûts qui ne se transmettent point; inhérents à tous les hommes, ils naissent naturellement avec eux partout où ils existent" (10: 4). In other words, the French novel is not a late product of a continuous evolution, but rather a sort of literary Minerva. Sade's first objective in the "Idée" is to have the originality of the French tradition recognized: he insists, for example, that Italian masters like Boccaccio, rather than influencing their French counterparts, were in fact influenced by French troubadours (pp. 7-8).

The first goal of this revisionist history is to highlight the superiority of the Classical French novel, and the center of the "Idée" is signaled by Sade's version of "enfin Lafayette vint," "après tout ce fatras . . . parut Mme de La Fayette" (p. 9).[10] But Sade's ultimate aim is to point out that, after a period of successful development (most notably in the hands of Rousseau), the genre brought into its own in France by Lafayette is currently at a standstill. Sade situates the "Idée" "dans un temps où tout semble être fait, où l'imagination épuisée des auteurs paraît ne pouvoir plus rien créer de nouveau" (p. 20). The new genius worthy of coming into Lafayette's legacy must

[9] Selections from all these texts are found in vol. 2 of H. Coulet's *Le Roman jusqu'à la révolution* (Colin, 1968). The preface to *Ibrahim* is generally, although not universally, attributed to Georges de Scudéry rather than Madeleine. Staël's *Essai,* published five years before Sade's "Idée," presents an overview of the eighteenth-century novel remarkably similar to Sade's. Sade records his admiration for *Delphine* in his *Cahiers personnels* for 1803 and 1804 ([Corrêa, 1953], p. 195); the "Idée" may provide an earlier record of his intellectual proximity to Staël.

[10] Sade's formulation is actually closer to Lafayette's own "Il parut alors une beauté à la cour."

seek inspiration from two sources. In the first place, he[11] must
have an excellent knowledge of the human heart, a knowledge
that may be acquired either through extensive travel or through
a more sedentary procedure, suffering: "[L]a main de l'infor-
tune, en exaltant le caractère de celui qu'elle écrase, le met à
la juste distance où il faut qu'il soit pour étudier les
hommes; . . . il faut avoir été leur victime pour savoir les apprécier" (p. 16). To revitalize the moribund novel, Sade calls
for a uniquely personal source of inspiration, an act of revenge
for victimization. And, since only misfortune can indicate to
the writer the proper perspective from which to study the
human heart, Sade implies that the prison cell is the ideal
place in which to compose a novel. Sade's prescription for the
new master of the novel reunites two semantic paths with a
common origin: the Latin *ingenium,* natural ability, gave rise
both to "génie" and to "engin," ruse or snare (in Sade's case,
the snare laid to entrap the victimizer). Like Rousseau's pedagogues, the writer destined to revitalize the novel would be
an engineer, "a layer of snares."

The second source of inspiration for the new genius was
in Sade's day more classic: "le romancier est l'homme de la
nature" (p. 16). Even Sade's description of what "l'homme
de génie" can learn by becoming nature's creature is characterized by a (predictably) Rousseauian vocabulary. He speaks
of "la fièvre du talent," "l'enthousiasme du génie," "cette soif
ardente de tout peindre" (p. 17). Yet this vision of the loss of
control and self-abandon, this rejection of all systems but a
"natural" one is not easily reconciled with the image that
immediately precedes it, that of genius as revenge for persecution. Sade's vision of the future of the novel culminates in
a paradox: for the writer, fidelity to nature means revenging
himself on his persecutors. This is a paradox we have already
encountered in what Sade calls the "pages brûlantes" of a

[11] Sade may eulogize the particular gift women writers have for the novel—
"ce sexe, naturellement plus délicat, plus fait pour écrire le roman" (p. 9)—
but the new genius he calls for is undeniably male.

"livre sublime" (*Julie*) by the writer he felt possessed "une âme de feu" and "un esprit philosophique," "deux choses que la nature ne réunit pas deux fois dans le même siècle" (p. 11).

"Sade parvient au bout du discours et de la pensée classiques," in Foucault's evaluation. "Il règne exactement à leur limite" (*Les Mots et les choses*). His statement is as intriguingly ambiguous as Man Ray's "portrait imaginaire." On the one hand, it contains in germ the philosophy that motivates the dominant tradition of recent Sade criticism: Sade must be situated "au bout du discours . . . classique" because he marks a sort of voluntary return of all the truths repressed in this discourse. This would seem to be the meaning of another of Foucault's striking formulations about Sade: "Il n'y a pas d'ombre chez Sade" (*Histoire de la folie*), a formulation that could serve as an epigraph for many recent readings of the divine marquis.[12] For example, Foucault has been echoed by Roger: "Sade ne ménage aucun recoin obscur au récit" (p. 135).

But this is to comment on only one aspect of Foucault's intuition. It is not sufficient to say that Sade brought all of Classicism's skeletons out of the closet. The marquis is not only a rebel striving to outdo the Classical model by pointing out its weaknesses. He is at the same time Classicism's heir, built of the same stones as the fortress of the Ancien Régime. It is only logical that the relationship between Sade's fiction and the novelistic models of the French Classical age must be more problematic than is generally allowed. For example, the incipit of the *120* openly proclaims its author's admiration for the Golden Age of French literature—"la fin de ce règne [Louis XIV's], si sublime d'ailleurs" (p. 1). Sade's own works of prose fiction have often been compared to the novelistic masterpiece of the Sun King's reign. Lely suggests that *La Princesse de Clèves* may have served as a model for *Adélaïde de Brunswick* (2: 643); Béatrice Didier contends that "on

---

[12] Foucault, *Les Mots et les choses* (Gallimard, 1966), p. 224; *Histoire de la folie à l'âge classique* (Gallimard, 1972), p. 553.

trouve de curieuses analogies entre *La Marquise de Ganges* et *La Princesse de Clèves*."[13] Such analogies are frequently encountered, and they are "curious" indeed, for the reader never knows which interpretation of Foucault's evaluation may be invoked to explain them.

The *120* provides the best illustration of what might be termed Sade's aggressive eulogy of Classical discourse. For example, its incipit follows the model established for the French novel by Lafayette's masterpiece. The opening of *La Princesse de Clèves* situates the novel in the last years of a reign. The novel's first business is to introduce the reader to the principal characters of that declining rule and to inform the reader about the structure of its waning power. The *120* repeats this pattern, but the "tone" that governs its repetition is not easily classified. Sade's choice of historical setting for the *120* and his careful mapping out of the actors and the strategies that govern the libertine court within a court cannot be viewed as a parody of the founding text of the Classical French novel. Here, as at every moment when the Sadean text aligns itself most closely with Classical discourse, the point of textual contact is signaled by a sort of narrative bravado that initially seems *almost* comic. Yet the purpose of the incipit of the *120* does not run counter to that of its predecessor. The beginning of Sade's novel is closer to a positive appraisal of Lafayette's understanding of the workings of power, but an appraisal that, nevertheless, makes clear that the insights it is prepared to offer are keener than those of its precursor.

In *Sade, Fourier, Loyola*, Barthes reminds us that the burnt-out, frozen landscape of Sade's fiction is not, for all its awesome timelessness, a-historical. Unlike the fairy tale and the science-fiction story, which also unfold in minimalist settings, the Sadean novel does not reject history. "Les aventures sadiennes ne sont pas fabuleuses: elles se passent dans un monde réel, contemporain de la jeunesse de Sade, à savoir la société

---

[13] Didier, *Sade: une écriture du désir* (Denoël/Gonthier, 1976), p. 123.

de Louis XV."[14] For the *120*, Sade shifts the setting from Louis XV's reign to the last years of Louis XIV's, only a slightly greater distancing. He revives the model for "historical" fiction established by *La Princesse de Clèves* by choosing a narrative that unfolds in the not too distant past, but in a past nevertheless just outside the collective memory of the writer's contemporaries. The exceptional precision with which the historical setting is inscribed into the incipit of the *120* is clearly intended to attract the reader's attention.

The *120*'s opening sentences—which bear an uncanny resemblance to Vauban's position in his *Projet d'une dîme royale* (1707)—portray Classicism and libertinism as leeches fattened on the blood of the French people and the vitality of the French state:

> Les guerres considérables que Louis XIV eut à soutenir pendant le cours de son règne, en épuisant les finances de l'Etat et les facultés du peuple, trouvèrent pourtant le secret d'enrichir une énorme quantité de ces sangsues toujours à l'affût des calamités publiques qu'ils font naître au lieu d'apaiser, et cela pour être à même d'en profiter avec plus d'avantages. La fin de ce règne, si sublime d'ailleurs, est peut-être une des époques de l'empire français où l'on vit le plus de ces fortunes obscures qui n'éclatent que par un luxe et des débauches aussi sourdes qu'elles. (p. 1)

The members of Sade's quatrumvirate are the survivors of the Classical wars. They build their fortress on the ruins of Classicism and of a glorious reign. Because they are nourished by its lifeblood, they are heirs to the Classical heritage, able to transmit its message to posterity. However, their time as heirs is destined from the outset to be of short duration. The last years of the Sun King's reign are qualified as a libertine utopia, because the dissolution of power and the crumbling of hierarchies create a space for their "débauches sourdes." But that

---

[14] Barthes, *Sade, Fourier, Loyola* (Seuil, 1971), p. 134.

space lies in the menacing shadow of its own destruction: "C'était vers la fin de ce règne et peu avant que le Régent eût essayé, par ce fameux tribunal connu sous le nom de Chambre de justice, de faire rendre gorge à cette multitude de traitants, que quatre d'entre eux imaginèrent la singulière partie de débauche dont nous allons rendre compte" (p. 1). In the incipit, the libertines are identified both as masters and as future victims—victims, indeed, of their own strategy. They intend to be the last of Classicism's heirs, and they would assure that its genealogy stops with them by bringing the Classical fortress down upon themselves. The libertines have been victorious during the Classical wars precisely because they share the responsibility for destroying the system of defenses that had protected both "the French empire" and their own "obscure" activities. They are among the few defenders able to hold out during the siege of Classicism, and they enjoy this distinction because they understand so intimately the functioning of the war machinery Vauban created. The Sadean heroes protect themselves in order to reap the profits of the disasters they provoke. The members of the *120*'s quatrumvirate illustrate what the true Vaubanian hero would be—he who can comprehend, make creative, and even master the perfectly matched offensive and defensive systems of Vauban's nonstop, geometrical war machine. Sade's assessment of France's Golden Age is less a critique of the strategies it developed than an attempt to put them to more effective, if short-lived, use.

Such a state of inconsonant alignment with Classicism is frequently evident in the *120*. For example, when the libertines decide to use colored ribbons to denote their division of the "subjects," they follow courtly practice as recorded in Classical novels like *La Princesse de Clèves*: "Les reines et les princesses avaient toutes leurs filles magnifiquement habillées des mêmes couleurs qu'elles étaient vêtues: en sorte que l'on connaissait à qui étaient les filles par la couleur de leurs habits."[15]

---

[15] *La Princesse de Clèves*, ed. Adam (Garnier-Flammarion, 1966), p. 140.

On the surface, the libertine variant follows its model line by line:

> Les amis étant bien aises de distinguer à tout instant de la journée ceux des jeunes gens . . . dont les pucelages devaient leur appartenir, décidèrent de leur faire porter, de tous leurs divers ajustements, un ruban à leurs cheveux qui indiquât à qui ils appartenaient. (p. 117)

The libertines, of course, realign the variant of the official system devised by earlier lovers (Henri II wears Diane de Poitier's colors, the princess weaves Nemours's colors around the Indian cane). In the *120*, those marked with color-coded ribbons do not wear them to communicate with a loved one through a form of more or less silent communication, but as a mark of their total and irrevocable victimization; they truly belong to those whose colors they wear. The libertines take the aristocratic system to what could be considered its logical conclusion by stripping it bare of its repressive elements. In the *120*, the Classical system—"l'on connaissait à qui étaient les filles" (*Clèves*, p. 140)—is literalized.

Yet, when the libertines unveil the convention's true colors, they reject only its implicit role; they accept and heartily approve its explicit role, the codification of one more aspect of life in their kingdom. Sade has his libertines "expose" this device of courtly love for what it is (or at least for what he takes it to be), but any comic effect that results from this exposure is inconsequential, given that he also shows how seriously the libertines take the refocused system of classification. They appreciate fully the purpose for which the system was intended, and they take evident satisfaction in putting their victims in order, and in doing so by means of a system of coded signs that serves as a constant reminder of their newly developed form of control.

In the *120*, Sade matches his historical distancing with a form of what might be termed architectural distancing. The result of this process is a fictive architecture that repeats the relationship, already noted in the novel, of dissonant alignment with regard to the structures of French Classicism. Critics have often contrasted the two types of châteaux created to shelter the Sadean passion plays. They note first the gracious and open *demeures* of eighteenth-century inspiration, such as Mme de Saint-Ange's country home in which the "instituteurs immoraux" of *La Philosophie dans le boudoir* devote themselves to the task of Eugénie's education. This is a château gracious enough to contain so feminine a space as a "boudoir délicieux" (3: 381), and a château so open that, as their pupil Eugénie remarks on several occasions, newcomers are able to enter that boudoir with great ease.

These elegant dwellings stand in sharp contrast to the fortresses surrounded by thick walls in concentric circles, of which Silling is perhaps the "classic" representative. Hénaff interprets this second type of château as intended to "convoquer d'un coup tous les signes de la forteresse féodale avec ses implications historiques."[16] He sees the Sadean *château fort* as emblematic of the feudal system, and contends that the *120* grants a privileged position to the fortress, and therefore to the feudal system it is intended to represent, because of the unlimited powers that system conferred on the nobility, powers the libertines reappropriate behind Silling's walls. Hénaff offers no justification for choosing to ignore Sade's own historical setting of his fiction, a setting that marks off far more restricted chronological limits for the *120*. Sade situates his novel just after the apex of the French monarchy in a decidedly post-feudal atmosphere in which nobles and financiers conspire to bring down the monarchy in order to create a paradise doomed to self-destruction. The period that serves as the historical setting for the *120* also provides a model for the defensive architecture of its fortress.

Silling is actually the polar opposite of the medieval defensive enterprise. Apparently challenging its enemies to renounce their offensive position at the sight of its collective might, the medieval fortress makes an open display of its protective lay-

---

[16] Hénaff, *L'Invention du corps libertin* (PUF, 1978), p. 168.

ers. The libertine fortress is no virile projection surmounting a pinnacle: the descriptions of its systems of protection note no towers jutting up over its walls to complete its domination of the landscape. On the contrary, Silling is camouflaged in the center of a forest, sunken first in a valley and then projecting even deeper "dans le fond des entrailles de la terre" (p. 48). The libertines burrow so deep into the earth for Silling's protection that Didier speaks of "le symbolisme utérin du château qui se manifeste par son caractère essentiellement souterrain de creusement infini" (p. 30). The Sadean fortified place erected at Silling has the hidden, devious, even discreet, nature of its defenses in common with Vaubanian fortifications. The Classical French fortress sits close to the earth, has its elaborate trenchwork dug into the ground. Its defenses are therefore so obliquely deceptive that the full panoply of its protective barriers is only visible from above.[17]

The *120* could be called the greatest literary monument to the age of the fortress, for few subjects are granted a more important place in Sade's novel than defensive military architecture. Silling is surely the ultimate Sadean *lieu clos*. The setting for the narration and the reenactment of the six hundred passions of the *120* is a fortress its creators intend to be more isolated and with more limited access than any utopia since the original Earthly Paradise. "Il fallait, pour y parvenir, arriver d'abord à Bâle; on y passait le Rhin, au delà duquel la route se rétrécissait au point qu'il fallait quitter les voitures. Peu après, on entrait dans la Forêt Noire, on s'y enfonçait d'environ quinze lieues par une route difficile, tortueuse et absolument impraticable sans guide" (p. 44). Like Candide and Cacambo when they make what is said to be an impossible

---

[17] The "modest" nature of Classical fortifications was responsible for the importance of engravings of traces during Vauban's lifetime, and the secrecy that surrounded them. Engravings—along with the *plans-relief*, the scale-model miniatures made of the most important places—provided the only opportunity of demonstrating the full extent of Vauban's defensive system to his contemporaries. Today, the aerial view is almost universally adopted for photographs of Classical fortifications.

journey into Voltaire's utopia, Eldorado, those who would travel to Silling find themselves embarked on a voyage that becomes increasingly more treacherous.

The libertine utopia's exterior line of defense is formed by natural barriers that would be the envy of any Vaubanian strategist. As they finally approach the Golden City, Voltaire's two wanderers find themselves surrounded on all sides by unscalable heights, their retreat apparently cut off.[18] By the time the voyager to Silling comes to the first unqualified obstacle, the "route absolument impraticable sans guide," his difficulties are only just beginning. After the barriers of the river and the forest, there are the rigors of the mountain:

> [O]n commençait à escalader une montagne presque aussi haute que le mont Saint-Bernard et d'un abord infiniment plus difficile, car il n'est possible de parvenir au sommet qu'à pied. Ce n'est pas que les mulets n'y aillent, mais les précipices environnent de toutes parts si tellement le sentier qu'il faut suivre, qu'il y a le plus grand danger à s'exposer sur eux. . . . [S]ans les secours de l'art, après avoir grimpé la montagne, il devient impossible de la redescendre. (pp. 44-45)

The dizzying heights and precipices of the mountain constitute the second "impossible" barrier protecting the libertine space against penetration. Yet even after two absolute dead ends have been reached and crossed, and the impossible has been twice defied, there remains an ultimate natural barrier: "Ce caprice singulier de la nature est une fente de plus de trente toises sur la cime de la montagne" (p. 45). The narrator's formulation, "ce caprice singulier de la nature," suggests an excess even in natural precautions, as though nature had conspired with the libertines by outdoing itself in the creation of the definitive defensive landscape.

[18] "Enfin ils découvrirent un horizon immense bordé de montagnes inaccessibles" (*Candide*, ed. R. Pomeau [Nizet, 1963], p. 148). Unlike the Black Forest mountains, however, the range that shelters Eldorado from the outside world is scaled without enormous difficulty with the aid of a "machine."

But the narrator has not completed his proof of the inaccessibility of Silling. In the continuation of his description, the hint of natural redundance is far surpassed by the seemingly infinite man-made precautions, precautions that quickly take on an air of wild excess. Following Vauban's practice, Durcet, master of the fortress and organizer of the libertine house party, uses these natural formations to ensure the isolation of his privileged group. He builds a bridge across the precipice, then has it destroyed as soon as all the future participants in the drama of Silling have arrived—"et, de ce moment-là, plus aucune possibilité quelconque de communiquer au château de Silling" (p. 45). Even the syntax of the phrase that marks the hermetic seal around the libertine *haut lieu* is excessive: its absolute nature is doubly signaled, by "aucune" and by "quelconque." From this point on, all the defenses are man-made, and their multiplication becomes staggering. Since Durcet controls the only nearby town (at the base of the mountain), the narrator affirms that "la barrière fut fermée." The town is inhabited solely by armed criminals in Durcet's employ, so the village in its entirety is an armed camp that constitutes a human, outer enclosure around Silling (p. 44). The libertine *place forte* is situated over and beyond nature's fortifications, in a valley "entourée de partout de rochers à pic dont les sommets touchent aux nues" (p. 45). "[C]est au milieu de cette petite plaine si bien entourée, si bien défendue, que se trouve le château de Durcet. Un mur de trente pieds de haut l'environne encore; au-delà du mur, un fossé plein d'eau et très profond défend encore une dernière enceinte formant une galerie tournante" (p. 45).

Even after the multiplication of the lines of defense, both natural and man-made, has become so great that the reader loses count of their number, the libertines are unable to put their fortifying mania to rest. The duke continues Durcet's work when he decides to fortify Silling from within. The libertines have brought in sufficient supplies to enable them to hold out for the duration of the siege (and in fact food never runs out, no matter how elaborate the meals become, so their calculations must have been made with a rigor worthy of Vauban). Since they have no need of contact with the outside world, the duke literally eliminates the very possibility of an escape route. The narrator recounts the ultimate enclosure: "[I]l fallait, dis-je, faire murer toutes les portes par lesquelles on pénétrait dans l'intérieur, et . . . on se barricada à tel point qu'il ne devenait même plus possible de reconnaître où avaient été les portes" (p. 49). Thus Silling's heroes wall themselves inside their utopia "comme dans une citadelle assiégée" (p. 49); the seal with which they make their fortress safe is so perfect that it enables them to reach a defensive ideal, the erasure of all means of penetration.

Once the doors have been effaced, the members of the quatrumvirate promulgate the rules intended to govern all aspects of life in the fortress during their stay, as though the guarantee of a hermetic seal around the space chosen for their activities frees them to begin those activities. However, the defensive obsession cannot be laid to rest so easily. Indeed, the very day after the rules are laid down, the duke "passa la matinée . . . à tout verifier, . . . et surtout à examiner avec soin la place, pour voir si elle n'était pas susceptible, ou d'être assaillie, ou de favoriser quelque évasion" (pp. 56-57). The duke's tour of inspection reiterates the essential lesson to be learned from Vauban's accounting and from his students' relationship to his "preventive" bookkeeping: the defensive strategist is doomed to continue his work ad infinitum, for he will always imagine the possibility of one more attack and therefore the necessity of a "final" defense. Indeed, the defense of Silling constitutes the most successful literary embodiment of the Vaubanian dream, for the efforts to protect the Black Forest *château fort* are marked by the tradition of defensive military speculation that existed in the wake of Vauban's theorizing. The story of Silling is situated at the limits of the myth of the perfect defensive system.

But the Sadean fortified place is more than a realization of Vauban's dream. Because the libertines double their external defenses with internal defenses, they alone in the Classical century of military strategy can be said to fulfill Montalembert-Laclos's dream and surpass Vauban. Sade attempts to ensure victory in his private war by applying Vaubanian strategy to life inside his novelistic fortress. In Vauban's plan for the Classical fortified place, for the rational fortress, no provision is made for revolt from within the *enceinte;* the enemy is positioned only outside its walls. At the initiation of a state of siege, any potentially unruly, weak, or useless individuals who find themselves inside the fortress are simply evicted to beg mercy of the enemy, or otherwise to fend for themselves. If the commanding officer of a place sees that he is about to be besieged, Vauban orders him to "obliger ceux qui sont inutiles dans un siege, comme les femmes, les vieillards, les enfans, de sortir de la place" (*Défense des places,* 1795 ed., pp. 195-96). The Classical defense simply eliminates the forces unable to follow its discipline, the forces that could cause a breakdown in its system of control.

Vauban also instructed the commander of a fortified place to lay waste to the no man's land surrounding the fortress: "Quelques jours avant l'arrivée des troupes ennemies, il faudra mettre le feu à toutes les maisons et bâtiments des dehors qui pourraient favoriser les gardes et les approches, ainsi qu'à tous les fourrages des environs, afin que l'ennemi n'en profite pas" (*Défense des places,* p. 198). His prohibition against natural proliferation is so sweeping that the Classical master of defense even forbids governors to allow flowers to be planted on the walls of the fortress in time of peace (*Défense des places,* p. 24). Once the commanding officer has emptied his place of all elements that cannot be governed by the laws of geometry, he is able to go on with his preprogrammed defense, reassured that all will henceforth be calculable.

It never occurred to Vauban to include more about the day-to-day existence of those left inside the fortress than the amounts of the various commodities they might consume. Those responsible for the defense of the fortified place are no more than statistics for him. In the *120,* Sade's demonstration of the greatness of Vauban's system, the perspective on the siege traditional in military strategy is reversed. The story is told from the point of view of the defenders of the fortress, yet the reader is never asked to look out in the direction of the attacking forces. On the contrary, our vision is directed inside the fortress, and not on account of the possibility of attack from within, but because in the *120* the scope of life inside the fortress is explored as an end in itself. When Sade fills in an area left blank in Vauban's treatises, he sheds light on the paradox shaped in the "Idée sur les romans," his positioning of literary genius at the intersection of natural inspiration and revenge for humiliation.

The opening paragraph of the *120* can be read as a confirmation of Vauban's assessment of the balance of power in France at the end of Louis XIV's reign: the "fin de ce règne" was weakened by too many wars, and these wars were characterized by too blind an indulgence in offensive strategy; the Sun King should have protected his kingdom against internal ravages, from the creeping power of "leeches." Sade situates the novel he composed on the eve of the Revolution at what he views as the limit of Classical French military strategy. The operation of Vauban's theoretically flawless system of defenses is rendered impotent because a monarch has become libertinism's puppet.

Following the model established by Lafayette in *La Princesse de Clèves,* Sade realigns history in order to make a place in it for his fiction. His rewriting betrays his dream of omnipotence. As his story begins, his characters have already brought France's Golden Age to its knees; in the *120* they will profit from the lessons to be learned from Louis le Grand's weakness in order to make their defenses airtight. The creator of the quatrumvirate implies that his literary production likewise stands at the logical conclusion of Classical aesthetics. The *120* will be *the* masterwork of the aesthetics of Classicism because it is purified of the weakness inherent in the literary products of the Age of Louis XIV—their authors' refusal to come to grips with the strategy on which they are founded. Sade's novel tells the story of a libertine war: "Comme ce tableau réglait . . . toutes les opérations de la campagne, nous avons cru nécessaire d'en donner copie au lecteur" (p. 107). The novel that recounts that story is itself an act of warfare, the ultimate attempt to win the battle of/with Classicism, a last skirmish fought just as the Ancien Régime was breathing its last.

The *120* is the most Classical of Sade's novels. For his libertine utopia, the marquis rejects both the picaresque dispersal he adopts in *Justine* and *Juliette* and the epistolary polyphony chosen for *Aline et Valcour* in favor of an eminently contained and single-minded vision. The product of this repression of novelistic excess is Sade's blueprint for the novel. In the *120*, Sade takes his reader inside the Classical fortress and shows him the ultimate manifestation of natural proliferation controlled by systematization. Sade's tabulating strategy is both more excessive and more rigorous than that of either Rousseau or Laclos. He uses his calculating rigor to make explicit a vision that previous literary fortifiers had only demonstrated implicitly: the Classical utopia is a fortress.

The *120* may be the ultimate work of prison literature. It was composed in a cell in the Bastille shortly before the French Revolution (1785). Moreover, it is a fiction confined by the limits of the paper on which it was written, since in order to protect it from his captors Sade wrote it on strips of paper that were rolled up and hidden between the stones of his cell wall. Under the circumstances, it seems almost inconceivable that the dream created by the prisoner is in fact a mirror image of the panopticon in which he created it: the *120* is truly the literary equivalent of the stones between which it was camouflaged. Sade is the first (literary) fortifier to portray life inside the fortress. And when he reverses the perspective on siege warfare, he reveals a *mise en abyme*. The external state of siege—which remains purely mythical in the *120*, since there is never the slightest indication of any plan to attack Silling—contains an internal state of siege, which in turn unfolds around the "heart" of the libertine enterprise, a prison cell.

In *Emile* and *Julie*, the *mise en abyme* mirrors a situation among characters: an *infans in machina* reveals the true goal of (adult) strategy. In Sade's carceral master text, the reflection in the self-conscious mirror is architectural. A place of confinement and a center of offensive/defensive strategy is built around a miniature reproduction of itself. Silling's fortification within a fortification is a *cachot*, the torture chamber hidden in the bowels of the fortified place and Silling's true inner sanctum.

> ... une espèce de cachot voûté, fermé par trois portes de fer, ... Et là, que de tranquillité! Jusqu'à quel point ne devait pas être rassuré le scélérat que le crime y conduisait avec une victime! Il était chez lui, il était hors de France, dans un pays sûr, au fond d'une forêt inhabitable, dans un réduit de cette forêt que, par les mesures prises, les seuls oiseaux du ciel pouvaient aborder, et il y était dans le fond des entrailles de la terre. (p. 48)

The fortified place within the fortified place is the only true libertine "home": "Il était chez lui." And the home the libertine creates for himself is a prison, a prison designed simultaneously to keep out and to keep in. The *cachot* in the bowels of Silling lies at the heart of the Classical drive to systematize.

The narrator of the *120* informs his readers that when they have finished taking away all the pieces of his novel "tout aura trouvé sa place" (p. 61). He would have the reader believe that the structure of the *120* is neither permanent nor definitive and that the place of Sade's book is elsewhere. It will be "à sa place" when it has been disassembled and its constitutive elements have been reassimilated into other systems. Yet Sade's invitation to a beheading cannot be reconciled with the insistence on strategy, system, and calculation that dominates the *120*. Sade is merely echoing the rhetoric of liberation developed by previous defensive novelists as a smokescreen for their own strategic obsessions. In fact the *120* conveys its author's conception of the proper place of fiction and demonstrates that the novel itself—and everything in it—is "à sa place," in its proper place. That place is obviously at the culminating point of the tradition of the Classical French novel, for the admiration Sade voiced for Lafayette and Rousseau in the "Idée sur les romans" was sincere. Foucault argues that Sade's *oeuvre* is a "gigantesque pastiche de Rousseau" (*Histoire de la folie*, p. 552). Foucault fails to make clear just what he means by this intriguing statement, but, as Gérard Genette has recently reminded us, "pure" pastiche occurs only in cases of imitation of a master writer in the absence of satirical intention, and the pastiche of Rousseau is no more parodic than the pastiche of Lafayette.[19] Yet Sade's use of pastiche in the *120* differs from the model Genette sets up in at least three important ways. Genette points out that pastiche is most often "playful" ("ludique," p. 32)—in some way a schoolboy's exercise—while Sade's transposition of Rousseau's theories has a more serious goal. Genette also stresses that pastiche is generally a form of stylistic transposition, as opposed to parody, a semantic transformation, whereas in Sade's case pastiche operates in parody's semantic domain (p. 35). (Laclos often echoes Rousseau's style; Sade repeats only his theories.) Finally, Genette remarks that pastiche is rarely hidden; there is a "pact," reminiscent of Lejeune's "autobiographical pact," whereby the *pasticheur* spells out for his reader both what he is doing and the model he is imitating (p. 141). Sade, however, includes no "pastiche contract" to guide his reader; like Laclos, Rousseau is not named in the *120*'s mute, semantic "pastiche." And Sade's very refusal to sign his echoes makes it difficult for readers to interpret them. Tony Tanner contends that Sade's châteaux can be viewed as the "nightmare mirror image of . . .. Julie's house, Clarens."[20] The alignment may be incongruous, but that incongruity should not be allowed to mask Sade's attempt to put his novel in the

---

[19] Genette, *Palimpsestes* (Seuil, 1982), p. 32.
[20] Tanner, *Adultery in the Novel* (Baltimore: Johns Hopkins Univ. Press, 1979), pp. 153-54 n. 10.

place occupied by the *Liaisons,* to have himself accepted as Lafayette's and Rousseau's heir. It is only fitting therefore that the *120,* Sade's fortress/prison/utopia, should lay bare the ethos of Rousseau's naturalism and that it should provide the ultimate statement on the meaning of liberation for Sade, and for the Classical age. Sade harnesses the violence contained by Classicism to his desire to have the genealogy of Classicism stop with his name: after him, the deluge.

===== ✳ =====

Re-membering the Body of Narrative

> Beau développement de la voûte du crâne (théosophie, bienveillance); point de saillies exagérées dans les régions temporales (point de férocité); point de saillies exagérées derrière et au-dessus des oreilles (point de combativité . . .); cervelet de dimensions modérées, point de distance exagérée d'une apophyse mastoïde à l'autre (point d'excès dans l'amour physique).
>
> En un mot, . . . son crâne était en tous points semblable à celui d'un père de l'Eglise.
>
> Dr. L.-J. Ramos, "Notes sur M. de Sade"[21]

Gilbert Lely refers to the "aspect massif et ténébreux" of the famous *rouleau manuscrit,* and indeed in its manuscript version the *120* is an alarming document (*O.c.,* vol. 13, p. lxxiv; vol. 2, p. 329), a document far more constrained than Laclos's claustrophobic manuscript. The essential fragility of the original manuscript—a roll of thin paper just over twelve meters long made up of small sheets twelve centimeters wide glued together—is counteracted by the manner in which Sade's

---

[21] Dr. L.-J. Ramos, the doctor who as a young man was with Sade on the night of his death, late in life examined the marquis's skull. A self-proclaimed student of phrenology, he offered this description of it. Appendix to Sade, *Cahiers personnels (1803-1804),* pp. 113-14.

handwriting fills the sheets. The imprisoned novelist blackened the paper with a nearly microscopic script, giving the fragile roll an appearance of formidable solidity. As Sade composed it, the *120* is a narrative without margins, almost without paragraphs, with few of the divisions or ruptures that conventionally serve to break the flow of narrative for readerly consumption, a text without the *failles* Barthes considered essential to readerly *jouissance*. Traditionally, critics have not taken the conditions of the *120*'s composition into account in their readings of the novel; they do not speak of the appearance of the manuscript, presumably because they consider that appearance to be determined by the constraints that governed the text's transcription. They place little emphasis on the fault-finding interventions with which the major sections of the *120* conclude, because these interventions would in all likelihood have been eliminated, had Sade been able to revise the manuscript for publication. Thereby they reduce to the status of mere curiosity those moments in the *120* when the voice of the narrator fuses with that of the author, who is taking himself to task because the narrative does not live up to the perfection of his master plan. Most significantly, critics ordinarily limit their reading of the novel to the finished introduction and first section, almost completely ignoring the three final parts, which exist in something apparently only slightly more elaborate than outline form. Thus Lely typically extols the introduction as "le chef d'oeuvre de Donatien-Alphonse-Françqis" and declares the first part worthy of comparison to the *Satyricon* (2: 334), but reserves no praise for the novel's later sections. In the reading of the *120* I propose here, I reverse what has become standard critical practice. I argue that the author's references to the compositional constraints and the "unfinished" sections must not be dismissed as falling outside the critic's domain because, on the contrary, they serve as the surest indicators of the nature and the scope of Sade's project in the *120*. In fact, the allegedly "incomplete" final sections may even be, more than the opening parts of the novel, the blueprint of Sade's dream for the French novel, the text that stands as his version of the logical culmination of the Classical novelistic heritage. As he worked on the *rouleau manuscrit*, Sade was working to discipline both the body of narrative and the body in narrative.

"Mettons, s'il vous plaît, un peu d'ordre à ces orgies," Mme de Saint-Ange imperiously commands in *La Philosophie dans le boudoir;* "il en faut même au sein du délire et de l'infamie" (p. 424). She might have changed her "even" to "above all," for this rallying cry to her fellow pedagogues and their eager pupil expresses precisely what is most perplexing, disturbing, and at times simply ludicrous in the behavior of all Sade's heroes: the libertine superhero is quite obviously one of the best housekeepers in fiction. Certainly the hero Rousseau proposes as the model of an efficient natural manager, Robinson Crusoe, could offer the libertines no competition in the scope of their endeavors: his domain, however well-run, is far too limited and rustic to challenge the lavish complexity of Silling's organization. Even Switzerland's most renowned literary housekeeper, Julie de Wolmar, cannot always compete with the members of the quatrumvirate when it comes to thinking of everything that needs to be kept under watchful surveillance and to becoming *l'oeil vivant* constantly on the lookout for trouble.

It is undoubtedly Julie's constant concern with imposing order for the smallest possible price that restrains her obsession with systematization to dimensions unworthy of the libertines' quest for a well-ordered fortress. For example, she makes an elaborate list of the kinds of after-dinner wines she serves the men in her life. At the end of her enumeration, the reader is surprised to learn that the many varieties she is able to put before them actually cost far less than one would imagine, because all the wines are locally grown in the perfect microcosm that surrounds her garden. ("Le rancio, le cherez, le malaga, le chassaigne, le siracuse dont vous buvez . . . ne sont en effet que des vins de Lavaux diversement préparés" [5: 2: 552]).

Mealtime at Silling is a subject on which the narrator dwells with loving care. Witness the example of the evening feast on 1 November: "Il y eut d'abord un service de potage au jus de bisque et de hors d'oeuvre composés de vingt plats. Vingt entrées les remplacèrent et furent bientôt relevées elles-mêmes par vingt autres entrées fines." The narrator's blow-by-blow account of the meal concludes, like Julie's, with his remarks on the wines that had accompanied each course: "A l'égard des vins, ils avaient varié à chaque service: dans le premier le bourgogne, au second et au troisième deux différentes espèces de vins d'Italie, au quatrième le vin du Rhin, au cinquième des vins du Rhône, au sixième le champagne mousseux et des vins grecs de deux sortes avec deux différents services" (pp. 87, 88). Also like Julie's, the narrator's excessively careful enumerations are always punctuated with precise monetary information, only he is eager to demonstrate how excessive the expenses were : "[P]as un seul de ces repas ne coûtait moins de dix mille francs" (p. 6).

The libertines' ostentatious opulence is the opposite of Julie's opulent frugality, but the contradictory impressions that the Sadean and the Rousseauian wine stewards wish to give of their lists should not blind the reader to the stewards' procedural affinities. The narrator of the *120* shares all of Julie's eagerness to keep the reader informed of every expense, to make certain the public is aware of the exact cost of each libertine feast. In *Julie,* the long and varied list of wines has cost surprisingly little to produce, whereas in the *120,* the necessary culinary variety has required a startling outlay. Yet both these literary budgets are ultimately inspired by the same delight in the pleasures of calculation, the same *jouissance* in the well-made and elaborate tally sheet.

The narrator in the *120* develops Robinson Crusoe's mania for drawing up lists into a true passion, a passion ultimately as unsettling as any of the libertine "passions" the novel enumerates. As Barthes has so convincingly argued, this obsessive bookkeeping is the primary distinguishing trait common to all Sade's heroes. Barthes characterizes Juliette as the archetypal shopkeeper. He describes her efforts to realize a Vaubanian dream of controlling the world's population: "L'imagination de Juliette est éminemment comptable: à un moment, elle met au point un projet numérique, destiné à corrompre sûrement, par progression géométrique, toute la nation française" (*Sade, Fourier, Loyola*, p. 34, n. 1; *O.c.*, vol. 8, p. 503).[22] In the *120*, these tables serve to tally up and distribute the objects of libertine passion, to regulate all aspects of their victims' lives. Thus the narrator includes a table to govern the whipping of disobedient victims, a table "des fautes avec à côté le nombre de coups" (p. 363), and the "tableau des projets du reste du voyage" (pp. 108-10), essentially the rules governing the distribution of the victims' virginity (the libertine to whom the virginity is assigned; the type of virginity assigned, frontal or dorsal; the date of the defloration). Then, of course, there are the unforgettable final tallies, recapitulative compilations that neatly set out the effects of the sojourn and that bear titles such as "sacrifiés," "nouveaux ménages," and "recapitulations" to show "l'emploi de tous les sujets" (pp. 429-31).

Whenever possible, the libertines arrange their lives and the setting for their lives in symmetrical formations. Their collective marriage contract is perhaps the best illustration of an extended arrangement in which the heroes' individual idiosyncrasies are shaped according to the demands of symmetry:

> [L]e duc, père de Julie, devint l'époux de Constance, fille de Durcet; . . . Durcet, père de Constance, devint l'époux d'Adélaïde, fille du président; . . . le président, père d'Adélaïde, devint l'époux de Julie, fille ainée du duc, et . . . l'évèque, oncle et père d'Aline, devint l'époux des trois autres en cédant cette Aline à ses amis, aux droits près qu'il continuait de se réserver sur elle. (p. 3)

A neat series of half-chiasmi contains the story of the one happy family that rules over Silling as tidily as if the arrange-

---

[22] In addition to his vision of the pig inheriting the earth in "De la cochonnerie," Vauban drew up a project estimating the growth of the French colonies until the year 2000.

ments its members had contracted did not defy transcription in a family tree. And this passion for symmetry continues to govern all the agreements made by the libertines: they divide up and dispose of their victims as neatly as if they were dealing with commodities as prosaic as those Vauban tallies for everyday life inside the fortress. Order carefully packages and contains the violent rupture at the heart of libertine contractual agreements.

In similar fashion, the libertines take a particular pleasure in enacting or having enacted before them tableaux "vivants" for which they arrange themselves and their subjects into positions whose neatness almost masks their complexity. At the end of the day's storytelling, the libertines multiply the pleasures of symmetry nearly ad infinitum, either to act out lessons in practical pedagogy that illustrate some of the day's stories, or simply for their own relaxation. Near the close of the ninth day, for example,

> Curval imagina de foutre Hyacinthe en cuisses et d'obliger Sophie à venir, entre les cuisses d'Hyacinthe, sucer ce qui dépasserait de son vit. La scène fut plaisante et voluptueuse; . . . et le duc qui, à cause de la longeur de son vit, était le seul qui pût imiter cette scène, s'arrangea de même avec Zélamir et Fanny . . . : Après eux, Durcet et l'évêque s'ajustèrent des quatre enfants et s'en firent aussi sucer. (p. 167)

The libertines demonstrate a consistent concern for introducing geometric precision into human contacts. In this manner, they are able to "freeze" the action in the scenes they stage, to make their tableaux "vivants" somehow strangely inanimate.[23] In addition, the concern for order consistently demonstrated by both characters and narrator in the *120* is a mirror

---

[23] Roger describes "la haine que Sade porte au tableau" (p. 119), which he feels results from painting's status as a closed space that the spectator cannot penetrate. He does not mention, however, a related Sadean passion, the desire to arrange all types of interpersonal contact into tableaux governed by mathematical permutations.

CHAPTER VI

image of their creator's desire to tame the body of his fiction. The standard novelistic model, in Sade's day as in ours, was organic. *Roman* and *nouvelle* generally told a story of development, of unfolding—if they did not cover the entire life cycle from birth to death, they were at least faithful to a "natural" or "logical" order in their constitutive episodes. The Sadean narrative model is opposed to this organic model as juxtaposition is opposed to development: Sade's text decomposes simply and "naturally" into fragments, narrative building blocks whose order seems at first highly unstable. "La rapsodie sadienne s'enfile ainsi sans ordre," in Barthes's characterization. "[L]e roman rapsodique (sadien) n'a pas de *sens*, rien ne l'oblige à progresser, mûrir, se terminer" (*Sade, Fourier, Loyola*, p. 144). However, while Barthes's evaluation may be true of Sade's work in general, it does not account for the particular narrative structure of the *120*.[24] In this novel, Sade attempts to find an answer to the question that haunts all novelists who explore the potential of nondevelopmental, inorganic narrative—from Cyrano to Flaubert to Huysmans. Once you have "liberated" narrative from a natural, organic model, how do you discipline the polymorphous body of narrative? How do you keep it in line and bring your inorganic narrative progression to a halt without having recourse to a deus ex machina on the model of the *Voyage dans la lune*, or to a reductio ad absurdum on the model of *Bouvard et Pécuchet*? From the Goncourts' diary, we know of Flaubert's "mad" obsession with what he called Sade's "dernier mot du catholicisme," with his "haine du corps," his "horreur de la nature."[25] Indeed the alliance between Flaubert and Sade may

[24] Like Foucault, Barthes uses *Justine* as the typical Sadean novel, as the text/lightning bolt that marks the culmination of the Classical age. The *120*, however, is far more closely related to the Classical French novel, because of its precision and its claustrophobic confinement.

[25] "Il y a vraiment chez Flaubert une obsession de Sade.... Il faut que chaque homme ait sa toquade" (Edmond and Jules de Goncourt, *Journal*, quoted by Françoise Laugaa-Traut, *Lectures de Sade* [Colin, 1973], p. 147).

even have been closer than Flaubert imagined. Sade created what might be termed a "catholic body," a body rendered somehow inorganic by a rigidly computed, "monastic" temporality and a mathematically charted narrative structure. He then developed a form to house that inorganic body, a narrative model with "natural" affinities to Flaubert's "frozen" form. Silling's defenses are made unassailable in order to protect the creation of the encyclopedia of libertine passion. Ultimately the encyclopedia becomes more than a subject for narrative and for orgy: in the last, "unfinished" sections, the novel is reduced to a listing of the entries in the libertine encyclopedia. Sade uses the principles of encyclopedic organization to give his text a logic and a shape—an appearance of inevitability normally absent in paratactic narrative. As the narrator of the *120* constantly proclaims, the building blocks of his text cannot be shifted or interchanged, for they possess a developmental logic all their own: Sade uses a fixed mathematical schema, a narrative accountability, to make parataxis the narrative equal of unfolding. To tame the body of narrative, Sade invents the narrative machine.

In the apostrophe to the *ami lecteur* that precedes his account of the first day's activities, the narrator reveals the strategy by which he gives the encyclopedia a life in narrative:

[O]n a fondu ces six cents passions dans le récit des historiennes. . . . Il aurait été trop monotone de les détailler autrement et une à une, sans les faire entrer dans un corps de récit. Mais comme le lecteur, peu au fait de ces sortes de matières, pourrait peut-être confondre les passions désignées avec l'aventure ou l'événement simple de la vie de la conteuse, on a distingué avec soin chacune de ces passions par un trait en marge. (p. 61)

The critical appraisal the narrator makes here is a key one for all Sadean narrative, and for the *120* in particular. He distinguishes between the narrative body (the "corps de récit"), in this case the lives of those telling stories, and the raison d'être of that narrative body, in this case the cataloguing of six hundred entries referred to as "passions."[26] The body of the novel is defined as the life stories of the four *conteuses,* the experiences from their pasts that allow each of them to frame the one hundred fifty passions assigned her for presentation to her audience. By implication, the house party at Silling, the "aventures" and "événements" in the lives of the four libertines that constitute the novel's frame narrative, is also characterized as narrative body. But this entire composite body exists only to stave off the boredom the reader, by implication too frivolous or feebleminded to endure a more rigorous presentation, would have experienced, had the six hundred entries simply been catalogued ("détailler") without the crutch ("l'événement *simple*") of biological or organic supplement ("la vie de la conteuse"). The narrative body— developmental fiction with all its narrative "riches" (chronology, situation in space, natural unfolding)—is the opiate of the masses, of those unable to comprehend pure, mathematical logic.

Barthes has argued in defense of the Sadean text that "Sade n'est ennuyeux que si nous fixons notre regard sur les crimes et non sur les performances du discours" (p. 41). Yet his argument is hardly valid in the case of the *120.* Initially, it is true, the reader is entertained by a lavish display of storytelling skill, as both the primary narrator and the first secondary

[26] Commentators generally consider "passion" a synonym for "perversion," as though Sade had in mind only the desires of his libertines. But the actual "passions" listed in the *120* seem more closely related to the word's etymological meaning, suffering or pain, and the term therefore appears to reflect the victims' perspective. From either perspective, the term has connotations of dynamism and unpredictability that are negated by Sade's static narration of the entries, just as the violence of "passion," "violent," and "éclatant" are contained by the frozen formality of the opening paragraph in *La Princesse de Clèves.* For a discussion of the strange equivocalness of Sade's use of "passion," see Roger, pp. 52ff.

narrator, the always charming Duclos, do their best to "distract" their publics from the content of their tales. Long before the novel is reduced to outline form, however, their narrative performances begin to be cut back. On the seventeenth day, for example, the primary narrator's performance territory is restricted. The normally lavish account of the evening meal is omitted, as is the story of the eighteenth day's activities prior to the post-prandial storytelling, because: "[I]l ne se passa absolument que des choses ordinaires" (p. 243). These untold events are judged "ordinaires," presumably because such narratives have become too repetitive. Sade realizes that similarity can make his development pass for repetition. Thus in the apostrophe to the *ami lecteur* the narrator directs him to pay attention to small differences: "étudie bien celle des passions qui te paraît ressembler sans nulle différence à une autre, et tu verras que cette différence existe" (p. 61). Ultimately Sade judges that paratactical narrative not strictly held in check is not worthy of the reader's attention.

This conclusion is supported by the fact that the first large-scale narrative omission on the seventeenth day is immediately preceded by a lengthy conversation between Curval and the duke on the necessity of keeping order in their activities and, also, on the possibility of secretly transgressing that order. As we learn here, the libertines do not always respect the code governing the "placement" of passion in the public domain (the space reserved for storytelling) within the confines of the chronological and physical spaces reserved for their private lives (for example, after lights out in their bedrooms, and in the evenings in the *cabinets* at the rear of the storytelling theater). In this passage, Curval is criticized for his persistent rule breaking. Just at this point when the code has been re-affirmed, Curval suddenly produces one hundred *louis* and declares that they "me serviront à payer une amende à laquelle je crains d'être bientôt condamné." "[C]e scélérat," the narrator comments, "prévoyait ses fautes d'avance et . . . il prenait son parti sur la punition qu'elles devaient lui mériter, sans se mettre le moins du monde en peine ou de les prévenir ou de les éviter" (p. 243). Curval's gesture here foretells more than his own future crimes: he is also a forerunner of Sade in his moments of self-criticism, even to the point of adopting a paradoxical mode identical to that elected by Sade: "Voilà cent louis, dit-il *en les recevant*" (p. 243, emphasis mine). Curval both pays out and takes in, serving simultaneously as corrector and corrected, and demonstrating thereby the totally self-contained nature of the libertine correctional process.

Yet despite this elaborate disciplinary procedure, Curval remains incorrigible. Ignoring repeated requests for order, he continually steps out of line. Indeed, by this point in the unfolding of the *corps de récit* (the seventeenth day), Curval's incorrigibility has become a narrative highlight: once the scene of disciplining and self-disciplining I have just described is over, the narrator puts an abrupt end to his account of the day's activities. The *120*'s narrative body gradually becomes *only* the account of tabulation and "corrections"—the imposition, reimposition, and policing of a code. This is true not only on the level of the story within the story, but also in the frame narrative, the tale of the quatrumvirate's exploits. Whereas nineteen pages are devoted to the account of the first day, the eighteenth day is passed over rapidly in only four pages, the nineteenth in five, and the twenty-second is dismissed in a mere two pages on the pretext that Duclos, who had been (nearly literally) dead-drunk the night before, was too tired to "flesh out" the numbered passions that were her lot for the day. Thus long before his account of the first month's activities is over, Sade turns increasingly to the outline form in which the description of the last three months of the pleasure party has come down to us.

The reader is informed at the outset that the text's performative aspects have only been included as a concession to the reader's inadequacies. Faced with the gradual disintegration of the narrative body, he can only conclude that the text that then emerges, encyclopedic bare bones stripped of narrative flesh and gleaming in their pure mathematical glory, is the master text, the text that in its pristine perfection serves as a worthy manifesto of the rigor that characterizes libertine "passion." The outline form in which we have three-fourths of the *120* is truer to the nature of the Sadean literary enterprise than the first one-fourth of the text in which we have, in Barthes's words, "crime" fleshed out by "performance." The "accident(s)" that have left us with an incomplete *120* have at the same time given us the archetypal Sadean text, his vision of narrative zero-degree.[27]

The final sections of the *120* provide us in several ways with what might be termed a theoretical utopia. As Barthes has demonstrated, the brutally "frontal" elements of Sade's lexicon take his reader to a linguistic extreme, to a territory normally reserved for scientific or mathematical languages—the destruction of connotation and the stabilization of language in the realm of pure denotation. "Par la crudité du langage s'établit un discours hor-sens, déjouant toute 'interprétation' et même tout symbolisme, ... sorte de langue adamique, entêtée à ne pas signifier: c'est, si l'on veut, la langue sans supplément" (pp. 137-38).[28] By the same token, in the *120* Sade takes his narrative to a Jakobsonian extreme: he constructs a text so obsessively devoted to fragmentation and then to the numbering and the placement of these fragments that it becomes a narrative feat—a pure illustration of the functioning of what Jakobson terms the axis of combination, or metonymy, and as total an exclusion as is conceivable of metaphor, or the axis of selection.[29]

[27] What Barthes saw as a "texte de jouissance" corresponds more closely to one of his earlier theoretical concepts, writing zero-degree.

[28] Barthes notes a similar drive in Flaubert's work. Commenting on *Bouvard et Pécuchet*, in *Le Plaisir du texte* (Seuil, 1973), he contends that "la langue littéraire est ébranlée, dépassée, *ignorée,* dans la mesure où elle s'ajuste à la langue 'pure,' ... à la langue grammairienne (cette langue n'est, bien entendu, qu'une idée)" (pp. 44-45).

[29] Barthes argues convincingly that this characteristic of Sadean narrative entertains a complicated and complicitous relationship with censorship of Sade's text: "Par un paradoxe qui n'est qu'apparent, c'est peut-être à partir de la constitution proprement *littéraire* de l'oeuvre sadienne que l'on voit le

Sade's celebration of the potential of combination reveals, not surprisingly, basic truths about narrative fragmentation and fragmented narrative. In the final sections of the *120*, almost the exclusive subject of the dislocated novel is the dislocation of the human body. When the novel's basic organizational principle is laid bare in these pages, it proves to be disarmingly simple. At least in "regular" months with thirty days, one day equals five numbers (five passions); one number equals one body—a body to be scarred, sewn, stuffed with hot coals, and cut into pieces by ever more complex machines that, like cookie cutters, punch out human flesh. The *120* translates, more vividly and with more variety than any other text, the implications for narrative of the body in pieces. It is the human body that is cut up, numbered, and tallied up by Sade's narrative without narrative body: accounting gives the body a new, inorganic life in time.

Behind this obsessive mutilation lies an equally obsessive totalizing vision. The libertine encyclopedia is *perfectly* complete: the six hundred passions are all that exist—"nous . . . avions . . . tout dit, tout analysé" (p. 61). This calculable perfection will make the body whole again. Sade reduces narration to computation because he is driven to find a system of accounting so flawless that it will replace natural development with systematic logic. For Sade, recounting is accounting, *conter* is *compter*.[30] His narrative preference proves etymologically sound: the first meaning of "recount" is "to narrate," but its less common uses include "to count up" and "to count over again"; likewise, the most common use of

---

mieux une certaine nature des interdictions dont elle est l'objet. Il arrive assez souvent que l'on donne à la réprobation morale dont on frappe Sade la forme désabusée d'un dégoût esthétique: on déclare que Sade est *monotone*. Bien que toute création soit nécessairement une combinatoire, la société, en vertu du vieux mythe romantique de l' 'inspiration,' ne supporte pas qu'on le lui dise" (p. 40).

[30] Sade may find "compter" preferable to "conter" because the former is faithful to a basic principle of libertine behavior: "Cachez le con, mesdames," snaps Gernande to Justine and Dorothée.

"account" is "to count up" or "enumerate," but it can also have
the sense of "to recount" or "narrate." Our English verbs are
derived from Old French in which "conter" was used for both
"to narrate" and "to count" until the thirteenth century, when
"compter" appeared as a learned spelling. And Old French took
its cue from Latin, where "computare" was used for both "to
give account of" and "to count."[31] When Sade makes the *120*
the account (a narrative/an adding up) of what is recounted
(retold/re-reckoned), he lays bare storytelling's original (fundamental?) complicity with computation: both "account for."

This union is made clear on several occasions by the verbs
chosen to describe the task of the secondary narrators, the
conteuses. Early on, the narrator defines the qualifications
responsible for the choice of the *conteuses:* "Il s'agissait donc
de trouver des sujets en état de *rendre compte* de tous ces
excès, de les analyser, de les étendre, de les détailler, de les
graduer, et de placer au travers de cela l'intérêt d'un récit"
(p. 28, emphasis mine). Here, as always in the *120*, the *récit*
comes last, while *rendre compte* (in its computational sense)
heads the list: the Sadean narrator is to "rendre un compte
exact" (p. 28). Furthermore, *conter* is consistently held in
check by *compter,* as the libertines pledge not to engage in
any activities "avant les époques où elles nous seront *comp-
tées*" (p. 242, emphasis mine).[32] In this example, "compter"
is used when the reader would expect to find "conter." Far
from being a lapsus, Sade's surprising choice of homonym
reveals that he intends not only to demonstrate the original
complicity between the two verbs but also to conflate them
and even to reduce *conter* to *compter.*[33]

[31] I am grateful to Karl Uitti for helping me support my original intuition
with sound philological information.
[32] Lely points out in his introduction to the *120* that Sade's manuscript
contains many "négligences" (p. lxxiv). On occasion, the reader may be
tempted to continue Lely's practice of correcting what seem to be evident
errors. In this example, Sade's use of the unexpected homonym is clearly an
intentional substitution.
[33] Sade's rejection of a third homonym in this series, "comte," may indicate
that his reduction of "conter" to "compter" is linked to a desire to restructure

CHAPTER VI

Leo Bersani and Ulysse Dutoit have analyzed a process they term "denarrativization," a process by which "a reading of related fragments" is substituted for "the reading of a coherently structured anecdote." Such a shift of focus, they allege, "freezes" or "contains" violence.[34] Yet Sade is not simply fighting against one type of order ("the coherently structured anecdote"). He is at the same time attempting to substitute a

the genealogical process, a desire also evident in his approach to novelistic structure. The author of the *120* is known in literary history as the *marquis* de Sade whereas he should have been known even during his lifetime as the *comte* de Sade. Had traditional onomastic procedure been followed, upon his father's death in 1767, Sade should have taken over his title, count. The documents included in Lely's biography make plain that, even though others began to refer to Sade as "count," he continued to refer to himself as "marquis." His correspondence reveals that he chose the title "count" for himself on only two occasions. During his captivity in the fort at Miolans in 1772-1773, Sade adopted the pseudonym, "comte de Mazan" (actually a title in his father's family), chosen for him by his sister-in-law, Anne de Launay (for example, Lely, vol. 1, p. 401). Then in January 1784, fearful that his wife's parents were trying to usurp his authority vis-à-vis his eldest son, Louis, Sade adopted his most forceful, fatherly tone in a letter to his son signed "Le Comte de Sade, votre père" (12: 423). He wrote to his wife the same day to announce this onomastic change (even though, with no further explanation, he immediately reverted thereafter to "marquis"): "[J]e dois vous prévenir que mon intention est de suivre l'usage établi dans toutes les familles, où le chef prend le titre de comte, et laisse celui de marquis à son fils aîné. Je ne ferai d'ailleurs, relativement à moi, que ce que le Roi veut sans doute que je fasse, puisque je n'ai pas un seul brevet, ni de ma charge, ni de mes emplois, pas une seule lettre de princes ou de ministres qui ne me soit adressé sous ce titre. Je vous dis cela afin que vous y accoutumiez le public qui, une différente habitude prise, changerait difficilement après ses idées. Et moi je ne changerai sûrement pas les miennes" (12: 425).

[34] I arrive at this interpretation of Bersani's and Dutoit's work by conflating two recent articles that, despite their radically different subject matter, deal with related issues. See "Merde Alors," *October* 13 (Summer 1980); "The Forms of Violence," *October* 8 (Spring 1979), esp. pp. 28-29. While I find Bersani's and Dutoit's analysis of the relationship between narrative form and the reader's response to violence highly stimulating, I disagree with their account of the narrative organization of the *120*. In my view, this is anything but a traditionally "coherent narrative" ("Merde Alors," p. 28). Their descriptions of Pasolini's *Salò* and Assyrian wall reliefs are actually closer to my interpretation of Sade's novel.

new type of order, attempting to find a new structure, above all a *perfect* structure. Just as Sade reduces language to denotation by making it function "mathematically," so he converts narrative to computation, in order to realize the sort of all-encompassing dream of a perfect system that is so typical of the late seventeenth and the eighteenth centuries, the age of dictionaries and encyclopedias.

Indeed, violence does seem "contained" by this frozen, mathematical text; for the purposes of calculation, bodies are no more than pieces in a giant *tableau*. Bersani and Dutoit argue that this is the danger of the Sadean *oeuvre:* in this text situated beyond difference, sexual or otherwise, violence becomes mathematical, symmetrical, aesthetically pleasing. As a result, they contend, placing their reading in a moral context, the reader experiences an aesthetic response to violence, a response that encourages what they term a "pleasurable identification" with the Sadean text. Their reading rejoins the stance of critics who contend that the *120* extends an invitation to its readers to reenact its passion play, to verify the perfection of its encyclopedic activities in their own lives.

In the *120,* however, violence may appear to be contained, but this containment is no more than a carefully constructed "optical" illusion. The computational system that disciplines the narrative activities of the *120* functions perfectly, or so the narrator would have us believe. Yet the periodic interventions of a voice that can only be identified as that of the novel's author serve to remind us that the all-controlling accounting machine is itself never completely under control. Sade strives desperately to make the cipherable work for him, but his novel constantly reaffirms a key revelation contained in a letter he wrote from the Bastille: "Le chiffral s'emploie contre moi" (Barthes, p. 183)—and the helplessness conveyed by his choice of a reflexive verb should not be underestimated. Just as the sequences in which the members of the quatrumvirate discipline themselves reveal that the libertines are incorrigible, so the computation of narrative error demonstrates that Sade's system of accounting can never be brought to a halt. The shape of Sade's ambivalent relationship to the *chif-fral* can be seen in the meanings of the word itself. A cipher is both an Arabic numeral and a secret code, either a fixed entity or a language created for disguised communication.[35] In Sade's *Journal inédit*, Arabic numerals become the basis of his secret code, as he makes operative a type of personal mathematics that resembles Rousseau's in significant ways.

In *Persecution and the Art of Writing*, Leo Strauss contends that persecuted writers defend themselves against their persecution by writing obliquely—in his words, by "writing between the lines." According to Strauss's theory, a writer "slants" his work, deflects and camouflages his meaning, in order to "perform the miracle of speaking in a publication to a minority, while being silent to the majority of his readers."[36] A writer can feel sure that, thus protected, his work's message will only be deciphered by a sympathetic audience. In the *Journal* he kept during his final period of detention in the hospital/prison at Charenton, Sade was capable of a type of "writing between the lines" so oblique that its laconism verges on muteness. Even the text's editor, Georges Daumas, admits that the *Journal* is a remarkably closed work: "Quant aux allusions dont le texte fourmille, elles sont pour la plupart très difficiles à élucider. Il est manifeste que M. de Sade n'écrivait que pour lui, et avec précaution, et qu'il était seul à pouvoir se comprendre."[37] In his *Journal*, Sade far surpasses the comparatively limited efforts at camouflage of a writer

[35] Following the same pattern, "code" gradually came to mean "secret language," in addition to its original meaning, "system." According to the OED, this semantic drift can first be noted at the turn of the nineteenth century, roughly the period during which Sade composed his prison *Journal*. I am grateful to English Showalter for suggesting that I explore this semantic evolution. John Lyons has suggested that the force in eighteenth-century intellectual life that most closely reproduces the semantic configuration I have been exploring with relation to Sade is Freemasonry. His intuition is intriguing, and I regret that I have not been able to explore it.

[36] Strauss, *Persecution and the Art of Writing* (Glencoe, Illinois: The Free Press, 1952), p. 25.

[37] Daumas, preface to the *Journal inédit* (Gallimard, 1970), p. 9.

like Rousseau. For example, when Rousseau seeks to veil a message destined only for a special public, he turns to methods familiar to readers of Strauss. In the *Confessions*, he describes the means he adopted to make his break with Diderot "public": "Je m'avisai d'insérer par forme de note dans mon ouvrage [*Lettre à d'Alembert*] un passage du Livre de l'Ecclesiastique qui déclaroit cette rupture et même le sujet assez clairement pour quiconque étoit au fait, et ne signifioit rien pour le reste du monde" (1: 497). Rousseau tempers the gesture by which he limits access to his work by leaving a breach in his defenses ("assez clairement pour quiconque étoit au fait") and by subsequently revealing the passage's secret.

Sade uses no such means to render his rejection of readers less radical. He protects his journal so thoroughly that he ultimately leaves much, if not most, of it incomprehensible to all but its original reader. Sade fortifies and finally silences his work by means of an accounting machine similar to that which animates the *120*, but unlike it because he rarely explains what is being tallied up. Numbers and tabulation are the dominant and perhaps the sole concern of the *Journal*. The reader cannot but be bewildered by the extraordinary accumulation of figures that dominates its pages. Some of the tallies are comprehensible, usually those that concern the entity a prisoner would be most likely to attempt to estimate, the length of his confinement: "Cette operation eut lieu à l'epoque juste de six ans et trois mois du total de ma detention et de 4 ans 6 semaines de Charenton, 4 ans et 39 jours" (p. 40, n. 2). More often, however, the numerically coded passages remain elusive, protecting their secret behind a wall of now silent calculations:

Le 7 M. de C. m'envoya chercher pour retarder la representation jusqu'au 17 mais ce n'etoit qu'un bel et bon lazi pour me faire un 17 et 23. Absurde betise beaucoup trop repété(e) d'autant plus que la representation n'eut

lieu que longtemps apres. L'almanach prouve que c'etoit
un 7 et 9. (pp. 54-55)

Sade, unlike Rousseau, never explains the rules governing the
utopian mathematical equations he senses in operation around
him. It is clear that he sees in these equations a revelation of
an (impossible) plenitude, but he gives no clue to aid in the
decipherment of that revelation. Sadean arithmetic locks his
journal away from his posterity; it enables him to retain final,
uncontested mastery over its secrets and their interpretation.

Barthes has argued that Sadean calculations play both a
generative and a liberating role: "Le chiffral est le commence-
ment de l'écriture, sa mise en position libératrice" (*Sade, Fourier, Loyola*, p. 183). Certainly, Sade indicates that calculation
enables him to see what might otherwise have remained hidden, that it introduced him to a highly refined, almost mystical,
form of understanding: "Au lieu de m'apporter 24 oranges
que j'avais demandé(es) on ne m'en apporta que 18 a 10s.
J'en fis offrir par Md. à M. de C. qui le $1^{e(r)}$ du mois n'en prit
que 3 et en laissa 9 ce qui forme le plus beau 13 et 9 possible"
(p. 54). Critics who view Sade, in Foucault's terms, as a "shad-
owless" representative of Enlightenment rationality can only
pass over in silence or dismiss as unimportant these moments
when Sade seems less a rational systematizer than a numer-
ologist.[38] Yet the phenomenon of Sade's "mystical" involvement with ciphers recurs throughout his work. For example,
for any attentive reader of Sade's correspondence, the drift
from system to secret language—from fixed, and therefore
controlled and controllable code, to personally suggestive, and
therefore unlimited and uncontrollable code—is also apparent, most evidently in Sade's letters to his wife.

As is often the case in defensive texts, the clinamen from
control to loss of control originates in a pedagogical act: Sade

[38] Thus Roger, who argues that "aucune magie là-dedans, aucun irrationnel
non plus," dismisses such numerological tendencies as a brief aberration,
whereas in reality they are frequently evident in Sade's writings during the
period of his most important literary productions (p. 150).

attempts repeatedly, although apparently without great success, to initiate his wife into the complexities of encoding and decoding, in order to render their communication impervious to interference from censors. His attempts to teach code reveal a seemingly paradoxical belief in the existence of "natural" signals. "Tout ce qui est affecté n'est plus naturel, et songez à l'importance de mettre de la nature dans le signal. . . . [V]ous vous efforcez à courir apres l'air naturel: les choses ne sont jamais faites exprès; c'est toujours le hasard qui les produit" (12: 174). This may well be the root of Sade's obsessive fascination with encoding, calculation and le chiffral. Sade, like Rousseau, wants to systematize nature and still have it be natural (spontaneous). He wants signals to function as signals, but maintains nevertheless that in order to be successful, the process of encoding must be produced by spontaneous generation ("chance"), rather than conceived by human intelligence.[39] Sade exposes himself as a cratylist of ciphers, convinced of the existence of a naturally perfect secret code, the uniquely perfect cipherable system whose signals, once found, cannot be misread, because they are naturally and inherently bound to the entity they represent. The inventor of a humanly imperfect system of communication could merely hope to protect his communication, whereas the (re)discoverer of the ur-code would be truly invulnerable, secure behind fortifications worthy of Vauban's mythic status.

Yet when Sade attempts to use calculation to achieve omnipotence, he discovers, like his predecessors, that the computational mania can never be put to rest. He begins to suspect that his wife is deliberately confusing her signals as a result of pedagogical interference from another master teacher, his hated mother-in-law, the présidente de Montreuil. Like Rousseau who believed Thérèse's mother to be an expert in "l'art de tirer d'un sac dix moutures," (Confessions, vol. 1, p. 419), outdoing him thereby at his own utopian mathematics, Sade

---

[39] Sade parallels here the reflection on "natural" citation by Laclos's editor in a footnote to letter 58 of the Liaisons.

fantasized that the présidente, his "enemy sister," was in possession of the ultimate code and had become mistress of "le chiffral." To his faithful Carteron (dit La Jeunesse, dit Martin Quiros), he confides a speech he imagined for his mother-in-law, in which he has her boast of having fulfilled his own most cherished dream: "[D]es cadrements de chiffres, des rapports, des ressemblances, il n'y a que mon favori Alberet et moi qui puissions exécuter ces choses-là" (12: 233). When he allows himself to turn the tables on the présidente in fantasy and to indulge in his own dream of omnipotence by imagining her death, his fiction reveals that the definition of genius proposed in the "Idée sur les romans" corresponds to Freud's notion of the *tu quoque* defense. He writes to his wife

Il faut que ta mère soit exactement . . . folle à enchaîner, de risquer les jours de sa fille pour former un *19 et 4* ou *16 et 9*, et ne pas être lasse de tout cela depuis douze ans. Oh, quelle indigestion de chiffres elle avait, cette vilaine femme! Je suis persuadé que si elle était morte avant l'irruption et qu'on l'eût ouverte, il serait sorti des millions de chiffres de ses entrailles. Il est inouï, l'horreur que ça m'a donné pour les chiffres et les entortillages! (12: 428)

Despite this avowed "abhorrence" of computation and secret codes, the drive to master calculation inspired by Sade's belief in the existence of the perfect code is not limited to the diary and the letters he wrote while in prison. The link between systematization and secrecy and the calculating obsession it inspires have a vital impact on less radically "mute" texts like the *120*. In the account of the siege of Silling, narrator and author are united in their attempt to perfect the computation of a narrative whose very title dedicates it to the passion for tabulation. Yet their attempt to use systematization for the purpose of textual fortification is constantly menaced by an enemy less conveniently exterior than the hated présidente: the threat of computational error.

Thus each section of the *120* concludes with an accounting

for error—"omissions que j'ai faites," "fautes que j'ai faites" (pp. 67, 345)—in which Sade takes himself to task for the deficiencies and the miscalculations in his encyclopedic account. The fear of error, error not even accounted for in the tallies that conclude each section, is reinscribed into the *120* at key moments: "Et n'ayant pas pu me relire, cela doit sûrement fourmiller d'autres fautes" (p. 345). Indeed, by the end of the third part, the encyclopedic project seems to have become a victim of internal corruption. When he concludes the activities of 31 January, Sade realizes that the total of the month's passions is not 150, but 151.[40] He makes no attempt to eliminate the telltale supplementary passion, but leaves a monument to error in the form of a parenthesis: "(Vérifiez pourquoi une de trop, et s'il y en a une à supprimer que ce soit cette dernière que je crois déjà faite)" (p. 388).

Each of Sade's fault-finding interpolations contains, in addition to the catalogue that computes error, a brief dialogue between the narrator-author and the imprisoned scriptor. This dialogue encircles the tabulations and eventually besieges them, for these self-reflections ultimately call attention to the problematic nature of calculation's function in the Sadean text. Initially, the dialogue's grammatical structure is relatively unobtrusive. Sade lists his faults and refers to himself in the first-person singular: "Fautes que j'ai faites." On occasion, when indicating a course of future action, he adopts the imperative: "Vérifiez pourquoi une de trop." In these brief comments, Sade's use of the second-person plural to address himself may seem mildly surprising. If the practice were no more developed than this, the reader could accept Lely's assessment of it as simply "une curieuse habitude de l'auteur" (2: 253, note).

However, in the final pages of the *120*, the form taken by the author's self-criticism seems far more exceptional than Lely would have it. The dialogue becomes more developed:

[40] Martin Pops points out that Sade "has inadvertently and comically omitted complex passion number 69, just as Sadean libertines exclude *soixante-neuf* from their sexual repertoires" ("The Metamorphosis of Shit," *Salmagundi* 56 [Spring 1982], pp. 40-41).

"Ne vous écartez en rien de ce plan: tout y est combiné plusieurs fois et avec la plus grande exactitude" (p. 432). Furthermore, the pronoun "vous," generally absent from the imperative constructions, is introduced: "A l'égard ... des supplices des vingt derniers sujets ... vous le détaillerez à votre aise" (p. 431). Faced with the growing presence of "vous," a pronoun it is surprising to find Sade use as a form of self-address, the reader cannot but view this dialogue as more than a mere "curiosity." "Ne faites surtout jamais rien faire aux quatre amis qui n'ait été raconté, et vous n'avez pas eu ce soin-là", (p. 432). In this instance, an author's dialogue with himself is more than a literary convention: it sounds as if there were two people in Sade. In these moments of self-humiliation, Sade becomes, like Curval in his disciplinary procedures, simultaneously master and victim, rulemaker-scorekeeper and rulebreaker.

By the "end" of the fourth and final stage of the house party, the adding machine has acquired such a life of its own that what stands as the *last* passion is doubly marked by its inconclusiveness. In the first place, the "final" passion is only the 148th of the month, so Sade frets that "Vérifiez pourquoi ces deux manquent, tout y était sur les brouillons" (p. 425). Indeed, the "last" passion, unlike the 597 that precede it, concludes with still another last tabulation, a list of fifteen "supplices" to which fifteen victims are subjected simultaneously in the course of this "passion-spectacle."

Because of the inconclusively conclusive nature of the 598th passion, it should come as no surprise that the *120* does not end here. What Sade refers to as "cette grande bande" closes with a final catalogue that demonstrates above all that the libertine encyclopedia can never be perfect, that the calculating energy that is omnipresent in the novel cannot be contained and put to rest in a completed form. The encyclopedic ambition of the *120* seems an encyclopedic madness when the reader learns that Sade cannot tell the complete story of libertine passions, that the encyclopedia he has just created is not big enough to include all the passions he can imagine. The *120*'s final tabulation is appropriately entitled "Supplices en supplément," and it proves that for Sade, just as for Rousseau before him, the supplement indicates the ultimate unraveling of his mathematics.[41] The *120* closes on an image of the drive to calculate exceeding the boundaries it had imposed. At the end of the third part, there was already one passion too many—with the "supplices en supplément," the Sadean adding machine approaches the ultimate in computation for its own sake.

The catalogue of "supplices en supplément," and thus the *120*'s entire account of libertine and narrative passion, ends with a properly obsessive instance of authorial self-guidance:

> Que dans le cahier de vos personnages, le plan du château, appartement par appartement, y ait une feuille, et dans le blanc que vous laisserez à côté, placez les sortes de choses que vous faites faire dans telle ou telle pièce.
> (p. 433)

This passage finally makes explicit a factor less prominently associated with the narrator's dream of totalizing perfection from the time of his apostrophe to the *ami lecteur,* the importance of spatial situation or architectural placement. For

[41] As Jane Gallop has reminded me, the equivalent in the domain of the quatrumvirate's passions of this mathematical unraveling is coprolagnia. Lely notes the enormous role played by this deviation in the *120* and characterizes this narrative excess as an "error"; for him, coprolagnia is the supplement that shatters the scientific pretensions of Sade's libertine encyclopedia. "[U]ne erreur dominante vient compromettre en maints endroits la valeur didactique d'un tel ouvrage: nous voulons dire la place monstrueusement exagérée que l'auteur réserve à l'abérration coprolagnique portée à ses derniers excès" (*Vie,* vol. 2, p. 256). Gallop views the insistence on coprolagnia as the true mark of Sade's perversity, as an effort for "the improper [to] maintain its impropriety there where it is in its place" (*Intersections* [Lincoln and London: Univ. of Nebraska Press, 1981], p. 49). The libertines' coprolagnic instinct can also be seen, in a revision of Lely's objection, as another manifestation of the supplement that causes the system of calculation to malfunction, of the fight against excess (in this case, they literally consume waste) that breaks down the barriers of systematization.

example, the narrator begins his "banquet" speech to the reader by declaring "c'est maintenant, ami lecteur, qu'il faut *disposer* ton coeur et ton esprit au récit le plus impur qui ait jamais été fait. . . ." (p. 60, emphasis mine). "Disposer" should not be understood in a metaphorical sense: a reader must get ready to approach this text by quite literally putting his heart in the right place. When the characters go to bed on the eve of the 120-day-long siege of Silling, spatial arrangement once again proves crucial: "Le lendemain devant retrouver, dès le matin, les choses sur le pied *d'arrangement* où elles avaient été mises, chacun *s'arrangea* de même pour la nuit" (p. 60, emphasis mine). The libertines lay themselves out for the night as carefully as the storytellers line up their passions, as though the entire master plan would go haywire if one of them were to get out of place. The end of the apostrophe to the *ami lecteur* reveals the nature of the threat that careful disposition is designed to ward off: "Mais comme il y a beaucoup de personnages en action dans cette espèce de drame . . . , on va *placer* une table qui contiendra le nom et l'âge de chaque acteur. . . . A mesure que l'on rencontrera un nom qui embarrassera dans les récits, on pourra recourir à cette table [pour] rappeler ce qui aura été dit" (pp. 61-62, emphasis mine). In other words, careful placement—of our hearts, of tables, and so forth—is necessary as a memory aid: what is out of place is out of mind.

This, then, is the *120*'s battle, the battle for memory. I have already described the novel's story as the siege of Silling, but upon reflection my metaphor may seem strange. The members of Sade's quatrumvirate complicate normal structures of siege warfare because they are both attackers and defenders. They make their defenses impregnable and stockpile their provisions in order to lay siege to their own fortified place—from within. The goal of their siege warfare, Sade's siege warfare, is to take over Silling, room by room, and to inscribe in its spaces—indelibly—an accounting for action: "dans le blanc que vous laisserez à côté, placez les sortes de choses que vous faites faire dans telle ou telle pièce."

In the *120*, Sade develops computation and combination as an alternative to the developmental unfolding and temporal sequence that normally serve to structure the novel. In a parallel move, Sade subverts the traditional elements that constitute a novel's setting by limiting geographical and architectural description to a form of ordered placement. Thus, he creates what might be termed a flattened or metonymic topography for this encyclopedia. In the *120*, situation in space means quite simply a particular type of framing, the placement of an activity in a certain place in a certain room—in other words, in its proper place. It is essential to note that Sade does not ask his readers to imagine the spaces of Silling, to give them a three-dimensional status in their minds. Instead, he literalizes the notion of space in the novel. The rooms in the libertine fortress are only architectural drawings, and the only space they occupy is on a page; setting means inscription of an activity in the blank areas of a two-dimensional backdrop.[42]

In *Sade, Fourier, Loyola*, Barthes stresses the importance of theatricality in Sade's novels. The obsession with the theatrical is of course evident in the *120*, but here Sade subjects theatricality to the same code that flattens and distributes spatialization in the novel. Silling's theater is a memory theater, to borrow the term devised in the 1530s by Guilio Camillo to characterize the enterprise that Frances Yates describes so eloquently in *The Art of Memory*.[43] As Yates reconstructs it, Camillo's Renaissance theater had nothing to do with drama or staging. The term refers to a backdrop on which, faithful to the centuries-old tradition of memory arts, Camillo proposed to inscribe written clues that would enable the viewer

[42] This geographical abstraction is responsible for Bersani's and Dutoit's assertion that Silling is a "fairy-tale" castle. See "Merde Alors," p. 26.

[43] The information on which the following section is based is drawn from Frances Yates's seminal study *The Art of Memory* (London: Routledge & Kegan Paul, 1966). The idea of applying Yates's findings in this context was suggested to me by Eugene Vance's stimulating article, "Roland and the Poetics of Memory," in *Textual Strategies*, ed. J. Harari (Ithaca, N.Y.: Cornell Univ. Press, 1979), pp. 374-403.

(the spectator of the memory theater) to reconstruct subjects for oratory. Camillo's theater can be interpreted as a visualization or a making concrete of all the arts of memory. From the outset, practitioners of the memory arts had instructed their students in the technique of spatially situating the concepts crucial to their discourse. During their orations, they were to imagine themselves in a familiar architectural space and to *place* their key rhetorical points in the interstices (between the columns, etc.) of that space.

When Camillo actually built such a space for memory, he was attempting to realize the full potential of the art of memory. He was not trying simply to teach a method that could be applied to individual situations. He intended instead to construct a fixed space that would house a system of actual written clues or stimuli so complete that it would permit any orator who had mastered it to stand in his theater and not only make any speech he wished but make it perfectly. As Yates points out, Camillo's contemporaries considered the potentialities of his theater so awesome that they made ever greater claims for it. For example, a visitor to Padua wrote Erasmus in 1532 that the spectator admitted to the theater and its secret became instantly the equal of the greatest master of oratory, Cicero, able to discourse on any subject as fluently as he.

Other arts of memory—that of Raymond Lull for example—are more scientifically abstract, more mathematical than Camillo's theatrical theory. If I choose to compare his memory art to Sade's encyclopedic monument to libertine passion, it is because of the extraordinary reputation Camillo enjoyed in his day for allegedly having brought a system to absolute perfection, for having attained status as a systematizer comparable to that enjoyed by Vauban. Indeed, the parallels between Camillo's career and Vauban's are striking. According to Yates, Camillo's contemporaries, like Vauban's, considered him "a divine man of whom divine things are expected" (p. 132). Moreover, in both cases these expectations were sustained despite the fact that few of their contemporaries were ever able to judge their work firsthand. Camillo displayed a wooden model of his theater—roughly the equivalent of the scale models of Vauban's fortifications—to a chosen few in Venice and in Paris, but he, like Vauban, was never to write any more than fragments of the great book that his supporters believed would preserve his secret for posterity. However, Camillo, also like Vauban, never intended to share his art (and therefore his "omnipotence") with the general public. He had planned to reveal his secret to only one man, also a king of France (in his case François I) (Yates, pp. 129-32). Finally, Camillo, like Vauban, attained a type of mythic status, since his fame continued to grow after his death—in Yates's analysis, "in spite of, or perhaps because of, the fragmentary nature of his achievement" (p. 135). This, then, is the position reserved for those who can control the union of system and secret language, who are able, in Sade's terms, to uncover the natural code of spontaneous signals. And this is the type of legendary status Sade had in mind for his own memory theater, *Les 120 Journées de Sodome*.

The points of comparison between Camillo's theater of memory and Sade's encyclopedic monument to libertine passion are numerous. Both are totalizing systems—like the reputed supreme master of the memory art, Sade sought to create a vehicle capable of "tout dire," "tout analyser." In the *120,* Sade constructed the literary equivalent of Camillo's legendary theater: in the interspaces of Silling's two-dimensional combinatory architecture, he was able to arrange *in order*[44] the ultimate discourse on libertine life. Sadean architecture is flattened and geometrical because its sole function is to aid computation in the creation of an all-inclusive, flawless system, a system that, once perfected, will enable its practitioner to build a theater of memory in any space (even in a prison cell in the Bastille) and in that theater to re-create the

---

[44] All accounts of the memory arts—from Cicero's to Martianus'—stress the central role played by order in drawing up memory's tally sheets: "[I]t is order which sustains the precepts of memory" (Martianus, quoted by Yates, p. 51).

CHAPTER VI

perfect libertine discourse—without recourse to the treacherous *brouillons* to which Sade so frequently alludes.[45]

One of the spaces inside Silling's concentric circles is described in a particularly detailed manner, the "champ de bataille des combats projetés," that is, "un cabinet d'assemblée, destiné aux narrations des historiennes" (p. 46). This attention is fully justified. In the *120* the *story* of sexual deviations comes to dominate the enactment of these "passions," so the room in which the verbal accounts take place becomes the real theater of war. The discussion of the room's topology is prolonged by a description of the participants' disposition around the half-circle in which the encyclopedia is created: the *historienne* on call "se trouvait alors placée comme est l'acteur sur un théâtre, et les auditeurs, placés dans les niches, se trouvaient l'être comme on l'est à l'amphithéâtre" (p. 46).

Sade uses the storytelling situation familiar from all the collections of *nouvelles nouvelles* (revived earlier in the eighteenth century by, for example, Marivaux in *La Voiture embourbée*) to give the *120* the "Classical" narrative distance and passivity Rousseau and Laclos found in the epistolary form. We do not witness most of the action directly; instead we see it thirdhand, as the libertines themselves are already listeners, voyeuristically imagining the "horrors" of the action on the basis of the storytelling by the *conteuses*. There is no action in most of the *120*, only a twice told, doubly controlled tale of an accounting for past events. Sade's (memory) theater,

---

[45] In several of the most obscure passages of his autobiographical writings, Sade appears to link the role played by secret numerical codes to the mastery of memory. In May 1780, Sade is afraid that the présidente has obtained certain of his licentious manuscripts which he had locked up in his *cabinet* at La Coste. In Lely's words, "il déclare, dans un beau défi, qu'il les reconstituera de mémoire, et les écrira une seconde fois" (*Vie*, vol. 2, p. 68). In the only entry for that month in his "Histoire de ma détention," Sade writes that "le major vint me voir au jardin, mais c'étoit à l'occasion de la sceine des chiffres sur le mur" (2: 120). If the "numbers on the wall" to which he alludes functioned as a memory aid, then this (theatrical?) "scene" could have been the source of his conviction that he would be able to reconstruct the lost manuscripts from memory.

like Camillo's (and like French Classical theater), is a theater of words rather than events. Combatants in the novel's battle for memory are required either to tell or to listen to a story, with the members of the quatrumvirate, the novel's heroes and the masters of Silling's defenses, choosing the passive role of listeners and spectators. The four *historiennes* are substitute figures for Sade, who is telling his story, all their stories, on a rolled-up manuscript, "cette grande bande," inside a somewhat smaller and more solitary half-circle than that dominated by his female avatars in Silling—his prison cell in the Bastille. Even the time slots they reserve for storytelling almost coincide. The *conteuses* tell their tales of passion every day from six until ten o'clock in the evening; we know from Sade's annotations that he completed the *rouleau manuscrit* by writing from seven until ten o'clock each evening (on only thirty-four consecutive days).

Just as the *120* takes us back to a primitive union between storytelling and calculation, so it reveals an original and equally fundamental complicity on memory's part, a complicity that is evident in the story of the invention of memory arts, as Yates reconstructs it from various accounts. Simonides of Ceos, credited from antiquity with the invention of a system of memory aids, is said to have come upon this system in a manner relevant to Sade's tale of a four-month-long *grande bouffe* that was always already poised on the brink of disaster. The father of the Classical art of memory was a poet.[46] At a banquet in Thessaly, Simonides recited a lyric poem that praised both his host, a nobleman named Scopas, and the twin gods, Castor and Pollux. Afterwards, his host refused to honor the contract that was to govern the poet's performance. He paid Simonides only half the price they had agreed upon for his poem, informing him that he could turn to the twin gods to settle the rest of their account. Shortly thereafter, a messenger informed the poet that two men wished to speak to him out-

[46] Simonides of Ceos was also the poet generally credited with being the first to demand payment for his poems (Yates, p. 28).

CHAPTER VI

side. Simonides followed the messenger from the banquet hall and during his absence the roof fell in, crushing his host and all his guests to death. Their bodies were maimed beyond recognition, and it was only because Simonides remembered exactly where each had been seated at the banquet table that the relatives were able to identify the bodies. Thus, the means chosen by Castor and Pollux to pay for their share of the panegyric gave Simonides the basis for the art of memory (Yates, pp. 1-2).

The story of the bard's mastery of the mnemonic art has much in common with the tale in the *120*. In both cases, memory (defined as the ability to list in order, to recount, to account for) is born of violence. The poet's task is to reconstruct the final banquet before the holocaust. The *120* is situated at the end of Louis XIV's reign, characterized by Sade as a period of financial and physical "exhaustion," and just before what he sees as the regent's attempt to "faire rendre gorge à cette multitude de [sangsues]," from among whom he chooses the heroes of his novel (p. 1). In both cases, memory is used to give account of a scene of violence, to provide a listing of bodies in pieces. In both cases, the poet adds up the maimed and those crushed beyond recognition, those who, in a sense, have no identity other than their place on the tally sheet. As one of his concluding gestures, the narrator of the *120* offers his reader a series of "recapitulative" tables that neatly provide the calculation of those "massacrés avant le premier mars dans les premières orgies," as well as the "sujets ... immolés ... depuis le premier mars" (p. 431).

Furthermore, in both these tales of conquest by memory, the poet is a survivor, not an infrequent phenomenon in "commemorative" literature—witness the examples of the bard spared from the *Odyssey*'s final massacre and of "seigneur Gilles" who survives the slaughter at Roncevaux to tell Roland's tale. What is noteworthy about the survivors of the banquet of memory is that they are not innocent of responsibility for the bloody tales they live to tell. In these cases, memory is also an accounting in the sense of a settling of a

320

score. Although those who recount Simonides' experience, from Cicero to Martianus to Yates, fail to comment on this aspect of his activity, the story of the invention of the memory art demonstrates that the violence that provides the poet's inspiration is in fact the poet's own act of revenge. When Castor and Pollux destroy both his patron and his public, they are acting as a projection of Simonides' desires.

Sade's encyclopedic novel is also an immense pedagogical treatise, his version of a "traité d'éducation naturelle." In all Sade's extended fictions, the libertines share an interest in pedagogy and the cast of characters frequently contains an "instituteur." However, in the *120* pedagogy is far more than an interest: it is the novel's central concern. The novel's didactic passion is reflected in its pedagogical subtitle, "L'Ecole du libertinage." "Il s'agit essentiellement d'une société éducative," in Barthes's formulation, "ou plus exactement d'une société-école (et même d'une société internat)" (*Sade, Fourier, Loyola,* p. 29). Thus all the controls the narrator and the *historiennes* exercise over their stories are justified as essential to the advancement of pedagogical concerns.

The narrator alleges that he includes so many tables of calculation just to maintain the reader's interest. For example, he explains the purpose of the "Tableau des projets du reste du voyage": "Il nous a semblé que, sachant après l'avoir lu la destination des sujets, il prendrait plus d'intérêt aux sujets dans le reste des opérations" (p. 107). According to his theory, the perfectly informed reader, the reader who has all the information about the characters, their environment, and their actions clearly laid out for him, the reader who therefore feels totally in control of the story he is reading, this reader is not likely to put that story down before he has learned all there is to learn from it. To make his point perfectly clear, the narrator even includes at the end of this "tableau" a résumé of its contents, a listing of the listings in the event that the length and complexity of the original entry had created any confusion in the reader's mind.

Nor is the pedagogical combination of repetition and recapitulation limited to this occurrence. The narrator includes résumés of all his most important résumés. "[C]et arrangement, qu'il est à propos de récapituler pour la facilité du lecteur," so he describes his strategy to keep his reader with him through the complexities of the libertines' marital arrangements (p. 3). Perhaps the most remarkable occurrence of this technique of doubling involves the presentation of the novel's cast of characters. Initially, the characters are described at some length and in an exceptionally detailed and systematic manner. After this first overview of the actors in the *120*'s drama, the reader finds himself at least as well-equipped to identify the principal characters as he would be after reading the first sixty pages of any other novel. He cannot but be slightly puzzled to encounter at this point a repetition in shortened form of the basic information about the cast of characters labeled "Personnages du roman de l'Ecole du libertinage." "A mesure que l'on recontrera un nom qui embarrassera dans les récits, on pourra recourir à cette table et, plus haut, aux portraits étendus, si cette légère esquisse ne suffit pas à rappeler ce qui aura été dit" (p. 62). Ever the pedagogue, the narrator of the *120* is careful to point out that should any reader find himself in a difficult situation and unable to remember one of the characters, he has only to turn back to the handy résumés.

Never has the task of reading been made so effortless. The narrator's technique is pedagogically sound, and through the combined effects of his tables and the system of cataloguing he employs, it is seemingly impossible for his reader to miss anything or to be even momentarily lost or confused. The dominant narrative ideology of Sadean fiction thus appears to be the antithesis of the code governing any work that could be termed modernist; the narrator of the *120* desires above all to make his tale as clear and as undemanding as possible. It is inevitable that the reader should wonder why Sade created a narrator so concerned with sharing control of his narrative with his reader and why Sade and his narrator are so interested in the question of the reader's sense of security.

Only once do the narrator's comments on the repetitions he so obviously relishes hint at an explanation for his concern. He contends that his pedagogical simplifications of his text are necessary to ensure the reader's *jouissance*. Just before he launches into the proclamation of the "code de lois" that governs life at Silling, the narrator pauses for an apostrophe to "notre lecteur," "qui, d'après l'exacte description que nous lui avons faite du tout, n'aura plus maintenant qu'à suivre légèrement et voluptueusement le récit, sans que rien trouble son intelligence ou vienne embarrasser sa mémoire" (p. 49). The Sadean narrator's version of the *texte de jouissance* is a narrative so well controlled that its reader will never find it necessary to make the slightest effort to recollect its details or to ponder its complexities. The narrator explains his attention to order and completeness as essential for the reader's liberation, as if the slightest movement in the direction of active participation in the "making" of the text would be fatal to the proper appreciation of it.

However, an obvious result of the form of reader passivity the narrator prescribes is a reluctance on the part of the reader to give up that passive stance in order to form an interpretation of the work. The insistence in the *120* on catalogues and computations is intended to "liberate" the reader from his usual hermeneutic concerns to the extent that he will eventually relinquish an essential part of the imaginative space generally permitted him by fiction. The *120*'s author/narrator refuses to allow the reader to forget or to become confused. In the process, he also attempts to deny him any interpretive freedom, the right to step out of the line the narrator traces for his reading. Under the guise of making life easier for his reader, the *120*'s authorial dictator moves to take over the reader's space.

"Au langage de la maîtrise, lié à celui de la propriété, de l'accaparement," Roger contends, "s'oppose directement le flot continu et dépersonnalisé du texte sadien, où la multitude des locateurs interchangeables font du langage, non le bien de quelques-uns, mais la production de tous" (p. 86). What

Roger calls "le flot continu et dépersonnalisé du texte sadien" is one of the most striking features of the *120*; it is this "neutralization" of language that explains the reader's difficulty in remembering and the narrator's compulsion to repeat. But it is impossible to accept Roger's assessment of this language as unpoliced, communally shared, and liberated from the "commander/obéir" dialectic that stymied the progress of the tutor's student in *Emile*.

Instead of exhilaration, the depersonalized flow of Sadean language only produces a numbing effect on the reader being harangued by it. The linguistic leveling process operative in the *120* takes the novel beyond pedagogy to didacticism, and the drive to impose at any cost the ideology serviced by this neutered voice destroys such potentially deviant forces as individualized psychology. The nondifferentiated Sadean language is neither liberated nor liberating: "le flot continu et dépersonnalisé" is indicative of the uncontested reign of the master teacher's language. The Sadean discourse can in no way be considered an attempt to share the speaker's traditional power with his audience, to become truly dialogic. The fact that all those in power sound alike and speak with the same language restrains the reader's urge to identification or projection. The dominant discourse in the *120* is a monolithic force that seeks to hold Sade's reader in check, to turn him into the victim of the master who has thought of everything.

Granted, readerly freedom is an elusive affair at best. No author, not even the author of the most extreme modernist texts, creates a text supple enough to allow the reader absolute interpretive freedom and accords his reader license to make of his work what he will. Yet this is just what the Sadean narrator-authorial projection claims to do—"C'est à toi à le prendre et à laisser le reste"; "choisis et laisse le reste" (p. 61). On the basis of these pronouncements, the *120*'s potential reader would imagine that he was about to embark on an experience with fiction in which he would be encouraged to be as active and creative a reader as possible. The image the *120* seeks to project of itself is of a type of narrative that corresponds to Benjamin's definition of storytelling, that is, a fiction that does not attempt to lead the reader through its narration from beginning to end. "It is half the art of story-telling to keep a story free from explanation as one reproduces it," Benjamin affirms. "It is left up to [the reader] to interpret things the way he understands them, and thus the narrative achieves an amplitude that information lacks."[47] For Benjamin, the appeal of storytelling lies in the space it leaves the reader to flesh out the narrative with his interpretive vision. He views such fictions as analogous to the city for Baudelaire's *flâneur*, as constructs open to their observer's personal contribution.

The fiction Sade shapes in the *120* is anything but a flexible construct, a set of building blocks put out for the reader to rearrange and reshape into a personal interpretation of the *120*'s story. The narrator holds out to the reader the freedom to use any of the encyclopedic building blocks he may find useful to construct his own encyclopedia. He then makes it clear that as he has arranged them, these blocks form a complete and perfectly ordered entity. Like the master's language, the *120*'s numbered passions add up to a monolithic structure, a narrative ruled by a pedagogical order so authoritarian that only a foolhardy participant at the *120*'s banquet could imagine that its narrator/author meant his invitation to deconstruct his edifice to be taken literally. The *120* is powerfully and indelibly marked by its author's struggle to bring it to structural perfection: Sade provides a fitting *mise en abyme* of his authorial activity in the image of his libertines erecting barriers around themselves so flawless that "il ne devenait même plus possible de reconnaître où avaient été les portes" (p. 49).

In *Les Liaisons dangereuses*, Merteuil, a self-proclaimed "new Delilah," betrays the man she typecasts as a "modern-day Samson," Valmont. She cannot fail to know the end of the Biblical story she adopts as her "emblem," that is, that

[47] Benjamin, "The Storyteller," *Illuminations* (New York: Harcourt, Brace and World, 1968), p. 89.

Samson will take revenge for his victimization by pulling the house down, crushing himself to death along with all the observers of his humiliation (the new Delilah, like her Biblical namesake, escapes, but she is obliged to flee the world of action—and of literature). Simonides also displaces his revenge by confiding it to the pugilistic twin gods (literally his enemy twins?). He, like Merteuil and unlike Samson, is not caught when the roof caves in, for the ultimate revenge of the poet with mnemonic gifts is to live to tell the tale of his victimization and his subsequent settling of accounts. Sade's narrator is cleverer still. His victimization has already taken place when his performance begins. He is, according to the logic of the "Idée sur les romans," in the novelist's proper place, "à la juste distance où il faut qu'il soit pour étudier les hommes" (10: 16). From this distance, he is able to control not only the outcome of the literary banquet, but its disposition as well. He invites the guests and shows them to their places at the table in the storytelling theater. He then proceeds to regale them with a tale of mastery that, as far as narrator and author are concerned, is actually a tale that demonstrates memory's power of control—six hundred passions (or very nearly so) all tidily put in their places, rolled up tightly, and tucked away between the stones, the stones destined to come tumbling down only a few days after the new Camillo is taken away.

Sade describes the *120* to his reader as "l'histoire d'un magnifique repas où six cents plats divers s'offrent à ton appétit" (p. 61). The reader may see Sade's novel as an invitation to a pleasure party; he may view its violence as aesthetically pleasing; but these ways of writing violence out of the Sadean text underestimate its goal. Memory is murderous. All those who are guests at the banquet at which the poet of memory performs have a sword of Damocles suspended over their heads, for the writer with mnemonic gifts also possesses death dealing powers.

═══ VII ═══

Under the Walls of the
Fortress of Classicism

Shy-Wang-Ti . . . a fait bâtir la grande muraille qui sé-
pare la Chine de la Tartarie, qui a six cents lieues de
circuit, trois milles tours, trente pieds de haut, quinze
d'épais. . . . Shy-Wang-Ti l'a fait construire en cinq
ans. . . . Eh bien! ce prince fit brûler tous les livres, et
défendit, sous peine de mort, d'en conserver d'autres que
d'agriculture, d'architecture, et de médecine. Si Rousseau
avoit connu ce trait historique, le beau parti qu'il en eût
tiré![1]

Diderot's reflections on the Great Wall of China contain in
germ both the Sun King's and Vauban's theories on the role
of defensive structures. The creative genius behind the *Encyclopédie,* like the founding father of France's *corps de génie,*
imagines that perfect fortifications would simultaneously protect against the unenlightened and create a territory so secure
that an intellectual golden age could flower within its confines.
He admires the magnificence of the emperor's defensive complex, but condemns the use of fortifications for dazzling, blinding control rather than enlightenment. Yet, as the example of
France's then recent Golden Age demonstrates, to the authors
of great defensive projects, books that do not bear the stamp
of their control also threaten their security. During the rule
of the builder of the great walls of France, few books had
been burned, and history had not been, as Borges phrases it
in his commentary on Shih Huang Ti's coupling of constructive and destructive operations, "rigorous[ly] aboli[shed]." Yet

[1] Diderot, *Lettres à Sophie Volland,* 3 vols., ed. A. Babelon (Gallimard,
1930), vol. 1, pp. 306-7.

history had been rewritten, so that ties with France's barbarian past could be severed, and so that a new genealogy could be crafted for the Splendid Century, a revised historical setting designed to put the brilliance of its accomplishments in a proper light. Inappropriate names from all ages were simply erased from the books. Names of moderns considered a credit to their country were displayed prominently, but were also subjected to a form of erasure: their authority was displaced, redirected to the source of all authority and glory. Louis XIV, the ultimate name in France's magnificent new history, orchestrated a realignment of the concept of authority, making it compatible with his own personal strategy. And the hollow, impersonal system of authority that corresponded to his Great Wall provided the central model for Classical discourse.

Diderot, an instinctive fortifier who, like Vauban, denies his own aspirations to invulnerability, infers that the Chinese emperor's characteristically Classical strategy would have won Rousseau's approval. Certainly in *Emile* Rousseau is even more stringent in his ban than Shih Huang Ti, for he judges only one book worthy of preservation. And the volume he would save from destruction is a work that would surely also have been spared by the builder of the wall that set the standard for all defensive complexes to come. Rousseau proposes a reading of *Robinson Crusoe* as the most perfect example of the type of book preserved by the emperor of China, "le plus heureux traitté d'éducation naturelle" (4: 454). He reads Defoe's novel as though it told only the story of one man's struggle for survival. The aspects of Robinson's insular existence that he intends to have Emile imitate—such as planting crops and raising animals—are precisely those that Defoe borrowed from accounts of shipwreck victims like Alexander Selkirk.[2] Rousseau omits from his fictional re-creation of Defoe's novel precisely those of its hero's activities that Defoe

[2] Selkirk's account and other contemporary narratives can be found in Charles Neider's *Great Shipwrecks and Castaways: Authentic Accounts of Adventures at Sea* (New York: Harper, 1952).

did not take from his narrative model, for no shipwreck account tells a tale of fortification. The territory of *Robinson Crusoe*'s fictionality is defined by the walls its title character repeatedly erects around himself. Indeed, the work Rousseau would have his pupil consult as a child's version of Diderot's epistemological fortress, as a rational dictionary of natural sciences and arts, is also a treatise on natural fortification. Robinson's basic instinctive drive is the desire to create a personal *pré carré*. He chooses a space that can be perfectly defended and proceeds to wall himself into that space behind a series of concentric fortifications. A true defensive *bricoleur*, he packs the walls of his fortress with fragments of the ship that brought him to the island, cramming them among stakes and tree trunks and backing this patchwork with dirt.[3]

If, however, Rousseau's suppression of all trace of Robinson's enclosures from his educational *enceinte* was intentional, he may have exaggerated the threat posed by Defoe's novel to his own territorial security. The founding text of the modern English novel portrays the urge to self-protection as man's fundamental instinct, but it limits the defense of territory to mere *fortification sauvage*, a drive that, while excessive (by his own account Robinson continues to perfect his outworks for the first sixteen years of his insular existence in the absence of any threat to his security [pp. 128, 130]), is exclusively self-protective and masks no urge for conquest. "[A] Man perfectly confus'd and out of my Self"—thus Robinson characterizes the panic that follows his discovery of the lone footprint in the sand (p. 121). He can only calm this panic by coming "Home to my Fortification." His formulation implies that he can only exist as himself within these walls, that the trace of the fortress marks the limits of Crusoe's self. Safe inside its walls, with his provisions neatly lined up and tallied and his spiritual books balanced, Robinson feels no "fluttering Thoughts" (p. 121), for the enclosed self is the self intact.

[3] Defoe, *Robinson Crusoe*, ed. M. Shinagel (New York: Norton and Co., 1975), pp. 126-27.

CHAPTER VII

Yet Defoe's hero is at the same time recurrently drawn to the life-threatening Other outside his miniature Great Wall. The solitary footprint that lies at the dead center of his novelistic trajectory might be taken for a realistic detail, a logical explanation for Crusoe's behavior and undeniable proof of the Other's existence, but in its solitary perfection, its durability—it is still intact when he returns to measure his own foot against it some five to seven days later (p. 125)—it stands as the trace of Robinson's desire for the cannibals who will justify his obsessiveness, and of his inability to mechanize his defensive instincts. Robinson's desire to tame wild creatures culminates in a parodically perfect colonialist utopia, but nature is merely brought into line, never geometrized: the "fluttering" that betrays a lack of control is constantly evident in his creations.

When Saint-Preux first penetrates the barriers that wall off Julie's secret garden from the larger *pré carré* of Rousseau's novelistic utopia, he expresses his admiration with what he imagines to be the ultimate compliment and compares the Elisée to desert islands visited on his great voyage: "O Tinian! ô Juan Fernandez! Julie, le bout du monde est à votre porte" (4: 11: 471).[4] Yet the mistress of Rousseau's Elysian fields, far from being flattered by his outburst, rejects the inappropriate compliment with a smile that ridicules her former teacher's naiveté: "Adieu, Tinian, adieu Juan Fernandez, adieu tout l'enchantement! Dans un moment vous allez être de retour du bout du monde" (p. 472). The garden created by *Julie's* *oeil vivant* and christened Elysium by his wife is not intended to be a re-creation of exotic natural profusion, of an actual desert island. Nor is it to be seen as a mere comforting domestication of natural forces, an attempt to make that desert island, as Defoe's shipwrecked Englishman did, a castle and therefore a home. Wolmar fortifies Julie's garden in order to transform it into a Classical masterpiece, not to render European nature

[4] Robinson Crusoe's model, Alexander Selkirk, was marooned on Juan Fernandez.

exotic and Other, not to humanize nature and make it comforting, but to mechanize it and make it inorganic. Defoe's hero leaves his personal touch all over the desert island so that he can feel at home. Rousseau's gardeners seek to depersonalize their domain; they feel secure when their absolute control—"il n'y a rien là que je n'aye ordonné," Julie proclaims (p. 472)—has made their garden into a horticultural wall. The footprint on Robinson's island demonstrates that, for him, the Other is recognizable and its threat identifiable. Thinking of his desert islands, Saint-Preux remarks that "je n'apperçois aucuns pas d'hommes," to which Wolmar replies "c'est qu'on a pris grand soin de les effacer" (p. 479). In a horticultural machine, all prints are equally threatening, for any trace of the human signals a lack of control.

This systematic erasure of all signs of human presence is evident in *Robinson Crusoe*'s French counterpart, *La Princesse de Clèves*, the text generally referred to as the first modern French novel and the novel whose impenetrability Rousseau admired and sought to emulate in *Julie*. Published only months before the signing of the peace of Nimwegen, Lafayette's masterpiece reveals a perfect comprehension of the role, as cornerstone of national and personal glory, already accorded Vaubanian strategy in the royal memoir fiction for that year. "On attaque le coeur d'un(e) prince(sse) comme une place" (*Mémoires de Louis XIV*, p. 258)—from all the moral tales recited for her edification and from the events of her own life that she evaluates as pedagogical exempla, Lafayette's princess learns one decisive lesson. Within the confines of the courtly enclosure, one is never alone and no actual space—no closet, no pavilion—is ever safe from penetration. In order to protect one's secrets from public disclosure, to guarantee one's territorial security, it is necessary to make oneself into a fortress. To this end, all forms of instinctive and personal self-expression, from blushes to true confessions, must be eliminated and replaced by automatic responses and cliché-ridden discourse.

In *La Princesse de Clèves*, Lafayette lays bare the real meaning of one of the basic tenets of novelistic theory in her day:

the Classical-modern French novel tells the story of the siege of virtue as a war of words in which the besiegers are more interested, à la Valmont, in proving that they can outmaneuver the besieged than in the conquest itself.[5] As Merteuil maintains, true strategic genius is first of all defensive and must operate from what early theoreticians and practitioners of the novel alike saw as the woman's place. The princess is unable to protect her narrative body, the text of her life, so she is obliged to flee the courtly theater where every actor aspires to the condition of all-seeing, all-knowing, yet impenetrable *oeil vivant*. Inside this royal *pré carré*, the victor of the *defense* of Metz is a perpetual voyeur laying bare "le coeur d'une princesse" as though she were always in an open (secret) pavilion. The groundwork for this realization is laid as early as the "canne des Indes" episode when the princess gazes at a painting representing Nemours as master of defensive strategy, even as Nemours himself, hidden more by his strategic superiority than by the "window" behind which he "places himself," looks straight into the secret of her desire.[6]

Rather than allowing the account of her emotional life to pass into the public domain and become anonymous in the way that Rousseauian tales of passion do in the *Liaisons*, the princess suppresses her story and becomes "inimitable," moving thereby beyond representation into what Lafayette's precursor, Scudéry, defined as the Sun King's space, the space of

[5] Huet, who understood so well the workings of the machinery of power at the Sun King's court, contends in his *Traité de l'origine des romans* (written as a preface to Lafayette's *Zayde*) that in France "Les Dames . . . n'ayant point d'autres défenses que leur propre coeur, elles s'en sont fait un rampart plus fort et plus seur que . . . toute la vigilance des Douëgnes. Les hommes ont donc esté obligés d'assieger ce rampart par les formes." He maintains that it is this transformation of the siege of virtue into a verbal art that defines the territory of the French novel: "C'est cet art qui distingue les Romans François des autres Romans" (*Zayde, histoire espagnole* [Barbin, 1670], p. 92).

[6] Lafayette, *La Princesse de Clèves*, ed. Adam (Garnier-Flammarion, 1966), p. 154. At the siege of Metz in 1552, Henri II's men held out under the assault of Charles V, who was forced to withdraw after three months.

magnificence—"il est au dessus de toute expression, et . . . on ne peut jamais le bien représenter" ("De la magnificence," *Conversations nouvelles*, p. 52). When she terminates her story, the princess reenters on her own (female) terms the dazzling, awesome *pré carré* of "magnificence" and "galanterie" in which the novel opens. This novelistic territory, like that of Laclos, is also in a sense beyond representation, but not because its creator seeks to be instinctively original and finds her space invaded by wilier strategists, but because she manages, as the Sun King did, to be a mechanical genius brilliantly empty of significance, an enigmatic façade of glittering clichés.

Wolmar claims that he erases human prints from his horticultural machine because artistic discretion is the essence of good taste: "L'erreur des prétendus gens de goût est de vouloir de l'art partout, et de n'être jamais contens que l'art ne paroisse; au lieu que c'est à le cacher que consiste le véritable goût" (4: 11: 482). But the real reason he, like all the Classical artists discussed here, insists that the evidence, the trace, of human intervention and artifice be kept *sous rature* is that he understands what the princess learns from her experience of a novelistic siege—that the human, the personal, is not considered beautiful in the aesthetics of Classicism because it is weak. When Rousseau's hero speaks of erasing footprints, he prefigures the project of literary fortification of a subsequent writer working in the shadow of the Classical literary fortress—Flaubert. Flaubert hoped that his writing would constitute "un mur tout nu," "un mur de l'Acropole." In his conception the prints to be erased become mortar, which must be kept to a bare minimum if he is to come as close as possible to the ideal creation—a "precise," "polished," "harmonious," "bare" wall: "j'ai eu bien du ciment à enlever, qui bavachait entre les pierres, et il a fallu retasser les pierres pour que les joints ne parussent pas."[7]

The basic tool at this builder's disposal, the standard block

[7] Flaubert, *Extraits de la correspondance ou Préface à la vie d'écrivain*, ed. Bollème (Seuil, 1963), pp. 271, 133.

from which he crafts his bare walls, is the *lieu commun,* the same stone that was chiseled, polished, and fitted together without mortar by his Vaubanian predecessors Lafayette, Rousseau, Laclos, and Sade.[8] Lafayette's use of the hyperbolic language of "magnificence" and "galanterie," Rousseau's "creation" of an immediately codified discourse often taken for the product of unique personal experience, Laclos's and Sade's experiments with pastiche and parody, and Flaubert's manipulations of both the already-said and the already-formulated, that is, his use of ready-made fragments from the vast number of sources he consulted for works such as *Bouvard et Pécuchet*—these diverse strategies have a common goal. These textual fortifiers are all working toward, in Borges's words, "the rigorous abolition of history." To that end, they develop techniques more devious than those employed by Louis's moderns in their attempt to settle historical accounts with their predecessors. The various uses of linguistic commonplaces just enumerated are oblique strategies that undermine traditional hierarchies of authority. They are the means by which the literary fortifier writes another's discourse into his own, using it as a stone to build a wall of the already-said. The discourse thus processed by these literary *bricoleurs* is hollowed out and rendered impersonal, and the names of the

---

[8] Rousseau, the master fabricator of a discourse of passion whose genius is defined by its situation on the border between spontaneity and artifice, created the eighteenth century's ultimate linguistic cliché and supplied Laclos and Sade with the basic stone for their walls. Thus, in the *Lettre à d'Alembert* Rousseau proclaimed that the rhetoric of passion in the *Lettres portugaises* was so perfectly expressed that the text could only be a novel, and a novel written by a man (note, pp. 138-39). Conversely, Merteuil uses the same reasoning as the basis for her argument that even though she knows *Julie* to be a novel, she is sure that "le fond en était vrai" (33: 68). Jean Fabre maintains that "les effusions en style de l'*Héloïse* offrent la plus subtile alternance ou le plus troublant amalgame de pastiche et de sincerité" (*Idées sur le roman* [Klincksieck, 1979], p. 161). The ambiguity of the rhetoric of passion in *Julie* may mark the realization of Rousseau's youthful dream of becoming a master *persifleur.* As he reasoned in *Emile,* "c'est de l'usage de tout dire sur le même ton qu'est venu celui de persifler les gens sans qu'ils le sentent" (4: 282).

originators of this discourse are repositioned once their language has been placed in the public domain.

These borrowed discourses—the discourse of magnificence as well as the language of passion—are reduced to dazzling hollowness by the machinating genius who builds a perfect wall, a wall with no loopholes. The personal and the instinctive are perfectly subjugated, and outside and inside cease to function as relevant distinctions in a literary economy in which *conter* is more than homonymic with *compter*. "La loi des nombres gouverne donc les sentiments et les images, et ce qui paraît être l'extérieur est tout bonnement le dedans," in Flaubert's formulation (p. 271). The desired result of such literary geometry, for Flaubert as for his Classical forerunners and for the Sun King who devised the most perfect model of such a strategy, is a textual Great Wall whose beauty will "crush" its spectator. "[O]n se sent écrasé sans savoir pourquoi" (p. 95).

Nowhere is Flaubert's affinity with the aesthetic of the literary age of the fortress more evident than in what may be the ultimate masterpiece of novelistic siegecraft, *Salammbô*.[9] Flaubert's fascination with the fortress can be read in different ways. For example, it can be seen as a form of nostalgia for an age when a sense of territorial security could be derived from the simple fact that borders were visible and therefore easier to police, for an age when a corresponding intellectual belief was still conceivable, that it was possible to systematize knowledge, to contain it and fix its limits within a perfectly complete encyclopedic form—surely a drive to which the author of *Bouvard et Pécuchet* was no stranger. But the prominence granted fortified places in Flaubert's work

[9] Carthage and Hamilcar (written Amilcar) were associated with the origin of the modern French novel. They figure prominently in the ultimate novelistic rendition of the discourse of magnificence, *Clélie,* composed by Lafayette's precursor, Madeleine de Scudéry, during the years (1654-1661) that taught the future Sun King the necessity of defensive strategy. See, for example, *Clélie, histoire romaine,* 10 vols. (Geneva: Slatkine Reprints, 1973), vol. 1, pp. 159-69.

also indicates an intersection of military and literary strategy. Even though in his day siege warfare had been replaced by more direct military confrontations, Flaubert dreams of a more mediated type of conflict, and not simply as a romanticized evocation, along the lines of certain nineteenth-century portrayals of Napoleonic warfare, of what was just outside the military experience of his age. Siegecraft was a system of martial strategy that the would-be master of the already-said understood instinctively and intimately to be the military equivalent of the wall of the Acropolis. Flaubert knew that the rightful antecedent of the space of neoclassical military encounters was not the medieval fortress but the ground-level fortifications of antiquity. First in *Salammbô*, then in the final tale of his last completed work, "Hérodias," he re-created the mechanized geometry of these ancient fortresses and the claustrophobic spaces within and under their walls. In the process, he rediscovered the implications of the literary state of siege in French Classicism.

Flaubert's Carthage is a novelistic space generated by a Vaubanian quest for territorial invulnerability. In an important early analysis of *Salammbô*, Sainte-Beuve characterized Flaubert's project in terms that evoke Louis XIV's creation of Versailles: "[S]on nouveau sujet . . . [était] presque inaccessible; l'impossible, et pas autre chose, le tentait."[10] Like Silling, Flaubert's Carthage is a tyrant's paradise, composed of multiple concentric ring walls that mark off enclosures within enclosures. Thus, both the temple and Hamilcar's palace are scale models of the entire fortified place—the temple a series of ever more secret sancta camouflaging the ultimate transparent obstacle, the *zaïmph*, and the palace a fortified maze concealing the existence of its master's "last" line of defense, the immense storehouses of his buried treasures. Thus protected, all of Carthage—its natural ornamentation, its inhabitants—moves ever closer to a realization of Flaubert's dream of perfectly frozen form. Exotic trees seem "immobiles comme

---

[10] Sainte-Beuve, *Nouveaux Lundis* (Michel Lévy, 1865), vol. 4, p. 34.

des feuillages de bronze" (p. 79); an early stage of Hannon's leprosy gives him the appearance of "quelque grosse idole ébauchée dans un bloc de pierre," "une chose inerte" (p. 38). Within Carthage's fortifications, the inside is truly the outside, and walls generate walls, all governed by "the law of numbers."

Yet all the mortar has not been removed from these ramparts, for the immense defensive machine that nurtures Carthage's illusion of invincibility is riddled with loopholes through which the barbarians, the archetypal enemy against whom all Great Walls are erected, penetrate its fortified body—the "brèche" in the big wall through which Mâtho and Spendius enter Mégara, the "ouverture étroite" in the "impenetrable" temple's defenses, the "fente, large d'une coudée," that "slices" the wall behind Tanit's chariot.[11] Thus the shape of Carthage's defenses generates the shape of the offense used against them, putting besieged and besieger on similar tactical ground, and ultimately making Same (Carthaginian) and Other (barbarian) interchangeable.[12] In the course of the war the reader joins in medias res in *Salammbô*'s opening pages, attacker and defender repeatedly shift position in their mutual pursuit of the *zaïmph*, the blatantly floating signifier that is the ur-mark of invulnerability, the façade that transforms its wearer—both Mâtho and Salammbô immediately wrap it around themselves—into a Sun King, a blinding, untouchable, hollow presence.

In their pursuit of a status that is, like the *zaïmph*, beyond representation, Hamilcar and Mâtho create a conflict that they know to be as theoretically "interminable" (p. 243) as Vaubanian strategy. They come to long for an end—"ils souhai-

[11] Flaubert, *Salammbô*, ed. Maynial (Garnier, 1961), pp. 77, 81, 82, 84. Flaubert's response to Sainte-Beuve's critique is included as an appendix in Maynial's edition.

[12] Sainte-Beuve criticized Flaubert for having amplified the proportions of the siege recorded in historical accounts, even though he realized that Flaubert had done so in order to create a tactical parallelism between Carthaginians and barbarians (*Nouveaux Lundis*, pp. 74-75).

taient ... une grande bataille, pourvu qu'elle fût bien la dernière" (p. 333)—but the machine they put into operation in their quest for invulnerability is as insatiable as the immense bronze god to whom the Carthaginians sacrifice their own children in the hope of regaining their lost power: "Des dévots avaient voulu ... compter [les enfants], pour voir si leur nombre correspondait aux jours de l'année solaire; mais on en mit d'autres, et il était impossible de les distinguer dans le mouvement vertigineux des horribles bras" (p. 298). The besieged cannot control the system put into operation for their defense. The appetite of its geometric proliferation guarantees its continuing functioning up to and even after the obliteration of the barbarians outside the walls.

The battle for Carthage is a perfect illustration of the theoretical conclusion of Vauban's system, for in it defense and offense are evenly matched. From his vantage point as writer, under the walls of the French Classical fortress, Flaubert gives a detailed account of the creation of an offense designed to destroy Carthage's fortifications. In fact, he goes into such detail in his enumeration of the machines devised for the siege and in his portrayal of the inorganic come alive in them that Sainte-Beuve takes the passage for an extended joke: "Evidemment l'auteur s'amuse" (p. 74). Hamilcar, the tyrant who defends civilization from behind the walls of his great palace, is opposed by the couple Mâtho-Spendius, whose partnership reveals the same complicity of forces as the Louis XIV-Vauban configuration. "Spendius enviait sa force [de Mâtho]; mais pour la conduite des espions, le choix des sentinelles, l'art des machines et tous les moyens défensifs, Mâtho écoutait docilement son compagnon" (p. 167). The infinitely machinating inventiveness of Spendius is the foundation of Mâtho's offensive threat. Indeed Sainte-Beuve calls Spendius the keystone of the entire novelistic fortress, the deus in Flaubert's machina. "[C]ar ce Spendius est comme le *nain merveilleux* du roman; à lui seul, il fait tout" (p. 75). Together, Mâtho and Spendius almost bring down the dazzling fortress that shelters the accouterments of civilization, but on occasion they separate to give battle on different fronts, and this division of forces is fatal to their project. The night before the final bloody slaughter, Mâtho thinks only of Spendius: "Si parfois des soupirs lui échappaient, c'est qu'il pensait à Spendius" (p. 335), just as the Sun King must have regretted "l'âme de tous [ses] sièges" as he was leading his nation ever closer to ruin.

But even if the barbarians do not succeed in razing Carthage's threatening Great Wall, their attack nevertheless makes plain the barbarism of the dazzling sophistication it protects. Under siege, the Carthaginians reveal themselves to be capable of a brutally primitive inventiveness in the tortures they imagine for their captives and in the weapons they create for their defense. Within the confines of the fortress under siege, their artistry turns into *bricolage,* and they use, for example, the hair of prostitutes and of the wives of the city's elders as strings for their catapults (p. 275). They build and rebuild with borrowed elements, incorporating everything inside the Great Wall into its defensive structure, using these displaced fragments like stones.

When at the novel's close Mâtho turns defender inside the walls of Tunis, its fortifications are so weak that he is obliged to practice the most basic form of *bricolage* as fortification: "Mâtho en boucha les trous avec les pierres des maisons" (p. 326). At this point the fortifying project has come full circle—prior to this Mâtho has often been in a defensive position but he has never attempted to construct fortifications— and the former besieger of a defensive system that aspired to invulnerability attempts to wall himself in. Mâtho stands here in Flaubert's position, as a creator so obsessed with the fortress of the already-said that he first tries to tear down its walls and then builds new walls with blocks both pre-cut and already-used. Editors of *Salammbô,* like editors of the *Liaisons,* devote much of their energy to the identification of the sources of the textual building blocks its author puts together as impersonally as possible. What the editors do not mention is that in Flaubert's case as in Defoe's, the mortar—in the sense of the fiction, the personal invention—with which he surrounds these fragments of foreign discourse is a story of the construction and the destruction of fortifications. Defoe added Robinson's exploits as natural fortifier to earlier shipwreck accounts; in a more Classical gesture, Flaubert added the siege to accounts of the war between the Carthaginians and the barbarians. In *Salammbô*, even the textual mortar is petrified, is an affair of stones.

Sainte-Beuve attacked *Salammbô* because he confused stones with mortar. He criticizes Flaubert on opposite, though interrelated, grounds. On the one hand, he objects to Flaubert's artistry because it is too petrified. Flaubert has "paved" his novel with "de cailloux de toute couleur et de pierres précieuses" (p. 69). As a result, *Salammbô* is "ingénieux" and "artificiel" (p. 53), a product of "travail" and "combinaison," that is, a work marked by mere talent rather than genius. For true genius, in Sainte-Beuve's description as in Fontenelle's characterization of Vauban, is always "happy," that is, spontaneous and unpredictable ("imprévu," *Nouveaux Lundis*, pp. 82-83). On the other hand, Sainte-Beuve also accuses Flaubert of having run out of the pre-cut stones (that is, historically documented facts) he needed to make a "true," a "real" "painting" (a historical reconstruction) and of having been forced therefore to use so much mortar ("invention au premier chef") that he had ultimately built a "poem" rather than a new Carthage (p. 47). While Sainte-Beuve correctly perceives the point in *Salammbô* where documentation ends and personal invention takes over, he fails to see that Flaubert's novelistic wall, unlike the ramparts of Carthage, is seamless. It is not that Flaubert did not find sufficient historical stones to rebuild the city's fortifications, but rather that he did not consider all the material he found strong enough to make invulnerable novelistic ramparts. When Flaubert imagined new elements, they were not "spontaneous" (a "poem"), but still more "artificial" and "ingenious" "combinations" and "constructions."

Flaubert responded with particular vehemence to Sainte-Beuve's criticisms of his novel. The "apology" he addressed to his critic reveals that he saw a link between Sainte-Beuve's accusation that *Salammbô* displays a "pointe d'imagination sadique" and his insistence that the actual siege of Carthage is of Flaubert's invention (p. 361). Despite the testimony to his "obsession" with Sade furnished by the Goncourts, Flaubert denied that he was "un disciple de de Sade," and responded to Sainte-Beuve's charge of literary sadism with his standard defense in such matters—detailed references to the sources on which his account was based. Thus, for example, he defends the "immolations d'enfants" in Carthage on the grounds that the Greeks practiced human sacrifices in other wars as late as St. Augustine's day (p. 361). On this score, however, even an especially lavish display of erudition does not succeed in distracting the reader's attention from the fact that, if he did not invent, as Sainte-Beuve claimed, the "supplices," the "mutilations," and the "horreurs" of the scenes of revenge and appeasement, he certainly displaced historical evidence to condense the maximal amount of torture within the limited confines chosen for his fiction.

It is exactly the type of historical compression practiced in *Salammbô* that ultimately renders inoperative Flaubert's use of erudition as defense. Sainte-Beuve contends that during the actual siege of Carthage, the barbarians did not have the technical expertise necessary for a proper assault and were only able to mount a limited effort that was no challenge to the Carthaginians' superior strategic genius: "Il y a loin de là à ce siège en règle, monumental, classique, à ce siège modèle qu'a imaginé l'auteur de *Salammbô*" (p. 70). To this objection to his inventiveness, *Salammbô's* author is forced to yield: "Vous avez raison, . . . j'ai forcé l'histoire, et comme vous le dites très bien, *j'ai voulu faire un siège*. Mais dans un sujet militaire, où est le mal?—Et puis je ne l'ai pas complètement inventé, ce siège, je l'ai seulement un peu chargé" (p. 361). For *Salammbô*, Flaubert collected fragments of history in order to construct a novelistic wall. He then built an unexpected turn of events into the straight line of historical documentation ("j'ai forcé l'histoire") when he added a siege. Flaubert does not admit that he "completely invented" the siege of Carthage: "[J]e l'ai seulement un peu chargé." Flaubert bent history to include a siege. Then, as he "weighed down" Salammbô's delicate body with exotic jewels, he "weighed down" that siege with lapidary accounts of strategic prowess.

Flaubert ends the section of his self-defensive letter in which he responds to Sainte-Beuve's two charges by addressing a third objection, his critic's feeling that his cast of characters should have included a "raisonneur," what Flaubert terms in a partial citation from his detractor, "un monsieur *sentant comme nous*" (pp. 361-62). He thus arrives at what he hints at several points is the unacknowledged foundation of Sainte-Beuve's objection, his inability to identify with or comprehend the barbarian, oriental Other (for example, pp. 355, 362). Throughout his letter, Flaubert maintains a distinction, essential to the microcosm of *Salammbô*, between the civilized (explicitly the Greeks, by implication the French like Sainte-Beuve) and the barbarians (semantically "the Other" for the Greeks, implicitly all peoples so disorganized, so "redundant" that the civilized representatives of order always have to "shorten" and "rearrange" the products of their creativity [p. 356]). Flaubert contends that Sainte-Beuve's attack is inspired by Flaubert's refusal in *Salammbô* to "franciser" this foreign disorder, this foreign sadism, a refusal that is anti-"Classical" (p. 355). *Salammbô's* author denies that he has any Classical aspirations; his genius, he infers, is incomprehensible to his compatriots because he is able to comprehend both besieged and besiegers, because he has tried to "appliqu[er] à l'Antiquité les procédés du roman moderne" (p. 355).

Flaubert's quarrel with Sainte-Beuve has important implications for the definition of a French national literary tradition. Sainte-Beuve denies the Frenchness of Flaubert's sadistic novelistic siege. Flaubert agrees that his genius does not correspond to the official national fiction from the Sun King's day to his own, but hints that it may be inherently French in another sense of the adjective, "classique dans le mauvais sens du mot" (p. 355). Sainte-Beuve contends that after *Madame Bovary* Flaubert's readers wanted from him "un autre sujet . . . également vivant, mais moins circonscrit, moins cantonné et resserré" (p. 32), that is, a new novel characterized by less siegecraft and more field battles. However, Flaubert knew that in the French tradition a truly Classical work could only be the story of a siege, a siege in Sainte-Beuve's terms "en règle, monumental, classique" (p. 70). *Salammbô* lays bare the true Frenchness of the magnificent walls and the monumental siege of Classicism, the complicity between its author's "pointe d'imagination sadique" and its invulnerable Vaubanian fortifications. Flaubert "burdened" the history of Carthage with this siege because he saw it as the perfect structure to illustrate the bond between violence and walls, walls that both define a contained, claustrophobic space and stand for artistic perfection. He re-created both the supplemental accounting for violence in Vauban's system and its ultimate recuperation of aggression.

The master of the already-said understood that all the fortifications of the Ancien Régime were composed of the same stones, that Silling was a reconstruction of Dunkerque or Versailles just as Versailles—according to the logic Borges uses when he speaks of Kafka's "precursors"—already contains Silling. What he terms the "procédés du roman moderne" are none other than the strategies for novelistic fortification systematized during the period when Versailles's ruler petrified himself and mechanized his domain. Even after the Revolution(s), Flaubert shares the dream of all "strong" Classical novelists, of becoming Classicism's heir and building the invulnerable textual fortress—the novel that will be the literary counterpart of the fortress's scandal, simultaneously blending into its surroundings (being *vraisemblable* or realistic) and standing out from them as a dare to those who would challenge its might.

Louis XIV's Commissioner of Fortifications molded a shape for the kingdom of France, transforming it into the fortified utopia that was the model for the literature of the Golden

Age. The literature the French call Classic was formulated inside a *pré carré,* sheltered by the invincible fortifications Vauban constructed. That literature remains a model, the original shape, for all French literature and plays a determining role in the formulation of all subsequent literary strategies. Baudelaire, brought to account on a literary morals charge in the same year as Flaubert because of his own refusal to make his textual production Classical in the good sense of the word, called the *Liaisons* a "livre typiquement français." Roger Laufer refers to Laclos's novel as a "triomphe de l'intelligence lucide et de la clarté française." What is perceived as archetypically French in the kingdom of letters has all the "clarity," all the "lucidity" of Flaubert's ideal, a wall of the Acropolis. Yet the transparency that characterizes the Classical French novel always veils—to transpose Starobinski's re-creation of Rousseau's basic schema—a fortified obstacle, a complex of defensive structures. The geometric accountability of this fortified art camouflages a literary machine with a movement of enormous complexity—structural and linguistic snares, ruses, and machinations—set in motion to achieve an impersonal containment of energy, yet generating in the process explosive and implosive detonations. "[O]n se sent écrasé sans savoir pourquoi" is Flaubert's description of the effect of such lucidly machinating art.[13]

Recently certain French architects have attempted to resurrect Vauban's dream of a utopian *pré carré.* In *Vivre à l'oblique,* Claude Parent argues that modern architecture can only be revitalized by a return to Vaubanian strategy: we must create structures that are at the same time defensive and dynamic, that simultaneously protect and foster creativity.[14] But

[13] In *Absorption and Theatricality: Painting and Beholder in the Age of Diderot* (Berkeley, Calif.: Univ. of California Press, 1980), Michael Fried argues that eighteenth-century French painters contrived increasingly complicated strategies to respond to the threatening presence of a viewer.

[14] Claude Parent, *Vivre à l'oblique* (n.p., 1970). See also Paul Virilio's *L'Insécurité du territoire* (Stock, 1976). In their study of Vauban (Fréal, 1971) M. Parent and Verroust discuss the pertinence of Vauban's architectural

even for generations that no longer live immediately under the walls of Vauban's Classical fortifications, it may still be impossible to accept a Vaubanian plan for oblique structure at face value and conceive of defensive systems independent of the (royal) aggressiveness to which they originally gave license. In the kingdom of letters, this seems especially true when current French critical practice proposes a vision of textuality that has much in common with the hollow literary *boulets creux* produced in the age of the Vaubanian fortress. When critics today proclaim the death of the subject in texts beyond representation, it is not clear whether, as some have argued, they are attacking literature, or whether French literary theory is not itself finally becoming Classical, entering its own age of the fortress.

---

practice today (p. 16). The threat of Vaubanian military architecture has been completely defused today. Thus, for example, in Strasbourg a park has been constructed around some of Vauban's outworks and grass allowed to grow on their slopes, so that they now seem tailor-made for children's rather than war games.

Index

INDEX

INDEX

fortifications (*cont.*)
   breaches in, 242, 245, 260, 267,
      337; language of, 28, 117, 132;
      literary, 6, 9, 117, 261, 266,
      309; Montalembert's system of,
      196-97; Vauban's system of, 36-
      37, 41
fortress, 280, 287, 329, 335; age of
   the, 7, 281; as art, 27; Classicism as, 66, 73, 271, 278, 287;
   fall of the, 270; groundplans or
   traces of, 54, 281n.17; impregnable, 25, 44, 46-47; literary, 4,
   73, 267; medieval, 280-81; as
   metaphor, 6, 26, 29, 60; under
   siege, 50-52, 284-86, 337-41;
   Vaubanian, 12, 29, 54, 119, 281.
   See also Bastille
Foucault, Michel, 3, 5, 7, 10, 26,
   275; *Histoire de la folie*, 109,
   229, 289; *La Volonté du savoir*,
   28
fragmentation, 136n.22, 296, 301-
   2, 304
frame narrative, 298
framing, 315. *See also* placement
France, 45, 200, 343; its modern
   shape, 26; as *pré carré*, 344. See
   also *pré carré*
Freemasonry, 306n.35
French Academy, 200n.11, 203,
   262
Freud, Sigmund, 29, 77, 97, 196,
   310; *Beyond the Pleasure Principle*, 5, 84-85, 117; *Dora*, 76,
   108-9, 242; *tu quoque* defense,
   76, 81, 85
frontiers, 8, 44-45, 74, 239, 335;
   France's "natural," 45, 74

Gallop, Jane, 313n.41
gardens, 330; Chinese, 174-75,
   177; French, 27, 174, 176; at
   Versailles, 64-65; as wall, 331.

See also Corpechot, Lucien; Le
   Nôtre, André
gastronomy, 292-93
genealogy, 14, 189, 303-4n.33,
   328; literary, 290, 292
Genette, Gérard, 229, 289
génie militaire. *See* engineer
genius, 47, 273-74, 286, 310, 340;
   French, 27-28, 342. See also *ingénieur*; originality
geography, importance of, in Vauban's system, 44, 74
geometry, 18, 54, 63, 113-18 pas-
   sim, 263, 285, 295, 330, 335.
   See also Classicism; space in the
   novel
Girard, René, 256
Goethe, Johann Wolfgang von, 63
Goncourt, Edmond and Jules de,
   296, 341
Great Wall of China, 59, 175, 327,
   335. *See also* Flaubert

Haudricourt, André, 174
Heloise, 122, 123n.13, 162, 190
Hénaff, Marcel, 280
historical setting of fiction, 286-87
Hoffman, Paul, 206
hollowness, 252-54, 328, 334-35.
   See also *boulet creux*; Sun King
home, 288, 329, 330
homme au masque de fer, 30
housekeeping, 174, 292-94. *See
   also* bookkeeping; gastronomy
Huet, Pierre Daniel, 23, 239-n.38,
   272, 332n.5
humiliation, 158-59, 286, 312, 326
Huysmans, Joris-Karl, 296

imposter, 262. *See also* mountebank
incorrigibility, 300, 305. *See also*
   fault finding; rule breaking
infantilism, 164-65, 169, 172

349

Library of Congress Cataloging in Publication Data

DeJean, Joan E.
  Literary fortifications.

  Includes bibliographical references and index.
  1. French fiction—18th century—History and criticism.
  2. Classicism.   3. Literary form.   4. Space and time in
literature.   5. Military art and science in literature.
  6. Fortification in literature.   I. Title.
PQ648.D39 1984   843'.4'09   84-42593
ISBN 0-691-06611-6 (alk. paper)

Joan DeJean is Associate Professor of French at Princeton University.